Chau Ju-kua

On the Chinese and Arab Trade

in the Twelfth and Thirteenth Centuries.

CHAU JU-KUA:

His Work on the Chinese and Arab Trade in the twelfth
and thirteenth Centuries, entitled Chu-fan-chï,

Translated from the Chinese and Annotated

by

FRIEDRICH HIRTH

and

W. W. ROCKHILL.

PARAGON BOOK REPRINT CORP.

New York
1966

Printed by order of the Imperial Academy of Sciences.

September 1911.   Permanent Secretary S. d'Oldenburg.

An unaltered and unabridged reprint
of the work first published St. Petersburg 1911

Printed in the United States of America

ARNO PRESS, N.Y.

Preface.

Chau Ju-kua (趙汝适), the author of the *Chu-fan-chï* (諸蕃志), i. e. «A Description of Barbarous Peoples», or «Records of Foreign Nations», deserves to be named among the most prominent writers on the ethnography and trade of his time. As throwing light on the mediaeval trade with the Far East, then in the hands of Arab or Persian merchants, his notes compete successfully with those of Marco Polo and the early Arab and Christian travellers. The authors of this volume have, therefore, endeavoured to furnish a translation, illustrated by notes derived from other sources, which it is hoped will place readers in the position to fully realize the value of this new Chinese source on an interesting historical subject.

The *Chu-fan-chï* is a rare and expensive work, obtainable only as part of certain voluminous collections of reprints. For the benefit of Sinological readers, therefore, Chinese characters and passages have been frequently added, and this has increased the difficulty of printing the book, credit for which is due to the Printing Office of the Imperial Academy of Sciences at St. Petersburg.

Friedrich Hirth.   W. W. Rockhill.

CONTENTS.

I*

Map.

INTRODUCTION.

When King Solomon, in the early part of the tenth century B. C., had opened relations with the Sabeans of the Southern coast of Arabia, the land of Punt of the Egyptians, he sent his ships from the head of the Red Sea to the land of Ophir, — generally believed to have been Guzerat or the
5 Malabar coast. Already at that remote time trade by sea was active between the ports on the south coast of Arabia, the principal of which was where Aden now stands, and Western India. The ships of the Sabeans carried the products of Arabia and India to the heads of the Red Sea and the Persian Gulf. By the former route they reached the cities of the Phoenicians; by the
10 latter they came to Media and Nineveh.

Although some accurate particulars concerning the sea-route between the Indus and the head of the Red Sea must have reached the Greeks through the voyages of Skylax of Karyanda, made about 512 B. C., it was not until Alexander the Great's invasion of India in 327 B. C., that real knowledge
15 of this vast region and of the sea-route leading there was given to the Western world. Notwithstanding the fact that the writers of the time of Alexander make no mention of the considerable coasting trade which was carried on in their time between the West and India through the medium of the Sabeans, they were certainly aware of its existence. We learn from Arrian[1] that, at
20 the time of his death, Alexander was entertaining the scheme of following up the explorations of Nearchus by another expedition to proceed from the mouth of the Euphrates to the head of the Red Sea, presumably for the purpose of diverting the great profits of the sea trade between India and Egypt from the Sabeans to the Greeks.

---

1) Hist. Indica, XLIII.

Fifty years later Ptolemy Philadelphus attempted to carry out this scheme by erecting on the Red Sea the ports of Arsinoë, Myos-hormos and Berenike; but it appears that the ships of Egypt went no further than the port of Aden, where the merchants of India came to sell their wares. The voyage from southern Arabia, Aden and Merbat to India was first made in 5 small vessels which kept close to the shore and followed its windings, but after sailing with the monsoons became known (sometime between B. C. 10 and A. D. 52), trade was greatly developed; larger ships were used (though the coasting trade was not abandoned) and a straight course was steered between the Somali, or rather Arabian coast, to Diul-Sindh or Bharoch, Manga- 10 lore or Nelisseram[1]. Though Nelkunda (Nelisseram, at the head of an estuary the mouth of which is a few miles to the north of Mt. Delli on the Malabar coast) was the farthest point habitually visited by Greek (and probably Sabean) merchants in the first century A. D., Ceylon and the coast of India as far as the Ganges were already known to them, presumably through the re- 15 ports of native traders.

By the middle of the second century Greek knowledge of the sea-route to the Far East, though here again the information appears to have been derived solely from native traders, extended to Tongking, where mention is made of the port of Cattigara, — the present Hanoi. Ptolemy had heard of 20 the various stages on the route between Ceylon and the Malay Peninsula, of the Andaman and Nicobar Islands (Bazakata), the Islands off the west coast of Sumatra (?Barusai), Sumatra (Sabadiu) and Kalah (Kozi), but beyond their geographical position he knew practically nothing[2], nor can I find anything in the works of succeeding geographers, — Pausanias, Solinus, Orosius, or 25 even Cosmas Indicopleustes, this last writing in the first half of the sixth century, — to show that the Greek traders had reached China (although there is no reason for denying that some adventurous traders may have got

---

1) Nearchus had already noticed the monsoon (Arrian, Hist. Indic., XXI. See also M° Crindle, Periplus, 135 n., where he notes that Vincent (in his Commerce and Navigation of the 30 Ancients) remarks that the account of the discovery of the monsoon given in the Periplus, naturally excites a curiosity in the mind to enquire how it should happen that the monsoon should have been noticed by Nearchus, and that from the time of his voyage for 300 years no one should have attempted a direct course till Hippalus ventured to commit himself to the ocean. He is of opinion that there was a direct passage by the monsoons both in going to and coming from India in use 35 among the Arabians before the Greeks adopted it. — The Periplus (§ 32) notes that such ships as come from the west coast of India (Limuriké) and Bharoch (Barugaza) too late in the season put into harbor at Merbat (Moskha) for the winter, where they dispose of their muslins, corn, and oil to the king's officers.

2) See Gerini, Researches on Ptolemy's Geography of Eastern Asia. 1909.   40

that far), — or that Chinese traders had visited Ceylon, or India, let alone the ports of Arabia or the Persian Gulf.

At a very early date Ceylon had become a flourishing country and entertained important commercial relations not only with India but with the
5 countries of the East, the Malay Peninsula, and probably Indo-China. Its pearls and precious stones, its ebony, muslins and tortoise-shell were carried to Nelkunda and Barugaza (Bharoch) in the first century of our era, and probably centuries before. The tortoise-shell from the Malay Peninsula (the island of Chrysé) reached those ports through it. In all likelihood the traders
10 of southern Arabia founded establishments in Ceylon at a very early date; however this may be, the commercial importance of Ceylon in the trade between the East and the West was coeval with the opening of this trade, and it retained its preponderance down to modern times.

The pilgrim Fa-hién, the first Chinese who has left a record of a voyage
15 from India to China (A. D. 413), came from Tamlook at the mouth of the Ganges to Ceylon to sail for Sumatra, and when in Ceylon he noted the signs of wealth of the «Sa-po traders» on the island, and it does not seem unlikely that these foreigners were Arabs from the Hadramaut and Oman coasts.

Cosmas in the sixth century says of Ceylon: «The Island being, as it is,
20 in a central position, is much frequented by ships from all parts of India and from Persia and Ethiopia and it likewise sends out many of its own. And from the remotest countries, I mean Tzinista (China) and other trading places, it receives silk, aloes, cloves, sandalwood and other products, and these again are passed on to marts on this side, such as Malé, where pepper grows, and to
25 Calliana, which exports copper and sasame logs and cloth for making dresses, for it also is a great place for business. And to Sindu (Diul Sindh at the mouth of the Indus) also where musk and castor is procured, and androstachys (possibly spikenard), and to Persia and the Homerite country (Yemen) and to Adulé (Zula on the African coast of the Red Sea). And the island
30 receives imports from all these marts which we have mentioned, and passes them on to the remoter ports, while, at the same time, exporting its own produce in both directions[1].

---

1) Cosmas Indicopleustes, Christian Topography, 365 (Hakluyt Soc. edit.). Among the products which Cosmas mentions as coming from China, the only real Chinese product is silk.
35 The ships which came to Ceylon from China got the eaglewood, cloves, sandalwood, etc., at the various ports in Indo-China and the Malay Archipelago at which they stopped. Edrisi (I. 51 Jaubert's transl.) makes a similar loose statement about the products of China brought to Aden. He says «The town of Aden is small but renowned on account of its port, whence sail the ships

It seems evident that, during ancient and mediaeval times, the sea-trade between Egypt and Persia on the one side, and India and the Far East on the other, remained nearly exclusively in the hands of the enterprising Arabs of the southern Arabian coast, who, in very early days, established stations at all the principal ports-of-call along the coast to the south of the Indus and thence ultimately to Canton where, as we shall see, they appear to have had a settlement or colony as early as A. D. 300. So far as can be gathered the Greeks took little or no share in this trade beyond the Malabar coast, and, as the sequel will show, there is absolutely no evidence to substantiate the assertion that the Chinese did either [1]. Greeks may have got to China, and Chinese may have travelled in the sixth century as far as Aden or the head of the Persian Gulf, to Hormuz, Siráf, Basra or Baghdad, but these were isolated cases of commercial adventure, and do not affect the conclusion reached.

It was in about 120 B. C. that China first heard of the countries of western Asia, of Syria (Li-kan) and of Chaldaea (T'iau-chï). This information came to it through Chang K'ién, who had been sent by the Emperor Wu-ti on a political mission to the Yüé-chï (Kushān) to solicit their aid against the Hiung-nu, who were pressing on the Chinese western frontier. Chang K'ién only heard of the countries of the west when in Parthia (An-si), and the information he brought home concerning them was of the vaguest. It was not until the end of the first century of our era that a Chinese, Kan Ying, reached Chaldaea and gained some exact information concerning it and the sea-route which led from the head of the Persian Gulf to Syria and Egypt. But Kan Ying went no further than the mouth of the Euphrates, probably to the Apologos of the Greeks, when frightened by the reported dangers of the voyage, he retraced his steps [2].

---

for Sindh, India and China. There is brought there from the last named country such merchandize as iron, damasked sword blades, shagreen skins, musk, aloes wood (gharu?), horses, saddles, pottery, pepper, both odoriferous and non-odoriferous (i. e., black pepper and long peppers), cocoanuts, *hermut* (a perfumed seed), cardamoms, cinnamon, galangal, mace, myrobolans, ebony, tortoise-shell, camphor, nutmegs, cloves, cubebs, divers grass tissues, and others rich and velvety, elephants tusks, tin, rattans, and other reeds, as well as the greater part of the bitter aloes destined for commerce».

1) As for example R. Beazley, Dawn of modern geography, I, 490, and E. Speck, Handelsgeschichte des Alterthums, I, 29.

2) See F. Hirth, China and the Roman Orient, 35 et seqq., 137 et seqq. and E. Chavannes, Les Pays d'Occident d'après le Heou Han Chou, in T'oung-pao, 2ᵈ ser. VIII. 176, et seqq. Chavannes (176. n. 3) thinks it possible that the name T'iau-chï may be an attempt to transcribe the Persian word *desht* «plain», which is found used by early Arab writers to designate the Desht Misan, the Mesene at the mouth of the Tigris.

Although China appears to have first become known to the Greeks through the expedition of Alexander, (Nearchus and Onesicritus mention the Seres, of whose longevity they had heard marvellous tales, but which they evidently supposed to have been an Indian tribe), the first accurate information
5 concerning China was supplied by the author of the *Periplus of the Ery-thraean Sea*, writing somewhere about 80 A. D. He refers (§ 64) to the country of Thina as lying beyond the Malay Peninsula (Chrysé) «Where the sea terminates outwards». For more precise information concerning the geographical position of China, we have to come down to the first half of the
10 sixth century, when Cosmas Indicopleustes stated that Tzinista «was bounded to the east by the ocean».

Although the author of the Periplus knew little of China's position, he supplied other reliable information concerning it. We learn from him that already in his time there came from a city in the interior of that country
15 much silk «both raw and spun into thread and woven into fine stuff», also furs and iron, which were brought overland through Baktria to Bharoch (Barugaza) and to Diul-Sindh at the mouth of the Indus (Barbarikon), or to Mangalore (Muziris) and Nelisseram near Mt. Delli, by way of the Ganges. Nothing, however, is to be found in the Periplus to indicate that the author
20 had the slightest idea of there being any direct communication by sea between India or Ceylon and China. «Had such existed», Bunbury justly remarks,[1] «even in the hands of native traders, it is hardly possible that our author could have remained so entirely in the dark as we actually find him with regard to all the countries beyond the Ganges».

25 Chinese records confirm the belief that China had no relations by sea with India and the West at the beginning of our era. The earliest mention of a mission, or more probably a private expedition, arriving from the West (Ta-ts'in) in China is referred to in the year 166 A. D., when a party of foreigners representing themselves as sent by An-tun (the Emperor Marcus
30 Aurelius Antoninus) arrived by sea in Tongking, and proceeded thence overland to the court of the Emperor Huan-ti. Sixty years later, in 226, another westerner came to China, also a merchant from Ta-ts'in, Ts'in-lun by name; he also landed in Tongking, and was sent overland to the court of the Emperor Sun-ch'üan. When Ts'in-lun started on the return journey, the Emperor sent one
35 of his officers with him, but he died on the way, and T'sin-lun returned alone[2].

---

1) Ancient Geography, ii, 476.
2) Hirth, Op. cit., 42, 47, 48. 173—178.

Although direct intercourse between China and Ta-ts'in may be said to have begun with the arrival of the mission of A. D. 166, we are told by the Chinese that down to the sixth century no Chinese and but few (if any) persons from Kamboja, Annam or Tongking had reached the Far West (Ta-ts'in), though merchants from those parts came frequently to Indo-China[1]. 5

Regular trade relations between China and the regions lying immediately outside its southern and south-western border, Tongking and India, may be said to have begun in the latter part of the second century before our era, after the conquest of Tongking by the Chinese[2]. The bulk of the trade with 10 the latter country appears to have been conducted over the land routes and to have been concentrated at a few marts in close proximity to the frontier, although there can be little doubt that a coasting trade must have existed from even earlier times between Canton and the people of Tongking (Kiau-chï). However, official trade between the two countries followed the land 15 route from Hanoi to K'in-chóu in south-western Kuang-tung, which remained for many centuries the center of Chinese overland trade with Indo-China.

The mission of exploration of Chu Ying to the countries south of China, which was undertaken in the first half of the third century, by order of the Emperor Sun-ch'üan, who had tried to open relations with Ta-ts'in by means 20 of the trader Ts'in-lun, travelled, it would seem, overland. The narrative of this journey has not reached us, but it does not appear to have resulted in establishing relations of any increased importance with the neighbouring countries of Indo-China[3], for it was not until the last quarter of the third century that we hear of a tribute mission (i. e. a trading venture) from Siam (Fu- 25 nan) coming to the court of China.

Notwithstanding the lack of enterprise on the part of the Chinese in the first centuries of the Christian era, they were becoming better known

---

1) Sung-shu, 97. Liang-shu, 54. See also Hirth, Op. cit., 46, 47, 180. The presence of people from western Asia (Hu-jön) in Canton prior to the year 300 is confirmed by a reference 30 to them at that city and to the fact that they had introduced the cultivation of the jasmine (yé-si-ming, Persian yásmín. See Nan-fang-ts'au-mu-chuang, 2,2. This work was written A. D. 300. Hirth, Op. cit., 270—272, and J. Amer. Orient. Soc. XXX. 23.

2) When Ch'ang K'ién was in the country south of the Oxus, called Ta-hia, he learned that it had commercial relations with India and received from it products of Ssï-ch'uan. Already 35 in the beginning of the second century A. D. there was a regular trade — route from southwestern Yünnan to Pegu. Hirth Op. cit., 179.

3) See Ma Tuan-lin's remarks on this mission and on the slowness of the development of Chinese foreign relations — commercial and political, in the 5th, 6th and 7th centuries. Hervey St. Denis, Ethnographie des peuples étrangers à la Chine, II, 410. 40

to the rest of the world. Commerce by sea with south-eastern Asia and the countries lying to the west was steadily increasing through the continued energy and enterprise of the Arabs and Indians[1].

The troublous times through which China passed in the fourth, fifth and 5 sixth centuries may have had much to do with retarding the development of commercial enterprise on the part of the people of the southern provinces, but piracy was probably more effective in keeping them off the sea. In the middle of the fifth century, Chinese living along the southern coast were so harried by the Tongking pirates, who plundered cities and towns, that the 10 Emperor Wön-ti of the Sung had to send, in 447, a punitive expedition into Indo-China, which laid the country waste and sacked the capital[2].

How hazy were the notions of the Chinese of the fifth century of India and the West, how slight the intercourse established with them, may be seen in the Sung-shu, the history of the period extending from A. D. 420 to 478, 15 and written about A. D. 500. In chapter 97 we read: «As regards the Roman Orient (Ta-ts'in) and India, far out on the Western Ocean (迴出西溟), though the envoys of the two Han dynasties have experienced the special difficulties of this route, yet trade has been carried on, and goods have been sent out to the foreign tribes, the force of the wind driving them far across 20 the waves of the sea. There are lofty (ranges of) hills quite different (from those we know) and a great variety of populous tribes having different names and bearing uncommon designations, they being of a class quite different (from our own). All the precious things of land and water come from there.......all this has caused navigation and trade to be extended to those 25 parts» (舟舶繼路商使交屬)[3]. From this we infer that at that time what trade there was between China, India, and the West was not in Chinese hands, and that the Chinese had but a vague notion of the lands whence the products of foreign countries were brought to them, and to which none of their people had ever gone. Additional evidence of this is furnished 30 by other dynastic histories covering the period from the end of the fourth to the beginning of the seventh centuries, in which we find all the products of Indo-China, Ceylon, India, Arabia, and the east coast of Africa classed as

---

1) In A. D. 414 the pilgrim Fa-hién embarked in Java on a large merchant ship bound for Canton. The people on board were «Po-lo-mön», a name used in those days by the Chinese to 35 designate the west coast of India from Kulam to the mouth of the Indus. Legge, A Record of Buddhist Kingdoms, 111—115. See also infra, p. 12.

2) Mᶜ Gowan, History of China, 209, 210.

3) Hirth, Op. cit., 46, 180.

«products of Persia (Po-ssï),» the country of the majority of the traders who
brought these goods to China[1].

In the seventh century Chinese maritime enterprise began to manifest
itself, and we hear of Chinese making at least one sea voyage of considerable
length. In the third year of his reign, A. D. 607, Sui Yang-ti sent a mission   5
by sea to Siam (Ch'ï-t'u) to open commercial relations with it. The explorers
were back in 610, and, from the fact that they received high official prefer-
ment, there is little doubt that the exploit was held to be a most extraordinarily daring one[2].

In 629 the famous pilgrim Hüan-tsang started on his travels through   10
Central Asia and India. He reached the south-eastern coast of India near
Ceylon, but the notions he brought back of the latter country were still of the
vaguest. He did not even know that it was an island. He heard of some islands
«some thousands of li» to the south and the west of Ceylon, but apparently
never a word reached him of intercourse by sea existing between India and   15
Ceylon and the countries to the east, Sumatra, Java, Indo-China and China.
The pilgrims to India who succeeded him followed at first the overland route

---

1) See Wei-shu, 102, Sect. Po-ssï. Sui-shu, 83, Sect. Po-ssï.

2) The explorers Chang Tsun and Wang Kün embarked at Canton in the month of
November 607 (10th moon), and, sailing day and night for 20 days with the monsoon, they passed   20
Tsiau-shï island (焦 石 山) and anchored S. E. of it at Ling-kié-po-pa-to island (陵 伽
鉢 拔 多 洲), which faces Lin-i (Tongking) to the W. and on which there is a temple
(神 祠 devālaya). Continuing S. they came to the Shï-tzï rocks (師 子 石), where there
are a great many contiguous islands and islets, whence continuing for two or three days they sighted
in the W. the hills of Lang-ya-sü (狼 牙 須). Thence S. by the Ki-lung island (雞 籠 島)   25
they came to the frontier of Ch'ï-t'u.

On the return voyage, on which they were accompanied by Siamese envoys, they noted
shoals of green flying-fish. After ten days they came to the high coast of Lin-i, when for a whole
day the ship sailed through a strip of yellowish, foul smelling water, which, it was said, was the
dung of a great fish. Following to the N. coast of the sea they came to Kiau-chï (Hanoi?), where   30
it seems that their sea voyage finished. See Sui shu, 82. Sect. Ch'ï-t'u.

Tsiau-shï island, is tentatively identified with the island of Tseu, Hon Tseu on the maps,
1½ miles S. E. of Mui (Cape) Duong, in the Ha-Tinh district on the coast of Annam, near Tourane.
(See Gerini, Asiat. Quart. Rev., 3d ser. XI, 156). Ling-kié-po-pa-to island, is identified by the same
(loc. sup. cit.) with Cape Varella. It is evidently the same as Mount Ling of Kia Tan (see infra,   35
p. 10) which Pelliot thinks may possibly be Cape Sa-hoi, N. of Quinhon. The Shï-tzï rocks,
Gerini thinks (p. 157) may be Pulo Sapatu of the Catwick group, or else Pulo Cecir de Mer not
far N. of Pulo Sapatu. Lang-ya-sü is identified by Gerini (p. 157) with the Lankachiu islands,
Koh Katu on the charts, intended for Koh Kachin (i. e., Koh Lankachiu) in the gulf of Siam,
opposite Swai Bay, a little below C'hump'hon Bay. Although the name Lang-ka-sü was applied   40
by mediaeval Chinese to several places in the Southern Seas widely apart, Gerini cannot, it would
seem, be far wrong. Ki-lung island, is tentativaly identified by Gerini (p. 158) with Koh-rang-kai
or «Hen's nest island», one of a group of 4 islets, S. of Lem (Cape) C'hong P'hrah, some
20 miles above C'hump'hon Bay.

by Balkh, Peshawar, Tibet and Nepaul, but in the latter part of the seventh
century the sea-route became nearly exclusively used[1], the port of embar-
kation being Canton, whence the travellers made western Java (Ho-ling), or
more usually Palembang in Sumatra. Here they changed ships and, taking
5 a course along the northern coast of Sumatra and by the Nicobar Islands,
came to Ceylon, where they usually took ship for Tamlook at the mouth of
the Ganges and thence reached the holy places of India by land. The voyage
took about three months, one month from Canton to Palembang, one to the
north-west point of Sumatra and one to Ceylon; it was always made with the
10 north-east monsoon in winter, and the return voyage to China in summer,—
from April to October — with the south-west monsoon.

It seems that by this time the sea-trade of the Hindus and Arabs with
the Malay Archipelago and China had assumed very considerable importance,
and this accounts partly for the fuller and more accurate accounts of the
15 countries of southern Asia and the Archipelago given in the Chinese Annals
of the sixth and seventh centuries.

The earliest Chinese testimony we have concerning this trade is of the
eighth century[2]. From it we learn that the ships engaged in this trade and
which visited Canton were very large, so high out of the water that ladders
20 several tens of feet in length had to be used to get aboard. The foreign
(Fan 番) captains who commanded them were registered in the office of the
Inspector of Maritime Trade (Shĭ-po-shĭ). This office (the existence of which, by
the way, proves the importance of this trade), before allowing the ships to clear
required that the manifests should be submitted to it, and then collected export
25 duty and also the freight charges. The export of «precious and rare articles»
was forbidden, and attempts at smuggling were punished with imprisonment.

With the exception of the chapters devoted to foreign lands in the
Annals, very little has come down to us concerning the extent of Chinese
geographical knowledge in the eighth century. One document of great value
30 has fortunately been preserved in the itineraries compiled by Kia Tan between
785 and 805[3]. The one dealing with the sea-route from Canton to the Per-

---

1) I-tsing mentions 60 Chinese pilgrims who in the latter part of the seventh century made
the journey to India. Of these 22 travelled overland and 37 took the sea-route. See Chavannes,
Mém. sur les Religieux éminents, passim.

35   2) T'ang-Kuo-shĭ-pu, by Li Chan, a work of the beginning of the ninth century, but
purporting to record historical facts concerning the period from 713 to 825.

3) Given in T'ang-shu, 43[b]. See also Pelliot, Deux itinéraires de Chine en Inde, 131
et seqq. (in B. E. F. E. O., IV). On Kia Tan, who died in 805, see Mém. conc. les Chinois, XVI,
151—152.

sian Gulf enables us to determine the extent of Chinese knowledge in this
direction, and leads us to believe that it was for a great part, — especially
that bearing on the route from Kulam to the Persian Gulf, — entirely second
hand, and supplied by the foreign traders who frequented Canton and
presumably often visited other cities of China. It is particularly interesting
to note that Kia Tan seems to have had no knowledge of the regular direct
route between Kulam-Malé and the Persian Gulf followed by Arab ships.
Why Kia Tan's informants should have told him only of the roundabout, little
followed coasting route from Kulam to the Persian Gulf must remain — of
course — a matter of conjecture; it may have been, however, that he was
not told of the regular course for the purpose of keeping the Chinese from
attempting to compete in the valuable trade, of which the Arabs and Persians
had a monopoly.

Kia Tan's sailing directions read as follows: «From Kuang-chóu towards
the south-east, travelling by sea for 200 li, one reaches Mount Tʻun-mön[1]
(屯 門). Then, with a favourable wind going westward for two days, one
reaches the Kiu-chóu rocks[2] (九 州).· Then southward, and after two days
one reaches the Siang-shï[3] (象 石), or «Elephant rock». Then southward,
after three days, one comes to Mount Chan-pu-lau[4] (占 不 勞); this mountain is in the sea at 200 li east of the country of Huan-wang[5] (環 王).

«Then southward, after two days journey, one reaches Mount Ling[6]
(陵). Then after a day's journey one comes to the country of Mön-tu[7] (門

---

1) Tʻun-mön is mentioned as one of the several passages leading out to sea from Sin-an-
hién, the next one mentioned being Ki-shui-mön, i. e. the passage known to sailors as Capsing-
moon, or Kapsuy-moon (see Kuang-tung-sin-yü, 2,15). The best known native map of the province,
the Kuang-tung-tʻu, has a village called Tʻun-mön-tsʻun on the coast of the continent right
opposite the northern spit of Lantao Isd. I suppose the following passage appearing in an early
account of the China Coast (Chinese Repository, V, 348) refers to this anchorage: «Just after
passing out of Kapshwuy Moon towards the northeast, there is a bay protected by the island
Chungyue (青 衣 ?) on the south, which affords good anchorage, is perfectly land-locked, and
was the principal rendez-vous of the pirates in the early part of this century. It was examined
by a party of English and American gentlemen last year, and pronounced to be one of the safest
harbors in the world».

2) Taya islands, N. E. point of Hai-nan. Pelliot, B. E. F. E. O., IV, 216.

3) Tinhosa island, or a point even farther south, Pelliot, ibid., 216.

4) Culao Cham. Pelliot, ibid., 200.

5) The kingdom of Huan-wang was practically the same as the Chan-chʻöng of the
Sung period. It included, in the Sung period, most of the Tongking and Annam coast
country.

6) Possibly Cape Sa-hoi, N. of Quinhon. Pelliot, ibid., 217. See also supra p. 8. Ling-
kié-po-pa-to island some writers think was Cape Varella.

7) Probably near Quinhon, but unidentified.

毒); then after a day's journey one comes to the country of Ku-tan[1] (古 笪); then after half a day's journey one reaches the territory of Pön-t'o-lang[2] (奔 陀 浪). Then after two days' travel one reaches Mount Kün-t'u-nung[3] (軍 突 弄). Then after five days' travel one comes to a strait which the Barbarians call Chï[4] (質). From the south to the north it is 100 li. On the northern shore is the country of Lo-yüe[5] (羅 越); on the southern coast is the country of Fo-shï[6] (佛 逝).

«To the east of the country of Fo-shï, travelling by water for four or five days, one comes to the country of Ho-ling[7] (訶 陵); it is the largest of the islands of the south. Then east(west?)ward, going out of the strait, after three days, one comes to the country of Ko-ko-söng-chï (or ti)[8] (葛 葛 僧 祇 or 祇), which is an island separated at the north-east point from Fo-shï. The people of this country are pirates and cruel; sailors dread them.

«On the northern coast (of the strait) is the country of Ko-lo[9] (箇 羅), and to the west of Ko-lo is the country of Ko-ku-lo[10] (哥 谷 羅). Then from Ko-ko-söng-chï, after four or five days' journey, one comes to the island (洲) of Shöng-töng[11] (勝 鐙). Then westward, and after five days' journey

---

1) Kaṇṭhara, the sanskrit name of the present Nha-trang. Pelliot, ibid., 217.

2) Panduranga, the present Phanrang, see infra, p. 51.

3) Pulo Condore. See infra, p. 50, n. 10.

4) Pelliot sees in this the Strait of Malacca. I agree with Gerini (J. R. A. S., 1905, 505) in thinking it was the Singapore strait.

5) The southern extremity of the Malay Peninsula, or Ligor. Gerini, Researches on Ptolemy's Geography of Eastern Asia, 820.

6) Eastern Sumatra. According to our text the voyage from Canton to E. Sumatra occupied 20 days; this is exactly the time taken by the pilgrim I-tsing to make it. Chavannes, Relig. émin., 119.

7) Java, but see infra, p. 78, n. 1.

8) Possibly the Brouwers islands, as suggested by Pelliot, op. cit., 339. Gerini, Researches, 816, 817 identifies this island with Pulo Medang, the old designation of which was Kūkor. It lies W. of the mouth of the Siak river, E. coast of Sumatra or Pulo Siak.

9) In all likelihood the Kalah of the Arabs of the ninth century, which Groeneveldt, Notes, 122, has identified with the present Kora on the W. coast of Malacca in about 7° N. lat. — Gerini, Asiat. Quart., 3d series, XIII, 133, and Pelliot, op. cit., 339 accept this identification. Gerini, Researches, 817, thinks Kia Tan's Ko-lo may be Kalapang near the Umbai river, just below Malacca.

10) Pelliot, Op. cit., 343 thinks this is the Qaqola (قاقلة) of Ibn Batuta, the Angkola river on the W. coast of Sumatra, and an affluent of the Batang gadis. This identification seems to me impossible since Ko-lo was on the Malay Peninsula, and the two seem to have been conterminous. Gerini, Researches, 444, n. 2 suggests, with great plausibility, either Kelantan or Ligor on the E. coast of the Malay Peninsula.

11) Pelliot, Op. cit., 354, thinks this may have been the Deli or Langkat district of Sumatra. Gerini, Op. cit., 817, says it is the Serdang district near Deli.

one comes to the country of P'o-lu¹ (婆露). Then after six days' journey
one reaches the island of K'ié-lan² (伽藍) of the country of P'o³ (婆).
Then northward, and after four days' travel one reaches «the country of the
Lion»⁴ (獅子); its northern coast is 100 li from the southern coast of
southern India. Then westward, after four days' journey one passes through 5
the country of Mo-lai⁵ (沒來), which is the extreme southern frontier of
southern India.

«Thence (from Mo-lai) northwest and passing by (經) more than ten
small countries, one comes to the western frontier of P'o-lo-mön⁶ (婆羅

1) Presumably some place in N. W. Sumatra, Perlak or Pedir. It may be the same on the 10
«kingdom of P'o» referred to in the next phrase, and of which the Nicobar islands were a
dependency.

2) There is little room for doubt that the island of K'ié-lan is one of the Nicobars. I-tsing
states that it took him ten days' sailing in a northerly direction from Kié-ch'a — which was some
place on the N. W. coast of Sumatra near Kia Tan's P'o or P'o-lu (if not identical with it) to reach 15
the Lo (裸) country, or «the country of naked people». Chavannes, Religieux éminents, 120.
Hüan-tsang was the first Chinese writer to mention the Nicobars by name, he calls them Na-lo-
ki-lo islands (那羅稽羅洲), a transcription of Sanskrit nārikera, «cocoanut», which he
and I-tsing and the Arab Relations state was the principal food of the islanders. The name used by
I-tsing may be an abbreviated from of that used by Hüan-tsang. K'ié-lan is also an abbreviated 20
form of the Sanskrit name, or rather a transcription of the two last syllables -kera. In the fifteenth
century the Chinese called these islands Ts'ui-lan (翠藍). Gerini, Researches, 396, suggests
with a high degree of probability that Ts'ui-lan-shan is but the phonetic transcript of Tilong-
chong, the native name of the north-easternmost of the Nicobars. The Sanskrit name Nārikera is
found in Necuveram, the name Polo gives to these islands. Yule, Marco Polo (2ᵈ edit.), II, 289— 25
292. See also Beal, Records, II. 251, Chavannes, Relig. émin., 100, 120; Geo. Phillips R.
A. S., 1895, 529.

3) Possibly the same as the P'o-lu in the preceding phrase. Gerini, Op. cit., 817, says
«P'o simply stands for bār, vār, and is thus a contraction of Nikobār, if not actually meant for
Bharu, in which case Chia Tan's P'o kingdom would recall the ancient Bharu kingdom». 30
According to Buddhist tradition, he says, the Bharu kingdom, as the result of a cataclysm,
became detached from the continent of India, forming a thousand islands which, according to the
scholiast, is identical with the island of Nālikera, mentioned by Hüan-tsang. Ibid. 399.

4) Fa-hién first used this name to designate Ceylon, which he was probably the first to
make known to his countrymen. It is a translation of the Sanskrit name Singhala. In the twelfth 35
century some Chinese writers, who had got their knowledge concerning the island from Arab
traders, wrote the name of the island Si-lan. See infra, Ch. XIII.

5) The Malabar coast and more particularly the port of Quilon. In the sixth century Cosmas
refers to the city of Malé, where there was a settlement of Christians — Christian Topography,
119. A century later Hüan-tsang calls this country Mo-lo-kü-ts'a (秝羅矩吒), in 40
Sanskrit Malakūṭa. The form Mo-la-yé (摩剌耶) or Malaya also occurs at about the same
time. The Arab Relations of the ninth century use the form Kulam-Malé (كولم ملى). In the Sung
period Quilon was called by the Chinese Ku-lin (故臨 or 古林), and in the Yüan period
Kü-lan (俱藍).

6) In another passage of these Itineraries, Kia Tan says «From the southern frontier of 45
Po-lo-mön by way of Mo-lai to Wu-la, all (this) is the eastern shore of the Green Sea» (緑海
the Arab name of the Ocean). Po-lo-mön meant therefore the whole of the west coast of India.

門). Then going north-west for two days, one comes to the country of Pa-yü [1]
(拔 颭). Then going ten days, and passing by (經) the western frontier of
T'ién-chu (天 竺 i. e., India) (and) five small countries, one comes to the
country of Ti-yü [2] (提 颭), in which country is the great river Mi-lan [3]
5 (彌 蘭), also called (一 曰) the Sin-t'ou (新 頭) river. It comes from the
mountains of P'o-lun [4] (渤 崙) in the north and flows westward; on arriving
north of the country of Ti-yü it empties into the sea.

«Again going westward from the kingdom of Ti-yü twenty days and
passing more that twenty little countries, one comes to the country of Ti-lo-
10 lu-ho (提 羅 盧 和), also called the country of Lo-ho-i (羅 和 異). The
people of this country have set up ornamented pillars (華 表) in the sea, on
which at night they place torches (炬) so that people travelling on board
ships at night shall not go astray. [5]

---

1) Presumably some port on the coast of the Guzerat peninsula, the Balabhi or Vala-
15 bhadra kingdom of the sixth and seventh centuries. The name suggests the island of Diu, an
important port in mediaeval times, but I do not know whether it existed in the eighth century.
2) This seems to be the Taïz (تيز) of mediaeval Arab geographers. According to Abulfeda
(II. Pt. 2, 111, Reinaud's transl.) Taïz was the port on the Indus for the Mekran and adjacent
countries. It was on the banks of the Indus, to the west, near the canal which left the river not
20 far from Mansurah (Brahmanābād). Ti-yü may, however, represent Daibul, which was on the
Indus at its mouth, and which was the principal port of Sindh in mediaeval times.
3) The Arabs called the Indus Nahr Mihrān. Since the time of Fa-hién the Chinese had
known of the Indus under its Indian name of Sindhu.
4) It appears probable that P'o-lun is the same country as Hüan-tsang's Po-lu-lo (鉢
25 露 羅) or Bolor, the modern Balti, the Palow of Marco Polo. It is possible, however, that
we should read K'un-lun (崑 崙), for Liang-shu, 54,16 says that the great river called Sin-t'au
(新 陶 Sindhu) has its source in the K'un-lun mountains.
5) Ti-lo-lu-ho, or Lo-ho-i does not occur in any other Chinese work I have seen. I am
inclined to look for this country on the Mekran coast, about a day's sailing S. E. of Cape
30 Mesandum. Geo. Phillips (J. R. A. S., 1896, 525) thinks the beacons referred to in our text were
near Al-Ubullah on the Tigris estuary, and he mentions passages in Masudi and Abulfeda to the
effect that marks are said to have been erected in the sea near Al-Ubullah (الأبلة), see Masudi,
Prairies d'or, I, 230; Lee's Travels of Ibn Batuta, 36 note, and Istakhri (Mordtmann's transl.,
18). If the indication given in the text as to the distance between the mouth of the Indus and the
35 point on the coast where the beacons were is anyway near correct — 20 days, it is quite impossible
that Al-Ubullah can be referred to, we must look for them not farther than the mouth of the Persian
Gulf. The most natural identification of the place where the beacons were erected seems to be
with Cape Mesandum on the Oman coast. The Arab Relations of the ninth century (Reinaud,
Relations, I, 14) state that on the coast of Oman there was a place called Aldordur, a very narrow
40 passage between two mountains which small boats passed through, but in which the China ships
could not enter. There were two rocks called Kossayr and Uayr; only a small portion of the rocks
was seen above water. See also Masudi, Op. cit., I, 240. These rocks are, I take it, the huge basalt
rocks seen some miles out at sea beyond Cape Mesandum. See W. G. Palgrave, Central and
Eastern Arabia, II, 317.
45   Marco Polo speaking of Kalhat, which stood near Cape Mesandum, says «This city of
Calatu stands at the mouth of the Gulf, so that no ship can enter or go forth without the will

«Again going westward one day one comes to the country of Wu-la[1] (烏剌).

«Now (乃) the Fu-li-la river — (弗利剌河) of the realm of the Ta-shï flows southward into the sea. Small boats ascend it two days and reach the country of Mo-lo (末羅), an important market (重鎮) of the Ta-shï[2].

«Again going overland (from Mo-lo?) in a north-westerly direction for one thousand li one comes to the capital of the Prince of the Mau-mön (茂門王), (which is called) the city of Fu-ta[3] (縛達城)».

By the beginning of the seventh century the foreign colony at Canton, mostly composed of Persians and Arabs, must have been a numerous one, for Islam seems to have been brought there between 618 and 626. There is even some evidence for believing that the Moslim had also settlements at that time in Ts'üan-chóu and Yang-chóu; Ts'üan-chóu, however, became of importance in their China trade only in the ninth century[4]. By the middle of the eighth

---

of the chief». He also notes that the chief of Kalhat was subject to Hormuz». Yule's Marco Polo, II, 448.

1) Wu-la is, I think, to be identified with Sohar in Oman, on account of the indications concerning its position given in the text. It is probably the same as Chau-Ju-kua's Wu-pa (infra, Chs. XXVI and XXVIII).

2) Mo-lo I am disposed to identify with Old Hormuz, which lay at a distance of two post-stages, or half a day's march, from the coast, at the head of a creek called Al-Jir, according to Istakhri, «by which after one league ships come up thereto from the sea». Le Strange, Lands of the Eastern Caliphate, 318. Ibn Batuta, Voyages, II, 230 calls Old Hormuz Mughostān, which may be the original of the Chinese name Mo-lo. On Old Hormuz, see Yule, Marco Polo, I, 113 and Heyd, Histoire du Commerce, II, 133. Assuming that the identification of Mo-lo with Hormuz is correct, it is interesting to note that this is the only reference in Chinese works to this great port of the Persian Gulf. This is another proof that the Chinese cannot have taken any personal part in the sea trade with Persia in the eighth century, as Geo. Phillips (J. R. A. S. 1895, 525) thinks they did. The Al-Jir of Istakhri is the present Mináb river.

3) Mau-mön is Arabic Momenīn «the Faithful». The title Ameer al Momenīn, or 'Commander of the Faithful' was first assumed by Omar (635—644). Caliph (Successor) of the Prophet of the Lord, was, he said 'too long and cumbersome a name, while the other was easier and more fit for common use.' Muir, Annals of early Caliphate, 285. This is the earliest occurrence of this title in Chinese works.

Fu-ta might be the city of Fostat, the modern Cairo, which is spoken of by Chau Ju-kua (infra Ch. XXXVI) as el Kahira (K'ié-yé). Fostat was founded in or about A. D. 641. It is possible, though, that the first character of this name is incorrectly written in our text and that it should be Po (縛) and that Baghdad is meant. This city was founded by the Caliph Mansur in 762.

4) W. F. Mayers, quoting the Min-shu, says that sometime between A. D. 618 and 626 four disciples of Mohammed are supposed to have brought Islamism to China. One taught at Canton, one in Yang-chóu and the two others at Ts'üan-chóu. China Review, VI, 276. The Pan-yü-hién-chï, as quoted by Edkins in Opium, Historical note, etc., 5, says Mohammed sent his mother's brother to China. See also Dabry de Thiersant, Mahométanisme en Chine, I, 86—97, and G. Devéria, Origine de l'Islamisme en Chine, 319—325.

century the Mohammedans at Canton, — which they called Khanfu, — had become so numerous that in 758 they were able, for some reason which has not come down to us, to sack and burn the city and make off to sea with their loot[1].

5   The earliest Arab narratives concerning the China trade date from the ninth century. They are those of a trader called Soleyman and of Ibn Wahab of Basra; the former made the voyage to China in the first half of the century, the latter in the second. They have been recorded by the Zeyd Hassan of Siraf in his little work entitled Salsalat-al-tewarykh, or «Chain of 10 Chronicles»[2]. From it we learn that at this time the products of China were very expensive and scarce in the markets of Basra and Baghdad, on account of the fires in Canton which frequently destroyed them, and also by reason of the frequent wrecking of the ships engaged in the trade and the acts of pirates. Some of the trade also went to the ports in the Yemen and to other 15 countries. The ships engaged in the China trade[3] sailed from Siraf on the coast of Fars, where the goods were brought from Basra, Oman and other places. They then went to Mascat, whence they sailed for Kulam-Malé, which port was reached in a month. Passing the Nicobar Islands they made directly for Kalah on the Malay Peninsula, which was reached in a month 20 from Kulam. From Kalah four days were employed to reach Pulo Condore, from which point a month's sail brought them to Canton.

On arriving at Canton each ship handed over its cargo to the agents of the Chinese Government, and it was stored until the last ship of the season's fleet arrived, when three-tenths of the merchandise was retained as import 25 duty and the balance handed back to the owners. The principal imports into

1) T'ang-shu, 10 and 258[b]. See also Bretschneider, Early Chinese and Arabs, 10—11 and Chavannes, Documents sur les Tou-Kioué, 173. Khanfu is Kuang (chóu) Fu. On the identity of Khanfu of the Arabs with Canton, see infra p. 20, n. 3 and 22, n. 1.

2) Text and translation published by Reinaud in Relation des Voyages faits par les 30 Arabes et les Persans dans l'Inde et à la Chine. See p. 12 et seqq. See also E. Dulaurier, Journ. Asiat., 1846, № 10.

3) The text reads «Chinese ships.» Masudi (Prairies d'or, I, 308) also speaks of «the ships of China which used to go to Oman, to Siraf, to Obollah and Basra, while the ships of those countries sailed directly for China.» The so-called «Chinese ships» may have been built in China, 35 but it seems highly improbable that they were owned or navigated by Chinese. Down to the end of the twelfth century the names of Aden and Siraf even were unknown to the Chinese. Chóu K'ü-feï, Ling-wai-tai-ta, II, 13 says distinctly that «when the Chinese traders (中 國 舶 商) wished to go to the countries of the Arabs they had to embark at Quilon on small boats (舟) on which, with a fair wind, they could make the voyage in a month. There is no 40 evidence that it was not the same in the time of Soleyman and Masudi.

China were, according to Soleyman, ivory, frankincense, copper, tortoise-shell, camphor, and rhinoceros horns [1].

The importance of the Moslim settlement in Canton in the ninth century may be guaged by Soleyman's statement that one of the Musulmans was appointed by the Chinese authorities to maintain order among his coreligionists and administer the law of Islam. On feast-days he said prayers, repeated the *khotba* and prayed for the welfare of the Caliph. From Chinese sources we learn that this organization was extended at a later date to the foreign settlements at Ts'üan-chóu, Hang-chóu and elsewhere, in all of which the Moslim had their *kadi* and their *sheikhs*, their mosques and their bazaars. A Chinese work of the beginning of the twelfth century [1] notes the following interesting facts concerning the foreign [2] (蕃) settlement of Canton:

---

1) Reinaud, Op. cit., I, 13, 33—35. Cf. also supra, p. 3 and infra, p. 19, n. 1. The Wei-shu, 102, the history of the period between 385 and 556, and written prior to 572, mentions among the products of Po-ssï (Persia), — by which it seems probable should be understood products brought or made known to China by Persians — coral, amber, cornelians, pearls, glass, both transparent and opaque, rock-crystal, diamonds (? *kin-k'ang*), steel, cinnabar, quicksilver, frank-incense, turmeric, storax, putchuk, damasks, brocaded muslins, black pepper, long peppers, dates, aconite, gall nuts and galangal. The Sui-shu, 83, which relates the events of the period extending from 581 to 617, and which was certainly written before 650, reproduces substantially the above list of Persian products, to which it adds gold, silver, *tush*, lead, sandalwood, various tissues, sugar and indigo. Most of these products came, of course, from India or from countries of south-eastern Asia, only a few being products of Arabia or countries bordering on the Persian Gulf. See also infra p. 19 for the lists of foreign imports into China at the end of the tenth century.

1) P'ing-chóu-k'o-t'an (萍 洲 可 談) by Chu Yü (朱 彧) II, 1—4. This work appears from internal evidence to have been written in the first quarter of the twelfth century. The latest date found in it refers to the period between 1111 and 1117. The father of the author was an official at Canton in the latter part of the eleventh century. All the quotations from this work are taken from Ch. II, p. 1—4. Hirth, The Ancient History of China, etc., 133.

2) By «foreigner» (*fan*) the author understands Moslim of all nationalities. He says they did not eat pork, and only ate domestic animals (fish and turtles excepted) which they had killed them-selves. Their women answered to the name of P'u-sa-man (菩 薩 蠻), the Chinese transcription of the name Musulman, the Bussurman of mediaeval Russian annalists, the Bisermin of Friar John of Pian di Carpine.

In Ibn Batuta's time (beginning of the fourteenth century) the Mohammedan quarter of Canton was inside the city; at Ts'üan-chóu they had a city of their own. Voyages, IV, 273. 269. As relating to the foreign Moslim settlement in Canton in the thirteenth century, the foll-owing, taken from Tung-nan-ki-wön (東 南 記 聞), a work written in the beginning of the Yüan dynasty, but referring to events during the previous Sung dynasty, is of interest. It says (3,6[b]): «Many Sea Lao (海 獠) live scattered about in Canton. The most prominent among them was a man surnamed P'u (蒲 Abu) who was by birth a noble of Chan-ch'öng. Later on he took up his permanent residence in China, to attend to his import and export trade. He lived inside the city where his home was furnished in the most luxurious fashion, for in wealth he was the first of the time.

«His disposition was very superstitious, and he loved neatness. For his prayers he had a hall in which was a tablet which served as a god (爲 像 主). Whenever there was a gather-

«In the foreign quarter (蕃 坊) in Kuang-chóu (Canton) reside all the people from beyond the seas (海 外). A foreign head-man (蕃 長) is appointed over them and he has charge of all public matters connected with them. He makes it his special duty to urge upon the foreign traders to send
5 in tribute (to the Chinese court). The foreign official wears a hat, gown, shoes, and (carries) a tablet just like a Chinese. When a foreigner commits an offense anywhere, he is sent to Kuang-chóu (Canton), and if the charge is proved (before the Chinese authorities?), he is sent to the foreign quarter[1]. (There he is) fastened to a ladder (木 梯 上) and is whipped with a rattan from head
10 to foot, three blows of a rattan being reckoned equal to one of the heavy bamboo. As foreigners do not wear drawers and like to squat on the ground, beating with the heavy bamboo on the buttocks proves most painful, whereas they do not fear beating on the back. Offenses entailing banishment or more severe punishments are carried out by the Department Magistrate of Kuang-
15 chóu»[2].

Somewhere about the ninth century, possibly even earlier, a portion of the southern sea-trade of China was diverted to Ts'üan-chóu, near Amoy, which had had commercial relations with Japan and Korea for centuries past, and where the Arabs found the products of those countries and of remote
20 parts of China not easily reached from Canton, besides probably receiving

---

ing (of his people) to feast (at his home), they did not use spoons or chopsticks: they had very large platters (lit. «big troughs» 巨 槽) of gold and silver in which was fresh water porpoise (鮭) and millet (or rice 粱 米) cooked together. They sprinkled rose (water) about, and put their right hands under their skirts, all picking up the food with their left hand».
25   1) Gambling appears to have been prohibited, but the game of chess was allowed. The P'ing-chóu k'o-t'an, loc. sup. cit., says «In the foreign quarter of Canton one sees foreigners playing the «elephant game» (i. e., the Chinese game of chess). They do not have rooks (車) or knights (馬), but a number of pieces made of ivory, rhinoceros horn, gharu wood or sandal-wood, which the two players move in turn according to certain rules. They play as an amusement (not for
30 stakes) and it is not usually inquired into». — The game was probably a kind of backgammon called *nerd*.
      2) From this it appears that the right to inflict capital punishment on foreign residents was reserved by the Chinese government. As regards mixed civil cases in which Chinese and foreigners were parties, we learn from another passage of the P'ing-chóu-k'o-t'an (2,3ᵃ) that there was at
35 Canton an office under the orders of the Superintendent of Merchant Shipping which received all complaints (of Chinese) for non payment of loans or interest on loans made to foreigners. The custom of the Cantonese was to ask of traders double the amount lent, irrespective of the period for which the money was lent. Payment was made in merchandise, which were taken at the market price at the time of settlement.
40   The Adjaib says that the moslim settlements in India had each their *honarmen*, who tried all cases against Musulmans according to the laws of Islam. Merveilles de l'Inde, 161. Apparently the same power was given the *honarmen* in China, though the carrying out of certain sentences was done by the Chinese authorities.

more favourable treatment from the local customs. Two centuries later this port became of nearly equal importance with Canton; the Arab settlement became much larger than at the latter place, and the fame of the city extended throughout the mediaeval world under its Arab name of Zaytun[1].

The troubles which broke out in China in the latter part of the ninth [5] century, when the revolted troops of the Tʻang Emperor Hi-tsung (874 — 889) sacked Soochow, Chang-chóu and Chʻö-kiang, and Fu-kién generally, interrupted for a time established trade relations, and caused the foreigners at Canton and Tsʻüan-chóu to seek refuge at Kalah on the west coast of the Malay Peninsula, and presumably Palembang; and at the former place the [10] ships from Siraf and Oman met those which came from China. Trade was carried on in this way down to at least the beginning of the tenth century, for Masudi says it was so at the time he visited that place[2]. It seems possible that the ships which plied at this time between China and the Malay Peninsula were really Chinese-manned ships. In the twelfth century, as is shown [15] further on, Chinese (Cantonese) sea-going junks went as far as Quilon on the Malabar coast, and this seems to be the farthest point west ever reached by them before the Ming dynasty.

At the end of the tenth century Canton and Tsʻüan-chóu had revived,

---

1) There has been much discussion concerning Zaytun, whether it was the present Tsʻüan- [20] chóu — east of Amoy, or Chang-chóu — west of that port. The conclusion now nearly universally accepted is that Zaytun of the Sung and Yüan periods (i. e., eleventh to fourteenth century inclusive) was Tsʻüan-chóu or Chinchew as it is now often called, but, that as used by the Portuguese in the sixteenth and seventeenth centuries, it may have meant Chang-chóu. Sir Henry Yule (Marco Polo, 2ᵈ edit., II, 223) summed up the discussion as follows: «Whether the application by foreigners [25] of the term Zayton, may, by some possible change in trade arrangements in the quarter century after Polo's departure from China, have undergone a transfer, is a question which it would be vain to answer positively without further evidence. But as regards Polo's Zayton, I continue in the belief that this was Tsʻwanchau and its haven, with the admission that this haven may probably have embraced that great basin, called Amoy Harbour, or part of it». Cordier in the 3ᵈ edit. of [30] Yule's Marco Polo (II, 239—241) accepts these conclusions.

As corroborative evidence of the identity of Tsʻüan-chóu with Zaytun during the Sung and Yüan periods, we find in the Yüan-shĭ, 94,25, that at about the time of Polo's departure from Zaytun, Inspectors of Maritime Shipping (shĭ-po-shĭ) were stationed at the following ports: Tsʻüan-chóu, Shang-hai, Kan-pu (near Hang-chóu, Polo's Ganfu), Wön-chóu, Kuang-chóu (Can- [35] ton), Hang-chóu and Kʻing-yüan (Ning-po). The places where the chief officers for collecting the customs revenues from foreign trade were stationed must have been identical with the places where that trade was carried on.

Abulfeda (Reinaud's transl. II, Pt. ii. 122—124) says «Khanfu (Canton) and Shinju — the latter known in our time as Zaitun—are the *bandar* or ports of China, and with them the ports [40] are also the places of customs». Shinju (a pretty close transcription of Tsʻüan-chóu by the way) was situated, he goes on to say, on a gulf or bay and at the mouth of a river, a half-day from the sea. Ships could come up to the fresh water river.

2) Masudi, Prairies d'or, I, 308.

for we learn that at that time they carried on direct trade with the Arabs, the Malay Peninsula, Tongking, Siam, Java, Western Sumatra, Western Borneo, and certain of the Philippine Islands, though, of course, the products of many other countries of the south and south-west were brought there too. 5 The annals of the Sung dynasty[1] supply a list of the principal articles of this trade, imports and exports, in or about 999. They were gold, silver, Chinese cash, coined money, lead, piece-goods of all colours, porcelain-ware, cotton fabrics, incense and scented woods, rhinoceros horns, ivory, coral, amber, strings of pearls, steel (pin-t'ié)[2], shells of turtles, tortoise-shell, cornelians, 10 ch'ö-kü shell[3], rock-crystal, foreign cotton stuffs, ebony and sapan wood.

So valuable had this trade become at the end of the tenth century, that not only was it made a Government monopoly, but, with the object of increasing it, a mission was sent abroad by the Emperor with credentials under the Imperial seal and provisions of gold and piece-goods to induce «the foreign 15 traders of the South Sea and those who went to foreign lands beyond the sea to trade» to come to China. Special licences to import goods were promised them.

The result of the Government's strenuous effort to increase this trade was only too soon felt; the Imperial storehouses were shortly packed with 20 ivory, rhinoceros horns, pearls, jade, incense and scented woods and all the precious merchandise of the southern seas. To find a market for these goods the local officials of the empire were ordered to induce the people to purchase them with «gold, piece-goods, rice and straw»[4].

The great value to China of this foreign trade may be estimated by the 25 steps the Government took to regulate it. We have seen (p. 9) that a

---

1) Sung-shï, 186,18[b].

2) Literally «hard iron». There is great uncertainty as to the nature of pin-t'ié (鑌 鐵). Bretschneider, Ancient Chinese, etc., 12, n. 2 — is disposed to think it was damascene 30 steel, especially sword blades. Perhaps it was the ondanique of which Marco Polo (I. 91) speaks as a product of Kerman, a word which Yule thinks may be Hundwaniy هِنْدُوانى, «Indian steel», which enjoyed great fame all over the East. Edrisi (I, 65) says that the iron preferred by the Indian smiths came from the Sofala coast of East Africa. There was a large amount of it carried yearly to India by ships from Sumatra or Java («the islands of Zabedj»).

3) Probably a large white shell of the cockle kind, plentiful in Sumatran waters. The 35 term is sometimes translated «mother-of-pearl». See infra Pt. II, Ch. XXXV.

4) Sung-shï, 186,19. It is imposible to determine the exact amounts of these imports, as we do not know the units of count, which varied greatly. The Sung-shï says that from 1049 to 1053 the annual importation of elephants' tusks, rhinoceros horns, strings of pearls, aromatics, incense, etc., was over 53,000 units of count. In 1175 the annual amount had risen 40 to over 500,000 units.

2*

maritime customs service existed in Canton in the eighth century, and Soleyman, the Arab, has informed us concerning it a century later. In 971 the Canton Inspectorate of Maritime trade was reorganized to meet the requirements of the rapidly increasing foreign intercourse and to secure to the Government a larger share of the profits. A few years later, between 976 and 983, this trade was declared a state monopoly, and private trading with foreigners was made punishable by branding on the face and exile to an island of the sea[1].

Still a few years later, but before 998, a General Customs Collectorate was established at the capital (King-shï, Marco Polo's Kinsay) and orders issued that all foreign aromatics and goods of value arriving in China, either at Canton, Ts'üan-chóu, the Liang-ch'ö (Ch'ö-kiang) Province, or even in Kìau-chï (Tongking)[2] were to be deposited in Government warehouses.

In 999 Inspectorates for Maritime trade were established at Hang-chóu and at Ming-chóu, — the present Ning-po, — and we are told that this was done «at the request and for the convenience of the foreign officials»[3].

The P'ing-chóu-k'o-t'an, previously referred to, throws some additional light on the Chinese Maritime Customs of the beginning of the twelfth century. «The Superintendency of Merchant Shipping (市 舶 司) at Canton», it says, «is an old institution; (originally) the Comptroller General of the grain transport was specially appointed for the management of merchant shipping affairs.

«In the reigns of T'ai-tsu and T'ai-tung (of the Sung dynastry, i. e., 960—997) he was called Superintendent of Merchant Shipping (市 舶 使).

«Ts'üan-chóu in the province (路) of Fu-kién, Ming-chóu and Hang-chóu in the province of Ch'ö-kiang (兩 浙), being all near the sea, had also Superintendencies of Merchant Shipping (Shï-po-ssï). In the beginning of the *chung-ning* period (1102) the three provinces had each its special official for the management of merchant shipping (提 舉 市 舶 官). Of the three, Kuang-tung was, however, the most prosperous. If, perchance, the officials and underlings (there) were extortionate, then the merchants went to the one making the lightest charge. So these three places (provinces) had their periods of prosperity and decline.

---

1) Sung shï, 186,18[b]. See also infra p. 21.

2) Kiau-chï was an integral part of China; most of its trade with China proper was centered at K'in-chóu in S. W. Kuang-tung.

3) Sung-shï, loc. cit. The fact that a Custom house was opened at Hang-chóu only in 999 disposes of the identification of this port with the Khanfu of the Arabs of the middle of the ninth century. Marco Polo's Ganfu is Kan-fu (or pu 澉 浦) near Hang-chóu.

«At one time the Court abolished (the superintendency) at Ts'üan-chóu and directed that (merchant) shipping should repair to Kuang-chóu; this did not please the merchants».

We know, on the authority of the Arab trader Soleyman[1], that in the middle of the ninth century thirty per cent. (in goods) was levied as duty on foreign imports at Canton. This tariff seems to have been maintained for centuries after, with only occasional lower rates[2]. The P'ing-chou-k'o-t'an supplies us with the following:

«On the arrival of any ships the Chief Commissioner (帥 漕) and the Superintendent of Customs examine the cargoes and levy duties, which is called 'taxing for release' (or 'clearance duties' 抽 解). On a basis of ten parts for the whole, pearls, camphor, and all articles of fine quality (細 色) pay (in kind) 1 part, (i. e., 10%). Tortoise-shell, sapan wood and all coarse grade articles pay (in kind) 3 parts (i. e., 30%). Besides this duty each official market (官 市) levies a small tax. After these charges are paid the remainder belongs to the merchants themselves.

«Ivory tusks of thirty catties weight or over, and gum olibanum, besides paying the 'clearance dues' must be disposed of exclusively at the official market, since they are 'licensed articles' (榷 貨, — i. e., sold only to those having received licenses to import them)[3]. Merchants who have rather large ivory tusks (and who wish to sell them elsewhere) must cut them into pieces of three catties or less (必 截 爲 三 斤 以 下) to escape the official markets. All prices on the official market are low, and other varieties of goods are so greatly undervalued on it that the merchants are displeased (or 'injured' 病) thereby.

«Should anyone, before the ship has paid its clearance dues, presume to remove from it any part of the cargo, even the smallest bit (lit., 'a hau worth,' i. e., a ten-thousandth part of a tael), all the remainder (of the cargo) is confiscated, and he is in addition punished according to the gravity of the offense. So it is that traders do not dare to violate the regulations»[4].

From another source[5] we learn that in 1144 an import duty of 40% was levied on all aromatic drugs and that, though in 1147 it would seem to have

---

1) Reinaud, Relation, I, 34.
2) See infra, p. 22.
3) Scented woods generally were also «licensed articles», and could only be sold to Government, or, as it is said in the text «in the official markets». See P'ing-chóu-k'o-t'an, loc. cit.
4) In the fourteenth century smuggling was punished at Zaytun by confiscation of the whole cargo. Ibn Batuta, IV, 265. Conf. also supra p. 20.
5) Sung-shï, 186,18[b].

been reduced to 10%, it was 50% in 1175, the duty being paid in merchandise. Some idea of the magnitude of this trade may be got from the fact that in 1175, and probably during a number of years preceding that date, the import duties amounted to 500,000 odd units of count (catties, strings, pieces, etc. according to the various articles).   5

The tariff would seem to have been lowered in the Yüan dynasty, for Marco Polo (II, 217) says of the customs of Zayton (Ts'üan-chóu) in his time: «The great Kaan derives a very large revenue from the duties paid in his city and haven; for you must know that on all the merchandise imported, including precious stones and pearls, he levies a duty of ten per cent; or in 10 other words takes tithe of everything; then again the ship's charge for freight on small wares is 30%, on pepper 44%, and on lign-aloes, sandal-wood, and other bulky goods, 40%; so that between freight and the Kaan's duties the merchant has to pay a good half the value of his investment though on the other half he makes such a profit that he is always glad to come back with 15 a new supply of merchandise». It may be, however, that the figures given on previous pages included freight which, we know, (at all events in the early part of the ninth century) was collected by the Inspector of Maritime Customs at the same time as the import duty. If this assumption is correct the Yüan tariff was practically the same as the earlier ones.   20

In the twelfth century Chinese contemporary writers agree in stating that the foreign trade was confined to Canton and Ts'üan-chóu[1], if not by law at least by custom.

Chóu K'ü-feï, writing in 1178, makes this point perfectly clear[2]. His statement contains so much other interesting matter on the southern sea trade 25 of China and shows so conclusively that this trade in his time was in the hands of the Arabs and other foreigners, that it is given here in full:

«The coast departments and the prefectures of the empire now stretch from the north-east to the south-west as far as K'in-chóu[3] (欽 州), and

---

1) The Khanfu and Shinju of mediaeval Arab writers. Additional proof of the identity of 30 Khanfu with Canton is supplied by Edrisi (I, 84. 90 Jaubert's transl.); he says that Lukin (Hanoi, the Chinese Kiau-chï) was four days sailing from Khancu (Khanfu), or 20 days by land. This city, he adds, was the end of the voyage for travellers from the West.

2) Ling-wai-tai-ta (嶺 外 代 答) by Chóu K'ü-feï (周 去 非), 3,10—11. 35 Chóu K'ü-feï was a native of Wön-chóu (溫 州) in Ch'ö-kiang, and when he wrote his book he held the position of Assistant Sub-Prefect in Kui-lin (桂 林), the capital of Kuang-si. It is highly probable that he collected his notes while in Canton, when on his way to his official residence.

3) K'in-chóu was the westernmost district of Kuang-tung on the Kiau-chï (Tongking) frontier. It is part of the Lien-chóu Fu of the present day.   40

these coast departments and prefectures (are visited) by trading ships (市 舶). In its watchful kindness to the foreign Barbarians (外夷) our Government has established at Ts'üan-chóu and at Kuang-chóu Special Inspectorates of Shipping, and whenever any of the foreign traders (蕃 商) have difficul-
5 ties or wish to lay a complaint they must go to the Special Inspectorate (提 舉 司).

«Every year in the 10th moon the Special Inspectorate establishes a large fair for the foreign traders and (when it is over) sends them (home)[1]. When they first arrive (in China) after the summer solstice, (then it is that)
10 the Inspectorate levies (duties) on their trade and gives them protection.

«Of all the wealthy foreign lands which have great store of precious and varied goods, none surpass the realm of the Arabs (Ta-shï). Next to them comes Java (Shö-p'o); the third is Palembang (San-fo-ts'i)[2]; many others come in the next rank.

15 «Palembang (San-fo-ts'i) is an important thoroughfare (衝) on the sea-routes of the Foreigners on their way to and from (China). Ships (on leaving it, on their way to China) sail due north, and having passed the Shang-hia-chu islands[3] (上 下 竺) and (through) the Sea of Kiau-chï (交 洋), they

---

1) The text reads 大 設 蕃 商 而 遺 之. It appears from Sung-shï, 186,19[a]
20 that in 1175 the Inspector of merchant shipping was ordered not to grant leave to unload to any ships from abroad until ten at least had arrived. He was then to levy duty — in goods, 50 per cent, on all goods not government monopolies imported under special licenses. All this latter class of goods had to go to the government saleshouse.

P'ing-chóu-k'o-t'an supplies some interesting details—referring presumably to the latter
25 part of the eleventh century, as to the rules observed by ships from foreign ports entering the port of Canton. «From the Siau Hai (小 海) at Kuang-chóu to Ju-chóu (island 辱 洲) is 700 li. At Ju island there is a lookout for ships; it is called Lookout № 1 (一 望). A little to the north are Lookouts № 2 and № 3. Beyond Ju island is the Warm Current (滄 溟). Merchant ships on reaching Ju island make a brief stop to say farewell, and setting sail after this is called
30 «putting to sea» (放 洋). When (ships) reach Ju island on their return, they exchange congratulations, and the soldiers at the port supply them with samshu and meat as well as provide them escort to Kuang-chóu. When they drop anchor at the Inspector of Foreign Customs' pavilion (at Canton) the Wu-chóu Inspection Office (五 洲 巡 檢 司) sends soldiers to keep watch on board, and this is called «putting up the barriers» (編 欄). On the subject of this Pavilion
35 and Wu-chóu islands, see infra p. 29, n. 1 and 2.

2) In another passage (2,11) the same writer says of San-fo-ts'i: «It is the most important port-of-call on the sea-routes of the foreigners from the countries of Java (Shö-p'o) in the east and from the countries of the Arabs (Ta-shï) and Quilon (Ku-lin) in the west; they all pass through it on their way to China».

40 3) Called T'ién-chu (天 竺) islands in the Sung-shï, 489. They are usually identified with Pulo Aor, S. E. of Tyoman, although some writers place them near Singapore.

come within the confines of China. Those wishing to make Kuang-chóu enter
that port by the T'un-mön[1] (屯 門), while those wishing to enter Ts'üan-
chóu make it by the Kia-tzï-mön[2] (甲子門).

«Ships coming from Java (Shö-p'o) go a little north-west (at first), but
when they have passed the Shï-ïr-tzï rocks[3] (十 二 子 石), they take the 5
same route as the Palembang ships from below (下 i. e., south) of the Shang-
hia-chu Islands.

«(Traders) coming from the country of the Ta-shï, after travelling south
to Quilon (Ku-lin) on small vessels, transfer to big ships[4], and, proceeding
east, they make Palembang (San-fo-ts'i). After this they come to China by 10
the same route as the Palembang ships.

«The (foreign countries) which are dependencies of Annam (Chan-
ch'öng) and Kamboja (Chön-la), are all near the southern part of the Sea of
Tongking (Kiau-chï), not half as far away as San-fo-ts'i and Shö-p'o, and
these latter in turn are not half as far away as the countries of the Arabs 15
(Ta-shï). A year is sufficient for all the foreigners to make the round voyage
to China, with the exception of the Arabs who require two years.

«As a general thing the foreign ships can make 1,000 *li* a day with a
good wind, but if they have the misfortune to run into a north wind and they
can neither find an anchorage on our territory or some place in which to run 20
to shelter and anchor in some foreign land, men and cargo will all be lost.

«As to Mo-k'ié (墨 伽) and Wu-ssï-li (勿 斯 里), it is not known
how many myriads of *li* away they are»[5].

———————————

1) On T'un-mön, see supra, p. 10, n. 1.

2) The present junk passage at the place known to mariners as Cupchi Point (甲 子 25
港), now an important station of the Kuang-tung province. «The junks pass between Turtle
Rock and the rock next to the northward». See Williams, Chinese Commercial Guide, 5th edit,
Appendix-Sailing Directions, p. 55. The Kia-tzï-mön appears to have been the safest anchorage
in the neighbourhood and a refuge shelter for junks sailing between Hongkong and Chinchew
waters. The Emperor Tuan-tsung, in his flight from the Mongol conquerors, made it the head- 30
quarters of his fleet before the final downfall of the Sung dynasty, in A. D. 1277. See T'u-shu-tsi-
ch'öng, Sect. 6. Ch. 1326, p. 4, and Kuang-tung sin-yü, 2,7 where a special paragraph. is devoted
to the Kia-tzï-mön.

3) These rocks are marked on Chinese maps of the sixteenth century as being N. of Carimata Island off the S. W. coast of Borneo. Phillips, J. C. B. R. A. S., XXI. 40, and maps.   35

4) The Arab *sambuks* (سنبوق) of those times were probably of about 100 tons burden,
like those of the present day. They were made of boards lashed together with coir ropes and
the seams pitched. Their weakness is often referred to in mediaeval Arab works. Conf. also infra,
p. 30, n. 4. It seems probable that at Quilon the Arabs transhipped to large junks of the Chinese
type which regularly made the voyage from Canton to Quilon.   40

5) Mo-k'ié is probably the Magreb-alaksà of the Arabs — «the remotest West, corresponding roughly with the present Morocco. Chau Ju-kua transcribes the name of the

This extract naturally suggests an inquiry into the general geographical knowledge of the Chinese concerning the world of the Barbarians in the time of this author. Fortunately he has left us a comprehensive and complete statement (the like of which is found in no other Chinese writer of the Sung
5 period) of his notions on the physical and political geography of the world in his time. It reads as follows:

«The Great (World)-encircling-Ocean-Sea bounds the Barbarians' countries; in every quarter there are kingdoms of them, each has its peculiar products, each its trading centre (都 會) from which it derives its (commer-
10 cial) prosperity. The (Barbarian) kingdoms due south have San-fo-ts'i as their commercial centre. Shö-p'o is the centre of those to the south-east. The countries to the south-west are so vast in extent that they cannot all be described. The nearest are Chan-ch'öng and Chön-la as the commercial centres of Wa-li[1] (宍 裏). The most distant is Ta-ts'in as the commercial centre of the coun-
15 tries of Western India[2]. Among the distant ones Ma-li-pa[3] (麻 離 拔) is the commercial centre of the countries of the Ta-shï, and beyond these there

---

same country Mo-k'ié-la (默 伽 獵). Wu-ssï-li, as used by Chau Ju-kua, is certainly Egypt; whether our author applies this name in the present case to the same country or to some other it is impossible to say. In another passage (3,8b) Chóu uses three characters with the same sounds
20 (勿 斯 離) for Mosul (al Mawsil).

1) Chau Ju-kua (infra, p. 54) mentions Wa-li as a dependency of Chön-la (Kamboja). Chóu K'ü-feï (2, 11a) says it was 60 days journey from P'u-kan on the Irrawadi, without mentioning any direction. It may have been either the Laos country or that of the Karens.

2) The whole of Western Asia is sometimes covered by this term in Chinese works. For
25 example in the modern work Hai-kuo-t'u-chï (30), Persia, Arabia, Syria and their ancient equivalents are discussed under the heading of Si-Yin-tu, i. e., Western India.

3) Ma-li-pa, or Ma-lo-pa as Chau also writes it, appears to be Merbat on the Hadramaut coast of southern Arabia. At the time of which our author writes, Aden was perhaps the most important port of Arabia for the African and Arabian trade with India and the countries beyond.
30 It seems highly probable that the Ma-li-pa of the Chinese must be understood as including Aden—of which they make no mention whatsoever, but which was one of «the great commercial centres of the Arabs». In another passage of his work (3,2) Chóu says that Ma-li-pa was reached from Lan-li (N. W. Sumatra) by ships sailing with the N. E. wind in some 60 days. It was also some 80 days by land from Mekka (Ma-kia). Chau Ju-kua says it was 120
35 stages from Ma-lo-pa to Ki-tz'ï-ni (possibly Ghazni) and 300 stages to Lu-meï (Rûm,—Syria, Rome or Constantinople?). There is nothing in these indications which can help us locate this place. The ancient Merbat or Robat was, according to Theo. Bent (Geogr. Journ. VI, 115—116, 124—125), near the modern Takha, about half way between Cape Risut and the modern Merbat. From Bent's examination of the locality, it had a good spacious
40 and commodious harbor with an island protecting the entrance. It is, he says, the Abyssapolis (Ἀβυσσάπολις) of Ptolemy, the Moscha (Μόσχα) of the Periplus. Ibn Khaldun uses the name Mirbat. See also Müller, Geogr. Graeci min. I, 282, § 32 and Mc Crindle, Periplus, 95.

is Mu-lan-p'i[1] (木 蘭 皮) as the commercial centre of the countries of the extreme west.

«To the south of San-fo-ts'i (here Sumatra) is the Great Southern Ocean-Sea and in this Ocean-Sea there are islands inhabited by a myriad and more of peoples. Beyond these to the south one cannot go.   5

«To the east of Java (Shö-p'o) is the Great Eastern Ocean-Sea, — where (the surface of) the waters begins to go downward (水 勢 漸 低); there is the kingdom of women. Still further to the east is the place where the *wei-lü* (尾 閭) drains (泄) into the world from which men do not return[2]. In a slightly north-easterly direction there is only Kau-li (N. W. Korea) and 10 Pai-ts'i (N. Korea).

«It is impossible to enumerate the countries in the South-Western Ocean, but if we take Tongking (Kiau-chï) as a central point, we have to the south of it Annam (Chan-ch'öng), Kamboja (Chön-la) and Fo-lo-an[3] (佛 羅 安). To the north-west of Kiau-chï is Ta-li (Yün-nan), the Heï-shui, or 15 'Black Water'[4] (黑 水), and the T'u-fan (the Tibetans), and beyond this to the west a big sea called the Sea of Ceylon[5] (細 蘭 海). In this sea is a big island called the country of Si-lan (Ceylon). Crossing westward there are again countries; in the south there is Ku-lin (故 臨, Quilon); in the north is Ta-ts'in (the empire of the Caliphs) and the T'ién-chu of Wang-shö-ch'öng[6] 20 (王 舍 城 天 竺 Central India).

«Still beyond (this Sea of Ceylon) there is another sea called the 'Eastern Sea of the Arabs', and beyond it to the west are the countries of the Arabs. The lands of the Arabs are very broad and their kingdoms very many, too numerous to enumerate. In the west beyond them is the sea called the «Western Sea 25

---

1) Mu-lan-p'i appears to be a transcription of the Arabic *Murābiṭ*, the Almoravides or Almorabethum, who reigned in northwestern Africa and in Spain between 1073 and 1147.

2) On this old notion of a hole in the Pacific into which the waters of the Ocean emptied, see infra, p. 75, and Chs. XXXVIII, 4, and XLVI.

3) Fo-lo-an is identified with Beranang on the Langat River, west coast of the Malay 30 Peninsula. Chau Ju-kua (Ch. VII) says it was a dependency of San-fo-ts'i.

4) According to the earliest geographical notions of the Chinese (Shu-king, Tribute of Yü, Pt. I, 71, Pt. II, 6) the Black Water formed the western boundary of China, and emptied into the Southern Sea. See Legge, Shu-king, Pt. III. Bk. I, 123, and Chavannes, Mém. historiq., I, 126, n. 2. Here the Irrawadi must be meant. See infra, p. 63, n. 1 another reference to the 35 Black Water by Chóu K'ü-feï, and a repetition of this whole passage in slightly different words.

5) This is the earliest use known in Chinese literature of the Arab name for Ceylon. See infra, p. 71, n. 2.

6) According to another passage of Ling-wai-tai-ta (3,4) this T'ién-chu was the country of Magadha. He mentions another Wang-shö-ch'öng as being located by some writers in Pin-t'o- 40 lung. See infra, p. 51, n. 1.

of the Arabs», and still beyond that is Mu-lan-p'i, and a thousand other kingdoms; and in the extreme West is the place where the sun goes in and of which we do not know»[1].

The earliest narrative of a voyage on the southern seas by a Chinese
5 which has come down to us is that of the pilgrim Fa-hién in the early part of the fifth century. He says that, desiring to return from India to China, he embarked at Tamlook[2] near the mouth of the Hoogly, on a large merchant vessel (商 人 大 舶) on which, sailing day and night, he came to Ceylon in fourteen days. Here he took passage on another large merchant ship (大
10 舶), on board which there were more than 200 men, and to which was attached a smaller vessel (舶) in case of damage to the larger one by the sea. Fa-hién speaking of the voyage says[3]:

«The Great Ocean (大 海) spreads out over a boundless expanse. There is no knowing east or west; only by observing the sun, moon and stars was
15 it possible to go forward. If the weather was dark and rainy the ship went forward as she was carried by the wind, without any definite course. In the darkness of the night only the great waves were to be seen, breaking on one another, emitting a brightness like that of fire, with huge turtles and other monsters of the deep (all about). The merchants were full of terror, not know-
20 ing where they were going. The sea was deep and bottomless, and there was no place where they could drop anchor (下 石, lit., «let down a stone») and stop. But when the sky became clear they could tell east and west, and the ship again went forward in the right direction. If she had come on any hidden rock there would have been no way of escape».

25 Arriving in Java (耶 婆 提) he took passage on another large mer-chantman, on which there were over 200 men. It carried provisions for fifty days and set sail on the 16th of the 4th moon (sometime in May). After steering a north-easterly course for a month, they encountered a «black wind»,

---

1) Ling-wai-tai-ta, 2,9.
30   2) Tamlook was already in Fa-hién's time the principal emporium of trade with Ceylon and south-eastern Asia, and it remained so for centuries after. It was visited by numerous Chi-nese pilgrims in the seventh century, but no mention is made of it as a great commercial center either by the writers of the T'ang or the Sung dynasties. Chóu K'ü-feï and Chau Ju-kua did not know of its existence.
35   3) Legge, Record of Buddhist kingdoms, 100, 112—113. Chavannes, Religieux éminents, 42, says, on the authority of the I-tsié-king-yin-i, Ch. 1, that the vessels called po (舶) were some 200 feet long and could carry from six to seven hundred persons. Ships called ch'uan (船) were, probably, of smaller dimensions.

accompanied by a heavy rain. «The sky continued dark and gloomy and the sailing masters (海 師) looked at one another and made mistakes». When seventy days or more from their start from Java were passed, they came to the conclusion that they had held a wrong course as they should have made Canton, at the ordinary rate of sailing, long before; so they altered their 5 course to the north-west and in twelve days made Lau-shan, near Tsingtau on the south-east of the Shan-tung Peninsula.

Such was the method of sailing ships in the fifth century, such it remained down to the twelfth; the skippers trusted—when venturing out of sight of land, to the regularity of the monsoons and steered solely by the sun, moon 10 and stars, taking, presumably, soundings as frequently as possible. From other sources[1] we learn that it was customary on ships which sailed out of sight of land to keep pigeons on board, by which they used to send messages to land. This custom appears to have been a very old one with the sailors of India, as it is found mentioned in Buddhist works dating from the fifth century B. C.[2]   15

By the twelfth century, the next period concerning which we have any information, navigation had made considerable progress, due principally to the application made of the compass or «south-pointing needle», as it is called by the Chinese, who had long known of the polarity of the needle, but had never applied it to this purpose[3]. The earliest mention of the compass 20

---

1) Yu-yang-tsa-tsu (酉 陽 雜 俎) by Tuan Ch'öng-shï (段 成 式). The author died in A. D. 863. Mayers, Chin. Readers' Man. 211. Wylie, Notes, 155, says he wrote towards the end of the 8th century. See also Giles, Chinese Biograph. Dict., 788. Tuan says (16,5), on the authority of Chöng Fu-li (鄭 復 禮), that «on the sea-going ships of the Persians many feed pigeons. These pigeons can fly several thousand *li*, and, when let loose, at a single flight 25 they return to their homes, thus serving as a letter of good news (平 安 信)».

2) The Kevaṭṭha Sutta of the Dīgha nikāya puts the following in the Buddha's mouth: «Long ago ocean-going merchants were wont to plunge forth upon the sea, on board a ship, taking with them a shore-sighting bird free. And it would go to the East and to the South and to the West and to the North, and to the intermediate points, and rise aloft. If on the horizon it 30 caught sight of land, thither it would go. But if not, then it would come back to the ship again». As Rhys Davids remarks, this is very probably the earliest reference in Indian books to ocean-going ships out of sight of land. J. R. A. S., 1899, 432.

The use of carrier-pigeons was probably introduced into China by the Hindu or Arab traders. The earliest mention of them in Chinese literature is connected with Chang Kiu-ling, 35 born in A. D. 673, and who was a minister of the Emperor Hüan-tsung. Watters, J. C. B. R. A. S., IV, 226.

3) Beazley, Dawn of modern geography, I, 490 says that the Chinese used the compass on their long voyages from Canton to Malabar and the Persian Gulf as early as the third century A. D. So far as I am aware there is absolutely no evidence that they made these long voyages 40 at the time mentioned, or that they had ever thought of using the compass for navigation. E. Speck, Handelsgeschichte des Alterthums, I, 29, 209 thinks the Chinese used the compass for

for navigation is probably the account of the Pʻing-chóu-kʻo-tʻan, which Chinese critics believe was supplied by the author's father during the latter part of the eleventh century. Another early mention is found under the year 1122.

The rather disconnected notes on Chinese sea-trade contained in the
5 Pʻing-chóu-kʻo-tʻan embody so much of interest on the general subject with which we are dealing that they are given in full. They run as follows:

«At the Shï-poʻs (Inspector of Foreign Trade) pavilion there is close to the water-side the Hai-shan-lóu[1] (海 山 樓); it faces Wu-chóu[2] (五 洲 'Five Islands'). Below this (the river) is called the «Little Sca» (小 海).
10 In mid-current for some ten odd feet the ships can take water (from the sea or river) aboard for use in crossing the sea; this water does not spoil, but water taken outside this limit of ten feet or more, and all ordinary well-water

---

navigation as early as the first century A. D. Reinaud, Géographie d'Aboulfeda, I, CCIII—CCIV, speaking of the oldest Arab references to the polarity of the magnetic needle, concludes his
15 remarks by saying: «These various pieces of evidence prove that at the end of the XII th and beginning of the XIIIth centuries the magnetic needle came into use (for navigation) at the same time in the East and in the West». It may well be, however, that the Arab traders engaged in the China trade got their knowledge of the polarity of the magnetic needle from the Chinese and applied it to navigation before the Chinese did. See Hirth, Ancient History of China, 126, 134.
20 Another early mention of the mariner's compass in Chinese works is that made by Sü-king in the narrative of his mission to Korea in 1122. He there describes the use of the «south-pointing floating needle» (指 南 浮 針) on the ships on which he sailed from Ning-po, as if it were a new invention. Edkins, J. C. B. R. A. S., XI, 128—134. A. Wylie, Magnetic Compass in China, quoting the Möng-kʻi-pi-tʻan of the Sung period, shows that the Chinese, or at least
25 a few of them, had some knowledge of the changes which take place in the magnetic elements, in the tenth to thirteenth century, but of the application of the magnetic compass to navigation no mention is made earlier than that of the Pʻing-chóu-kʻo-tʻan.

E. H. Parker, China Review, XVIII, 197 says that the Sung-shu makes mention of a «south pointing ship» (指 南 舟) during the Tsin (晉) dynasty (A. D. 265—313), but this
30 is not sufficient evidence to show that the compass was used at that date for sea navigation. J. Chalmers, China Review, XIX, 52—54 arrives at the conclusion that the «south-pointing chariots» mentioned in early Chinese records did not lead to the discovery of the compass».

It is of interest to note that no reference occurs in any Chinese works of the Tʻang or Sung periods to the astrolabe, an instrument which must have been in very general use on the
35 Arab ships of those times.

1) The Hai-shan-lóu, according to the Yü-ti-ki-shöng, the geography of the Southern Sung dynasty, 89,11, is enumerated among the «sights worth seeing» of Canton. It was a building commanding a fine view of the surrounding country, and situated in a locality called Ki-mu-kan-li (極 目 干 里) «in the south of the city». The local chronicles, quoted in the Tʻu-shu-tsi-
40 chʻöng, Sect. 6. 1313,2, describe its situation as «outside the south-gate of the prefectural city defenses». This seems to involve that the Shï-poʻs office was in the southern suburbs of Canton city and on the north shore of the Pearl River.

2) On Wu-chóu or Five Islands, see also supra, p. 23, n. 1. They cannot be identified at present. The same remark applies to the Little Sea (Siau-hai), though it may be the Bay of
45 Lintin below the Bogue, since in a temple inscription of this neighbourhood, the Siau-hai is opposed to the Ta-hai, the latter being east of the former. Pʻei-wön yün-fu, 40,35.

cannot be stored (on board ship), for after a time it breeds insects. The cause
of this is unknown [1].

«Ships sail in the eleventh or twelfth moons to avail themselves of the
north wind (the north-east monsoon), and come back in the fifth or sixth
moon to avail themselves of the south wind (the south-west monsoon).   5

«The ships are squarely built like grain measures («bushels» 斛). If
there is no wind (i. e., if the sails are not used) they cannot remove the
masts, for these are firmly planted, and the sails hang down on one side (of
them), — one side close to the mast, around which they move like a door (on
its hinges). They have mat-sails. These ships are called kia-t'u [2] (加 突), 10
which is a foreign word [3] (方 言 也).

«At sea they can use not only a stern wind, but wind off or toward
shore can also be used. It is only a head-wind which drives them backward.
This is called «using the wind of three directions» (使 三 面 風). When
there is a head-wind they can heave the anchor (矴 石) and stop.   15

«The Governor of Kuang-tung in the fifth moon prays to the god Föng-
lung (豐 隆 神) for wind.

«On large kia-ling (Kling?) [4] sea-going ships (甲 令 海 舶 大 者),
every several hundred men, and on small ones a hundred and more men,

----

1) Kuang-tung-sin-yü, 4, 6,25, contains an account of springs of brackish (or fresh) water 20
in the sea (海 中 淡 泉), six of which were along the Kuang-tung coasts, two of these
seeming to have been on the coast of Sin-hui-hién near the Bogue. Our author assumes, I take
it, that a submarine spring sends a column of fresh water to the surface where it spreads out,
while the lower strata of the sea remains salt-water, this prevents the formation of certain
organic growths containing the germs that will breed insects in ordinary spring-water.   25

2) kia-t'u is pronounced ka-tat in Cantonese, and the second syllable stands for tür or
tur. Final r is quite commonly represented by final t in old inscriptions, as in the name T'u-küé
which represent Türk of the Old Turkish stone inscriptions preserved in alphabetical script. Katur
is probably the word Catur said to have been in use on the coast of Malabar as the name of a
special kind of sailing ship in the early days of the Portuguese. Yule & Burnell, Anglo-Indian 30
Glossary, s. v. Catur, say «Jal (Archéologie Navale, II, 259) quotes Witsen as saying that the
Caturi or Almadias were Calicut vessels, having a length of 12 to 13 paces (60 to 65 feet), sharp
at both ends, and curving back, using both sails and oars. But there was a larger kind 80 feet
long, with only 7 or 8 feet beam». This, it is true, does not tally with the description of our
Chinese author, who compares the ship to a grain measure, hu, the characteristic shape of 35
which is that of the frustum of a pyramid, — an impossible type, even for this remote period, for
distant ocean craft. See, however, the picture of an Arab ship of about this period in Van der
Lith and Devic's Merveilles de l'Inde, 91. Our word «cutter» is derived from Catur (or
kattira).

3) Fang-yen lit. «local term», in the title of a well-known ancient work, means «terms 40
not usual in the standard language of China», being some kind of provincialism; but it also occurs
in the sense of a regular «foreign word». P'ei-wön-yün-fu, 13A, 85.

4) The Kling are usually called Ho-ling (訶 陵) in Chinese mediaeval works; my
suggestion is quite gratuitous. It is certain that the Kling were the principal foreign traders

choose one of the more important traders as head-man (綱首) who, with an assistant head-man — (副綱首), manages various matters. The Superintendent of Merchant Shipping (at Canton) gives them a certificate (朱記) permitting them to use the light bamboo for the punishing of their followers.
5 When one (of the company) dies, they (i. e., the head-men) make an inventory of his property.

«Traders say that it is only when the vessel is large and the number of men considerable that they dare put to sea, for over-seas (海外) there are numerous robbers, and they plunder, moreover, those who are not bound for
10 their (the robbers') country. For instance, if a ship be bound for Chan-ch'öng and by chance get off her course and enter Chön-la, both ship and cargo are confiscated and the men are bound and sold, (the robbers and the people of the place) saying: «It was not your purpose to visit this place»[1].

«In foreign lands, though there may be no tax on commerce, there is
15 an insatiable demand for presents. No matter whether the cargo is large or small, the same demands are made; consequently small ships are not profitable. Sea-going ships are several tens of *ch'ang* in breadth and depth (深濶).

The traders divide the space by lot among themselves and store their goods therein. (Each) man gets several feet (of space for storing his goods)
20 and at night he sleeps on top of them.

«The greater part of the cargo consists of pottery (陶器), the small pieces packed in the larger, till there is not a crevice left.

«At sea they are not afraid of the wind and the waves, but of getting shoaled, for they say that if they run aground there is no way of getting off
25 again. If the ship suddenly springs a leak they cannot mend it from the inside, but they order their foreign slaves[2] (lit. 'devil slaves' 鬼奴) to take knives

---

at this time in Java, Sumatra, and possibly China. The ships here described were certainly not Chinese, either in build or crew. Chau Ju-kua calls the ships which traded between Ts'üan-chóu and the Arab countries of the West «Fan-po» (番舶). When he speaks of Chinese junks he,
30 as well as the other writers of his time, call them «Ts'üan (chóu) ships», or even Chung-kuo (i. e., Chinese) ships». — In the early part of the 14th century Ibn Batuta (Voyages, IV, 90) remarks «Chinese ships only are used in navigating the Sea of China ... These vessels are built at Zaytun (Ts'üan-chóu) and at Sin-kalan» (Canton).

1) Abd Alrazzāk in the narrative of his mission to the court of China, to which he was
35 sent by Shahrokh, refers to this practice as being followed on the west coast of India in bis time, Calicut only excepted. Reinaud, Géogr. d'Aboulfeda, I. CDXXXIII.

2) P'ing-chóu-k'o-t'an, 2, 4ª, says of these «devil slaves», that «in Kuang (Canton) rich people keep (畜) many «devil slaves», who are very strong, being able to carry several hundred catties. In their language and tastes they are strange. Their disposition is gentle, and they do
40 not run away. They are also called «wild people» (野人). They are black in colour, as black

and oakum (絮) and mend it from the outside, for the foreign slaves are expert swimmers, and do not close their eyes under water.

«The ship masters know the configuration of the coasts (地理); at night they steer by the stars and in the day-time by the sun. When the sun is obscured they look at the south-pointing needle[1] (指南針) or use a line a hundred feet long with a hook (鈞), with which they take up mud from the sea bottom; by its smell they determine their whereabouts. In mid-ocean it never rains; whenever it rains (they know) they are nearing an island (*or* headland 山).

«Traders say that when they get in calms the water of the sea is like a mirror. The sailors then catch fish by taking (a line with) a hook (on it) as large as a man's arm, on which they fasten a chicken or duck as bait. When this is swallowed by a big fish they follow it (in a small boat?) as it makes off, but not till half a day (is passed) does it grow tired enough for them to

---

as ink. Their lips are red, their hair curly and yellow. Both sexes are found among them; they are natives of the islands beyond the sea (of China 海外). They live (in their native land) on raw food; when caught and fed on food cooked with fire, it purges them daily and this is called «changing the bowels» (換腸). Many during this treatment sicken and die, but if they do not they may be reared and become able to understand human speech (i. e., Chinese), though they themselves cannot (learn) to speak it.

«There is a variety of wild men from near the sea (近海野人) which can dive in water without closing the eyes; these are called «K'un-lun slaves» (崑崙奴).

The slaves who were «natives of the islands beyond the Sea (of China)», may have been African negroes, in which the Arabs of those times carried on a large traffic. The effect of the change of diet on these blacks, making them able to understand Chinese, is based on the Chinese notion that purging of the bowels is a result of mixing hot with cold food, and that these people had to become used to the food and water of China and have the old washed out of them, before they could understand Chinese.

The «K'un-lun slaves» were in all likelihood Malays or Negritos of the Malay Peninsula and the islands to the south. I-tsing calls the Malay language «language of K'un-lun» — Cha-vannes, Relig. émin., 63, 159, 183. In A. D. 976 an Arab brought to the Court of China, «a K'un-lun slave with deep set eyes and black body». Sung shĭ, 490. The practice of keeping black slaves continued in China down to the latter part of the fourteenth century, perhaps even to much more modern times. In 1370 among the presents brought to the Court of China by a mission from Malacca were «little foreign slaves» (番小廝). The following year a mission from Borneo brought «little black slaves» (黑小廝). Nan-yüé-pi-ki. 7,16,17. The same work- (whether referring to the time when it was written, latter part of eighteenth century, or to past ages does not appear) says that «many families (in China) buy black people to make gate-keepers of; they are called *kui-nu* or «devil slaves», or *heĭ siau ssĭ* «black slaves or servants». Duarte Barbosa in the early part of the sixteenth century says that many slaves were shipped from the island of Sunda to China. Descript. of East Africa, etc. (Hakl. Soc. edit.), 196.

F. W. Mayers, China Review, IV, 182 in translating the passage of this P'ing-chóu-k'o-t'an was under the impression it referred to the Ming period. He mentions the fact that in 1381 the king of Java sent 300 black slaves as a present to the Chinese Emperor.

1) See supra p. 28, n. 3.

get near it, and it is another half a day before they can secure it. Should a wind come up suddenly, they abandon it. If they catch a large fish which is not fit to eat, they open its belly and take out the small fish which it has swallowed and which are eatable. There may be not less than several tens
5 in one belly, each one weighing several tens of catties[1]. All kinds of big sea fish follow the ships, rising and sinking (around them), and there is nothing thrown overboard that they do not eat. When a man sickens, he fears dying on ship-board, for usually before the breath has left his body, he is rolled up in several layers of matting and thrown into the sea, and, as it is desired to
10 have the body sink, several earthenware jars are filled with water and tied in the matting before it is thrown overboard. The crowd of fish have devoured the body and the matting before it can get down very far.

«There are saw-fish (鋸 鯊) hundreds of feet long, with snouts like saws, and when they strike a ship they cleave it asunder as though it were
15 a piece of rotten wood.

«When the ship is in mid-ocean, if suddenly there is seen in the distance (something like) a clump of islands covered with dried trees, and the skipper has reason to believe that there is no land in that place, they (know) that it is the sea-serpent (lit., «the dragon-monster» 蛟 龍). Then they cut off
20 their hair, take fish-scales and bones and burn them, upon which it will gradually disappear in the water.

«All these are dangers, from the most of which there is no escape. Traders give heed to the bonzes' saying: 'To cross the sea is dangerous, but pray, and you will see to the vault of heaven (於 空 中), and in nothing
25 will help fail you'. On their arrival at Kuang-chóu they make the bonzes presents of food, which is called a 'Lo-han feast'».

Chóu K'ü-feï, writing a generation later, thus describes the great ships which sailed the Southern Sea, and the method of navigating them:

«The ships which sail the Southern Sea and south of it are like houses.
30 When their sails are spread they are like great clouds in the sky. Their rudders are several tens of feet long. A single ship carries several hundred men. It has stored on board a year's supply of grain. They feed pigs and ferment liquors. There is no account of dead or living, no going back to the mainland when once they have entered the dark blue sea. When on board
35 the gong sounds the day, the animals drink gluttonly, guests and hosts by

---

1) The Arab relations of the ninth century mention fish caught in the Indian Ocean which were 20 cubits long. On opening it a smaller fish of the same species was found in its belly, and in the belly of the smaller fish a still smaller one. Reinaud, Relations, I, 2.

turn forgetting their perils. To the people on board all is hidden, mountains, land-marks, the countries of the foreigners, all are lost in space. If (the ship's master) says 'to make such and such a country with a favourable wind, in so many days, we should sight such and such a mountain, the ship must (then) steer in such and such a direction'; but if it happens that suddenly the wind 5 falls and is not strong enough to sight the mountain on the given day, it must change its bearing. But if the ship has been carried far beyond (the land-mark), it has lost its bearings, it is blown hither and thither, gets in shoal water, comes on hidden rocks; then it is broken to pieces (lit., 'the tiles are broken'). The big ship with its heavy cargo has naught to fear of the 10 great waves, but in shallow water it comes to grief[1].

«Far beyond the Western Sea of the Arabs' countries lies the land of Mu-lan-p'i (Southern Spain). Its ships are the biggest of all. One ship carries a thousand men; on board are weaving looms and market places. If it does not encounter favourable winds it does not get back to port for years. 15 No ship but a very big one could make such voyages. At the present time the term 'Mu-[lan]-chóu' is used (in China) to designate the largest kind of ship»[2].

----

1) One is inclined to infer from this passage that the compass, if used at all, did not play much of a role in navigation at the time. The captains of the ships appear to have counted on the wind carrying them from one land-mark to another in a given time and kept approximately 20 on their course by means of some star.

Ling-wai-tai-ta, 6,9, says that there grew on the coast hills of K'in-chóu (欽 州) two very remarkable kinds of timber. One is called tzï-king-mu (紫 荆 木 lit., «purple thorn»). The wood is of the colour of red cosmetic and straight grained, and of a girth that two men can reach round. Used for roof beams it will last for hundreds of years.   25

The other kind of timber is called wu-lan mu (烏 婪 木). It is used for the timbers of sea-going junks, and is the most wonderful thing in the world. Foreign (蕃) ships are as big and deep as a great room. They sail the Southern Ocean for tens of thousands of li, and the lives of thousands or hundreds of men depend on one timber. Other varieties of timber are not more than 30 feet in length and are good enough for junks with a capacity of 10,000 bushels (斛), 30 but these foreign ships carry several tens of thousands of bushels, and might break in two if they encountered storms on the deep sea. But this timber of K'in-chóu is dense and tough and about 50 feet long, and is not affected by the wicked winds and angry waves ..... It is truly a treasure in the heaving billows! A couple of these logs (柂) are worth at K'in-chóu only a few hundred strings of cash. At Canton and Wön-ling (i. e., Ts'üan-chóu) they are worth ten times as much, for 35 only one or two-tenths of this timber is sent there as its length makes it difficult to transport by sea».

2) Ling-wai-tai-ta, 6,7,8. I fancy that the Mu-lan-p'i ships had no more real existence than the other enormous products of the same country, such as grains of wheat 3 inches long, melons 6 feet around, pomegranates weighing 5 catties, citrons or lemons of 20 catties, etc., which the same work (3,4) mentions. See also Chau Ju-kua, infra Ch. 35. The largest ships 40 known in China were those called po (see supra, p. 27, n. 3). All mediaeval western writers refer to the great size of the ships seen in China. Marco Polo (II, 231—235) speaking of «the ships in which merchants go to and fro amongst the Isles of India», says they had crews of at least 200 mariners, and every great ship had certain large barks or tenders attached to it».

In the preceding pages an attempt has been made to trace briefly the rise and development of the maritime intercourse between China and southern and south-western Asia down to the latter part of the twelfth century, when Chau Ju-kua, whose «Description of the Barbarous Peoples» (Chu-fan-chï) is
5 translated in this volume, takes up the subject and tells of what the Chinese at the beginning of the twelfth century knew of the foreign countries, peoples and products of Eastern and Southern Asia, Africa and Europe.

Chau Ju-kua was, as appears from the genealogical Records in the Annals of the Sung[1], a descendant of the Emperor Tai-tsung in the eighth
10 generation through the Prince of Shang, a younger brother of the Emperor Chön-tsung (A. D. 998—1023).

We know nothing concerning him beyond the briefest kind of notice of his work in Ch'ön Chön-sun's (陳振孫) Descriptive Catalogue of his family library, written about the middle of the thirteenth century[2]. It is there said, after
15 giving the title of Chau Ju-kua's book, and by way of explanation: — «The Inspector of Foreign Trade (Shï-po-shï) in Fu-kién, Chau Ju-kua, records (in this book) the several foreign countries and the merchandise which comes from them».

This is little indeed, and yet it enables us to see the reason for Chau
20 Ju-kua's interest in foreign peoples and trade, to determine the probable source of the information contained in those portions of his book, which cannot be traced to any previous written source, and it helps also to fix approximately the date before which the Chu-fan-chï must have been written[3].

This is exactly the style and size of ships Fa-hién has told us (supra, p. 27) he sailed on from
25 Ceylon in A. D. 412. Ibn Batuta, Voyages, III, 88—91 says the largest class of Chinese ship — which he calls Junk — had a crew of 1,000 men, viz., 600 mariners and 400 soldiers, and each vessel had three tenders. These ships need not have been much larger than the ordinary Chinese sea-going merchant junk (po) of the time — they were probably literally packed with people. In 1612 Sir Henry Middleton stopped off Aden a ship of Surate with 1,500 persons aboard.
30 Captain John Saris had this ship measured. It was long «from stem to sterne-post, one hundred three and fiftie foot. From the top of her sides in bredth, two and fortie. Her depth, one and thirtie». Purchas, His Pilgrimes, III, 193, 396 (Mac Lehose edit.).

We have to come down to the beginning of the fifteenth century, to Chöng Ho's famous expedition to the West, to find mention in Chinese works of ships of the Mu-lan-p'i type.
35 In this expedition there were ships measuring 440 feet in length and 180 feet beam. It is perhaps unnecessary to add that we may doubt the correctness of these measurements.

1) Sung-shï, 231, 233. See Hirth, J. R. A. S., 1896, 57 et seqq.

2) Wylie, Notes on Chinese literature, 60. The title of this work it Chï-chai-shu-lu-kié-ti (直齋書錄解題).
40 3) From a remark our author makes in his chapter on Baghdad it is possible to assign his work to about the middle of the thirteenth century.

That the Inspector of Maritime Trade at the great port of Ts'üan-chóu
in Fu-kién should have been interested in foreign trade and peoples, that he
should have had peculiar facilities for obtaining information on the subjects
from the foreign sailors and traders who frequented his port, and that his
statements should be found clear, matter-of-fact, and often agreeing with the 5
narratives of mediaeval Arab writers and giving information concerning
countries of the West never known to the Chinese from personal observation,
is all made clear to us by Ch'ön Chön-sun's few words.

Notwithstanding the use made of Chau's book by Ma Tuan-lin and
others, it has remained very little known in China, solely, it is to be suppos- 10
ed, through the habit of nearly all Chinese writers of incorporating bodily
into their writings the work of others without giving the names either of
the authors or of their books. The numerous Chinese biographical works with
all their fullness, are, with the one exception of Ch'ön Chön-sun's, absolutely
silent as to our author. His name is mentioned neither in the biographical 15
section of the Sung Annals nor, apparently, in the minor records of those and
of later times, such as the Biographical Treasury of the Ming dynasty (Wan-
sing-t'ung-p'u), the first general biographical record published after the life-
time of Chau Ju-kua.

The Chu-fan-chï, though of great value for a knowledge of the oriental 20
sea-trade of the Sung period, is but seldom quoted in Chinese works. Much
of it was incorporated by Ma Tuan-lin in his great Encyclopedia, and T'o-t'o
made frequent use of it in his Annals of the Sung dynasty, in both cases, as
is usual with Chinese authors, and as Chau-Ju-kua did himself with his
chief authority, Chóu K'ü-feï, as well as with the many others he quotes, 25
without a single word of acknowledgment. A comparison of the complete
text of the Chu-fan-chï with the extracts made from it by Ma and T'o-t'o
shows how much valuable information we would have lost if we knew this
work only through their quotations. The same would be true of Chóu K'ü-feï,
if we knew his Ling-wai-tai-ta only through Chau Ju-kua's frequent, but 30
not always comprehensive, extracts. The one completes and frequently elu-
cidates the other, besides both having great intrinsic value.

Chau Ju-kua's chief authority is Chóu K'ü-feï; in a number of sections
of his work he confines himself to quoting him textually, and in a still larger
number he adds but a phrase or two (and that not always wisely) to Chóu's 35
text. He has also used the various dynastic histories, the T'ung-tién and a few
other works. The most interesting part of his work, and, so far as the number of countries is concerned, the largest, is that in which he has set down

the information supplied him directly by Chinese and foreign traders of the
lands they had visited and concerning the products of their soil. The facts he
there records are not to be found in any other known Chinese work either of
the thirteenth or of subsequent centuries; he was the first, so far as we know,
5 to make known to China the names and some few facts, at least, concerning
many countries and localities of south-western Asia, of Africa and of the Mediterranean Sea.

The sections of the Chu-fan-chï based exclusively, it would seem, on oral
information furnished the author by Chinese and foreign traders, are those
10 dealing with San-fo-tsʻi, Tan-ma-ling, Ling-ya-ssï-kia, Fo-lo-an, Sin-tʻo,
Kién-pi, Lan-wu-li, Si-lan, Su-ki-tan, Nan-pʻi, Hu-chʻa-la, Ma-lo-hua, Tsöng-
pa, Wu-pa, Chung-li, Wöng-man, Ki-shï, Pi-ssï-lo, Wu-ssï-li (Egypt),
O-kön-to, An-to-man, Cha-pi-sha, Ssï-kia-li-yé, Mo-kié-la, Po-ssï, Ma-i,
San-sü and Pi-shö-yé.

15   In some chapters, while most of his information must have been supplied
him by traders, he has added to it paragraphs taken from Chóu Kʻü feïʻs
work. These are the chapters on Chan-chʻöng, Pin-tung-lung, Chön-la, Pʻu-
kan, Shö-pʻo, Chu-lién, the Ta-shï, Pi-pa-lo and Ki-tzï-ni.

In the chapters on Ta-tsʻin, Tʻién-chu, Wu-ssï-li (Mosul), Lu-meï, Mu-
20 lan-pʻi, Ma-kia, Pai-ta, Kʻun-lung-tsöng-ki, Sha-hua-kung, Ma-lo-nü and
Nü-kuo, he either quotes nearly verbatim the Ling-wai-tai-ta, or takes practically all his information from the Dynastic histories, the Tʻung-tién or some
other minor work, adding occasionally a few words of his owu.

The chapter on the island of Hai-nan is very largely taken from the
25 Dynastic histories and from the Ling-wai-tai-ta, but it contains also much
valuable original matter.

The chapters on Sin-lo and Wo are practically entirely copied from the
Dynastic histories without any regard to the periods to which they refer. These
chapters have consequently less value than any other portion of this work, though
30 they are useful as showing the knowledge possessed by Chinese of these countries in the days of Chau Ju-kua.

The second part of Chau's work, which is devoted to a description of the
principal foreign products mentioned in the first part, contains a considerable
amount of information, which the author probably got from traders at Tsʻüan-
35 chóu; he, however, makes frequent use of the Yu-yang-tsa-tsu and the Ling-
wai-tai-ta, and has based his statements for the most part on the same authorities mentioned previously in writing many of the articles. In this second part,
chapters XIX and XLI are verbatim quotations, without the addition of a

word, from the Ling-wai-tai-ta, and in chapters IX, XVIII, XXIII, XXIV,
XL and XLII he has made good use of this same work.

Geographical studies, though extensively applied to every part of China
proper during the twelfth and thirteenth centuries, were treated with considerable contempt where foreign countries were concerned. The enthusiasm for 5
geographical records shown by the men of the Fan Chöng-ta, Chóu Kʻü-feï
and Chau Ju-kua kind, was certainly rare and unappreciated in their times;
the public taste was not given that way. Chang Kʻién and Pan Chʻao, the
early explorers of the West, had become national heroes, it is true; Fa-hién
and Hüan-tsang, the Buddhist pilgrims, had in their time occupied public 10
attention in a high degree, but Confucian learning was the order of the day
at the end of the twelfth century, when Chu Hi was writing his great Com-
mentaries on the Confucian classics. The antiquities of China, the history of
its art, the philosophy of the classical and Tauist schools, Buddhist chrono-
logy, the poetry of the past and present, all were studied with an ardour 15
worthy of a period which may justly be called the age of renaissance in
China. But the knowledge of foreign countries was an obscure, unprofitable
hobby, taken up only by a few officials whose special duties disposed them to
make these researches, and which in no way appealed to the public fancy.
Confucian philosophers actually threw discredit on what was then known of 20
the geography of foreign parts, and one of the well-known essayists of the
period, Chʻöng Ta-chʻang, tried in his Kʻao-ku-pién to prove the untrust-
worthiness of all geographical information on foreign lands.

The first publication of the complete text of the Chu-fan-chï was, it
would seem, in the early part of the fifteenth century, when it was incorpor- 25
ated in the great collection of Chinese literary works called the Yung-lo-
ta-tién (永 樂 大 典). In this ponderous and extremely rare manuscript
collection it remained buried until 1783, when it was unearthed by a learned
Han-lin and a great lover of literature, Li Tʻiau-yüan (李 調 元), and incorporated in his collection known as the Han-hai (函 海). From this, the 30
first printed copy, it would seem, of this book ever published, another edition
was made in Chang Hai-pʻöngʻs (張 海 鵬) collection entitled Hiau-tsin-
tʻau-yüan (學 津 討 原), which was brought out in 1805. These two versions are practically identical[1].

---

1) G. Pauthier was the first Western writer to make use of Chau Ju-kuaʻs work. He 35
translated (in 1857) the chapter on Ta-tsʻin in his De lʻauthenticité de lʻinscription nestorienne de
Si-ngan fu, 53. Abbé Huc also translated this chapter at about the same time, in his Christianisme en Chine I, 74, n. In the Journal Asiatique, 1861, L. de Rosny made some use of it, also

Such as it is, Chau Ju-kua's work must be regarded as a most valuable source of information on the ethnology of the nations and tribes known through the sea-trade carried on by the Chinese and Mohammedan traders in the Far East about the period at which it was written.

5   His notes to a certain extent are second-hand information, but notwithstanding this, he has placed on record much original matter, facts and information of great interest. The large percentage of clear and simple matter-of-fact data we find in his work, as compared with the improbable and incredible admixtures which we are accustomed to encounter in all oriental authors of
10 his time, gives him a prominent place among the mediaeval authors on the ethnography of his time, a period particularly interesting to us, as it preceeds by about a century Marco Polo, and fills a gap in our knowledge of China's relations with the outside world extending from the Arab writers of the ninth and tenth centuries to the days of the great Venetian traveller.

---

15 in his Peuples orientaux connus des anciens Chinois, 48—49 (2d edit., 1886). F. Hirth translated
    the entire work during the years 1885 to 1895, and during his stay at Chungking (1893—95)
    revised his translation with Mr. H. E. Fraser, then British Consul at that port. He published
    the chapter on Ta-ts'in in his China and the Roman Orient (1885) 92—96, and other portions of
    it in his Die Länder des Islam (T'oung-pao, V, 1894), Das Reich Malabar (Ibid. VI, 1895), Chi-
20 nesiche Studien, 29—43, Die Insel Hainan nach Chao Ju-kua (Bastian Festschrift, 1896), Aus
    der Ethnographie des Tschau Ju-kua (Sitzungsberichte der philos.-philol. und histor. Classe der
    K. Bayer. Akad. d. Wissensch. 1898, III) and in Journal Royal Asiatic Society, 1896, 57—82,
    477—57. More recently P. Pelliot has made use of this work in Bull. de l'École Franç.
    d'Extrême Orient, IV, as has also G. Schlegel in a series of articles in the T'oung-pao, referred
25 to in subsequent notes to our text. So far as I am aware Chóu K'ü-feï's Ling-wai-tai-ta was
    first made known to Western students in 1899 by Tsuboi Kumazo in his paper entitled Cheu
    Ch'üfe's Aufzeichnungen über die Fremden Länder, published in the Actes du XIIe Congrès
    des Orientalistes à Rome, 1901, I, CXL. Since then Pelliot has made some use of it in
    his study mentioned above.

PART I.

Preface by the Chinese Editor,

Li Tʻiau-yüan, called Yü-tsʻun of Tʻung-shan.

―――――

The two chapters of the Chu-fan-chï, compiled by Chau Ju-kua of the Sung dynasty while holding the post of Inspector of Foreign Trade in Fu-
5 kién, are a collection of miscellaneous notes on foreign countries and their products. The fact that these accounts are very minute and agree exactly with what we hear and see of these countries at the present day leads us to the conclusion that Chau Ju-kua's sketches are drawn from the observations of eye-witnesses and more than merely theoretical lucubrations.

10   When the writer of this notice lived in Canton as Literary Chancellor, he had taken this book with him and, subjecting it to careful revision, could not but admire the accuracy of its detail, thus illustrating the truth that even those of later times who survey the same field obtain no small assistance towards a wider knowledge of their subject (by the use of works of earlier times).

―――――

1.

TONGKING.

Kiau-chï (交 趾).

Kiau-chï, the ancient Kiau-chóu[1] (交 州), to the east and the south
5 reaches to the sea and borders on Chan-ch'öng (占 城). To the west it
communicates with the Pai-i Man[2] (白 衣 蠻); to the north it comes down
to K'in-chóu[3] (欽 州).

The various dynasties (of China) kept troops continually stationed (in
Kiau-chï), although the revenues (derived from it) were extremely small, while
10 the military occupation on the contrary was extremely expensive. In view of
these facts the Government of our present dynasty, out of affection for the
army and for the weal of poor humanity, deemed it advisable that our troops
should no longer be kept in this pestilential climate for the purpose of guarding
such an unprofitable territory, and in consequence the territory was held
15 merely for the collection of tribute.

The king (of Kiau-chï) bears a Chinese surname[4].

The clothing and food of the people are practically the same as in the
Middle Kingdom, with the exception that both sexes go barefooted.

Every year on the fourth day of the first moon they kill oxen to have
20 a feast with their kinsfolk. The great annual feast-day is the fifteenth of the
seventh moon[5], when all families exchange civilities and give entertainments,
and officials present their superiors with live animals, in consideration of
which those who have received such presents give a feast in return on the
sixteenth. On New Year's day they pray to the Buddha, but they do not
25 make presents to their ancestors (as we do in China).

When they are ill they do not use medicines. During the night they do
not keep lamps burning. Among their musical instruments the best are
those (covered with) boa-constrictor's skin. They do not know how to manufacture paper and writing brushes, so those from our provinces are in demand.

45

The products of the country are *ch'ön-hiang* (gharu wood), *p'öng-lai*
(gharu wood), gold, silver, iron, cinnabar, cowries, rhinoceros horns, elephants,
kingfishers, *ch'ö-kü* (shells), salt, lacquer, tree-cotton (木 綿) and *ki-peï*
(cotton 吉 貝)[6].

Tribute is sent annually to the Court (of China).   5

Although this country does not participate in the foreign trade (of China),
the author has included these notes as an introduction to the (account of the)
neighbouring country (of Chan-ch'öng).

Ships after ten full days' sailing (from Kiau-chï) reach the country of
Chan-ch'öng.   10

Notes.

1) Down to the beginning of the Han dynasty (B. C. 206) Kiau-chï was a portion of Nan-
yüé (南 越). During the reign of Wu-ti (B. C. 140—86) Nan-yüé was conquered and divided
into nine prefectures (郡), one of which was Kiau-chï (交 阯), and in it the seat of government was placed, which resulted in the name of Kiau-chï being applied to the whole of the   15
country. See Ma Tuan-lin, Wön-hién-tung-k'áu, 330,12. During subsequent centuries, down to the
year 670, the name of Kiau-chï or Kiau-chóu (州) was given to at least a portion of the territory known by that name in the Han period. In 670 Kiau-chï was absorbed by a larger administrative district called An-nan (安 南), and after this the name of Kiau-chï was applied to the
Song-kai delta district, perhaps to the whole of the present Tongking. The name Kiau-chï may   20
be the transcription of a native name Kesho, by which Hanoi was known down to very recent
times. Chavannes, Rélig. émin., 53. It may also possibly be the original of Kattigara, used by
Ptolemy and other classical writers to designate Kesho, though the name Kiu-tö (九 德, in
Cantonese Kau-tak), that of one of the Tongking prefectures on the Chinese frontier, lends itself
better to that identification from a linguistic point of view. In A. D. 264, Kiu-tö is mentioned as an   25
official sub-division, and it is especially identified with the seat of the ancient Yüé-shang tribes, the
probable starting-point of nautical enterprise in high antiquity. Tsin-shu, 15, 16—17. Kiau-chï is
certainly the original of Marco Polo's Caugigu and of Rashideddin's Kafchikué (كفجيكوه Kaf-
tchehkoueh, i. e. كنجيكوه Kancheh-koueh), Hist. des Mongols publ. par. Quatremère. I p. XCVI
and note on p. XCV), the last syllable in both these names representing *kuo* (國 in Cantonese *kwok*)   30
«kingdom». It may also be the original of our modern name Cochinchina (Pelliot, B. E. F. E.
O., III. 291 n.), although other writers (as Devéria, Rel. de la Chine avec l'Annam, 1) trace this
name back to Kiu-chön (九 真), one of the old prefectures of Kiau-chï.

2) The Pai-i Man are, I imagine, the same as the Pai Ts'üan (or Man), the western branch
of the aboriginal tribes called Ts'üan (爨) or Man (蠻), which in the tenth century occupied   35
southern Yün-nan. Hervey St. Denis, Ethnogr., ii. 271—288. The Lolos of the present day are
thought by some to be their descendants.

3) K'in-chóu in Lién-chóu-fu in the extreme west of Kuang-tung province. It was the nearest
Chinese port to Kiau-chï territory and the centre of trade with that country. See supra pp. 6 and 22.

4) Sung-shï, 488,2 sqq., supplies some of the Chinese surnames of the kings of Kiau-chï.   40
We find among them the well-known family name of Ting (丁), Li (黎), Li (李) and Ch'ön (陳).

5) Bowring, Siam, I, 158, mentions the fifteenth of the sixth moon as a holiday, when
the king sends presents to the bonzes. The eighth and fifteenth days of the moon are considered
holy by the Siamese, the same writer states. I cannot, however, find that the fifteenth of th
seventh moon was at any time a particularly great festival in Siam or China.   5

6) On these various products, see Part II of this work. Ling-wai-tai-ta, 7,8 says that
Kiau-chï was a great market for amber.

2.

ANNAM.

Chan-ch'öng (占 城).

The sea-route to the east of Chan-ch'öng[1] leads to Kuang-chóu (Canton); to the west it borders on Yün-nan; to the south it reaches to Chön-la; to the north it confines on Kiau-chï, whence it communicates with Yung-chóu[2] (邕 州). From Ts'üan-chóu one can make this country in twenty days' sailing with a favourable wind.

The country extends from east to west 700 *li*; from north to south 3000 li. The capital is called Sin-chóu[3] (新 州). They use the designations «district city» (*hién* 縣) and «market town» (*chön* 鎮).

The (capital) city walls are of brick and are flanked with stone towers.

When the king shows himself in public he is seated on an elephant or is carried in a kind of cotton hammock (or *juan-pu-tóu*[4] 軟 布 兜) carried by four men. On his head he wears a golden cap and his body is ornamented with strings of pearls. Whenever the king holds his court, encircling his throne are thirty women attendants carrying swords and bucklers or his betel-nut. At audiences the officials present make one prostration and stop. When the business has been concluded, they again make a prostration and retire. The forms of prostration (拜) and salutation (揖) are the same for women as for men.

In cases of adultery both the man and the woman are put to death. Theft is punished by cutting off the fingers and the toes.

In battle they bind five men together in one file (結甲走); if one runs, all who belong to the same file are doomed to death. If a Chinese should be left by a native while lying dangerously wounded, the latter is treated as a murderer and put to death.

The people of this country are fond of cleanliness, they bathe from three to five times daily. They rub themselves with a paste made of camphor and musk and perfume their clothes with fumes of various scented woods.

During the whole year the climate is agreeably warm; there is neither extreme cold nor heat.

Every year on New Year's day they lead a chained elephant through the city, after which they turn it loose. This ceremony is called «driving out

evil» (逐 邪). In the fourth moon they play at boat-sailing, when they have
a procession of fishing boats and look at them[5].

The full-moon day of the eleventh moon is kept as the winter solstice.
At that time cities and towns all bring the king the products of the soil and
of their industry.   5

The people usually plough their fields with two buffaloes. Among the
various kinds of cereals they have no wheat; but they have millet, hemp and
beans. They do not cultivate tea, neither do they know how to make fermented liquors. They only drink the juice (or «wine») of cocoanuts. As to
fruits, they have the lotus, sugar-cane, bananas and cocoanuts. The country 10
also produces elephants' tusks, the *tsién*, *ch'ön* and *su* (varieties of gharu
wood), yellow wax, ebony, white rattans, *ki-peï* cotton, figured cotton stuffs,
silk, damasked cotton gauzes (綾 布), white muslins (or *po-t'ié* 白 疊毛),
fine bamboo matting, peacocks, rhinoceros horns and parrots[6].

The cutting of scented wood in the mountains is conducted under 15
government control; the tax paid the government is known as «the scented
wood poll-tax», just like the Chinese «salt poll-tax». Once the full amount
due has been paid, the people may trade in it on their private account[7].

Money is not used in trade; they barter with wine, rice and other food
substances; with these they settle their accounts yearly.   20

When it happens that any one of the people has gone into the mountains
and has been killed by a tiger, or has been dragged into the water by a crocodile, the relatives submit the case to the king. The king then orders the
high-priest of the realm to invoke the gods, to recite incantations and to
write out charms, which are scattered about at the place where the person 25
was killed. Then the tiger, or the crocodile, comes of itself to the spot; after
which an order must be secured to kill it. If, however, the complaint about
the killing is only an illusion, the result of magic, and the officials can get no
light on the matter, they order the complainants to pass through a crocodile
pool. If they have not spoken truth, the reptiles will come out and eat them; 30
but if they have been truthful they may go through it ten times and the crocodiles will flee away[8].

They buy people to make slaves of them; a boy is priced at 3 taels of
gold, or the equivalent in scented wood[9].

On the arrival of a trading-ship in this country officials are sent on 35
board with a book made of folded slips of black leather. In this they write
out in characters in white a list of the goods. After the ship has been sear-
ched, the cargo may be landed, and, with the exception of two-tenths claimed

by the government, is set free for barter. If there be goods omitted from the manifest they are confiscated.

Foreign merchants trade in camphor, musk, sandal-wood, lacquer-ware, porcelain, lead, tin, samshu and sugar.

5   The dependencies of this country are[10]:

Kiu-chóu (舊 州)   Wu-ma-pa (烏 馬 拔)
Wu-li (烏 麗)   Lung-yung (弄 容)
Jï-li (日 麗)   P'u-lo-kan-wu (蒲 羅 甘 兀)
Yüé-li (越 裏)   10 Liang-pau (亮 寶)
10   5 Weï-jui (微 芮)   Pi-ts'i (毗 齊)
Pin-t'ung-lung (賓 瞳 龍)

This country (of Chan-ch'öng) had only infrequent relations with former Chinese dynasties. During the *hién-tö* period of the later Chóu (951—960) it sent its first tribute mission. During the *k'ién-lung* and *k'ién-tö* periods of 15 the present dynasty (960—967) it sent native products as tribute.

In the sixth year of the *t'ai-p'ing-hing-kuo* period (981)[11], Li Huan (黎 桓) of Kiau-chï informed the Emperor that he wished to return ninety-three Chinese prisoners of war to the Imperial Capital. The Emperor T'ai-tsung ordered them to stop at Kuang-chóu and provided them with sub-20 sistence. From that time (Chan-ch'öng) has constantly presented tribute, and has been enabled through the presents so freely bestowed by the Imperial bounty to express its admiration for Chinese civilization.

A five to seven days' journey south of this country brings one to the kingdom of Chön-la (Kamboja).

25   **Notes.**

1) During the Sung dynasty the kingdom of Chan-ch'öng extended along the greater part of the Annam and Tongking coasts, to within two days sailing of (the town of) Kiau-chï. Sung-shï, 489,1. It corresponded roughly with the old kingdom of Lin-i (林 邑), which, in the seventh century became also known to the Chinese, through the travels of Hüan-tsang, by its 30 Buddhist Indian name of Mo-ho Chan-po (摩 訶 瞻 波) or Mahā Champa, from which in turn have been formed the various Chinese names given this country, Chan-ch'öng, Chan-p'o (占 婆) and Chan-pa (占 八 or 贍 八), the last mentioned being occasionally used during the Mongol dynasty. Yüan-shï, 23. In the middle of the eighth century the name Lin-i was changed to that of Huan-wang (環 王), which designation it retained until the beginning of the 35 ninth century, when it was called Chan-ch'öng. In 1177 Chan-ch'öng conquered Chön-la, but in 1199 it was in turn conquered by the latter country, the dynasty overthrown and a native of Chön-la placed on the throne. Our author mentions these latter events in his chapter on Chön-la, reproducing some facts from the Ling-wai-tai-ta, 2,11.

2) Yung-chóu was the name by which was known during the T'ang dynasty the present 40 Nan-ning (南 甯) in the Tso-kiang circuit in the province of Kuang-si. Playfair, Cities and Towns of China, 244. № 5116.

3) Pelliot, B. E. F. E. O., IV, 202—208 calls attention to the fact that the Tung-si-yang-k'au (a sixteenth century work), 9, and the Ming-shï, 324, apply the name of Sin-chóu to the port of

Binh-dinh, Thi-nai, which we call Quinhon. This town, he adds, is the same as Sha-ban of the Annamese, which was their capital in the early part of the fourteenth century. In another passage (op. cit., 198—202) Pelliot places the capital of Chan-ch'öng near the Quang-nam river in Annam, at the present village of Dong-duong, anciently called Indrapura. Ling-wai-tai-ta, 2,10 says the capital was called Chan-ch'öng like the kingdom. Gerini, Researches, 238, says it is the 5 same as the Senef of the Arabs.

4) Ling-wai-tai-ta, 10,14 says that in Tongking, Chan-ch'öng and Chön-la there was a kind of litter (肩 輿) made of cotton cloth. It had one pole, a covering of overlapping pieces of matting, and was borne by four men. In Annam is was called *ti-ya* (柢 亞 鳥).—This is certainly the *juan-pu-tóu* of our text. Ling-wai-tai-ta, 2,13 calls it also *juan-tóu*. Our author elsewhere 10 speaks of a *pu-tai-kiau*, which must be the same thing. This litter, as used in Chön-la, is described in Chön-la-föng-t'u-ki, Pelliot, B. E. F. E. O., II, 172. Schlegel, T'oung-pao, VI, 163, suggests that *juan-pu-tóu* is the transcription of a Singalese word *handul*, which, according to the Mer-veilles de l'Inde (118. § LXV), was a kind of hammock. It may be a foreign word, but I do not think that *handul* is the one it represents. 15

5) The time of year chosen for this boat festival or boat racing seems to connect it with the rise of the rivers. In Siam a boat festival was kept when the Meinam had reached its highest point. Bowring, Siam, I, 9, 101.

6) Ling-wai-tai-ta, 2,10 says «The native products of the country (of Chan-ch'öng) include famous aromatics, rhinoceros and elephants. The soil is of white sand with but very little arable 20 land, and there are no sheep, swine nor vegetables. The people gain their livelihood by gathering scented woods. They do not hold markets». *Su*, which is rendered by «millet» in the text, is in more modern works used for «maize, Indian corn». *Po-tié* is a foreign word (probably Turki ﭐﺧﺘﻪ *pakhta*) for «cotton», see infra Pt. II, Ch. XXIII. On «ebony» (烏 橭 木) and the other products here mentioned, see also Pt. II. 25

7) Pigafetta, First Voyage round the World, 156 (Hakl. Soc. edit.), describes the mode of hunting for gharu-wood in Chan-ch'öng, but he confounds this product with rhubarb. In Chiempa, he says, «there grows the rhubarb, and it is found in this manner: men go together in companies of twenty or twenty-five to the woods, and at night ascend the trees, both to get out of the way 30 of the lions, the elephants, and other wild beasts, and also to be able better to smell the odour of the rhubarb borne to them by the wind. In the morning they go to that quarter whence they have perceived that the odour comes, and seek for the rhubarb till they find it. This is the rotten wood of a large tree, which acquires its odour by putrefaction. The best part of the tree is the root, but the trunk is also good, which is called Calama». *Calama* is *kālambak*, one of the names 35 in use among the peoples of the Malay Archipelago for gharu-wood.

8) Liang-shu, 54,7 speaking of Fu-nan (roughly Siam) says that criminals were thrown to wild beasts kept for the purpose, or to crocodiles. If they were not devoured by them, their inno-cence was held to have been proved.

9) Ling-wai-tai-ta, 2,10 says «The people (of Chan-ch'öng) buy male and female slaves (奴 婢), and the ships carry human beings as cargo» (舶 舟 以 人 爲 貨). 40

10) None of the authorities available are of any assistance in identifying the dependencies of Chan-ch'öng. Ling-wai-tai-ta, 2,10 says only «The dependencies (or the dependency) of Chan-ch'öng are (is) Pin-t'ung-lung and (or) Pin-to-ling». Ma Tuan-lin says «The southern province of Chan-ch'öng is called Shï-peï-chóu (陁 備 州), the western Shang-yüan-chóu (上 源 州) and the northern Wu-li-chóu» (烏 里 州). The last named province is, presumably, the 45 second of the list in our text. Sung-shï, 489,1, repeats what Ma says, adding only that there were 38 departments (or cities, 州) in all Chan-ch'öng. By P'u-lo-kan-wu one is inclined to think our author transcribes the name Pulo Condore, though these islands were always called during the Sung period K'un-lun-shan (崑 崙 山), a transcription, according to Crawfurd, of the native name Pulo Kohnaong. In Kia Tan's sailing directions (supra p. 11) we have another form 50 of this name, Kün-t'u-nung.

11) This was the year in which the founder of the first Li dynasty ascended the throne of Annam. See J. C. B. R. A. S. XVII, 51. On Chan-ch'öng, see G. Maspero, Le Royaume de Champa, in T'oung-pao, 2d. Ser. XI. pp. 165—220.

3.

PANRANG.

(Coast of Cochinchina).

Pin-t'ung-lung (賓 瞳 龍)

5   The ruler of the country of Pin-t'ung-lung[1] wears the same kind of head-dress and clothing as that of Chan-ch'öng. The people cover their dwellings with palm-leaves, and protect them with wooden palisades. They send yearly products of the country as tribute to Chan-ch'öng.

     At the present day there is (counted) among the saints (lo-han) the 10 Venerable Pin-t'óu-lu (賓 頭 盧), from whom this country derives its name, corrupted into Pin-t'ung-lung.

     There are some also who say that the foundations of the hut (舍 基) of Mu-lién (目 連) are still extant (in this country)[2].

     In the fourth year of the period *yung-hi* (987) (this people), in company 15 with Ta-shï (Arabs), brought tribute to the court of China[3].

Notes.

     1) The identification of this territory with the Panrang coast of Cochinchina, the Sanskrit Pāṇḍuraṅga, first pointed out by Hirth, Aus der Ethnographie des Tschau Ju-kua, has been accepted by all subsequent writers. See H. Finot, B. E. F. E. O., III, 630—648. The name 20 appears in the earliest Cham inscriptions under the form Panrang and Panrān. All the Chinese forms of the name — and we know of nine, point to an original form Pandaran, and this conclusion is supported by local chronicles. The earliest mention of Pandaran in Chinese works is in T'ang-shu, 222[b], where it is given as Pön-t'o-lang (奔 陀 浪). The transcription of the name was apparently never settled, for Ch'óu K'ü-feï uses two forms and Sung-shï three in the three 25 brief references it makes to this country. Pelliot, B. E. F. E. O., III, 649—654, has translated and studied with his usual thoroughness all the Chinese references to Pandaran.

     Our author takes most of his information from Ling-wai-tai-ta, 2,10, which reads as follows: «Pin-t'ung-lung (or) Pin-t'o-ling (賓 陁 陵) is a dependency of Chan-ch'öng. The foundations of the hut of Mu-lién are in Pin-t'o-ling. It is even said by some (或 云) that Wang-30 shö-ch'öng (王 舍 城) is in this country.

     «In the second year *ki'en-lung* (of the Sung, 961 A. D.) it brought objects of tribute (to the Court of China). Again in the 8th moon of the third year (962) it came with tribute. In the first year *yüan-yu* of Chö-tsung (of the Sung, 1086) in the 12th moon it again came with tribute, when it received 2600 strings of cash from the Imperial bounty».

35   2) The references in the texts of both Chóu K'ü-feï and Chau Ju-kua to the Lohan Pin-t'óu-lu — better known by his Sanskrit name of Arhat Piṇḍola (Bhāradvaja), to the great disciple of Gautama, the Lohan Mu-lién — in Sanskrit Maudgalyāyana, and to Wang-shö-ch'öng — in Sanskrit Kuçāgārapura, the old capital of Magadha in Central India, remain unexplained. None of the inscriptions or texts studied by Finot throw any light on these curious Chi-40 nese traditions, which are found repeated, with only unimportant changes, in Chinese works

of the fifteenth and seventeenth centuries. See also infra p. 101, line 2 the tradition referred
to in 1015 by the envoys from Chu-lién (Coromandel) that the tomb of the Si-wang-mu was 100 li
E. of Pin-t'ung-lung.

The derivation of the name of the country from that of the Arhat Piṇḍola seems purely
fanciful. Conf. Hirth, Op. cit., 500 et seqq.   5

3) The tribute mission of Pin-t'ung-lung in 987 is not mentioned in the Sung-shï, but this
work notes (490,18) a tribute mission from that country to China in 997, and this is the only one it
records. Pelliot, Op. cit., 650, shows by the Sung-shï that the tribute missions from Pin-
t'ung-lung mentioned in the passage from Ling-wai-tai-ta translated in Note 1, and there recorded
under the years 961, 962 and 1086 were from Chan-ch'öng generally, not from this dependency 10
alone.

4.

KAMBOJA.

Chön-la (眞 臘).

Chön-la lies to the south of Chan-ch'öng; in the east one comes to the 15
sea; in the west one comes to P'u-kan (蒲 甘); in the south one comes to
Kia-lo-hi[1] (加 羅 希).

From Ts'üan-chóu a ship, with a good wind, can reach this country
within a month or more.

The country covers altogether fully 7000 square *li*. The capital of the 20
kingdom is called Lu-wu[2] (祿 兀). There is no cold weather.

The king's clothing is in all respects similar to that of the king of
Chan-ch'öng, but the ceremonial at his court is more elaborate. When he
goes out in his carriage of state it is drawn by a pair of horses[3] or he
has oxen.   25

The administrative divisions of the country do not differ from those of
Chan-ch'öng.

The officials and the common people dwell in houses with sides of bamboo
matting and thatched with reeds. Only the king resides in a palace of hewn
stone. It has a granite lotus pond of extraordinary beauty with golden bridges, 30
some three hundred odd feet long[4]. The palace buildings are solidly built and
richly ornamented[5]. The throne on which the king sits is made of gharu-wood
and the seven precious substances; the dais is jewelled, with supports (竿) of
veined wood (ebony?); the screen (behind the throne) is of ivory.

When all the ministers of state have audience, they first make three 35
full prostrations at the foot of the throne; they then kneel and remain thus,

with hands crossed on their breasts, in a circle round the king, and discuss the affairs of state. When they have finished, they make another prostration and retire.

In the south-west corner (of the capital) there is a bronze tower (臺),
5 on which are twenty-four bronze pagodas guarded by eight bronze elephants, each weighing four thousand catties [6].

There are some two hundred thousand war elephants and many horses, though of small size.

(The people) are devout Buddhists. There are serving (in the temples)
10 some three hundred foreign women; they dance and offer food to the Buddha. They are called *a-nan* (阿 南) or slave dancing-girls [7] (妓 弟 [read 娣]).

As to their customs, lewdness is not considered criminal; theft is punished by cutting off a hand and a foot and by branding on the chest.

«The incantations of the Buddhist and Tauist priests (of this country)
15 have magical powers. Among the former those who wear yellow robes may marry, while those who dress in red lead ascetic lives in temples. The Tauists clothe themselves with leaves» [8]; they have a deity (神) called P'o-to-li (婆 多 利) which they worship with great devotion.

(The people of this country) hold the right hand to be clean, the left
20 unclean, so when they wish to mix their rice with any kind of meat broth, they use the right hand to do so and also to eat with.

The soil is rich and loamy; the fields have no bounds. Each one takes as much as he can cultivate. Rice and cereals are cheap; for every tael of lead one can buy two bushels of rice.

25   The native products comprise elephants' tusks, the *chan* and *su* (varieties of gharu-wood), fine and coarse *shóu* (gharu-wood) (細 香 粗 熟 香), yellow wax, kingfisher's feathers (Note: Of which this country has great store), dammar resin and gourd dammar, foreign oils, ginger peel (薑 皮), «gold coloured incense» (*kin-yen-hiang*), sapan-wood, raw silk and cotton
30 fabrics (線 布) [9].

The foreign traders offer in exchange for these gold, silver, porcelain-ware, satinets, kittysols, skin (covered) drums, samshu, sugar, preserves and vinegar.

The following foreign (番) (countries or localities) are all dependencies
35 of this kingdom:

Töng-liu-meï (登 流 眉)	San-lo (三 濼)
Po-ssï-lan (波 斯 蘭)	5 Chön-li-fu (眞 里 富)
Lo-hu (羅 斛)	Ma-lo-wön (麻 羅 間)

Lü-yang (綠 洋)   10 Wa-li (窊 裹)

T'un-li-fu (吞 里 富)   Si-p'öng (西 棚)

P'u-kan (蒲 甘)   Tu-huai-sün[10] (杜 懷 潯)

From of old this country had maintained close neighbourly relations with
Chan-ch'öng, and sent it yearly a tribute of gold; but on the fifteenth of the 5
fifth moon of the fourth year of the *shun-hi* period (of the Sung, i. e., 1177) the
ruler of Chan-ch'öng surprised the capital (of Chön-la) with his fleet, and on
the refusal of their demands for peace (the people) were slaughtered. From
that time the bitterest enmity and a thirst for revenge existed (in Chön-la). In
the fifty-sixth year of the cycle in the *k'ing-yüan* period (i. e., 1199) (Chön-la) 10
invaded Chan-ch'öng with a powerful army, made the sovereign prisoner,
put to death his ministers, and nearly exterminated the people, after which it
made a man of Chön-la sovereign of Chan-ch'öng, and down to the present
day it has remained a dependency of Chön-la[11].

In the *wu-tö* period of the T'ang (618—627) this country (of Chön-la) 15
entered for the first time into relations with the Middle Kingdom. In the
second year of the *süan-ho* period (1120) it (first) sent a tribute mission
(to the reigning dynasty).[12]

This country confines to the south on Kia-lo-hi,[13] a dependency of
San-fo-ts'i.   20

Notes.

1) Chön-la, or Kamboja, included in the Sung period the present Lower Cochinchina, a
considerable portion of Lower Siam and of the Malay Peninsula. The origin of the name Chön-la
or Chan-la (占 臘) as it was also written during the Sung period, (see Sung-shï, 489,6), remains
unexplained. The earliest mention of Chön-la in Chinese works occurs in the seventh century. Its 25
first mission to China was in 616. Sui-shu, 82. T'ang-shu, 222[b], says it was called Chön-la or Ki-mié
(吉 蔑). The form Chan-la was adopted in 1199 after the conquest of Chan-ch'öng mentioned
in our text. Ming-shï, 324. During the Yüan period the older form Chön-la was again used.
During the Ming period this country was called Kién-pu-ch'ai (柬 埔 寨) or Kan-pu-chï
(甘 孛 智), both transcriptions of the native name of the country Kamboja. See Tung-si- 30
yang-k'au, 3,6, and Pelliot, B. E. F. E. O. II. 123—13). Ki-mié, pronounced Kat-mīt in Cantonese,
may be a transcription for Kmir, or Khmer. Cf. Gerini, 776.

On P'u-kan, identified with Pagan on the Irrawadi between the mouth of the Shindwin
and Prome, see infra, Ch. VI. Kia-lo-hi was a dependency of San-fo-ts'i and probably in the Malay
Peninsula, see infra, p. 66, n. 10.   35

2) In the seventh century the capital of Chön-la was called I-shö-na-ch'öng (伊 奢 那 城)
i. e., Īsānapura. Sui-shu, 82. The name Lu-wu would seem to point to Lovēk, the ruins of which
city are still visible 10 kil. N. of Udong. Bergaigne, Inscriptions, 122, but Pelliot, Op.
cit. II, 132. n. 3, 141 and IV. 237, says that Lovek only became the capital of Kamboja in the
fifteenth century. «When Chau Ju-kua wrote, he says, the capital was certainly Angkor, and its 40
name was Kambupuri or Yaçodharapura» — consequently Angkor is here referred to. In the
eighth century the capital of Southern Chön-la was, according to T'ang-shu, 222[b], Po-lo-ti-pa.

3) Ibn Batuta, IV. 245, speaking of the Sultan of Mul Djauah (Siam) says «no one in this
country, save only the Sultan, owns horses. The people ride elephants».

4) This «lotus pond» may be the «Northern Lake» mentioned in the Chön-la-föng-t'u-ki, and which Aymonier has identified with the Preah Réach Dak near the great monument of Prakhan at Angkor Thom. Pelliot, B. E. F. E. O. II, 144.

5) The Chön-la-föng-t'u-ki (Pelliot, Op. cit. 144) says «counting from the outer gate
5 the palace was from five to six *li* around. The tiles of the private apartments are of lead, those of the outer buildings of earthenware and yellow .... The Council hall has golden window frames; to the right and left are square columns bearing forty or fifty mirrors along the sides of the windows. Underneath are represented elephants».

6) The Chön-la-föng·t'u-ki (Pelliot, Op. cit, 142) describes a golden tower in the
10 center of the capital and one *li* north of it a higher tower of bronze, which was very imposing. One li N. of it was the Palace. Aymonier says that this bronze tower is the monument of Ba Phun in Angkor.

7) *A-nan*, as here written, is the usual transcription of the Sanskrit word *ānanda* «joy, happiness». — The almeh or dancing-girls are usually called in India *deva-dāsī* («slave of a
15 god») or *rāmjani*. Conf. Reinaud, Relation, I, 134, what he says of the «courtizans of the Bodda». Marco Polo, II, 329, speaking of the province of Maabar says: «They have certain abbeys in which are gods and goddesses to whom many young girls are consecrated .... And when the monks of a convent desire to make a feast to their god, they send for all these consecrated damsels and make them sing and dance before the idol with great festivity. They also bring
20 meats to feed their idol withal; that is to say, the damsels prepare dishes of meat and other good things and put the food before the idol, and leave it there a good while, and then the damsels all go to their dancing and singing and festivity for about as long as a great Baron might require it to eat his dinner .... This is performed by these damsels several times every year until they are married». See also infra p. 92. «Buddha» here means «idol», see infra p. 90 n. 5 and p. 92.

25   8) Quotation from Ling-wai-tai-ta, 2,11, which in turn seems to have been partly taken from Sui-shu, 82,7–8. The name of Tauist was often used by Chinese mediaeval writers to designate the followers of various forms of worship of Hindu origin.

P'o-to-li, the divinity they specially revered, may represent the sanskrit Bhadra, used in the Cham inscriptions to designate Siva. The Chön-la-föng-t'u-ki mentions among these religions
30 of Chön-la «the Tauists, who are called Pa-ssï-weï (八思惟)». Finot has suggested that this is the name Pāçcepatas, that of a Sivaite sect, and mentioned in an inscription of Angkor. Pelliot, B. E. F. E. O. II, 149—151. The Sui-shu, 82,8 says in connexion with the worship of P'o-to-li in Chön-la, «Near the capital is a mountain called Ling-kié-po-p'o (陵伽鉢婆); on the summit of the mountain there is a temple (神祠 Sanskrit, *devālaya*) which is con-
35 tinually guarded by 5000 soldiers. To the east of the city there is a spirit (神 *deva*) called P'o-to-li, to whom human flesh is offered in sacrifice. The king of this country (of Chön-la) goes every year thither and sacrifices a human being in the night. There are also 1000 men guarding (this spot)». Our author, in all likelihood, derived his information concerning P'o-to-li from this passage, as no mention is made of P'o-to-li in Ling-wai-tai-ta, which concludes its reference to
40 the religious systems of Chön-la by saying: «In this country, when looking at the sky, they constantly see in one corner (of the heavens) a few marks (or stains), and the people say: 'it is a place to which Nü-kua (女媧) did not get'». This is an otherwise unknown extension of the Nü-kua legends, the origin of which has to be looked for in all probability in the north of China. If not observable by the naked eye, the knowledge of those starless holes in our firmament known
45 as the «coal-sacks» near the Southern Cross, may have become familiar to the Kambojians through their Indian relations or the reports of Indian or Arab l.c. travellers, whose attention might have been attracted by the phenomena in the southern seas. Cf. Hirth, The Ancient History of China, etc., 10. On Nü-kua, see F. W. Mayers, Manual, 162.

49   9) The Chön-la-föng-t'u-ki gives the name of some other Kambojian products not mentioned
50 by our author; they are *hua-huang* (畫黃 lit., «painter's yellow», gamboge), a kind of lacquer called *tzï-köng* (紫梗), oil of lucrabau seeds (大風子油), *kiang-chön* (降眞 myrcitica iners) and some pepper. See Pelliot, B. E. F. E. O. II, 166. *Kiang p'i* or «ginger peel» is the skin of the ginger root which is peeled off in order to improve its appearance and

make it better adapted as a table luxury; it contains more effective medical properties than the inner parts and, therefore, constitutes a specialty in Chinese drug-shops, quite distinct from both the fresh and dried varieties of ginger. The Pön-ts'au-kang-mu, 26,53, treats of it in a separate paragraph. *Kiu-yen-hiang*, probably benzoin, see infra, Pt. II. Ch. V. All that the Ling-wai-tai-ta, 2,11, has to say of the products of Chön-la is: «It is extremely rich in famous aromatics; those of   5 Töng-liu-meï being the best. The aromatics of no other foreign country can compare with them». Most of the products mentioned here are described in detail in Part II.

10) Assuming that the lists of dependencies of Chön-la, as given in the works of Chóu K'ü-feï and Chau Ju-kua, refer to the times at which they wrote (which, however, is not always true, in the case of Chau at least), it is not surprising that the list (11 names) of Chau should 10 include names not found in the earlier one (7 names), for during that time Chön-la had extended its dominion at the expense of Chan-ch'öng and, it would seem, of the small states in the northern and north-eastern parts of the Malay Peninsula. Chau included also P'u-kan in his list of dependencies of Chön-la. In this he seems to have erred, for in the twelfth century Pagān was a powerful and independant state. See Phayre, Hist. of Burma, 49 et seqq.   15

(1) Töng-liu-meï appears in both lists. See infra, Ch. V. — (10) Wa-li is in both lists; concerning it Chóu K'ü-feï says (2,11) that it was 60 days journey from P'u-kan on the Irrawadi, but he does not say in what direction. In another passage (see supra p. 25 n. 1) he says that Chön-la was the commercial centre of the Wa-li countries. It may have been the Laos or Karen country. So far as known this name does not occur in any other Chinese work. — (11) Si- 20 p'öng, which occurs in both lists, remains unidentified. — (4) San-lo (which may also be read San-yau) is Chóu's San-po (三 泊). The first syllable may be an attempt to transcribe the name of the country called in the Khmer inscriptions Syām (kut) and which not long after Chau Ju-kua's time became Sién (暹). Syām kut was situated to the N. of Lopburi on the lower Ménam. San-lu and San-po may, however, stand for a name like *Sambuk*. — (6) Ma-lo-wön, 25 Chóu's Ma-lan (麻 蘭), may be the same as Mo-liang (莫 良) mentioned by Chóu Ta-kuan (1296) and which Pelliot (B. E. F. E. O., II, 173) says is the Malyan of Cham inscriptions. The country has not been located. Gerini, Researches, 495, mentions, on the authority of a Siamese Chronicle of the middle of the fourteenth century, a locality (or district) called Worawāri or Varavāri as a tributary state of Siam in the south (Malay Peninsula). There is at least some similarity 30 of sound, between this name and the Chinese Ma-lo-wön. — (2) Po-ssï-lan does not occur in Chóu's list; it seems to be the Pa-ssï-li (八 厮 里) of Chóu Ta-kuan's list. Ma Tuan-lin and the Sung-shï (489,11) say it was S. E. of Chön-la proper; it stood, however, S. E. of Chön-li-fu, which is conclusively identified by Gerini (Researches 524) with Chanthabun, so we know its approximate location. — (3) Lo-hu has been conclusively identified with the country of Lvo, Lavo 35 or Lahōt, the modern Lopburi on the lower Menam. Gerini, Asiat. Quart., 3d series, XIII, 119; Pelliot, Op. cit. II, 235, 264. — (5) Chön-li-fu is Chan-li-p'o (占 里 婆) in the earlier list. According to Ma Tuan-lin (Hervey St Denis, Ethnographie, II, 488) and Sung-shï, 489,11, it was situated N. W. of Po-ssï-lan, S. W. of Chön-la proper and N. E. of Töng-liu-meï. Chóu Ta-kuan's list has in it a Chön-p'u (眞 蒲), which may be the same. He says it was on the 40 border of Chön-la and could be reached from Chan-ch'öng in 15 days sailing with a good wind. Sailing from it S. W. ¼ W. one reached the mouth of a river. Gerini, Researches, 524, identifies Chön-li-fu with Chanthabun on the E. coast of the Gulf of Siam. The Ling-wai-tai-ta 10,17 says «A holy Buddha was born in the city of Chan-li-po in the kingdom of Chön-la».—(8) T'un-li-fu, (7) Lü-yang, and (10) Tu-huai-sün are unidentified; it seems likely that they were in the 45 north-eastern part of the Malay Peninsula. Chóu K'ü-feï's list contains one name not found in Chau's, it is Ti-la-ta (第 辣 撻); it also remains unidentified.

11) From Ling-wai-tai-ta, 2,10, we gather some additional details concerning this war and its causes. In 1171 an official of the military district of Ki-yang (吉 陽 軍) in Hai-nan, a Fukienese by birth, was blown by a typhoon to Chan-ch'öng. That country was then at war 50 with Chön-la, and, using only elephants to attack with, it was unable to gain a complete victory. The Chinaman advised the king to organize cavalry, and offered his service to instruct his soldiers in the use of the bow on horseback. The king, pleased with the advice, sent a junk to Ki-yang to

buy horses. It purchased «some tens», and with them he was able to gain a victory over Chön-la.
The following year the king sent a number of men to Ki-yang to buy more horses, but, as that
district had none for sale, they went to K'iung-chóu on the northern coast of the island. The
authorities of K'iung-chóu refused to allow them to purchase horses, and the Chan-ch'öng people
5 left in anger and did not come back again. Ma Tuan-lin, who also tells this story, says that the
Chan-ch'öng people on being refused permission to buy horses, devastated a portion of the island
and carried off a number of the people as prisoners.

　　　12) T'ang-shu, 222[b] says that in 707 Chön-la was divided into Northern Chön-la, or Dry
Chön-la, and also Wön-tan (文 單) and P'o-lóu (婆 鏤), and Southern Chön-la, which was
10 on the sea-coast, with much marsh land, whence it was also called Wet Chön-la. After 707 these
two sections of Chön-la appear to have sent separate tribute missions to the Court of China.
Gerini, Researches, 832, says Wön-tan was Upper Kamboja, and P'o-lóu he thinks (824) may
have been Kwāla Baloh in North Pahang.

　　　13) On Kia-lo-hi, see infra, p. 66.

15

5.

LIGOR (?).

(Malay Peninsula).

Töng-liu-meï (登 流 眉).

　　　The country of Töng-liu-meï is to the west of Chön-la[1]. Its ruler wears
20 flowers in his hair, which is done up in a knot; on his shoulders (he wears)
a red (garment) covered over with white (肩 紅 蔽 白)·

　　　On audience days he ascends an open platform, for they have altogether
no palace buildings of any kind.

　　　Palm-leaves are used as dishes in eating and drinking; neither spoons
25 nor chopsticks are used in eating; fingers serve the purpose.

　　　There is a mountain called Wu-nung (無 弄) (where) Shï-kia (i. e.,
Sakya-muni Buddha) (after his) nié-pan (i. e., nirvāṇa) manifested himself
(示 化); the event being commemorated by a bronze elephant (at this
place) [2].

30　　　The products (of Töng-liu-meï) are cardamoms, the tsién, ch'ön and su
(varieties of gharu-wood), yellow wax and red kino gum [3].

Notes.

　　　1) This name does not appear in Chinese works anterior to the Sung dynasty. The earliest
mention of Töng-liu-meï seems to be in the Ling-wai-tai-ta, 2,11, where the same characters as
35 here are used to transcribe the name. Sung-shï, 489,11, also writes the name in the same way. The
only indication we have as to its location is the brief reference in Sung-shï (loc. cit.) that it

was fifteen stages (程) by sea N. of Lo-yüë (the southern portion of the Malay Peninsula) and S. W. of Chön-li-fu (mentioned in the preceding chapter). Gerini Researches, 524, identifies Töng-liu-meï with Taluma, an ancient state on the E. coast of the Malay Peninsula, but whether near Patani or in the Ligor roadstead, he cannot say. — Pelliot, B. E. F. E. O., IV, 233—234, places Tan-liu-meï at Ligor or Lakhon, otherwise called Sri Dharmaraja, the Muang Lakawn of 5 our maps on the east coast of the Malay Peninsula.

2) This paragraph is very obscure, and seems to contain a strange jumble of misstatements for a writer who must have been somewhat familiar with Buddhist history. The Buddha Gautama is said to have entered the womb of his mother under the shape of an elephant. I do not understand how he can have shown himself after his death under this shape. The Bodhisattva 10 Samantabhadra manifested himself riding an elephant on O-mi-shan in Ssï-ch'uan, and a great bronze elephant commemorates the event. Some such manifestation by a P'u-sa may have taken place at Töng-liu-meï.

3) The Ling-wai-tai-ta, 2,11, says that the gharu-wood from Töng-liu-meï was the best in the world. See infra, Pt. II. Chs. XI[a], XI[b], and XI[c].   15

6.

PAGĀN.
(Burma).

P'u-kan (蒲 甘).

Both the officials and the people of P'u-kan[1] gather their hair in a knot 20 on the forehead, binding it with a piece of coloured silk; the chief of the country alone is distinguished by a high golden cap (or hat 冠).

In this country there is great plenty of horses; the people ride them without saddles.

Regarding their customs, they are very devout followers of the Buddhist 25 religion; all the priests wear yellow robes.

«The lord of the country holds his court in the early morning, when the officials each carry a flower which they present to him, while the priests repeat Indian (梵) words praying for his long life. The flowers are fixed on the king's head; those which are left over are taken to the temples and 30 offered to the Buddha» [2].

There is in this country a temple dedicated to the Marquis Chu-ko Wu [3].

In the first year king-tö of the present dynasty (1004) (P'u-kan) sent a mission (to China) with tribute, together with the kingdom of San-fo-ts'i and Ta-shï (Arabs), when they had an opportunity of witnessing the Feast of 35 Lanterns. In the fifth year ts'ung-ning (1106) (P'u-kan) again sent tribute [4].

Notes.

1) The Ling-wai-tai-ta, 2,11, from which nearly the whole of this chapter is taken, reads as follows: «The kingdom of P'u-kan is five day's journey from the kingdom of Ta-li (S. W. Yün-nan), and from Wa-li (a dependency of Chön-la referred to previously) it is sixty days thither. Its boundary line (隔) is the «Black-water muddy River» 黑 水 淤 泥 河 the Irrawadi?), where begin the kingdoms of the West—which cannot (all) be known (不 可 通). The king of the country of P'u-kan and the officials wear golden caps (or hats), in shape like a rhinoceros horn. They have horses and they ride them without saddles. The king's palace has tiles made of tin (錫); in the interior the ornamentation of the rooms is in gold and silver. There are several tens of Buddhist temples, and all the priests wear yellow robes...» (Then follows the passage forming the fourth paragraph of our text. After this the chapter concludes with the following:) «In the 2d moon of the fifteenth year ts'ung-ning of Hui-tsung (of the Sung, 1103), P'u-kan sent tribute to the Court of China».

The name of P'u-kan does not appear to occur in Chinese works earlier than the Ling-wai-tai-ta, and the tribute mission of 1103 — which is duly recorded in Sung-shï (20,4) seems to be the first appearance of P'u-kan at the Chinese Court, for the Annals for the *king-tö* period (1004—1007) do not bear out our author's statement of a mission from P'u-kan in that year, nor his other statement that one from San-fo-ts'i came there also in that year. The Annals (Sung-shï, 7,3) do, however, mention, under the year 1004 the presence at Court of a mission from P'u-tuan (蒲 端) together with missions from Chan-ch'öng and the Ta-shï (Arabs). Again under the years 1007, 1020, 1030, 1042, 1050, 1053, 1056 and 1061 P'u-tuan is recorded to have sent missions to Court. Ma Tuan-lin (Ethnographie, II, 586) begins his very short account of P'u-kan with the mission of 1106. Can P'u-tuan, about which we know nothing, save that Ma Tuan-lin (Op. cit, II, 538) tells us that it was reached by sea after some seven days sailing from Chan-ch'öng, be an earlier form of P'u-kan? It seems probable.

The article on P'u-kan in the Sung-shï (489,11), while supplying absolutely no information on its geographical position or concerning its people, says that when the P'u-kan mission of 1106 arrived at Court, the President of the Board of Rites (probably after a protest from the P'u-kan envoys) stated that, when in the *hi-ning* period (1068—1077) Chu-lién (Coromandel Coast, the country the nearest to P'u-kan of which the Chinese were cognizant) sent a mission to Court, the king of Chu-lién had been written to by the Board of Rites on plain white paper, as he was a vassal of San-fo-ts'i. P'u-kan, he went on to say, was an important (and independent) kingdom, and should not be treated like the princelet (of Chu-lién); it should be addressed with the same forms as the Ta-shï (the Caliph) or the sovereign of Kiau-chï. See also infra p. 96.

The identity of P'u-kan with Pugān or Pagān on the Irrawadi between the mouth of the Shindwin and Prome is generally accepted. In the eleventh and twelfth centuries P'u-kan ruled over Burma from Bhamo south — including Pegu and Arakan — the latter state, at all events, was under its suzerainty. The kingdom of Pagān was overthrovn by the Mongols, who captured the capital in 1284. Phayre, Hist. of Burma, 18—54.

Schlegel, T'oung-pao, IX, 90, tried to show that P'u-kan was Pahang in the Malay Peninsula — a country known to Chinese mediaeval writers as P'öng-höng (彭 亨), but his argument was extremely weak and his identification has not been accepted by any subsequent writers. If there could be any doubt as to the identity of P'u-kan with Pagān, we might refer to the account of the Mongol conquest of Mién or Burma, contained in the Yüan-shï, 210,5, where a victory over P'u-kan (written as in our text) in 1287 is said to signify the complete pacification of Mién resulting in the payment of an annual tribute of local produce. Again in the Yüan-ch'au-chöng-Mién-lu (元 朝 征 緬 錄) or «Account of the war of the Yüan dynasty against Burma», and which dates from the Mongol period, there are a number of passages in which P'u-kan is mentioned as a dependency of Mién.

2) Quotation from Ling-wai-tai-ta, see supra, n. 1.

3) Better known as Chu-ko Liang. He is credited with having led an expedition into the heart of Burma somewhere about A. D. 225. Giles, Chin. Biograph. Dict. 180.

4) See supra, n. 1, § 2.

7.

PALEMBANG.

(Eastern Sumatra).

———

San-fo-ts'i (三 佛 齊).

San-fo-ts'i [1] lies between Chön-la and Shö-p'o. Its rule extends over 5 fifteen *chóu* (州, provinces, or towns). It lies due south of Ts'üan-chóu.

In the winter, with the monsoon (順 風), you sail a little more than a month and then come to Ling-ya-mön (凌 牙 門), where one-third of the passing merchants (put in) before entering this country (of San-fo-ts'i) [2].

A large proportion of the people of this country are surnamed 10 «P'u» [3] (蒲).

The wall of the (capital) city is built of bricks, and measures several tens of *li* round.

When the king goes out he sits in a boat; his body has a *man-pu* [4] (縵 布) wrapped around it. He is sheltered by a silk umbrella and guarded 15 by men bearing golden lances.

The people either live scattered about outside the city, or on the water on rafts of boards covered over with reeds, and these are exempt from taxation [5].

They are skilled at fighting on land or water. When they are about to 20 make war on another state they assemble and send forth such a force as the occasion demands. They (then) appoint chiefs and leaders, and all provide their own military equipment and the necessary provisions. In facing the enemy and braving death they have not their equal among other nations.

They have no stringed copper cash, but use chopped off lumps of silver 25 (鑿 白 金) in their business transactions.

During most of the year the climate is hot, and there is but little cold weather. Their domestic animals are very much like those of China.

They have wine of flowers, wine of cocoanuts, and wine of areca nuts and honey, all fermented, though without yeast of any kind, but they are 30 intoxicating to drink [6].

In writing documents on official affairs they use foreign (番) characters [7], and the king's signet is used as a seal. They also know Chinese characters, which they use in sending memorials to (our) court.

The laws of the country are very severe; adultery exposes man and woman to the severest form of punishment (i. e., death)[8].

When the king dies the common people go into mourning by shaving their heads; his personal followers (or courtiers) choose, however, voluntary death by leaping into the blazing pyre; this is called «living and dying together»[9].

There is (in San-fo-ts'i) a (kind of) Buddha (*i. e.*, image) called «Hill of Gold and Silver», (金 銀 山) and it is cast in gold. Each succeeding king before ascending the throne has cast a golden image to represent his person[10], and they are most particular to make offerings of golden vessels to these images, and the golden images and golden vessels all bear inscriptions to caution future generations not to melt them down.

When any one in this country is dangerously ill he distributes his weight in silver among the poor of the land, and this is held to be a means of delaying death[11].

They style their king *Lung-ts'ing*[12] (龍 精). He may not eat grain, but is fed on *sha-hu*[13] (沙 糊); should he do otherwise, the year would be a dry one and grain dear. He also bathes in rose-water; should he use ordinary water, there would be a great flood.

(The king) has a high cap (or hat) of gold, set with hundreds of jewels and very heavy. At great court ceremonies no one but the king is able to wear it; all other people are unable. When the throne becomes vacant all the king's sons are assembled, the cap is handed them and he who is able (to bear its weight) succeeds to the throne.

There is an old tradition that the ground in this country once suddenly gaped open and out of the cavern came many myriads of cattle, which rushed off in herds into the mountains, though the people all tried to get them for food. Afterwards the crevice got stopped up with bamboo and trees and disappeared[14].

Exclusive of the native products, which include tortoise-shell, camphor, the *chön*, *su* and *chan* (varieties of gharu-wood), a coarse *shóu* (孰) (variety of gharu-wood), laka-wood, cloves, sandal-wood and cardamoms, there are also pearls, frankincense, rose-water, gardenia flowers, *wu-na-ts'i*(?), myrrh, aloes, asa-foetida, putchuk, liquid storax, elephants' tusks, coral-trees, cat's-eyes, amber, foreign cotton stuffs and sword blades. All these (latter) are products of the Arab (Ta-shï) foreigners (大 食 諸 番)[15].

The foreign traders (番 商) who gather together in this country give in exchange gold, silver, porcelain-ware, silk brocades, skeins of silk, silk gauzes, sugar, iron, samshu, rice, dried galangal, rhubarb and camphor.

This country, lying in the ocean and controlling the straits (lit., gullet 咽喉) through which the foreigners' sea and land (lit., ship and cart) traffic in either direction must pass, in olden times used an iron chain as a barrier to keep the pirates of other countries in check. It could be kept up or lowered by a cunning device. If a merchant ship arrived it was lowered. After a number of years of peace, during which there has been no use for it, it has been removed and (now) lies coiled up on the shore. The natives reverence it like a Buddha, and vessels coming there sacrifice to it. When rubbed with oil it shines like new. Crocodiles do not dare pass over it to do mischief.

If a merchant ship passes by without entering, their boats go forth to make a combined attack, and all are ready to die (in the attempt). This is the reason why this country is a great shipping centre.

The following are all dependencies (of this country)[16]:

Pöng-föng (蓬豐)　　　　　Tan-ma-ling (單馬令)

Töng-ya-nöng (登牙儂)　　10 Kia-lo-hi (加羅希)

Ling-ya-ssï-kia (凌牙斯加)　Pa-lin-föng (巴林馮)

Ki-lan-tan (吉蘭丹)　　　　Sin-t'o (新拖)

5 Fo-lo-an (佛羅安)　　　　Kién-pi (監篦)

Jï-lo-t'ing (日羅亭)　　　Lan-wu-li (藍無里)

Ts'ién-mai (潛邁)　　　15 Si-lan (細蘭)

Pa-t'a (拔沓)

This country began to have relations with China during the *t'ién-yu* period of the T'ang (A. D. 904-907). During the *k'ién-lung* period of the present dynasty (960—963) it sent tribute three times. In the third year *shun-hua* (992) it reported that it had been invaded by Shö-p'o, and besought that an Imperial manifesto be issued authorizing it to render obedience[17].

In the sixth year *hién-ping* (1003) it reported to the Throne that a Buddhist temple had been erected in the country, there to pray for the Emperor's life, and a wish was expressed that a name and a bell be bestowed upon it. The Emperor, approving the wish, ordered that *Chöng-t'ién-wan-shóu* (承天萬壽) should be the title of the temple, and also presented it with a bell.

Down to the *king-tö*, *siang-fu* and *t'ién-hi* periods (1004—1022) and in the *yüan-yu* and *yüan-föng* periods (1078—1094) this country sent a number of tribute missions, when Imperial messages with cordial assurances were conveyed to it[18].

This country to the east is conterminous with Jung-ya-lu (戎牙路), [Note: Also called Chung-kia-lu[3] (重迦盧)].

Notes.

1) All Chinese writers have identified San-fo-ts'i with Palembang, the north-eastern coast of Sumatra. The form San-fo-ts'i appears to have been first used in the Sung period. The earliest Chinese form of the name was Shï-li-fo-shï (室利佛誓 or 逝), which occurs in
5 I-tsing's writings, in the latter part of the seventh century. In the eighth century Kia Tan uses the abbreviated form Fo-shï (佛逝). Shï-li-fo-shï and San-fo-ts'i point to an original Indian form Çrī-Bhōja, and Fo-shï and Fo-ts'ï (for that form also occurs) to an original Bhōja. The form Çrī-Bhōja is the original of Serboza, the name used by the Arabs in the ninth century to designate the island of Sumatra. See Schlegel, T'oung-pao, 2d series, II, 122—138, 167—182,
10 329—377 and Gerini, Researches, 429, 481—483.

San-fo-ts'i was the kingdom of Menang-kabau, the parent country of the Malays in Sumatra. «Its original limits to the eastern side of the island were the great rivers of Palembang and Siak, and to the west those of Manjuta and Singkel». Crawfurd, Hist. Indian Archipel. II, 371. Marsden (Hist. Sumatra, 268 n.) says that before the name Menang-kabau came into use
15 the country (or the capital?) was called Syndo-Cauda. The empire of Menang-kabau extended at one time over the whole island, and, even in the latter part of the eighteenth century, all the Sultans of Sumatra derived their authority from its chief. Marsden, op. cit., 267.

In or about 1377 San-fo-ts'i was conquered by the Javanese, and the name disappears from Chinese works. We find instead Pa-lin-föng (巴林馮), P'o-lin-pang (浡淋邦)
20 and Kiu-kiang (舊港). Explanations of the last mentioned name, have been offered by Groeneveldt, Notes on the Malay Archipel., 76, and by Schlegel, T'oung-pao, 2d Ser. II, 172; but neither of them is more than a guess, the latter a particularly poor one. See also on the subject of San-fo-ts'i, Chavannes, Relig. émin., 36, n. 3 and 64, n. 1, and Pelliot, B. E. F. E. O. IV, 331—348. Gerini, Researches, 628, is of opinion, however, that Pa-lin-föng was probably
25 Berembang in Deli, 3°42′ N. lat., and not Palembang. I doubt it.

Chóu K'ü-feï, from whose work our author has largely drawn, uses the name San-fo-ts'i in a more restricted sense than Chau Ju-kua, applying it only to a port of that name. Here is what he has to say of it: «San-fo-ts'i is in the Southern Sea. It is the most important port-of-call on the sea-routes of the foreigners, from the countries of Shö-p'o (Java) on the east and from the
30 countries of the Ta-shï (Arabs) and Ku-lin (Quilon) on the west; they all pass through it on their way to China.

«The country has no natural products, but the people are skilled in fighting. When they are about to fight, they cover their bodies with a medicine which prevents swords wounding them. In fighting on land or on water none surpass them in impetuosity of attack; even the
35 Ku-lin people come after them. If some foreign ship, passing this place, should not enter here, an armed party would certainly come out and kill them to the last.

«This country has great store of rhinoceros, elephants, seed-pearls (?珠璣) and medicinal aromatics. It is a custom of this people to make rafts to float on the water and to live on them».
40 For other passages in the Ling-wai-tai-ta bearing on San-fo-ts'i, see supra p. 23.

2) The text reads 冬月順風月餘方至凌牙門經商三分之一始入其國. Some Chinese scholars, consulted on the meaning of this ambiguous phrase, think the passage may be mutilated and that it implies that a levy of one third *ad valorem* was made on merchandize at Ling-ya-mön (Linga Strait and Island) before merchants
45 were allowed to proceed to San-fo-ts'i. This interpretation seems forced; it appears much more likely that Ling-ya-mön was a convenient harbour for ships coming from the west and from Chan-ch'öng when sailing for San-fo-ts'i, and that many of them stopped there. However, there is nothing inconsistent with the facts in the explanation, for Chau Ju-kua tells us that the people of San-fo-ts'i and of other parts of the Malay Archipelago were great pirates, and it may well be
50 that merchant-junks found it to their advantage to put into Ling-ya-mön and pay a toll to escape worse. In the fifteenth century the people of the island of Linga still lived by piracy, according to Chinese accounts. Groeneveldt, Notes, 80.

The name Ling-ya-mön has not been found in any other Chinese work of this period, but in the fifteenth century we meet with the name Lung-ya-mön (龍 牙 門) as that of the Linga Strait and Island. Groeneveldt, Notes, 97; Geo. Phillips. J. C. B. R. A. S. XXI, 39; Pelliot, B. E. F. E. O., IV, 218. The sixteenth century Tung-si-yang-k'au, 9,7 says that junks sailing from Ch'ang-yau-sü (長 腰 嶼 Pulo Senang, better known as Bam Island. (Gerini, Researches, 5 815, not Singapore Island, as suggested by Phillips, loc. cit.), on their way to Chan-peï (Djambi, in Sumatra) passed the Lung-ya Peak (龍 雅 大 山). This seems to point without a doubt to some point on Linga. Ling-ya-mön appears to have been a trading depot of the Arabs in the twelfth century. See infra, Pt. II, Ch. XXIV.

3) P'u stands for Bū, an abbreviation of Abū «father», which precedes so many Arabic 10 names. The phrase 多姓蒲 «many are surnamed P'u», occurring here and there in Chinese ethnographical literature may safely be taken to indicate Arab settlements. Hirth, Die Insel Hainan, 487, note.

4) The words man (縵), kan-man (敢 縵), tu-man (都 縵), ho-man (合 縵) or man-pu (縵 布) are used in Chinese works of the mediaeval period to designate the 15 garment known to us by the Malay name of sarung or sarong. These Chinese names are derived from Sanskrit kambala — probably through some intermediate form. Takakusu, Record of Buddh. Religion, 12, n. 1; Pelliot, B. E. F. E. O., III, 268, n. 5 and IV, 283 n. 2. See also Crawfurd, Hist. Malay Archipel. I, 208.

5) The greater part of this and the following paragraph are taken from the Ling-wai- 20 tai-ta, see supra p. 63 n. 1. The Tanka or boat population of Canton are similarly exempted from the ground-tax. The description here given of the town of San-fo-ts'i might apply to Palembang of the present day. «The city is a large one, extending for four or five miles along a fine curve of the river, which is as wide as the Thames at Greenwich. The stream, is, however, much narrowed by the houses which project into it upon piles, and within these again, there is a row of houses 25 built upon great bamboo rafts which are moored by rattan cables to the shore or to piles, and rise and fall with the tide». A. Wallace, Malay Archipelago, 94 (10th edit.).

6) Conf. what is said in Ch. XIV on Shö-p'o concerning the drinks of the Javanese. It is possible that the «wine of flowers» is nipa arrak — which is made with the liquor drawn from the stems of the flowers of the nipa palm. «Wine of cocoanuts» is, of course, toddy, which in 30 Sumatra, however, is made usually from the gomuti palm. Crawfurd, Op. cit., I, 398.

7) The Sung-shï, 489,12ᵃ quotes this paragraph, but substitutes Sanskrit (梵) for «foreign» (番) characters. Either of these two readings may be justified. The Kavi character was used in the kingdom of Menang-kabau for writing Sanskrit in the seventh century of our era. Lassen, Indische Altherthumsk. IV, 463. The same authority says (ibid. IV, 472, n. 1) that other Sanskrit 35 inscriptions found in the same country were written in various other scripts not traceable to any system in use in Western India. The P'ing-chóu-k'o-t'an, 2,3–4, says that San-fo-ts'i had books, and that the people were able mathematicians. Traders reported that these people could calculate future eclipses of the sun and moon; the Chinese, they added, were unable to read their books. The San-fo-ts'i people did not make use of Chinese characters, it seems hardly necessary 40 to remark. Chinese versions of letters from their rulers addressed to the Court of China were rendered into Chinese — on arrival of the envoys at Canton or Ts'üan-chóu, and presented by them — with the original missives — at Court.

8) Crawfurd, Op. cit. III, 130 remarks that among all the tribes of the Archipelago adultery is still considered among the most heinous offences. 45

9) The Ling-wai-tai-ta, 2,12ᵇ states that the same custom obtained in Java (Shö-p'o), see infra, p. 80, n. 10. Conf. also the story told in the Adjaib of the king of India who became the balāndjar of his parrot and who had to kill himself when the parrot was killed by the cat. Van Lith and Devic, Merveilles de l'Inde, 115.

10) Conf. Lassen, Indische Alterthumsk. IV, 938. 50

11) A similar custom has existed in various parts of India from ancient times. It was called tulādāna or «weight gift». It is still observed in Travancore — perhaps elsewhere. Thomas Coryat, in a letter from the Mogol's Court at Asmere in 1615, referring to the Great Mogol

(Selim's) birthday, which was celebrated while he was there, says that «for that day he weighed himselfe in a paire of golden Scales, which by great chance I saw the same day (a custome that be observes most inviolably every yeare) laying so much gold in the other Scale as countervaileth the weight of his bodie, and the same he afterward distributed to the poore». Purchas, His
5 Pilgrimes, IV, 473: See also Sir Thomas Roe's Embassy, II, 411 (Hakluyt Soc. edit.) and Lassen, Op. cit. III, 810. IV, 273.

12) *Lung-ts'ing* transcribes probably some Malay word. The first syllable may stand for *Arung* «king», by which some of the princes in the Malay states were called. Crawfurd, Op. cit. I, 12. In Sumatra, or more properly in the Rejang country, the princes were called *Pangeran*—
10 but this may not always have been the case. Marsden, History of Sumatra, I, 387.

Sung-shï, 489,12 says that the style or mode of address to (號) the king of San-fo-ts'i was «Chan-peï» (詹 卑) or «Djambi». Djambi was a town which, after the Javanese conquest in 1377, became the capital of eastern Sumatra. It was, however, an important place already in the eleventh century, for in 1079 and in 1088 it sent a tribute mission to the Court of China. See
15 infra, p. 66, n. 18. It may be that the name Chan-peï came to be used as equivalent to San-fo-ts'i, and that the Sultan was usually spoken of as «the Djambi Raja».

13) *Sha-hu*, in Malay *sagu*, the term used among all the western tribes of the Archipelago for the sago palm and the farina extracted from it. Crawfurd, History, I, 387, and infra, p. 84.

14) This tradition may be in some way connected with what we are told of the native
20 etymology of the name Menang-kabau. Marsden (Hist. Sumatra, 266) says it is derived from *menang* «to win» and *carbow* «a buffalo»; «from the story, which carries a very fabulous air, of a famous engagement on that spot, between the buffalos and tigers; in which the former are reported to have acquired a complete victory». See also Marre, Histoire des Rois de Pasey, 103. 125—12, and Gerini, Researches, 641.
25 15) On these various products, see infra, Pt. II.

16) The earliest date assigned for the first invasion or migration of the Sumatrans to the Malay Peninsula is the middle of the twelfth century — 1160, and Crawfurd (History, II, 373 et seqq.) is inclined to think it was even later.

(1) P'ŏng-fŏng is generally identified with Pahang on the E. coast of the Malay Peninsula.
30 Bretschneider, Chin. Rev. IV, 387; Pelliot, B. E. F. E. O. IV, 344, n. 4. Gerini, J. R. A. S. 1905, 499 and Researches, 599, without attempting to identify it, thinks it must be looked for on the N. coast of Sumatra, where he locates most of the dependencies of San-fo-ts'i. The localities which he mentions as the probable equivalents of the Chinese names, have, at all events, names which resemble them in sound. Some of his identifications appear correct, some possible, two
35 quite impossible — Sin-t'o and Si-lan.

(2) Tŏng-ya-nŏng, identified with Trengganu or Tringgano on the Malay Peninsula. It is mentioned at the end of the fourteenth century as a dependency of the Mājapāhit empire. Phillips, J. C. B. R. A. S. XXI, 40. Pelliot, Op. sup. cit. IV, 344, n. 6. Gerini, J. R. A. S. 1905, 498 and Researches, 626, is sceptical as to this identification; he thinks Tŏng-ya-nŏng looks more like
40 Trieng-gading on the N. Coast of Sumatra, a little to the N. of Samalangan. See also Schlegel, T'oung-pao, 2ᵈ Ser. II, 132.

(3) Ling-ya-ssï-kia, is identified with Lengka-suka of the Mājapāhit empire, the original capital of Kedah, near Kedah Peak (Gūnong Jerai), on the W. coast of the Malay Peninsula. Pelliot, Op. sup. cit. IV, 345, 405—408. Gerini, J. R. A. S. 1905, 495. 498 and Researches,
45 825. See infra, p. 68.

(4) Ki-lan-tan is the Kalenten of the Mājapāhit empire, Kalantan on the Malay Peninsula. The Tung-si-yang-k'au, 9,6 says Ki-lan-tan was the name of the (country at the) mouth of the Ta-ni (大 泥 i. e., Patani) river. Gerini, Researches, 626, reading the Chinese name incorrectly Kia-ki-lan-tan, suggests a place called Gigieng in North Sumatra.
50 (5) Fo-lo-an, Beranang on the Langat river, W. coast of Malay Peninsula. See infra p. 69.

(6) Jï-lo-t'ing has not yet been satisfactorily identified. Gerini, Researches, 627, says it was very likely Jelatang on a small stream, a little to the south-west of the present Jambi town in 1°42'5 lat. See also Schlegel, T'oung-pao, 2ᵈ ser. II, 134.

(7) Ts'ién-mai remains doubtful. Schlegel, op. sup. cit., 135 thought it was Djambi, but that name we know was transcribed Chan-peï. Gerini, Researches, 627 takes this name to represent Semāwi or Semāwei, vulgo Semoy on the bight of that name, into which debouches the Pasei river, North Sumatra.

(8) Pa-t'a may possibly be the country of the Batta in N. Sumatra, as suggested by 5 Schlegel (loc. cit.). Gerini, op. cit., 627, thinks it, Pedada or Pidada — the Pirada of de Barros between Samalangan and Pasangan, North Sumatra.

(9) Tan-ma-ling was probably a district about the mouth of the Kwāntan river in Pahang, on the E. coast of the Malay Peninsula. See infra, Ch. VIII n. 1.

(10) Kia-lo-hi. In a previous passage (supra Ch. IV p. 52) our author says that Chŏn-la (Kam- 10 boja) confined to the S. on Kia-lo-hi; it would appear therefore that it should be sought for in the Malay Peninsula, south of Tŏng-liu-meï which was the southernmost dependency of Chŏn-la, and which is placed, with some degree of probability, in Ligor on the E. coast of the Malay Peninsula. See supra Ch. V p. 57. Whether Kia-lo-hi was the same as the Kia-lo-shŏ (迦羅舍) of the Sui-shu (3,12ᵃ) and the Kia-lo-shŏ-fu (迦羅舍弗), Ko-lo-shŏ-fŏn (哥羅舍分) 15 and Ko-lo-fu-sha-lo (哥羅富沙羅) of the T'ang-shu, 222ᵇ, I am not prepared to say. Pelliot (op. cit. IV, 360 n.) says that all these forms point to a sanskrit form Kalaṣapura, and that a city of that name seems to have existed in Indo-China or the Malay Peninsula, but where is not known. Gerini (Asiat. Quart. 3ᵈ ser. XIII, 133) identifies Ko-lo-fu-sha-lo with Koli badara, the present Kalantan, and (in his Researches, 627) he seems inclined to locate Kia- 20 lo-hi on the E. coast of Sumatra or on some neighbouring island. He admits that the name is a very puzzling one. Schlegel (T'oung-pao, 2ᵈ ser. II, 136) says Kia-lo-hi was contiguous with the present Cape Camboja.

(11) Pa-lin-fŏng is Palembang, see supra, p. 63, n. 1.

(12) Sin-t'o, or, as our author in another passage, transcribes the name Sun-t'a, is the western 25 portion of the island of Java, or possibly only a small part of it on the Straits of Sunda. See infra Chs. XI and XV, from which either conclusion seems possible. Gerini, Researches, 628, takes Sin-t'o to be Barbosa's Zunda-kingdom, S. W. Sumatra, corresponding to the present Indrapura district. It cannot be believed that Sin-t'o was used by Chau Ju-kua to designate any other country than that lying in Java near the Straits of Sunda. 30

(13) Kién-pi is Kampar on the E. coast of Sumatra. See infra, Ch. XII, from which it appears that in Chau Ju-kua's time it had become independent of San-fo-ts'i. Gerini, Researches, 628, thinks some district on the west coast of the Malay Peninsula may be meant.

(14) Lan-wu-li, the Ramni of Arab mediaeval travellers, the Lamori of Marco Polo. It was the N. part of the W. coast of Sumatra. See infra, Ch. XIII. 35

(15) Si-lan, the Singalese form Silam — shortened from Sihalam (Pāli Singhala), the island of Ceylon. See infra Ch. XIII, p. 73, where it is said, not only that Ceylon sends a yearly tribute to San-fo-ts'i, but that it is ruled by Nan-p'i (Malabar). In the latter half of the eleventh century the Coromandel coast (Chu-lién) was also tributary of San-fo-ts'i. See Sung-shǐ, 489,11 and supra, p. 59.

17) The Ling-wai-tai-ta, 2,12 says: «In the 9ᵗʰ moon of the first year kién-lung (of the 40 Sung, 960) the king of San-fo-ts'i, by name Hi-li-ta-hia-li-tan (Hilita Sultan?) presented tribute to the Chinese Court. Again in the 5ᵗʰ moon of the second year kién-lung (961), and also in the third year (962) in the 3ᵈ and 12ᵗʰ moons». The Annals of the Sung (Sung-shǐ, 1,9–12) state that in 961 people from San-fo-ts'i came to Court and offered presents. The following year two official missions appear to have come to the Chinese Court, one under a person bearing the Chinese name 45 of Li Li-lin (李麗林) — perhaps a Chinese resident of the country. In another passage of the Sung-shǐ (489,13) we read of a mission from San-fo-ts'i in 983 which presented among other things a rock-crystal image of the Buddha. See also Groeneveldt, Notes, 64. 67.

18) The Ling-wai-tai-ta, loc. cit., says «In the second year yüan-fŏng of Chŏn-tsung (1079) in the 7ᵗʰ moon a mission from the kingdom of Chan-peï (詹卑 Djambi) came to Court with 50 tribute; and again this country sent tribute in the year 1088».

19) Jung-ya-lu was to the east of Sin-t'o, the dependency of San-fo-ts'i in Western Java. In another passage (infra, p. 84) our author tells us that Jung-ya-lu was the same as Ta-pan

(Tuban) and that it was to the W. of «Great Shŏ-p'o» and of Su-ki-tan, — Central Java. Crawfurd, History, II, 297, says that in the twelfth century mention is made of a state of Janggolo in the present district of Surabaya in eastern Java.

Gerini, Researches, 451, 812, would place Jung-ya-lu in western or southern Sumatra.

8.

KWANTAN (?).

(Malay Peninsula).

Tan-ma-ling (單 馬 令).

The kingdom of Tan-ma-ling[1] is under a ruler who is addressed as Siang-kung[2] (相 公).

The city is surrounded by a palisade six or seven feet thick and over twenty feet high, strong enough to be mounted for fighting purposes.

The people of this country ride buffaloes, wear their hair done in a knot behind (打 鬈) and go barefooted.

Officials live in wooden houses, the common people in bamboo cottages, the walls being filled in with leaves and the poles fastened with rattan.

The native products comprise yellow wax, laka-wood, the *su* (variety of gharu-wood) incense, ebony, camphor, elephants' tusks, and rhinoceros horns.

The foreign traders barter for them with silk parasols, kittysols, silks of Ho-ch'ï[3] (渮 池 綪 絹), samshu, rice, salt, sugar, porcelain basins, bowls and the like common and heavy articles, and bowls of gold and silver.

Jï-lo-t'ing, Ts'ién-mai, Pa-t'a and Kia-lo-hi are of the same kind (類 此) as this country[4].

This country (of Tan-ma-ling) collects together such gold and silver vessels as it receives, while Jï-lo-t'ing and the other countries make assorted collections, and these they offer to San-fo-ts'i as tribute.

Notes.

1) Takakusu (Record of the Buddhist Religion, XLIII—XLV) thought he saw in this name the Tanā Malayu of de Barros' list of Sumatran kingdoms. Schlegel (T'oung-pao, 2ᵈ ser. II, 130) looked for it also in Sumatra. Pelliot, B. E. F. E. O. IV, 328, while not trying to locate this district, calls attention to the fact that there is an important affluent of the Pahang river called the Tembeling. Gerini, J. R. A. S., 1905, 498 identifies our Tan-ma-ling with Temiling or Tembeling, the name of a cape and a hill near the mouth of the Kwāntan river in Pahang, on the E. coast of the Malay Peninsula. «Probably, he says, it (Tan-ma-ling) is the old designation borne by the present Kwāntan district, and should not be confounded with Tembeling or Tembelang,

the name of an island district on one of the tributaries of the Pahang River». As our author states (infra Ch. IX § 1) that a land-route existed between Tan-ma-ling and Ling-ya-ssï-kia, which we have good reason to believe was about Kedah on the W. coast of the Peninsula, it seems safe to conclude that Tan-ma-ling cannot have been very far from where Gerini has located it.

2) This may possibly be paraphrased «he is addressed by a title which is the equivalent 5 of Siang-kung or 'Minister of State' with us in China». The native title generally used appears to have been that of Mantri, which Crawfurd (op. cit. III, 34) says is the denomination of the first class of the nobility in Malay governments. There is also the title of Pangeran, which is that of princelets of Sumatra. See Marsden, Hist. Sumatra, 173.

3) A district of Ho-ch'ï existed during the Sui dynasty (589—618) in the province of 10 Shen-si; it was identical with the present Huang-hién. See Playfair, Cities and Towns of China, № 1776. According to the local Gazetteer (see T'u-shu-tsi-ch'öng, 6. Ch. 1416,3) silk was produced in abundance in this district. Perhaps sericulture was continued in it down to the days of which our author wrote, or perhaps some silk stuff still bore in the trade the name of this once famous silk. 15

4) All of these dependencies of San-fo-ts'i are mentioned in the preceding chapter and in Note 16, p. 65—66. By «same kind» the author probably means that the people of these various districts were of the same race and that their habits, natural products, etc., were similar.

9.

LENGKASUKA. 20

(Malay Peninsula).

Ling-ya-ssï-[kia] (凌 牙 斯 [加]).

Ling-ya-ssï-(kia)[1] can be reached from Tan-ma-ling by sailing six days and nights; there is also an overland road (between the two countries).

The ruler of the country wraps himself in a sarong (縵) and goes 25 barefooted. The people of the country cut their hair and also wear sarongs.

The native products are elephants' tusks, rhinoceros horns, the *su*, *chan* and *shöng-hiang* (varieties of gharu-wood) and camphor.

Foreign traders barter there in samshu, rice, Ho-ch'ï silks and porcelain-ware. They calculate first the value of their articles according to their equi- 30 valents in gold or silver, and then engage in barter of these articles at fixed rates. As for example, one *töng*[2] (墱) of samshu is equal to one tael of silver or two mace of gold, two *töng* of rice are equal to one tael of silver, ten *töng* being equal to one tael of gold, and so forth.

(Ling-ya-ssï-kia) sends yearly tribute to San-fo-ts'i. 35

Notes.

1) Though written here without the final syllable *kia*, the name is correctly given in the list of dependencies of San-fo-ts'i (supra, p. 62). It is the Lengkasuka of the Mājapāhit empire, the

original capital of Kedah, near Kedah Peak (Gūnong Jerai), on the W. coast of the Malay Peninsula. Pelliot, B. E. F. E. O. IV, 345, 405—408. Gerini, J. R. A. S. 1905. 495, 498. Schlegel,
T'oung-pao, 2ᵈ Ser., II, 131 read the name Ling-ga-sze and placed it in Sumatra.

    2) *Töng* is explained in Chinese Buddhist works as a «Buddhist weight», which means
that it is an Indian term, here, *tola*. In the present case it seems to indicate a dry measure; both
Marsden (op. cit. 155) and Crawfurd (op. cit. I, 271) say that among the Malays everything
is estimated by bulk and not by weight. Marsden adds that the use of weights was apparently
introduced among them by foreigners.

10.

BERANANG.
(Malay Peninsula).

Fo-lo-an (佛 囉 安).

    The kingdom of Fo-lo-an can be reached from the kingdom of Ling-ya-
ssï-kia in four days; one may also follow the overland road[1].

    To this country there came flying two Buddhas, one with six arms, the
other with four arms. Should ships try to enter the confines (of Fo-lo-an),
they would be driven back by the wind; this is popularly ascribed to the
magic power of (these) Buddhas.

    The Buddhist temple (of Fo-lo-an) is covered with bronze tiles and is
ornamented with gold. The fifteenth of the sixth moon is kept as the Buddha's
birthday with crowded processions accompanied with music and the beating
of cymbals. The foreign traders take part in them[2].

    The native products comprise the *su* and *chan* (varieties of gharu-wood),
laka-wood, sandal-wood and elephants' tusks. Foreigners barter for them with
gold, silver, porcelain, iron, lacquer-ware, samshu, rice, sugar and wheat[3].

    It sends yearly tribute to San-fo-ts'i. Its neighbours P'öng-föng, Töng-ya-
nung and Ki-lan-tan are like it.

Notes.

    1) Gerini, J. R. A. S. 1905. 498, places Fo-lo-an at Beranang on the Langat river, W.
coast of Malay Peninsula; this satisfies the requirements of this and the last paragraphs of our
text. Earlier writers, misled by a wrong reading of the Chinese text, tried to locate this country
in Sumatra. Schlegel, T'oung-pao, 2ᵈ Ser., II, 134, said it was Puluan in Palembang residency.
    The Ling-wai-tai-ta, 2,12 says of Fo-lo-an: «The chief of Fo-lo-an is appointed from San-
fo-ts'i. The country produces aromatics with which those of the «Lower Coast countries» (i. e.,
Java, see Pt. II, Ch. XI) cannot compare in aroma or strength.

«There is here (in Fo-lo-an) a Holy Buddha which the princes of San-fo-ts'i come every year to burn incense before».

2) Kuan-yin (Avalokiteçvara) is usually represented with six or four arms. The images referred to may have been of this deity. We learn from another passage in Chau's work (infra, Ch. XXXIX) that the celebration of this festival on the 15th day of the 6th moon, was an important 5 one for sailors for securing good weather on their voyage back to China, and that they kept it as well in Borneo as in Fo-lo-an. According to de Groot, Les fêtes annuellement célébrées à Emoui (Amoy), I, 199, the principal annual feasts of Kuan-yin kept in Fu-kién, are on the 19th of the 2d, the 6th and the 9th moon. That on the 19th of the 6th moon is believed by some to be the goddess's birthday. The 15th of the 6th moon, the same author states (op. cit. I, 394) is also cele- 10 brated in Fu-kién as the mid-year festival. It may well be that these two festivals, especially as the second one, in some of its features at least, is also connected with the worship of Kuan-yin in one of her manifestations (P'o-tsu, 婆 姐), were celebrated by sailors on the same day. Schlegel, T'oung-pao IX, 404 says that the 15th of the 6th moon was the feastday of Ma-tsu-p'o (媽 祖 婆), the patron saint of sailors. De Groot (op. cit. I, 262) says that Ma-tsu-p'o's 15 birthday was the 23d of the 3d moon. I do not know when the cult of Ma-tsu-p'o's became general, at all events the particular «Buddha» referred to by our author was evidently a patroness of sailors, hence the presence at her feast of «the foreign traders» both in Fo-lo-an and in P'o-ni.

3) Fo-lo-an is mentioned in another passage of this work (infra, Ch. XXII) as one of the two principal ports of South-eastern Asia to which the Arab traders came, the other was, of 20 course, San-fo-ts'i.

11.

SUNDA.

(Western Java).

Sin-t'o (新 拖). 25

In the kingdom of Sin-t'o[1] there is a harbour (or anchorage 港) with a depth of sixty feet. Wherever one travels, by water or by land, one meets with the people's dwellings all along the two shores (兩 岸 民 居).

The people are also given to agriculture; their houses are made of poles stuck in the ground, roofed over with the bark of the coir-palm[2], the par- 30 titions being made with wooden boards (tied) with bits of rattan.

Both men and women wrap round their loins a piece of cotton, and in cutting their hair they only leave it half an inch long.

The pepper grown on the hills (of this country) is small-grained, but heavy and superior to that of Ta-pan (Eastern Java)[3]. The country produces 35 pumpkins (東 瓜), sugar-cane, bottle-gourds (匏), beans and egg-plants.

As, however, there is no regular government in this country, the people are given to brigandage, on which account foreign traders rarely go there[4].

Notes.

1) In the chapter on Su-ki-tan (infra, Ch. XV) our author says that Sukitan confined to the W. on Sin-tʻo and to the E. it adjoined Ta-pan (Tuban). In another passage (infra, Pt. II. Ch. XXVII) our author states that Su-ki-tan, Ta-pan, Pai-hua-yüan, Ma-tung and Sin-tʻo (新拖) are
5 places in Shö-pʻo. In a footnote — (infra p. 84, whether by the author or his editor Li Tʻiau-yüan does not appear), the name of this country is written Sun-tʻa (孫他), and there seems no doubt that the western portion of the island of Java is meant; it would even appear that Sin-tʻo must have extended well to the E. of Java, for our author has told us previously that San-fo-tsʻi extended as far E. as Jung-ya-lu in the present district of Surabaya, although it is
10 difficult to reconcile this with our author's remark that Sukitan — a portion of Shö-pʻo — was con-terminous on the W. with Jung-ya-lu — or Ta-pan as it was also called. Schlegel, Tʻoung-pao, 2ᵈ ser. II, 136, 137 tried to locate Sin-tʻo in Sumatra, because he found there several places called Sindar, Sindur, Sintu and Sindu. See also Gerini, Researches, 450—456; 628.

2) Nipa palm, not coir palm, leaves are universally used by the Malays for thatching.

15 3) Crawfurd, op. cit., I, 482, says that Java produces the worst pepper in the Archipel-ago. Maffei, Istorie dell' Indie Orientali, I, 275 (as quoted by Gerini, Researches, 453, note) speaks of the «pepe molto eccellenti» of Sunda.

4) The people of Sunda resisted for a long time the power of the Javanese, and were only finally reduced by Kaden Panka, who ascended the throne in 1156 and transferred his capital to
20 Pajajaran in the west of the island for the purpose of subduing and keeping under control the people of Sunda. This prince is reported to have introduced rice culture into Sunda. See Lassen, Indische Alterthumsk. IV, 476. It seems likely that the absence of any regular government, to which our author refers, may have been a result of the war going on at the time to which this notice of Sunda relates, some fifty years earlier than the time at which Chau wrote. It also explains
25 the absence of any mention of rice among the native products of this part of Java. Crawfurd, however (op. cit. I, 358). considers rice «an indigenous product in the Archipelago and its culture a native art, — and that *one* improved tribe taught and disseminated that art».

12.

KAMPAR.

30 (Eastern Coast of Sumatra)

Kién-pi (監篦).

The kingdom of Kién-pi[1], lying right at the mouth of the road (當路口), is much resorted to by trading ships as an anchorage. It can be reached from the San-fo-tsʻi country in half a month's sailing.

35 Formerly it was a dependency of San-fo-tsʻi, but, after a fight, it set up a king of its own.

The country produces tin (白錫), elephants' tusks and pearls.

The people are fond of archery, and those who have killed a great number of men boast with one another over the length of their tally scores[2]
40 (符標榜互).

Five days' journey by water brings one to the kingdom of Lan-wu-li.

Notes.

1) Kampei or Kampé of the Javanese histories, the modern Kampar on the E. coast of Sumatra. Kampé is mentioned in the fifteenth century as a dependency of the Mājapāhit empire. Pelliot, B. E. F. E. O. IV, 344. Takakusu, Record, etc. XLIII, quoting the Sung-shï, 489, 5 read the name wrongly Lan-pi, and identified it with Djambi. The identification with Kampar does not admit of doubt. Marsden (op. cit. 288) appears to place Kampar W. of San-fo-t'si and E. of the Rakan river. Chóu K'ü-feï, 2,13 says «The kingdom of Kién-pi comes every year to trade in this country (of Ku-lin) elephants and cattle, and the Ta-shï (Arabs) deal in horses. Formerly they used to come to this kingdom to sell goods». This, and the indications furnished by our author, would lead us to extend Kién-pi to near the N. W. extremity of Sumatra. On the 10 other hand the existence of tin in Kién-pi points to the E. part of the island; Crawfurd (History, etc., III, 450) says that in geographical distribution tin is confined to the island of Banca, the Malay Peninsula, and the islets on the coasts, with Junk Ceylon.

2) Probably the people made notches on the backs of their swords or on the scabbards of the number of persons they had killed, or the number of heads they had taken. 15

13.

LAMBRI. ISLAND OF CEYLON.

Lan-wu-li (藍無里). Si-lan (細蘭).

The products of the kingdom of Lan-wu-li[1] are sapan-wood, elephants' tusks and white rattan. 20

The people are warlike and often use poisoned arrows.

With a north wind one comes within twenty odd days to the kingdom of Si-lan[2], which is under the rule of Nan-p'i[3] (南毗). Sailing from Lan-wu-li, one knows that one is nearing Si-lan by continual flashing of lightning[4].

The king (of Si-lan) is black, his hair unkempt and his head uncovered. 25 He wears no clothes but has a cotton cloth of different colours wrapped around him; on his feet he wears sandals of red leather, tied with golden strings. When he goes forth he rides an elephant or is carried in a litter (軟兜). All day he chews a paste of betel nut and pearl ashes.

His palace is ornamented with cat's-eyes, blue and red precious stones, 30 cornelians and other jewels; the very floor he walks upon is so ornamented. There is an eastern and western palace, and at each there is a golden tree, the trunk and branches all of gold, the flowers, fruit and leaves of cat's-eyes, blue and red precious stones and such like jewels. At the foot of these trees are golden thrones with opaque glass (琉璃) screens. When the king holds 35 his court he uses the eastern palace in the forenoon and the western in the afternoon. When (the king) is seated, the jewels flashing in the sunshine, the glass (screens) and the jewel-tree shining on each other, make it like the glory of the rising sun.

5   Two attendants are always present holding a golden dish to receive the remains of the betel nut (paste) chewed by the king. The king's attendants pay a monthly fee of one i[5] (鎰) of gold into the government treasury for the privilege of getting the betel nut (paste) remains, for it contains «plum flower», camphor[6] and all kinds of precious substances.

10   The king holds in his hand a jewel five inches in diameter, which cannot be burnt by fire, and which shines in (the darkness of) night like a torch[7]. The king rubs his face with it daily, and though he were passed ninety he would retain his youthful looks.

The people of the country are very dark-skinned, they wrap a sarong 15 round their bodies, go bare-headed and barefooted. They use their hands in taking up their food; their household utensils are of copper.

There is (in this country of Si-lan) a mountain called Si-lun-tié[8] (細 輪 疊), on the top of which there is a huge imprint of a man's foot, over seven feet long, and a like imprint is visible in the water (of the sea) within 20 a distance of over 300 li from the mountain. The forest trees on the mountain, little and big, all bend towards it (as if reverencing it).

The products (of Si-lan) include cat's-eyes, red transparent glass (玻 璨), camphor, blue and red precious stones. The products of the soil are cardamoms, *mu-lan* bark (木 蘭 皮) and both coarse and fine perfumes[9]. 25 Foreign traders exchange for them sandal-wood, cloves, camphor, gold, silver, porcelain-ware, horses, elephants and silk stuffs.

This country sends a yearly tribute to San-fo-ts'i[10].

Notes.

1) So far as is known, Chóu K'ü-feï was the first Chinese writer to mention this section of 30 Sumatra, which he calls (3,2) Lan-li (藍 里), but concerning which he only says that it took a merchant junk from Canton forty days to reach it. Chóu's transcription reproduces very closely the name used by the Arab travellers of the ninth and subsequent centuries to designate Sumatra, Al-Ramni. As used, however, by Chóu K'ü-feï, our author and by Marco Polo (who writes the name Lamori), it designates the northern portion of the W. coast of Sumatra, commencing from 35 the neighbourhood of Achin Head. Yule, Marco Polo, II, 281, 283. See also Cordier, Friar Odoric, 135, 137.

The Chinese missions of the beginning of the fifteenth century wrote the name Nan-(Lan-)p'o-li (南 浡 利) or Nan-(Lan-)wu-li (南 巫 里), and in these forms the name occurs in the Ming-shï (325), although the same work has Na-(La-)mo-li, yang (那 沒 梨 洋) «the Sea 40 of Lambri». The Ming-shï says that Nan-p'o-li (i. e., the principal port of that district) was three days' sailing from Su-mön-ta-la (蘇 門 荅 剌) — the Samara of Polo, the Samuthrah of

Ibn Batuta, and placed by Yule (op. cit. II, 277) near the head of the estuary-like Gulf of
Pasei, called in the charts Telo (or Talak) Samawe. To the N. W. of Nan-p'o-li, the Ming-
shï adds, a high mountain called Mau-shan (帽 山) or «Hat mountain» rises out of the sea.
This is Pulo Rondo or Pulo Way off Achin. Gerini, Researches, 385. See, however, Phillips,
J. C. B. R. A. S. XXI, 221, and Groeneveldt, Notes, 100.   5

2) Chóu K'ü-feï appears to have been the first Chinese writer to speak of Ceylon as Si-lan,
which, it would seem, he must have heard of from a Singhalese who probably shortened the sound
Sihalam (the Pali form for Singhala) into Silam. See Yule, Marco Polo, II, 296, n. 1. The Yüan-
shï, 97, uses the form Ki-lan (急 蘭), which represents the same native form, and the Ming-
shï, 326 has Si-lan (錫 蘭). Marco Polo also used the form Seilom. The mediaeval Arabs 10
called the island Serendib—from the Pali Singhala-dîpa, and this name we find our author using
in a subsequent passage, under the form Si-lun-tié to designate (as did also the Arabs) Adam's Peak.
Fa-hién, in the fifth century, was the first Chinese to mention Ceylon, he called it Shï-tzï-kuo,
«the kingdom of the Lion», in Sanskrit Singhala. Hüan-tsang, in the seventh century, transcribed
the name by Söng-k'ié-lo (僧 伽 羅), while I-tsing used the form Söng-ho-lo (僧 訶 羅). 15
The name Lang-ya (狼 牙) was also used, transcribing the Sanskrit Laṅkā, one of the old
names of Ceylon. On the Chinese knowledge of Ceylon, see Tennent, Ceylon, I, 583—604, and
also for some additional references to it by Chóu K'ü-feï, supra, p. 26. Schlegel, Tʻoung-pao,
2ᵈ ser. II, 133 made out that Si-lan was not Ceylon but a Sumatran tribe, the Silan of Deli.

3) Nan-p'i, roughly speaking, comprised as its dependencies the whole of the western coast 20
of India, though it applied more particularly to the Malabar coast. See infra, p. 89, n. 1. The
Malabars invasion of Ceylon began in A. D. 515 and ended in 1153, when Prakrama Bahu, having
driven them out of Ceylon, was crowned «sole king of Lanka». He carried the war into the Dekkan,
and reduced Pandya and Chola, making their sovereigns his tributaries. He carried his arms into
Kamboja and Arramana in the Malay Peninsula (probably between Arracan and Siam). He died 25
in 1155, after the most glorious reign in the annals of Ceylon. «Within thirty years from the
decease of Prakrama Bahu, the kingdom was reduced to such an extremity of weakness by con-
tentions amongst the royal family, and by the excesses of their partisans, that the vigilant Malabars
seized the opportunity to land with an army of 24,000 men, reconquered the whole island, and
Magha, their leader, became king of Ceylon A. D. 1211... From the beginning of the 13ᵗʰ century 30
to the extinction of the Singhalese dynasty in the 18ᵗʰ, the island cannot be said to have been
ever entirely freed from the presence of the Malabars». Tennent, Ceylon, 394—418. See, however,
supra, p. 62, where Si-lan is mentioned as a «dependency» of San-fo-ts'i, and supra, p. 73, where it
is said Si-lan sent yearly tribute to San-fo-ts'i. In the early part of the twelfth century and
again in the early part of the thirteenth Ceylon, or a part of it, were under Cholian rule. Tennent, 35
op. cit. I, 402 et seqq.

4) «The lightnings of Ceylon are so remarkable, that in the middle ages they were as
well known to the Arabian seamen, who coasted the island on their way to China, as in later
times the storms that infested the Cape of Good Hope were familiar to early navigators of
Portugal. In the Mohit of Sidi Ali Chelebi, translated by von Hammer, it is stated that to 40
seamen, sailing from Diu to Malacca, «the sign of Ceylon being near is continual lightning, be it
accompanied by rain or without rain; so that 'the lightning of Ceylon' is proverbial for a liar».
Tennent, Ceylon, I, 60 n.

5) An i weighed 20 taels; it seems only to have been used for weighing gold.
6) See infra Pt. II. Ch. I.   45
7) Hüan-tsang speaks of the great ruby over the vihāra of the Buddha's tooth in Ceylon.
Beal, Records, II, 218. Cosmas Indicopleustes tells of a wonderful luminous gem of the king of
Taprobane which was «as large as a great pine-cone, fiery red, and when seen flashing from a
distance, especially if the sun's rays are playing round it, is a matchless sight.» Christian Topography, 365 (Hakluyt Soc. edit.).   50
8) Our author is, so far as is known, the only Chinese who has used this name to designate
Adams' Peak. Si-lun-tié, in Cantonese Sai-lun-tīp, is the name Serendib, used by the mediaeval
Arabs to designate the peak, although originally applied by them to the Island of Ceylon itself.

Reinaud, Relations, etc. I, 5. Ibn Batuta, Voyages, IV, 179—182 says: «The mountain of Serendib is one of the highest in the world; we saw it from the open sea, although we were distant from it nine days' journey .... The impress of the noble foot, that of our father Adam, is seen on a black and high rock, and in an open space. The foot is embedded in the rock,
5 the imprint deeply sunk; its length is eleven spans. The people of China came here in past times; they cut out of the stone the impress of the big toe and around it, and have placed this fragment in a temple of the city of Zeitun (Ts'üan-chóu-fu) to which they come from the most distant provinces». From this it appears that the Buddhist legend that the impress of the foot on Adams' Peak was that of the Buddha, had grown up before the fourteenth century; it
10 was unknown apparently to early Chinese writers. Fa-hién lived in Ceylon for two years, but makes no mention of the Peak. In the seventh century Hüan-tsang speaks of the Ling-k'ié-shan (駿 [or 稜] 伽 山), «the mount of Laṅkā or Ceylon» — as the spot where the Buddha preached the *Laṅkāvatāra sūtra*, but he makes no mention of the footprint (Beal, Records, II, 251), nor did I-tsing writing a little later, though he refers in several places to the
15 Buddha's tooth. In the fifteenth century Adams' Peak is called Si-lan-shan (錫 蘭 山) in Chinese works. See also Tennent, Ceylon, II, 132—141, and E. Dulaurier, Etude sur l'ouvrage intitulé Relation des Voyages, 51, 54.

9) On glass, both opaque and transparent, see infra, Pt. II. Ch. XXXII. It does not appear that camphor was ever procured in Ceylon; it was probably imported there from Sumatra. The blue and
20 red precious stones are sapphires and carbuncles. On the precious stones of Ceylon, see Tennent, op. cit., I, 32—40, II, 590—592. «Mu-lan bark» is evidently the bark of the *kumbuk* of the Singhalese — called *maratha-maram* by the Tamils; *mu-lan* transcribing the Tamil word *maram*. It is the Pentaptera tomentosa, Rox., and «is chiefly prized for its bark, which is sold as medicine, and, in addition to yielding a black dye, it is so charged with calcareous matter that its ashes,
25 when burnt, afford a substitute for the lime which the natives chew with their betel». Tennent, op. cit. I, 99.

10) The previous reference to Si-lan as a «dependency» (屬 國) of San-fo-ts'i, and the present one are irreconciliable with the statement made in the beginning of this chapter that Si-lan is «under the rule of» (管 下) Nan-p'i, unless we suppose that these statements refer
30 to two different periods or to different portions of the island.

14.

JAVA,

Shö-p'o (闍 婆).

The kingdom of Shö-p'o, which is also called P'u-kia-lung[1] (蒲 家 龍),
35 is in a south-easterly direction from Ts'üan-chóu, (whence) ships start, as a rule, during the winter, for, sailing day and night with the north wind, they can arrive (in Shö-p'o) within about a month.

«East (of Shö-p'o) you come to the (Ocean)-Sea and to where the waters flow downward; there is the kingdom of women». Still farther east is the
40 Wei-lü, the end of the habitable world[2] (尾 閭 之 所 泄).

Sailing the sea half a month (to the west from Shö-p'o?) one comes (至) to the K'un-lun (崑崙) country. To the south (from the port or chief city of Shö-p'o?) the sea is reached in three days' journey (日程).

Sailing (泛海) five days (from Shö-p'o), one comes to a country of the Ta-shï (Arabs). Westward one comes to the sea in forty-five days' journey. 5 Northward one comes to the sea in four days' journey (from the chief city?).

Sailing north-west (from Shö-p'o?), in fifteen days one arrives at the country of P'o-ni (渤泥); furthermore (又) you come in ten days to the kingdom of San-fo-ts'i. You arrive in seven days more (又) in the kingdom of Ku-lo (古邏). Again (又) seven days and one comes to Ch'ai-li-t'ing 10 (紫歷亭) and reaches (抵) Kiau-chï, (whence) one makes (達) Kuang-chóu (Canton)[3].

There are two kinds of monasteries (寺 i. e., religious systems) in the kingdom (of Shö-p'o); the one is called that of the «Blessed Buddha» (聖佛), the other that of the «shö-shön»[4] (捨身).   15

There is a hill on which live parrots and it is called «Parrot Hill» (鸚鵡山).

The king wears his hair in a tuft (or knot), on his head is a golden bell; he wears a silken robe and leather shoes[5]. His throne is a square seat, and his officers at their daily audience bow three times when withdrawing. 20 When he goes forth he rides an elephant, or is carried in a chair[6] (腰輿), followed by a company of from five hundred to seven hundred armed soldiers.

When any one of the people sees the king, he squats down until he has passed by.

Three sons of the king are made Fu-wang (副王 Royal Deputies).   25

Of officials they have Ssï-ma-kié (and) Lo-ki-lién (司馬傑落佶連), who conjointly manage the affairs of Government as the Tsai-siang (宰相 Ministers of State) do in China[7]. They have no monthly salaries, but at intervals they are given a liberal supply of native produce.

Inferior to them are three hundred and more civil officials, who divide 30 among themselves the government of the cities, the treasury and the government granaries. The commanders of the troops receive an annual salary of twenty taels of gold, and the soldiers of the army, 30,000 in number, also receive fixed annual pay in gold in various amounts.

As to the customs of the country, in seeking for a woman in marriage, 35 they do not employ go-betweens, but make presents of gold to the woman's family in order to marry her.

They do not inflict corporal punishment and imprisonment on criminals

(不設刑禁犯罪者); they are fined an amount in gold varying according to the gravity of their crime. As to robbers or thieves, they are put to death.

In the fifth moon they make pleasure trips in boats; in the tenth moon
5 they visit the hills, either riding hill ponies (山馬) or carried in a litter (軟兜).

Of musical instruments they have the flute, the kettle-drum and the castanet (板); they are, furthermore, skilled in pantomimes (舞).

The hills are full of monkeys. They are not afraid of man, but if one
10 calls «siau-siau» (霄霄 or if one whistles?) they come out, and if one throws fruit before them a big monkey, called «the monkey king» by the natives, first comes forward to eat, and the crowd of smaller monkeys eat what is left of his meal[8].

In this country there are bamboo gardens where they have pig-fighting
15 and cock-fighting.

The dwellings are of imposing appearance and painted in greenish tints (金碧). Traders (賈人) going there are put up in visitors' lodges, where food and drink both plentiful and good (are supplied them).

The natives dress their hair and wear clothes which are girt around
20 their chest and reach down to the knees[9].

When they are sick, they take no medicines, but simply pray to their local gods (神) or to the Buddha.

The people have personal names but no surnames. They are quick-tempered and of a pugnacious disposition, and when they have a feud with
25 San-fo-ts'i, both parties seek to join in battle[10].

In the twelfth year yüan-kia of the Sung dynasty (A. D. 435), this country entered into communication with China, but after that intercourse was broken off until the third year shun-hua of the present dynasty (992)[11], when it again performed the ceremony of sending tribute to our Court.

30 It is a broad and level country, well suited to agriculture. It produces rice, hemp, millet, beans, but no wheat. Ploughing is done with buffaloes. The people pay a tithe-rent. They make salt by boiling sea water. The country also abounds in fish, turtles, fowl, ducks, goats, and they kill horses and buffaloes for food[12].

35 The fruits comprise big gourds, cocoanuts, bananas, sugar-cane and taro (芋). They have also elephants' tusks, rhinoceros horns, pearls, camphor, (龍腦), tortoise-shell, sandal-wood, aniseed, cloves, cardamoms, cubebs (蓽澄茄), laka-wood, mats, foreign sword blades (番劍), pepper, betel-

nuts, sulphur, saffron (紅花), sapan-wood and parrots. They also pay attention to the raising of silkworms and the weaving of silk; they have various coloured brocaded silks (繡絲), cotton (吉貝), and damasked cotton gauzes (or damasks and cotton cloth 綾布).

No tea is raised in this country. Their wine is derived from the cocoanut [5] and from the inner part of the *hia-nau-tan* (蝦猱丹) tree, which tree has not been seen by the Chinese, or else it is made by fermenting (the fruits) of the *kuang-lang* (桄榔, sago palm) and of the areca palm; all of these (liquors) are clear and well-flavored [13] (亦自清香).

«As to cane sugar, it is brown and white (or brownish white?) in colour [10] and very sweet to the taste.

«They cast coins in an alloy of copper, silver, white copper (鍮), and tin; sixty of these coins are equal to one tael of gold; thirty two are equal to half a tael of gold» [14].

Foreign merchants use in trading gold and silver of various degrees of [15] fineness (夾雜金銀), vessels made of gold and silver, silk stuffs, black damasks (皂綾), (*ssï*)-*ch'üan-kung* [15] (川芎), orris-root, cinnabar, copperas, alum, borax, arsenic, lacquer-ware, iron tripods and green (or blue 青) and white porcelain-ware.

There is a vast store of pepper in this foreign country (此番) and the [20] merchant ships, in view of the profit they derive from that trade, are in the habit of smuggling (out of China) copper cash for bartering purposes. Our Court has repeatedly forbidden all trade (with this country), but the foreign traders, for the purpose of deceiving (the government), changed its name and referred to it as Su-ki-tan [16] (蘇吉丹). [25]

Notes.

1) Although it is possible that the Chinese may have heard of Java as early as the middle of the third century A. D., under the name of Chu-p'u (諸蒲; see Pelliot, B. E. F. E. O. IV, 270), it was in the early part of the fifth century that authentic mention was made of it by the pilgrim Fa-hién, who gave it its Sanskrit name Yé-p'o-t'i (耶婆提 i. e., *Yavadvipa*). In 433, [30] and again in 435 Javanese came to the Chinese Court, at which time their country is referred to by the Chinese (Sung-shu, 5) as the island of Shö-p'o (闍婆洲). From this time on relations were maintained between the two countries. In the sixth and seventh centuries, the Chinese wrote the name Shö-p'u (社蒲), and the first character was not infrequently erroneously written Tu (杜), as in Ma Tuan-lin, 332. In the Mongol period Java was known to [35] the Chinese by the name of Chau-wa (爪哇), sometimes wrongly written Kua-wa (瓜哇), and this name has continued in use ever since; though in the Ming period it was also known as Shun-ta (順塔), Hia-kiang (下港) and P'u-kia-lung. See Tung-si-yang-k'au, 3,1. In the fifth century the Chinese are believed to have referred to Java under the names of Ho-lo-tan (呵羅單) and Ho-ling (訶陵), the latter being presumably a transcription of the name [40] Kalinga, from which part of India the Hindu settlers in Java had for the most part come. Groeneveldt, Notes, 15; Gerini, however, thinks that Ho-lo-tan was in Siam and Ho-ling in the

Malay Peninsula. Asiat. Quart., 3[d] ser. X, 384, and XIII, 137. More recently, Gerini, Researches, 458 et seq., has arrived at the conclusion that Shö-p'o was a part of the Malay Peninsula, below the Krah Isthmus, and that the name is probably the last glimmering of Tuba, Jaba, or Saba, «the country of the Java (or Jawa) race», i. e., the Malays. He does not think that the name Shö-p'o
5 can have ever been applied by the Chinese to any part of Sumatra. «It is, he says, a most egregious mistake to localize the term Java or Jaba, with its variant Sava or Saba, to the present island of Java alone, since it was the common designation for the whole archipelago, or, at any rate, for those portions of it that had been settled by the Javana or Yavana race, besides being the name of several regions on the Indo-Chinese mainland» (p. 461—463). The above conclusion
10 being accepted, Gerini (541) says Fa-hién's Yé-p'o-t'i «must be identified either with the east and north coasts of Sumatra, or with a portion of the seabord of the Malay Peninsula on or about Malacca Strait». As to Ho-lo-tan, Gerini (542) says it was «possibly Gurōt in the Ghirbi district, west coast of the Malay Peninsula»; Ho-ling, according to him (544) was probably the east coast of the Malay Peninsula at Tanjong Gelang or Puling, 4° N. lat.; and perhaps the
15 eastern portion of the country of Ho-ling referred to previously as on the west coast of the Malay Peninsula about Gūnong Geriang and abreast of the Langkāwi islands.

     Readers may judge for themselves whether all these identifications can fit in with the details of our text. Schlegel, T'oung pao, X, 258 et seqq. and 2[d] ser. IV, was of opinion there were two Shö-p'o, one in Sumatra (Java minor), the other in Java (Java major). He looked upon
20 Chau Ju-kua's account of Shö-p'o, as a jumble, referring here to Sumatra, there to Java and still in other places to the Malay Peninsula. Pelliot, B. E. F. E. O. IV, 269 et seqq., has conclusively shown, it would seem, that Schlegel's suggestions on this point are quite untenable.

     As to the name P'u-kia-lung, the identification first made by Groeneveldt (Notes, 40) with Pekalongan on the N. coast of Java, is generally accepted. This was presumably the chief
25 center of Chinese and foreign trade in the Sung period.

     The apparent error into which our author has fallen in this paragraph of placing Shö-p'o S. E. of Ts'üan-chóu may be through his having used the general indications supplied by Chóu K'ü-feï (2,12[b]) as to the position of this island, while overlooking the fact that Chóu gives its bearing from Canton. But even from Canton it is rather south or south-west. The more likely
30 explanation of the position assigned by both writers to Java may be that junks sailing from Ts'üan-chóu and Canton had to steer S. E. in order to obviate the strong N. E. monsoon prevailing in the winter. Quite a number of errors in the directions of the compass as placed on record in mediaeval Chinese texts can be thus accounted for, as for example, the placing of Tsöng-po (off the E. coast of Africa) to the south of Guzerat; ships were forced by the winds
35 prevailing at the season of the year when the voyage from Guzerat to the E. Africa coast was made, to steer in a southerly direction to be driven where they would go. See infra, Ch. XXIV.

     The Ling-wai-tai-ta, 2,12[b], from which our author takes this paragraph, reads as follows: «The kingdom of Shö-p'o, also called P'u-kia-lung, is in the south-east of the sea. Its position being downward (i. e., in the S. as compared to the countries of Annam in the N., which are held
40 to be «upwards», or «above») causes it to be called the «Lower Coast». In the eleventh and twelfth moons of the year ships can reach there from Kuang-ch'óu with the monsoon and sailing day and night in one month».

     2) The phrase in quotation marks is taken from the Ling-wai-tai-ta, 2,9. See also supra, p. 26 and infra, Ch. XXXVIII. 4. The Chinese believed that the waters which poured continually into
45 the great World-Ocean-Sea flowed out again through a great hole called the Wei-lü. The surface of the Ocean began to incline downwards somewhere E. of Java at the mythical Kingdom of Women, so the waters flowed continually eastward into the great gulf, which, however, overflowed every few years. Masudi, Prairies d'or, I, 342, says that in the boundless and unknown sea east of the Sea of Sanf (i. e., Champa, Annam) are volcanic islands and beyond them is an island on
50 which the sound of music can be heard. «Sailors, he adds, who have been in those parts pretend that it is there that Dedjdjâl (the Antichrist) has set his abode». There seems some connexion between this Arab story and the Chinese one.

     3) This paragraph and the two preceding ones were reproduced with some change in the

Sung-shï, 489,14—15, the most important one making the time used in sailing from Shö-p'o to San-fo-ts'i 15 days instead of 10, as stated in our text. Ma Tuan-lin, 332 agrees on this point with our text. Groeneveldt, Notes, 15 has translated this passage from the Sung-shï, as has also Pelliot, B. E. F. E. O. IV, 296. The only difficulty in it is the vagueness or rather uncertainty of the meaning of the character *yu* (叉); apparently it has not in each phrase 5 quite the same meaning.

K'un-lun as here used may mean either K'un-lun-shan, i. e., Pulo Condore, or the country of the K'un-lun or Malays. See supra p. 32 n. It may also be the same as Ku-lun, a piratical state referred to in a subsequent passage (infra, p. 84), but this is doubtful. The Arab settlement referred to in the second paragraph may have been in western Java, our author's Sin-t'o. In 10 another passage (infra, Ch. XXXIX) our author says it was 45 days sailing from Shö-p'o to P'o-ni, i. e., the W. (or S) coast of Borneo; in the present case a straight course is probably meant, while in the latter the course taken may have been by way of San-fo-ts'i, the Malay Peninsula, and thence eastward. Ku-lo is, it would seem, the Ki-lo Ta-nung of a subsequent passage (infra, p. 88) situated possibly on the Perak coast. As to Ch'ai-li-t'ing, Groeneveldt, Notes, 16, thinks 15 it may have been an island about the entrance to the Gulf of Siam. Gerini, Researches, 514, suggests, with much more probability, that the Cherating river on the E. coast of the Malay Peninsula, 4°10′ N. lat., is the locality referred to. On P'o-ni (Borneo) see infra, Ch. XXXIX.

Schlegel, T'oung pao, 2^d ser. IV was of opinion that these three paragraphs in our text referred to the Malay Peninsula. He also corrected our text in the last paragraph and would read 20 «sailing north-east (from Shö-p'o) in fifteen days one arrives in the kingdom of P'o-ni». This correction is not needed, it would seem, for the reason given in a previous note on the courses junks have to sail with the monsoons.

4) *Shö-shön*, «to give up, to renounce the world, to enter the priesthood». Probably the Brahmans, or some kind of Hindu ascetics are meant. Brahmanism, at the time of which our 25 author writes, was tolerated in Java where Buddhism was, however, the predominant religion. Lassen, Indische Alterthumsk. IV, 467.

5) Ling-wai-tai-ta, loc. cit., has «The king of this country wears his hair in a knot behind his head; the common people shave their heads, leaving only a short top-knot. They like to wrap round their bodies cotton sarongs with gaudy patterns». 　　　　　　　　　　　　　　30

6) *Yau-yü*, literally «waist-carriage». It was carried by hand, like the so-called «Palace chairs» or *Kién-yü* (肩 輿) in use in the Palace of Peking at the present day.

7) Ma Tuan-lin, op. cit., 332, gives the title of these officials as Lo-ki-lién, as does also the Sung-shï, 489,15. Schlegel, T'oung-pao, X, 276 suggested that the last four characters in our text (Kié-lo-ki-lién) represent a Malay form *kedekaran*, «a council of warriors». Pelliot, B. E. 35 F. E. O. IV, 311, says that no such Malay word is known to exist. He suggests that Lo-ki-lién may represent the Malay *rakyran* or *rakarayan*, which appears in inscriptions in Java in conjunction with the word *mantri*, «minister», which in our text corresponds to the Chinese title Tsai-hiang. The Sung-shï, loc. cit., says there were four Lo-ki-lién who jointly managed the affairs of the kingdom. The T'ang-shu, 222^b, says there were in Java thirty-two high Ministers of 40 State (大 夫), the highest of whom was the Ta-tso-kan-hiung (大 坐 敢 兄). The dependencies of Shö-p'o are enumerated in the chapter on Su-ki-tan, infra, p. 83.

8) Ibn Batuta, op. cit., IV, 175, says that he was told in Ceylon of the monkeys of that country having chiefs whom they obeyed as a sovereign. They supplied him with bananas, when he, his young, and the four principal monkeys ate them while the others looked on. The 45 Sung-shï, 489, gives the story as told in the text, on the authority of the Javanese envoy to China in 992.

9) Conf. supra, n. 5.

10) The Ling-wai-tai-ta, loc. cit., says: «The inhabitants (of Shö-p'o) prize courage and are given to quarrelling and fighting. When the prince or some prominent official dies, all his 50 personal attendants vow to follow him; so when the corpse is burned, they go with dancing into the flames, and when the bones are thrown into the water, they jump in afterwards without the slightest hesitation and drown themselves». Our author says (supra, p. 61) that this custom prevailed in San-fo-ts'i.

11) Our author errs here, as the T'ang-shu, 222[b] mentions a number of missions from Java to the Court of China from A. D. 627 to 873. The reason for the omission of any mention of them was presumably because our author did not know that the Ho-ling of the T'ang period was identical with Shö-p'o. The Sung-shï, 489, gives a detailed account of the mission of 992. It
5 mentions also tribute missions in 1109. In 1292 Java, or a part of it, was invaded and possibly conquered by the Chinese. Groeneveldt, Notes, 14—34.

12) Ling-wai-tai-ta, loc. sup. cit., says «The native products (of Shö-p'o) are pepper, sandal-wood, cloves, white cardamoms, nutmegs and the *chön* variety of gharu-wood». Raffles, Java, I, 106, refers to the fondness of the Javanese for horse and buffalo meat.
10   13) The Sung-shï, 489,15 reproduces this paragraph, changing only the last four characters to 亦 甚 香 美, which justifies the translation given above. *Hia-nau-tan*, lit., «extract of *hia-nau*»; *anao* is the Malay name of the gomuti palm whose sap supplies the *toddy* of Java. The liquor itself is called in Malay *tuwak*. Crawfurd, History, etc., I, 40. Schlegel, T'oung pao, X, 267 suggested that *hia-nau-tan* was a Malay word *kedjutan*. Pelliot, op. sup. cit., IV, 310 while
15 rejecting this identification could suggest nothing better. The Ling-wai-tai-ta, loc. sup. cit., has: «They make wine from the cocoanut and also from the sap of a tree».

14) These two paragraphs are quoted from the Ling-wai-tai-ta, loc. sup. cit. *T'ou* is certainly in this passage the «white copper» of the Chinese and Koreans. The *t'ou-shï* (鍮 石) mentioned in Chinese historical works as a product of Persia, may represent Uiguric *tutsch*, Kazanic
20 *tudsch*, *tuus* (sic), possibly Italian *tausia*, from which German *tauschiren* «to damascene» is derived. See T. Watters, Essays on the Chinese Language, 359. Both Ma Tuan-lin (Hervey St Denis, op. cit., II, 496) and the Sung-shï, 489,15, referring to the currency of Shö-p'o say: «They cut up leaves of silver to make coins for business purposes; one coin of which is exchanged by government for 1 *hu* 2 *t'ou* (approximately 12 bushels) of rice». Crawfurd, History, etc., I, 281 says:
25 «Among the extensive and curious variety of ancient relics which Java has afforded, and particularly when a great variety of brass and tin coins has been found, no gold coin has ever been discovered, and silver coins on only one or two occasions .... The Mahomedans, shortly after establishing their religion in the Archipelago, seem to have taught the natives the use of gold as a coin. All the coins which we discover are stamped with Arabic letters, and bear the names of
30 the Mahomedan sovereigns by whom they were coined ... A brass coin, impressed with a number of fantastic figures and characters, which are at present unintelligible, formed the most ancient currency of Java ... This was the currency of the Buddhist sovereigns, whose empire was at *Mojopahit*. The Mahomedans who succeeded them coined a smaller money of the same metal». We gather from what our author says in the text, and particularly from his remarks concerning
35 the currency of Su-ki-tan (infra, p. 82), that there was a great scarcity of money in Java. See also infra, n. 16, and p. 82.

15) No explanation has been found of the nature of the stuff called *tsau-ling*, lit., «black damask». The *ssï-ch'üan-kung* is a species of levisticum, Hanbury, Science Papers, 260, Bretschneider, Materia medica, p. 100—102. In the chapter on Sukitan, our author says (infra, p. 83)
40 that the headaches from which the pepper-gatherers of Java suffered so greatly yielded to doses of this medicine; hence presumably its importance as an import from China.

16) Chinese copper cash appear to have been in great demand in the Archipelago. Among the return presents made the San-fo-ts'i mission of 1079 by the Chinese Government were 64,000 strings of cash (Sung-shï, 489). The same work (180) says that «after the appointment of Inspectors
45 of Foreign trade (Shi-p'o-shï) in Ch'ö-kiang, Fu-kién and Kuang-tung, the traffic of merchant ships between China and foreign countries had the effect of scattering abroad the copper cash coined for the use of our country. For this reason the exportation of cash to any place beyond the straits near Hang-chóu was prohibited. In the 9th year *shun-hi* (1182) an Edict was issued making the local authorities of Ch'ö-kiang responsible for the unlawful exportation of copper cash.
50 In the 9th year *kia-ting* (1216) the High Commissioners for the inspection of government affairs began their Report as follows: «Since the appointment of Inspectors of Foreign trade, the issue of copper cash to ships engaged in foreign trade at the open ports has been forbidden. At the end of the *shan-hing* period (about 1163) the Ministers drew attention to the irregularities arising from the

Inspectors of Foreign trade at Ts'üan-chóu and Canton, as well as the two Mint Inspectors of the south-western Provinces, allowing vessels to clear with return cargoes containing gold and copper cash. How could the local authorities be held responsible for such infraction of the law, if the four officers referred to were habitual law breakers themselves?»

It appears that similar complaints led to the repeated complete prohibition of the 5 exportation of cash, although during certain periods it was not strictly enforced. Thus in 1234 an Edict was issued prohibiting the exportation of cash «by Ocean going ships»; this seems to involve a partial restriction only, since traffic with Shö-p'o (Java) was specifically prohibited, and since the restriction could be easily evaded by clearing ships for another country — as Chau Ju-kua tells us traders did. 10

See also Schlegel, T'oung pao, 2ᵈ ser. IV, 236—238.

15.

CENTRAL JAVA.

Su-ki-tan (蘇 吉 丹).

Su-ki-tan is a branch of the Shö-p'o country. To the west it borders 15 on Sin-t'o, to the east it adjoins Ta-pan[1] (打 板).

There is a mountain of immense height called Pau-lau-an (保 老 岸). When approaching the coast foreign ships first sight the five lofty peaks of this mountain, always covered with clouds[2].

The king of this country wears a turban of cotton cloth of variegated 20 colours and goes barefooted. When walking about he is shaded by a black or white umbrella, and more than five hundred attendants follow him, bearing every sort of weapon and wearing hats of various shapes, — some like a tiger's head, some like a deer's, others like the head of an ox, of a sheep, a fowl, an elephant, a lion or a monkey; and little flags of coloured silk are stuck 25 in the side (of the hats).

Among the natives, the men cut their hair, but the women wear a coiffure; they all wrap their bodies in cloth, but go barefooted and wear a loin-cloth.

The people use as a medium of trade pieces of alloyed silver cut into bits 30 like dice and bearing the seal of the Fan-kuan (番 官) stamped upon it. Six of these counters are worth one tael of «trade gold» (貨 金), and each one may be exchanged for from thirty or forty up to a hundred shöng (pecks) of rice. For all their other trading they use (this money) which is called «Shö-p'o kin»

(«Java money»); from which it may be seen that this country is (identical with) Shö-p'o³.

Dwellings are built in the same fashion as in Sin-t'o. There is much rice in this country; very wealthy families keep as much as ten thousand piculs
5 in their granaries.

There is a tree called *po-lo-mi* (波 羅 密 the jack-fruit). The fruit is like a pumpkin, the skin like that of the chestnut, the pulp like that of the mandarin orange. It is extremely sweet and well-flavoured⁴. There are also lichees, bananas and sugar-cane, in all respects the same as those of China,
10 with this difference, however, that the lichee, when sun-dried, will cure bowel complaint; that the bananas grow a foot long, and sugar-cane to the height of ten feet.

The juice of the latter, with the addition of a drug, is brewed into a liquor superior to (that derived from) the cocoanut⁵.

15 The products of the soil are, on the whole, not different from those of Shö-p'o. There is a great abundance of pepper. At the right season and in good years, twenty-five taels of «trade money» (貨 銀) will buy from ten to twenty packages (包) of pepper, each package holding fifty pecks (*shöng*). In years of dearth, or in times of disturbance, the same sum will buy only half
20 that amount.

The pepper-gatherers suffer greatly from the acrid fumes they have to inhale, and are commonly afflicted with headache (malaria) which yields to doses of (*ssï*)-*ch'üan-kung*.

As cinnabar is much used in cosmetics (搽 抹) by the Barbarian
25 women and also for dyeing the finger nails and silk clothing of women, foreign traders look upon these two articles as staples of trade⁶.

Traders are treated generously; they are not charged expenses for either harborage or board.

This country is adjacent (連) to the following countries, all of which
30 are dependencies of Shö-p'o⁷:

Pai-hua-yüan (百 花 園)	Ma-li (麻 藶)
Ma-tung (麻 東)	10 Niu-lun (牛 論)
Ta-pan (打 板)	Tan-jung-wu-lo (丹 戎 武 囉)
Hi-ning (禧 甯)	Ti-wu (底 勿)
35 5 Jung-ya-lu (戎 牙 路)	Ping-ya (平 牙)
Tung-ki (東 峙)	I-wu (夷 勿)
Ta-kang (打 綱)	15 Nu-ku (奴 孤)
Huang-ma-chu (黃 麻 駐)	

6*

The country of Ta-pan connects to the east with Great Shö-p'o, it is (also) called, (號) Jung-ya-lu. (Note: Also written Chung-kia-lu (重迦盧). The houses which the people of this country build are like those of China. The country being a level plain, intersected by an anchorage (港), there is trade both by water and by land.   5

The native products are bay-salt (青鹽), sheep and parrots.

The foreign head-men[8] (番官) are brave and fierce; they take wives from the pirate states of the eastern borders. The people of the latter, under pretext of visiting relatives (married to the Fan-kuan and on board their ships), ships were frequently plundered (in this way). Matters went so far that captives 10 were considered a most valuable commodity, each one being worth two or three taels of gold. For this reason trade (with this country) was presently broken off.

(Note[9]: By «pirate states», Tan-chung-pu-lo (丹重布囉), Pa-li (芭離), Sun-t'a (孫他) and Ku-lun (故論) are to be understood).

The countries of Ta-kang, Huang-ma-chu, Ma-li, Tan-jung-wu-lo, 15 Ti-(wu), Ping-ya, I-wu and Nu-ku are situated on islands; each of them has its own chief, and they have vessels plying between them. There is but little agriculture, but there are many old trees, the inner parts of which produce *sha-hu* (sago), which looks like wheat flour. The natives by mixing water with it, make it into pellets of the size of peas. After being sun-dried it is packed 20 up and stored like grain. They also mix it with fish or meat and make a porridge. They are fond of sugar-cane and bananas. The former is crushed and by adding a certain substance (lit., drug) is caused to ferment and is made into wine. They have also the *weï-pa*[10] (尾巴) tree, whose pith being taken out and the juice extracted yields wine.   25

The natives (of these countries) are strong fellows, but savage and of a dark bronze colour. They wrap (a cloth round) their limbs and tattoo their bodies. They cut their hair and go barefooted. They use no vessels in eating or drinking; in their stead they bind leaves together, which are thrown away when the meal is finished.   30

As a standard of exchange the people use only pecks and pints of sago. They do not know either how to write or how to count.

They erect stages with wooden poles stuck in the ground and reaching to a height of twenty feet or more; on the top they build houses with walls and roofs of the same type as those made by the Sin-t'o people.   35

The native products include sandal-wood, cloves, cardamoms, fancy mats, foreign cotton cloth (番布), iron swords and other weapons.

Among these islands those of Tan-jung-wu-lo and Ma-li[11] are rather more extensive than the others; they raise large numbers of horses for military service and they have a slight knowledge of writing and counting. The native products are laka-wood, yellow wax, fine aromatic substances and tortoise-shell.

5   Although Tan-jung-wu-lo has such products, the people instead of attending to (legitimate) business, prefer going to sea for piracy, and so foreign traders rarely come there [12].

Notes.

1) The name Su-ki-tan does not appear in the Ling-wai-tai-ta or the Sung-shï, nor does
10 it occur in Crawfurd's list of mediaeval Javanese states. It seems to be of Indian origin, possibly *çuka* «parrot» and *dāna* «gift». The name Sukatana is found as that of a Javanese colony in southern Borneo. Lassen, Indische Alterthumsk. IV, 533, and A. Marre, Madjapahit et Tchampa, pp. 95—97, in Recueil de Mémoires, Centenaire de l'Ecole des Langues Orientales, 1895. Gerini. Researches, 451, suggests that Su-ki-tan was Sukadana in S. E. Sumatra.
15   It seems impossible, with only the references of Chinese authors of the Ming period to guide us, to locate Sukitan more closely than it is in the text, i. e., between the Sundas on the W. and Tuban on the E. In the Ming period Sukitan was apparently a much more extensive region. The Tung-si-yang-k'au, 4,13 says of it: «its chief place is Ki-li-shï (吉力石 i. e., Gersik) .... The people of this country go to Yau-tung (饒洞 i. e., Yortan, S. of Surabaya
20 on the Brantas river) to trade with the Chinese .... The neighbouring countries are Ssï-lu-wa (思魯瓦 i. e., Surabaya) and Tu-man (猪蠻 i. e., Tuban). Groeneveldt, Notes, 54. Our author in two passages conveys the impression that he uses the name Su-ki-tan as being identical with Shö-p'o.

2) The Tung-si-yang-k'au, 4,13[b] quotes the Ming I-tung-chï as follows: «The Pau-lau-an
25 mountain is in the country of Su-ki-tan. All foreign ships sight this mountain before arriving. The summit has five peaks and there are clouds on it all the year round. (Chinese) sailors call it Pa-na ta-shan (巴哪大山). The Ki-li-mön shan (吉里門山) faces the Pau-lau shan. Its western side extends into a very broad spit (or «promontory» 尾)». There can be no doubt as to the Ki-li-mön shan being Pulo Krimun, consequently Pau-lau-an (lit. «the
30 mountain (on) the cliffs of Pau-lau» [or Pulo]) must be the Tanjong (Cape) Pautuman of our maps.

3) *Fan kuan* «Foreign official», probably the resident head-man of the Foreign settlement. The silver «dice» here referred to were probably made by the Arab traders and bore the «chop» of their head-men. See also supra, pp. 60 and 69. The text reads 其他貿易悉用 是名曰闍婆金可見此國郎闍婆也.

35   4) «Of the Jack fruit (Artocarpus integrifolia) two species occur in the Indian islands, the common Jack, and the Champadak .... Rumphius suspects that it is not an indigenous product of the Indian islands, but that it was brought from the continent of India by stranger merchants». Crawfurd, op. cit., I, 422. See also infra, Pt. II, Ch. XVII.

5) Crawfurd, op. cit., I, 412 says: «The Indian islands are the countries in which the
40 banana grows to greatest perfection, and is found in greatest variety. There are at least sixteen distinct species or varieties of the cultivated banana, and five species of wild». In another passage (infra, Pt. II. Ch. XXVIII) our author states that cubebs grew in Sukitan. Crawfurd, Hist. Ind. Archipel., I, says cubebs only grow in Java.

    The use to which our text says the juice of the sugar-cane was put agrees with what
45 Crawfurd tells us (I, 476): «The natives of the country, to this day, are unacquainted with the art of extracting sugar from the cane, which they rear solely with the view of using it in its raw state, as a common esculent vegetable». The «drug» used in brewing *arrak*, the liquor here referred to, is *toddy* or palm wine which enters into its composition.

    6) On pepper, see infra, Pt. II, Ch. XXVII, and Crawfurd, op. cit., I, 479—486. On the *ssï-*

ch'üan-kung, see supra, p. 81, n. 15, it appears from this passage to have been, as also cinnabar, considered as a staple article of Chinese trade.

7) Crawfurd, op. cit., II, 297 et seqq., says: «The latter portion of the twelfth century is the earliest period of Javanese history to which I can with confidence refer. From this time, down to the establishment of Mahomedanism, at the close of the fifteenth century, a number of 5 considerable, but independent states, existed in Java, and the religion of the people was a modified Hinduism .... The following are the chief (states) which existed in the three centuries which preceded the conversion to Mahomedanism: Doho, Brambanan, Madang-kamolan, Jangola, Singhasari, Pajajaran, and Mojopahit ... The ruins of Doho are in the fertile district of Kadari, about the centre of the island, counting by its length and towards the southern coast ... The 10 state which existed at Brambanan flourished about 1266 and 1296 of Christ .... Tradition hands down to us the name of Madang-kamolan, and, in the district of Wirosobo, the ruins of a palace are still discernible .... Janggolo and Singhasari, the first in the district of Surabaya, and the last in that of Malang, both towards the eastern part of Java, are said to have flourished at the same time .... Pajajaran about forty miles from the modern city of Batavia, is pointed out by 15 tradition as the only ancient state of considerable extent, which ever flourished in the country of the Sundas .... The probability is, that it flourished during the end of the thirteenth, and the beginning of the fourteenth centuries of the Christian era. The origin of .... Mojopahit remains as undetermined as that of Pajajaran .... All accounts agree that Mojopahit was destroyed in the year .... 1478 of Christ, and, from presumptive evidence, it is inferred that it may have been 20 founded about a century and a half before .... The ruins of the city of Mojopahit are still visible in the district of Wirosobo».

Chau Ju-kua places the following states on or near the island of Java: (1) Pai-hua-yüan, (2) Ma-tung, (3) Hi-ning, (4) Jung-ya-lu also called Chung-kia-lu or Ta-pan, (5) Niu-lun, (6) Tung-ki, (7) Sin-t'o or Sun-t'a.   25

Pai-hua-yüan is probably Pejajaran of Crawfurd's list, Ma-tung is his Medang-kamolan, Hi-ning possibly his Singhasari, Jung-ya-lu is his Janggolo (see supra, p. 66, n. 16(19), aud Sin-t'o the Sundas (see supra, p. 66, n. 16(12) and pp. 70—71). Niu-lun and Tung-ki are unidentified. The latter may be a Chinese name, it means «Eastern Cape». Schlegel, T'oung pao, 2ᵈ ser. IV, 238 thinks Ma-tung is Batang in E. Java, and Hi-ning probably Giling Trawangan near Bali, but he only bases 30 these identifications on the fact of the names of these localities resembling phonetically the Chinese.

Chau Ju-kua places the following localities of his list on islands not close to Java: (7) Ta-kang, (8) Huang-ma-chu, (9) Ma-li, (10) Niu-lun, (11) Tan-jung wu-lo, (12) Ti-wu, (13) Ping-ya, (14) I-wu, (15) Nu-ku. Nᵒˢ 7 and 8 remain unidentified. Schlegel, loc. sup. cit., suggests that Takang is possibly the old name of Sumarang. Infra, Pt. II. Ch. XII we are told 35 that Ta-kang supplied sandalwood. Ma-li (or Pa-li) is the island of Bali. Niu-lun is unidentified; Schlegel, loc. sup. cit., thinks it the same as the Ku-lun pirate state mentioned in another passage of this chapter; he would place it in E. Java. Tan-jung wu-lo suggests Malay Tanjong Pulo or an Indian form Tanjong pura, and it appears that in the fifteenth century this name was applied by the Javanese to Borneo. Pelliot, B. E. F. E. O., IV, 224. Schlegel, loc. sup. 40 cit., says Tan-jung wu-lo must have been on the E. coast of Java. Ti-wu, in Cantonese dialect Ti-mat, is the island of Timor. In another passage (infra, Ch. XXXIX) the name is written Ti-mön, and this is the usual transcription. Ping-ya, in Cantonese dialect Pang-ga suggests Banca. Schlegel, loc. sup. cit., divides the last six characters in the list into two names only, Ping-ya-i and Wu-nu-ku, but this does not enable him to identify them. In Pt. II, Ch. XIV we are told that 45 Huang-ma-chu and Niu-lun produced nutmegs, we may therefore presume that these islands were near Ceram, Gilolo, Ternate or Amboyna. See Crawfurd, History etc. I, 505. I-wu and Nu-ku, supposing the names are to be read in this way, suggest nothing.

8) Probably here as in other passages meaning the head-men of the Arabs and other foreign traders settled in the various localities on the islands.   50

9) This note, like the others, may be by the Ming editor of the Chu-fan chï, as the name of the places mentioned are written, not as Chau does in the text, but as they were written at a later period. Pa-li is Bali, and Ku-lun may be Gurong off W. coast of Borneo.

10) Weï-pa, in Cantonese dialect mi-pa, the nipa palm. It is cultivated in some of the islands of the Archipelago solely for the liquor it yields, though its leaf, or *atap*, is the usual thatch of the Malays. See also infra, Ch. XXXIX.

11) The text reads Tan-jung ma-li wu-lo, but there can be no doubt that this is an error of a copyist.

12) Schlegel, T'oung-pao, 2[d] ser. IV, 240 says that this paragraph shows that Chau Ju-kua «has confounded Java with Djava on the Malay Peninsula, at all times the favourite haunt of the Malay pirates».

16.

MALABAR.

Nan-p'i (南 毗).

The Nan·p'i country is in the extreme south-west[1]. From San-fo-ts'i one may reach it with the monsoon (便 風) in a little more than a month.

The capital of the kingdom is styled (號) Mié-a-mo (蔑 阿 抹), which has the same meaning as the Chinese expression *li-ssi*[2] (禮 司).

The ruler of the country has his body draped, but goes barefooted. He wears a turban and a loin-cloth, both of white cotton cloth. Sometimes he wears a white cotton shirt with narrow sleeves. When going out he rides an elephant, and wears a golden hat ornamented with pearls and gems. On his arm is fastened a band of gold, and around his leg is a golden chain.

Among his regalia is a standard of peacock feathers on a staff of vermilion colour; over twenty men guard it round. He is attended by a guard of some five hundred picked foreign women (番 婦), chosen for their fine physique. Those in front lead the way with dancing, their bodies draped, barefooted and with a cotton loin-cloth. Those behind ride horses bareback; they have a loin-cloth,. their hair is done up and they wear necklaces of pearls and anklets of gold, their bodies are perfumed with camphor and musk and other drugs, and umbrellas of peacock feathers shield them from the sun[3].

In front of the dancing-women are carried the officers of the king's train, seated in litters (袋 bag) of white foreign cotton, and which are called *pu-tai-kiau* (布 袋 轎), and are borne on poles plated with gold and silver[4].

In this kingdom there is much sandy soil, so, when the king goes forth, they first send an officer with an hundred soldiers and more to sprinkle the ground so that the gusts of wind may not whirl up the dust.

The people are very dainty in their diet; they have a hundred ways of cooking their food, which varies every day.

There is an officer called *Han-lin* (翰 林) who lays the viands and drinks before the king, and sees how much food he eats, regulating his diet so that he may not exceed the proper measure. Should the king fall sick 5 through excess of eating, then (this officer) must taste his faeces and treat him according as he finds them sweet or bitter.

The people of this country are of a dark brown complexion, the lobes of their ears reach down to their shoulders. They are skilled in archery and dextrous with the sword and lance. They love fighting and ride elephants in 10 battle, when they also wear turbans of coloured silks.

They are extremely devout Buddhists[5].

The climate is warm; there is no cold season. Rice, hemp, beans, wheat, millet, tubers and green vegetables supply their food; they are abundant and cheap.

They cut an alloyed silver into coins; on these they stamp an official 15 seal. The people use these in trading.

The native products include pearls, foreign cotton stuff of all colours (i. e., coloured chintzes) and *tou-lo mién* (cotton cloth)[6].

There is in this country (a river called the) Tan-shui kiang (淡 水 江) which, at a certain point where its different channels meet, becomes very 20 broad. At this point its banks are bold cliffs in the face of which sparks (lit., stars) can constantly be seen, and these by their vital powers fructify and produce small stones (秀 氣 鍾 結 產 爲 小 石) like cat's-eyes, clear and translucid. They lie buried in holes in (these) hills until some day they are washed out by the rush of a flood, when the officials send men in little 25 boats to pick them up. They are prized by the natives[7].

The following states are dependencies of this country (of Nan-p'i)[8]:

Ku-lin (故 臨)	Föng-ya-lo (馮 牙 囉)
Hu-ch'a-la (胡 茶 辣)	Ma-li-mo (麻 㕧 抹)
Kan-pa-i (甘 琶 逸)	Tu-nu-ho (都 奴 何) 30
Pi-li-sha (弼 離 沙)	A-li-jo (啞 㕧 喏)
5 Ma-lo-hua (麻 囉 華)	10 Au-lo-lo-li (嗷 囉 囉 㕧)

This country (of Nan-p'i?) is very far away and foreign vessels rarely visit it. Shï-lo-pa-chï-li-kan, father and son, belong to this race of people; they are now living in the southern suburb of the city of Ts'üan-(chóu-fu)[9]. 35

Its products are taken thence to Ki·lo Ta-nung[10] (吉 囉 達 弄) and San-fo-ts'i, and the following goods are exchanged in bartering for them: Ho-ch'ï silks, porcelain-ware, camphor *(chang-nau)*, rhubarb[11], *huang-lién*

(黃 連), cloves, lump-camphor *(nau-tzï)*, sandal-wood, cardamoms and gharu-wood[12].

Ku-lin may be reached in five days with the monsoon from Nan-p‘i. «It takes a Ts‘üan-chóu ship over forty days to reach Lan-li (藍 里 i. e., Lan-wu-li); there the winter is spent, and, the following year, a further voyage of a month will take it to this country»[13].

The customs of the people are, on the whole, not different from those of the Nan-p‘i people. The native products comprise cocoanuts and sapan-wood; for wine they use a mixture of honey (蜜 糖) with cocoanuts and the juice of a flower, which they let ferment[14].

«They are fond of archery; in battle they wrap their hair in silken turbans»[15].

For the purpose of trade they use coins of gold and silver; twelve silver coins are worth one gold one. The country is warm and has no cold season.

Every year ships come to this country from San-fo-ts‘i, Kién-pi and Ki-t‘o[16] (吉 陀), and the articles they trade with are the same as in Nan-p‘i.

«Great numbers of Ta-shï live in this country. Whenever they (i. e., the inhabitants) have taken a bath, they anoint their bodies with *yü-kin* (鬱 金), as they like to have their bodies gilt like that of a Buddha»[17].

Notes.

1) Or more correctly «the country of the Nan-p‘i», or Nairs of Malabar. The name Nan-p‘i does not occur, it is believed, prior to Chau Ju-kua. In the light of the list of dependencies of Nan-p‘i given by our author in a subsequent passage of this chapter, the supremacy of the Malabars extended from Nellore to Cambay, and, as we have learned from a previous passage (supra, p. 72), comprised also the island of Ceylon.

The Si-yang cháu-kung tién-lu, 3,3, which is a record of the famous expedition of the eunuch Ch‘öng-Ho, about A. D. 1430, speaking of the inhabitants of Calicut, says that there were five castes, the Nan-p‘i, the Hui-hui or Moslims, the Chï-t‘i (哲 地) or Chittis, the Ko-ling (革 令) or Klings, and the Mu-kua (木 瓜) or Mukuva, a name applied to the fishermen of the western coast of the Peninsula near Cape Comorin. Phillips, J. R. A. S. 1896, 342, gives the first name as Nan-k‘un (南 昆), but is of opinion that it also transcribes the name Nair. The characters *k‘un* and *p‘i* differ so slightly that a copyist may have easily confounded them.

The time here stated as necessary to make the voyage from San-fo-ts‘i to the Nan-p‘i country is the same as that usually given to make the voyage from the former port to Quilon. In a subsequent passage (infra, p. 89) our author says it takes a ship sailing with the monsoon five days to reach Quilon from Nan-p‘i; it would appear therefore that Nan-p‘i, or the principal port of the Nan-p‘i, was really, as our author says, «in the extreme south-west» of the Peninsula.

2) *Mié-a-mo*, in Cantonese dialect *Mit-a-mat*, may be the same as the Ma (or Mo)-li-mo of Chau's list of dependencies of Nan-p‘i, and both may transcribe the name Malabar, which country in another passage (Pt. II, Ch. XXVII) he calls Wu-li-pa (in Cantonese Ma-li-pat). Li-ssï means «controller of sacrifices, priest». No explanation suggests itself.

3) Edrisi (I, 177 Jaubert's transl.) speaking of the Raja of Malwa — the Balhara, says: «He has troops and elephants .... He wears on his head a golden crown .... He rides much on horseback, particularly once a week accompanied solely by women, numbering a hundred; they

are richly attired, wear on their feet and wrists rings of gold and silver, their hair is done in tresses. They play at games and at sham fights while the king precedes them .... He owns many elephants and in this consists the principal force of his army».

4) *Pu-tai kiau*, lit. «Cotton-cloth-bag sedan-chair». On the S. W. coast of India this form of palanquin is called *manjil;* it is a hammock-litter. Yule & Burnell, Glossary, 456, sub voce 5 Muncheel. Ralph Fitch when in Pegu (1583—1591) travelled in Delingeges «which are a kind of coches made of cords and cloth quilted, & caried upon a stang betweene 3 or 4 men». Hakluyt, Princ. Navigations, V, 486 (Mac Lehose's edit), see also supra, p. 47.

5) Here, as in speaking of Hu-ch'a-la (Guzerat) and various other countries of India, Chau uses the word Fo (Buddha) in the sense of «an image of a god», not in its literal sense. In 10 speaking of Ta-ts'in (Baghdad) he says the sovereign «worships Buddha, does reverence to Buddha». In another passage he calls Mohammed a Buddha, and in another Brahma Fo. In Chapter XL on Ma-i (the Philippines) he calls the stone images of gods «Buddhas». There is some excuse for his confounding Hindu with Buddhist worship, as he does several times. Ma Huan in the 15th century makes the same blunder, he says the king of Cochin was a devout 15 Buddhist. J. R. A. S. 1896, 342.

6) This cotton-cloth is probably «the buckram which looks like tissue of spider's web» of which Polo speaks, and which Yule says was the famous muslin of Masulipatam. Yule, Marco Polo, II, 348. Conf. infra, Pt. II, Ch. XXIII.

7) It may be more correct to translate the first line of this paragraph: «There is in this 20 country a river of brackish water» or what is called a tidal-river. Cat's-eyes were procured in Ceylon (supra, p. 73. Cf. infra, Pt. II. Ch. XXXII). It may be that the river referred to was in Ceylon — a dependency of Nan-p'i. Conf. Reinaud, Relation, I, 127.

The P'ing-chóu-k'o-t'an, 2,4, speaking of the customs of the foreigners who frequented Canton says: «The men wear on a finger of the hand precious stones «set in gold or tin, according 25 as the wearer is rich or poor. These they call «finger-rings» (指 環 子). The people of Kiau-chï place particular value on this habit, one ring being worth as much as a hundred pieces of gold. The finest (precious stone) is called «cat's-eye», and it is a jade stone (or «of jade colour»? 乃 玉 石 也). It is so brilliant and flashing that it seems alive, and (close) examination does not disclose the reason of this. There is also the *mo-so* stone (摩 娑 石 bezoar stone) 30 which is an antidote for the poison of reptiles. Worn in a finger-ring, if one is poisoned and licks it, one is at once cured; so it may well be considered a life preserver» (衞 生).

8) Ku-lin, in Cantonese Kō-lām is Quilon, see supra, p. 12 and infra, p. 91. n. 17. Hu-ch'a-la, in Cantonese Hu-ch'a-lāt is Guzerat, see infra p. 92. Kan-pa-i, in Cantonese Kōm-p'ā-yat is the city of Cambay, the Kambayat of the Arabs. Pa-li-sha is probably Bharoch. Edrisi (I, 175. Jaubert's 35 transl.) says that Bharoch (Baruh i. e. بروج) was a station for ships coming from China. Ma-lo-hua, in Cantonese Mā-lō-wā is Malwa. Föng-ya-lo, in Amoy dialect Bang-ga-lo is probably Mangalore. Ma-li-mo, in Amoy dialect Ma-li-bwat is probably Malabar. See supra, p. 89, n. 2. Tu-no-ho may be the Tāna or Tannah of Arab geographers and of Marco Polo, on the island of Salsette near Bombay. A-li-jo may be the Ras Haili of Abulfeda, the country of Hili of Rashideddin and Ibn Batuta 40 between Mangalore and Fandarsina (i. e., Pandarani, 16 miles N. of Calicut), the kingdom of Eli of Polo. Ao (or Ngao)-lo-lo-ni may be Cannanore or Nellore — the Nilawar of Wassaf which divided Malabar from Mábar, and which Ma Huan in the 15th century calls Hön-nu-ïr (狠 奴 兒). Phillips, J. R. A. S. 1896, 345. See also Yule, Marco Polo, II, 315, 374—376.

9) Two paragraphs farther on he tells us that Nan-p'i is five days sailing nearer the 45 N. W. coast of Sumatra (Lan-wu-li) than Quilon. It may well be that it was not frequently visited by ships engaged in the China trade, for their principal port of call was Quilon. The name of the two Nairs living in Ts'üan-chóu in Chau's time may have been Shï-lo-pa and Chï-li-kan, there is nothing in the text to indicate how these six characters should be read. Ma Tuan-lin, op. sup. cit., II, 587, after quoting this paragraph adds: «since then (the arrival of these two Malabars in 50 China) many ships (of China?) have visited that country». On the Malabar coast and its trade in the middle ages, see Heyd, Hist. du Commerce, II, 146—149.

10) Identified by G e r i n i, Researches, 629, with Kwāla Terong, or Trong, probably on the Perak coast.

11) The mention of a sea-trade in rhubarb at this period is very interesting. H e y d, Hist. du Commerce, II, 667 had suspected its existence. H i r t h, J. N. C. B. R. A. S. XXII, 108.

12) *Huang-lién* is the rhizoma of the Coptis teeta, Wall. B r e t s c h n e i d e r, Materia medica, 68, 70. Pepper is not mentioned in this chapter as a product of Malabar, but in a note in a subsequent chapter (Pt. II, Ch. XXVII) this omission is repaired, not by the author, I think, but by the first editor.

13) The phrase in quotation marks is taken from the Ling-wai-tai-ta, 2,13 with the change of «Kuang(-chóu) ship», to «Ts'üan(-chóu) ship». Considering the great importance of the port of Quilon in the sea-trade between China and the West, it is surprising that both Ch ó u K'ü-feï and C h a u J u-k u a have so very little to say concerning it. On Quilon, see Y u l e, Marco Polo, II, 363—365. C o r d i e r, Voyage d'Odoric, 106 et seqq.

14) P o l o (II, 364) mentions the wine of Ku-lin (Coilum) which he says was made from (palm) sugar, and «capital drink it is, and very speedily it makes a man drunk». The Kambojians had a drink which the Chinese called *mi-t'ang tsiu* (蜜 糖 酒), to prepare which they used half honey and half water, adding a ferment. See Chön-la-föng-tu-ki as quoted by P e l l i o t, B. E. F. E. O. II, 170, and infra, Pt. II. Ch. XXIII.

15) Quotation from Ling-wai-tai-ta, 2,13. In another passage of the same work (see supra, p. 63, n. 1) the courage and impetuosity of the Ku-lin people is referred to as second only to those of the San-fo-ts'i men.

16) On Kién-pi, see supra, pp. 71—72. Ki-t'o may transcribe an original Karta. From its association in this passage with Palembang and Kampar, it may be looked for in Sumatra. G e r i n i, Researches, 628 says Ki-t'o «is Kat-to = Telok Kruit, West Sumatra?» The name does not occur elsewhere, neither does that of Ki-lo. P e l l i o t, B. E. F. E. O. IV, 352, n. 5 suggested for Ki-t'o Kedah on the Malay Peninsula, but G e r i n i, J. R. A. S. 1905, 495—496 says there is not a vestige of evidence to show that the name of Kedah existed before the end of the 15th century. The Ling-wai-tai-ta, 2,13 says: «Every year Kién-pi takes elephants and cattle, and the Arabs (Ta-shï) take horses to trade in this country (of Ku-lin)». This passage appears to be the basis for C h a u J u-k u a's remarks, he has only added the names of San-fo-ts'i and Ki-t'o, presumably because they were adjacent to Kién-pi and in Sumatra. It seems just possible that Ki-t'o may be the same as the pilgrim I-tsing's Kié-ch'a (羯 茶), which was on the extreme N. E. coast of Sumatra, and the last port-of-call (at least in the seventh century, but very probably also in later days) for ships going from San-fo-ts'i to India. C h a v a n n e s, Relig. éminents, 105.

17) Quotation from the Ling-wai-tai-ta, 2,13, which adds: «The king of the country worships Heaven. He who kills an ox forfeits his life. Chinese traders with big ships who wish to go to the country of the Arabs, must tranship at Ku-lin to smaller boats before proceeding farther. Although they may get (to their destination) in one month with a southerly wind, it may be two years before they can get back (to China)». The text goes on to state that «the people of Ku-lin are black, they wrap their bodies in white cotton cloth, wear their beards and all their hair loose and uncovered. They wear red leather shoes, so they look when walking as if they had the painted feet of a *lo-han* .... The king wraps his body in cotton-cloth, when he goes out he is carried in a litter (*juan-tóu*) of cotton cloth, or else he rides on an elephant. The inhabitants are devout Buddhist». On this last remark, see supra, p. 90, n. 5. The remark about the people smearing their bodies with turmeric occurs twice in the Ling-wai-tai-ta, first in connection with Ku-lin, and secondly as a custom of Nan-ni-hua-lo.

Yü-kin is produced by a plant which remains indetermined; it is a native of the south of China, and is most probably a species of Curcuma. H a n b u r y, Science Papers, 254. This seems to be borne out by the probable etymology of the word, which is pronounced *wat-kam* in Cantonese (old sound described by K'ang-hi's authorities as 紆 物 切 = *hat* and *kam*, gold), and may thus represent Persian كَرْكَم *karkam* and Hebrew כַּרְכֹּם *karkôm*, Arabic كُرْكُم *kurkum*,

from which the botanical name Curcuma is derived. Hirth, J. C. B. R. A. S. XXI, 221. This
need not necessarily involve that Curcuma is here covered by the word, though it would appear
that India furnished the root in ancient and mediaeval times. Flückiger, Pharmakognosie des
Pflanzenreiches, 368 (3ᵈ edit.). The Liang-shu, 54,17, says that *yü-kin* was procured solely
from Ki-pin (Kapisha, or rather Kashmir).   5

17.

GUZERAT.

Hu-ch'a-la (胡 茶 辣).

The kingdom of Hu-ch'a-la[1] rules over a hundred cities (州) and
more; its (principal) city has a four-fold wall.   10

The inhabitants of this country are white and clean looking; both men
and women wear double rings hanging down from holes in their ears; they
wear close fitting clothes with a cotton sarong wrapped around them. On
their heads they wear white hoods (白 氎), and on their feet shoes of red
leather. They are forbidden to eat flesh.   15

There are four thousand Buddhist temple buildings, in which live over
twenty thousand dancing-girls (妓) who sing twice daily while offering food
to the Buddha (i. e., the idols) and while offering flowers. When offering
flowers they tie them in bunches with cotton thread, of which they use three
hundred catties every day[2].   20

There are over four hundred war-elephants and about one hundred
thousand cavalry horses. When the king goes about he rides an elephant;
on his head he wears a cap. His followers ride horseback and carry swords.

The native products comprise great quantities of indigo, red kino,
myrobolans and foreign cotton stuffs of every colour. Every year these goods 25
are transported to the Ta-shï countries for sale[3].

Notes.

1) This is the earliest mention in Chinese works of the name Guzerat. In the preceding
chapter our author states that it was a dependency of the Malabars; I cannot verify this statement.

2) Guzerat was famous for its many temples, Hindu not Buddhist, most of which were 30
situated on the south-western coast, in the territory of Okamandala. Lassen, Indische Alterthumsk.
I, 134. Polo (II, 350) goes so far as to say that all the Abraiaman (Brahmans) in the world come
from that province (of Lar — possibly roughly the same region to which Chau refers). The word
«Buddhist» and «Buddha» are here used for «idol». See supra, p. 90, n. 5. On the dancing-girls,
conf. supra, p. 55 n. 7. and infra, p. 95.   35

3) Polo (II, 383) says: «In this province of Gozurat there grows much pepper, and ginger,
and indigo. They have also a great deal of cotton. Their cotton trees are of very great size, growing
full six paces high, and attaining to an age of 20 years». He also refers (II, 363) to the fine

indigo of Coilum (Quilon) and describes its preparation, and he mentions the indigo of Cambaet as very abundant (II, 388). The «foreign cotton stuffs of every colour» of our author were probably chintzes. Polo refers repeatedly (II, 379, 385, 388) to the «delicate and beautiful buckrams», «the export of good buckram and cotton», etc., from places in Chau's Hu-ch'a-la. The omission of any
5 mention of pepper among the products of Guzerat by both Chóu K'ü-feï and Chau Ju-kua has been remarked on previously, supra, p. 91, n. 12. All mediaeval writers, Eastern and Western, remark on the great number of horses brought by the Arabs to the Malabar coast. Chóu K'ü-feï refers to it; supra, p. 91, n. 16.

———

18.

MALWA.

———

Ma-lo-hua (麻 囉 華).

10

The kingdom of Ma-lo-hua borders on that of Hu-ch'a-la[1]. This country rules over sixty odd cities, and it has land routes[2].

The manner of dressing and the local customs are the same as those of
15 Hu-ch'a-la.

Of products white cotton cloth is very common. Every year two thousand oxen, or more, laden with cotton stuffs are sent over the roads to other countries to barter.

Notes.

20   1) No other reference to Malwa has been found in any other Chinese author of the period. Chóu K'ü-feï does not mention it, nor does Ma Tuan-lin, the Sung shï, or any subsequent writers.
     2) Ibn Batuta, Voyages, III, 182 says its sovereign was the most powerful of the infidel rulers of India. He also (IV, 28) speaks of the beauty of the people of this country, especially the women. By «it has land routes» (有 陸 路) must be meant that it had only land routes and
25 no sea-coast, and this is quite true of Malwa.

———

19.

CHOLA DOMINION.

(Coromandel Coast).

———

Chu-lién (注 輦).

30   «The kingdom of Chu-lién is the Southern Yin-tu (印 度) of the west»[1].
To the east (its capital) is five *li* distant from the sea; to the west one comes to Western India (西 天 竺) (after) 1500 *li;* to the south one

comes to Lo-lan (羅 蘭) (after) 2500 *li;* to the north one comes to Tun-t'ien (頓 田) (after) 3000 *li*[2].

This country had not from olden times carried on trade (with China). By water one comes to Ts'üan-chóu after some 411,400 *li*[3].

«If you wish to go to this kingdom, then you must change ships at 5 Ku-lin to go there. Some say that one can go there by way of the kingdom of P'u-kan»[4].

In this kingdom there is a city with a seven-fold wall, seven feet high, and extending twelve *li* from north to south and seven *li* from east to west. The different walls are one hundred paces distant from each other. Four of 10 these walls are of brick, two of mud, and the one in the centre of wood. There are flowers, fruit trees, and other trees planted (on them?).

The first and second walls enclose the dwellings of the people, — they are surrounded by small ditches; the third and fourth walls (surround) the dwellings of the court officers; within the fifth dwell the king's four sons; 15 within the sixth are the Buddhist (i. e., idol) monasteries (佛 寺) where the priests dwell; the seventh wall encloses over four hundred buildings forming the royal palace.

There **are thirty-one** (*sic*) *pu-lo* (部 落); of these twelve are in the west, namely: 20

    Chï-tu-ni (只 都 尼)

    Shï-ya-lu-ni (施 亞 盧 尼)

    Lo-pa-li-pi-pa-i (羅 琶 離 鼙 琶 移)

    Pu-lin-pa-pu-ni (布 林 琶 布 尼)

 5 Ku-tan-pu-lin-p'u-töng (古 檀 布 林 蒲 登)   25

    Ku-li (故 里)

    Po-lun-ts'ön (婆 輪 岑)

    Pön-t'i-kié-ti (本 蹄 揭 蹄)

    Yen-li-ch'ï-li (閻 黎 池 裔)

 10 Na-pu-ni (那 部 尼)   30

    Chö-ku-lin (遮 古 林)

    Ya-li-chö-lin (亞 里 者 林)

Eight are in the south, namely:

    Wu-ya-kia-li-ma-lan (無 雅 加 黎 麻 藍)

    Meï-ku-li-k'u-ti (眉 古 黎 苦 低)   35

 15 Shö-li-ni (舍 里 尼)

    Mi-to-lo-mo (蜜 多 羅 摩)

    K'ié-lan-p'u-töng (伽 藍 蒲 登)

Möng-k'ié-lin-kia-lan (蒙伽林加藍)

Pa-li-pa-li-yu (琶里琶离遊)

20 Ya-lin-ch'ï-möng-k'ié-lan (亞林池蒙伽藍)

and twelve are in the north, namely:

5   Fa-lo-yé (撥羅耶)

Wu-mo-li-kiang (無沒离江)

Chu-lin (注林)

Kia-li-möng-k'ié-lan (加里蒙伽藍)

25 Ts'i-kié-ma-lan (漆結麻藍)

10   Wu-chö-mong-k'ié-lan (握折蒙伽藍)

P'i-lin-k'ié-lan (皮林伽藍)

P'u-löng-ho-lan (蒲稜和藍)

Pau-pa-lai (堡琶來)

30 Tién-chu-li (田注离)

15   Lu-so-lo (盧娑囉)

Mi-möng-k'ié-lan [5] (迷蒙伽藍)

When any one among the people is guilty of an offense, one of the Court Ministers (侍郎) punishes him; if the offense is light, the culprit is tied to a wooden frame and given fifty, seventy, or up to an hundred blows
20 with a stick. Heinous crimes are punished with decapitation or by being trampled to death by an elephant.

At state banquets both the Prince and the four Court Ministers (侍郎) salaam (膜拜) at the foot of the throne (階), then the whole (company present) break into music, song and dancing. He (the Prince) does not drink
25 wine, but he eats meat, and, as is the native custom, dresses in cotton clothing and eats flour-cakes. For his table and escort he employs «fully a myriad dancing-girls (妓), three thousand of whom are in attendance daily in rotation» [6].

When contracting marriage, they send, in the first place, a female go-between with a gold (or) silver finger-ring to the girl's home. Three days
30 afterwards there is a meeting of the man's family to decide upon the amount of land, cotton, betel nuts, wine and the like to be given as marriage portion. The girl's family sends in return (a?) gold or silver finger-ring, *yüé-no* cloth [7] (越諾布) and brocaded clothing to be worn by the bride to the (intended) son-in-law. Should the man wish to withdraw from the engage-
35 ment, he would not dare reclaim the marriage gifts; if the girl should wish to reject the man she must pay back double.

As the taxes and imposts of the kingdom are numerous and heavy, traders rarely go there.

«This country is at war with the kingdoms of the west (of India?). The government owns sixty thousand war-elephants, every one seven or eight feet high. When fighting these elephants carry on their backs houses, and these houses are full of soldiers who shoot arrows at long range, and fight with spears at close quarters. When victorious, the elephants are granted 5 honorary names to signalize their merit».

«The inhabitants are hot-tempered and reckless of life; nay, in the presence of the king they will fight man to man with swords and die without regret».

«Father and son, elder and younger brother, have their meals cooked 10 in separate kettles and served in separate dishes; yet they are deeply alive to family duties»[8].

The native products comprise pearls, elephants' tusks, coral, transparent glass, betel nuts, cardamoms, opaque glass, cotton stuffs with coloured silk threads (色 絲 布), and cotton stuffs.   15

Of quadrupeds they have goats and domestic cattle; of birds, pheasants and parrots; of fruits, the *yü-kan* (餘 甘) the *t'öng-lo* (藤 蘿), Persian dates (千 年 棗), cocoanuts, the *kan-lo* (甘 羅), the *k'un-lun* plum (崑 崙 梅), and the *po-lo-mi* (jack-fruit)[9].

Of flowers, they have the white jasmine (白 茉 莉), the *san-ssï* (散 20 絲), the *shö-ts'i-sang* (虵 臍 桑), the *li-ts'iu* (麗 秋), the blue, yellow and green *p'o-lo* (婆 羅) the *yau-lién-ch'an* (瑤 蓮 蟬), the red canna (? 紫 水 蕉)[10].

Of grain they have green and black beans, wheat and rice; the bamboo is indigenous.   25

In former times they did not send tribute to our court, but «in the eighth year of the *ta-chung* and *siang-fu* periods (A. D. 1015), its sovereign sent a mission with pearls and like articles as tribute. The interpreters, in translating their speech, said they wished to evince the respect of a distant nation for (Chinese) civilization». They were ordered by Imperial Decree to 30 remain in waiting at the side gate of the Palace, and to be entertained at a banquet by the Associates in the College of Court Annalists. By Imperial favour they were ranked with the envoys of K'iu-tz'ï. It happened to be the Emperor's birthday, and the envoys had a fine opportunity to witness the congratulations in the Sacred Enclosure (聖 院)[11].   35

«In the tenth year *si-ning* (1077) they again sent tribute of native produce. The Emperor Shün-tsung sent an officer of the Inner Department (i. e., a Chamberlain) to bid them welcome»[12].

The remaining countries (of India), Nan-ni-hua-lo (南 尼 華 羅) and others, are more than a hundred in number; they are all included under the term of «Western» (*lit.*, Western Heaven 西 天).

Concerning Wang-shö-ch'öng (王 舍 城), tradition says that north of
5 Kiau-chï (Tongking), «one comes to Ta-li (Yün-nan), and west of Ta-li one comes to Wang-shö-ch'öng in less than forty days' journey».

Kia Tan (賈 耽) in the Huang-hua-ssï (or si)-ta-ki (皇 華 四 [or 西] 達 記), says that to go from An-nan (安 南) to T'ién-chu (天 竺), there is an overland route which one can take to get there. Yet as Ta-mo (達 摩)
10 came sailing across the sea to P'an-yü (番 禺, Canton), we may fairly ask whether the sea journey is not more expeditious than the long overland one [13].

P'öng-k'ié-lo (鵬 茄 羅) of the West has a capital called Ch'a-na-ki [14] (茶 那 咭). The city walls are 120 *li* in circuit. The common people are combative and devoted solely to robbery. They use (pieces of) white conch
15 shells (矿 螺) ground into shape as money. The native products include fine swords (寶 劍), *tóu-lo* cotton stuffs (堍 羅 綿) and common cotton cloth (布).

Some say that the law of the Buddha originated in this country, for Hüan-tsang, the master of the Tripiṭaka in the T'ang period, (when) he got
20 the Buddhist Classics (to bring to China), had already reached the West (西 天).

«Nan-ni-hua-lo (南 尼 華 羅) [15] city has a triple wall. The inhabitants morning and evening bathe and besmear their bodies with *yü-kin* (turmeric) so as to look like golden coloured images (*lit.*, Buddhas) [16]. «A large propor-
25 tion of them are called P'o-lo-mön (婆 羅 門, Brahmans), as they are genuine descendants of Fo (佛).

«The walls of their rooms and the mats they sit on are besmeared with cow-dung, which they look upon as a clean substance. In their houses they set up altars, three feet high and which are reached by three steps, and on which
30 daily in the morning they burn incense and offer flowers»; this is called «the offering to Fo» [17] (供 佛).

When Arab (Ta-shï) foreigners come to this country, they give them seats outside the doors and lodge them in separate houses supplied with bedding and household utensils [18].

35 When a woman is guilty of adultery she is put to death, and the officials make no enquiry about it.

7

The native products include the best quality of putchuck, and fine white flowered (or dotted) cotton stuffs (細白花蘂布). The people eat much butter [19] (酥酪), rice, beans and vegetables: they rarely eat fish or meat.

«A road leads to the Western Regions (Si-yü); when there are raids (on Nan-ni-hua-lo?) by the light horsemen of the Western Regions, the only 5 resistance they offer is to lock their gates. In a few days provisions run short, and (the raiders) withdraw of their own accord» [20].

Notes.

1) Quotation from the Ling-wai-tai-ta, 2,13[b]: «Southern Yin-tu of the West», means the peninsular part of India. Chu-lién is Chola or Soladesam, of which Kanchi (Conjeveram) was the 10 ancient capital. From Sola was formed apparently Sola-mandala or Chola-mandala, which the Portuguese made into Choromandel and the Dutch into Coromandel. Yule, Marco Polo, II, 354. Polo speaks of «the kingdom of Ma'abar called Soli, which is the best and noblest Province of India». According to Yule, it was in Polo's time in all likelihood Tanjore, but we are told by Tennent (Ceylon, I, 394 et seqq.), using Singhalese chronicles, that the Chola dominion at various 15 times before that had included most of southern India. As used by Chóu K'ü-feï and Chau Ju-kua, I think it should be understood to correspond to the Ma'abar of the Arabs, just as Nan-p'i does to their Malabar. According to Rashideddin «Ma'abar extended from Kulam to the country of Siláwar, 300 parasangs along the shore. Its length is the same. It possesses many cities and villages of which little is known .... Large ships, called in the language of China, «Junks», bring 20 various sorts of choice merchandise and cloths from Chin and Máchin, and the countries of Hind and Sind». Elliot, Hist. of India, I, 69.

In the seventh century Hüan-tsang mentions a kingdom of Chu-li-yé (珠利耶) between the lower Krishna and the Pennar rivers. (See, however, A. Cunningham, Anc. geog. of India, 545). The next mention of this country is in the Ling-wai-tai-ta. Ma Tuan-lin (op. cit., II, 25 571—582) reproduces Chau's notes, omitting from them, however, all the passages he has taken from Chóu K'ü-feï. The Sung-shï does likewise. In the Yüan period the name Chu-lién was not used; it was replaced by the appellation Ma-pa-ïr (馬八兒 Ma'abar). Yüan-shï, 210. It is there stated that Ma'abar is the largest of all the kingdoms of India. See Pauthier, Livre de Marc Pol, 603—605.   30

Chinese writers of the Ming period speak of the Cholas as So-li (鎖俚 or 所里). Groeneveldt, Notes, 40. G. Phillips, J. R. A. S., 1896, 342. The Sung-shï, 489,20 also calls these people So-li.

Additional evidence as to the location of Chu-lién is supplied by Chóu K'ü-feï's statement-which forms the fourth paragraph of this chapter. It was between Quilon and Burma (P'u-kan) 35 on the coast. The route followed by the Chola mission to China in 1015 (see infra) which took them by «the Cholian (part of) Ceylon» (娑里西蘭) is likewise evidence of some value. Still another indication is found in the statement made by the Sung-shï, 489,11 (see supra, p. 59), that the envoys who came in 1106 to the Chinese court from Burma (P'u-kan) insisted that they should be treated with more ceremony than those from Chu-lién which was a vassal of San-fo-ts'i. 40 From Singhalese sources (Tennent, Ceylon, I, 402) we learn that in the beginning of the twelfth century (and how long before is not stated), and again in the beginning of the thirteenth, Ceylon (or a part of it) was under Cholian rule. It was easy for the P'u-kan envoys to make out Chu-lién itself, instead of its dependency Ceylon, a feudatory state of San-fo-ts'i.

2) Ma Tuan-lin and the Sung-shï reproduce textually this paragraph (the former writer 45 giving erroneously the distance between the capital and the sea as 5000 li). Yule, Marco Polo, II, 319 places the principal sea-port of the Chola kingdom at Kaveripattanam, the «Pattanam» par excellence of the Coromandel Coast, and at one of the mouths of the Kaveri. He says that there seems to be some evidence that the Tanjore ports were, before 1300, visited by Chinese

trade. The only Lo-lan known to mediaeval Chinese is mentioned in the T'ang-shu, 221[c], and is identified with the capital of Bamian in Afghanistan. I think our text is corrupt here and that the character *lo* should be changed to *si* (西 or 悉), and that we should read Si-lan, our Ceylon. Both Ma and the Sung-shï say that 2,500 *li* south-east of Chu-lién was «Si-lan-ch'ï-kuo (悉 蘭
5 池 國) with which it was at war. Of course the distance mentioned is absurd, but all figures connected with Chu-lién in Chinese accounts are inexplicably exaggerated.

As to Tun-t'ién, which our author says was 3,000 *li* N. of Chu-lién, I am constrained to suggest that the text is again corrupt, or that our author's authority — which remains unknown, knew not of what he wrote. Tun-t'ién (in Cantonese Tun-t'in) is not mentioned in any other
10 Chinese work. It seems just possible that we should correct the text to read «to the east one comes to Tun-sun» (頓 遜), which is supposed to have been near the southern extremity of the Malay Peninsula.

3) The envoys, who came to the court of China in 1015 are reported to have said that it had taken them over three years to make the journey, but, according to their own statement (see
15 infra p. 101. line 7), they were only under sail during that time 247 days. It is within the bounds of probability that they said they had sailed 41,000 *li*, which would be at the rate of about 165 *li* a day, or else that the Chinese, to whom they narrated their journey, estimated that they must have sailed that number of *li* during the 247 days they were under way. Purchas (His Pilgrimes, I, 110 et seqq.) discussing the extreme slowness of navigation for coasting voyages in early centuries,
20 estimates 32 miles a day as the average run for the whole voyage, counting all the delays, stops at night, etc.

Ma Tuan-lin and the Sung-shï reproduce this paragraph of our text. Ma sums up his chapter on Chu-lién by saying: «If one considers seriously, all that we have related concerning this kingdom of Chu-lién, situated at exactly 411,400 *li* by sea from Kuang-chóu-fu, and the
25 journey from which took 1,150 days, one only establishes three facts worthy of credence, that Chu-lién was a country very remote from China, that it had never had intercourse in olden times with the Empire, and that it offered tribute for the first time in the middle of the *ta-chung* and *siang-fu* period (A. D. 1015)». As to the supposed letter of the king of Chu-lién presented to the Emperor on this occasion, Ma says, there can be no doubt that it was of Chinese composition and did not
30 show any evidence whatever of foreign composition.

The Yüan-shï, 210, says that it was 100,000 *li* from Ts'üan-chóu to Ku-lin (Quilon), and 15 days sailing from there to Ma-pa-ïr (Ma abar, i. e., Chu-lién).

4) Quotation from Ling-wai-tai-ta, 2,18[b]. See supra. p. 91. n. 17.

5) Pu-lo represent probably Sanskrit *pura*, «city, town, fortress». The thirty-two names given
35 in this list may be those of localities subject to the Cholas, or, more probably, they are the names of various places, scattered all over peninsular India, which our author probably heard of from some Hindu, or Arab, trader — for this list seems quite original with Chau Ju-kua. It is reproduced by Ma Tuan-lin and the Sung-shï without a change, omission, addition or remark. There is nothing to indicate how this long list of characters should be divided, where one name ends and another
40 begins. The divisions adopted are purely arbitrary, based on general analogy of sound with known Indian names, and by placing such recurring groups of characters as p'u-töng (Sanskrit, *patam*), k'ié-lan (Sanskrit, *glan, galam*), möng-k'ié-lan (Sanskrit, *mangalam*), and others which seem to be final syllables, at the end of the various groups.

It is only possible to suggest the following identifications. Chï-tu-ni may be Chitor; Pu-lin-
45 pa-pu-ni, in Cantonese Po-lam-pa-po-ni, Brahmapura. Ku-t'an-pu-lin-p'u-töng may be Kaveri-pattanam. Ku-li may be Koil, and Pön-t'i-kié-ti Bundelkhand. Na-pu-ni may be Nagpur. Ya-li-tu-lin, Elichpur. Meï-ku-li-ku-ti, may be Mutapili, Polo's Mutafili near Masulipatam. Mi-to-lo-mo suggests Madura, and K'ié-lan-pu-töng, Kalingapatam. Mong-kié-lin-kia-lan recalls Mangalore, Po-lo-yé, Vallabhi and Shö-li-ni Abulfeda's Schāliyat (Jaliat). Other arrangements of the characters are
50 possible; for example, in the pu-lo in the north, instead of reading Chu-lin and forming out of the nine characters which follow two names, one might read Chu-lin-k'ié-li-möng, K'ié-lan-ts'i and Kié-ma-lan; in this case K'ié-lan-ts'i, in Cantonese Ka-lam-ts'at recalls Kalindjar.

Conf. the list of kingdoms in India given by Yule, Marco Polo, II, 419—421.

6) The words in quotation marks are taken from the Ling-wai-tai-ta, loc. cit. Con-

7*

cerning the kings of Chu-lién, Ma Tuan-lin and the Sung-shǐ (loc. cit.) supply a few additional
facts of considerable interest. They say: «At the present time it is stated that the ruling sovereigns (of Chu-lién) have reigned for three generations». The first mission from Chu-lién to
China, in 1015, stated that the king of their country was called Lo-ts'a-lo-tsa, which probably
stands for Rāja-rāja. In 1033 the Chu-lién envoy said his king was called Shǐ-lo-lo-cha yin-to-   5
lo-chu-lo, which may well be Sri Rāja Indra Chola; and in 1077 the king of Chu-lién, his envoy
stated at that time, was Ti-hua-kia-lo, standing probably for Déwar Kala (or Kara or Deva-kula).
Rashideddin (Elliot, Hist. of India, I, 69) says the king of Ma'bar was called Dewar, which
means in the Mabar language, the «lord of wealth». The words «at the present time» very
probably mean «at the time of the mission of 1077», and this date would appear to be the latest 10
for any of the information given by Sung writers concerning Chu-lién, their earliest information
going back to 1015, when the first mission came to China. Cf. Gerini, Researches, 609,624.

The Ling-wai-tai-ta, after the words quoted in our text has «the king's cap has on it
lustrous pearls and other jewels». Duarte Barbosa speaking of the king of Calicut, says «This
king has a thousand waiting women, to whom he gives regular pay, and they are always at the 15
court, to sweep the palaces and houses of the king: and this he does for state, because fifty would
be enough to sweep … And these women do not all serve, but take turns in the service …». Duarte
Barbosa, Descript. coasts of East Africa and Malabar, 111. (Hakl. Soc. edit.).

7) Probably a kind of very fine muslin, made in various localities of western Asia. Our
author mentions «white yüé-no cloth» as a product of Baghdad and of Ki-tz'ï-ni (Ghaznï), and 20
«gold spangled yüé-no cloth» as a manufacture of Damascus (Lu-meï). See infra, Pt. II, Ch. XXVII.

8) Quotation from the Ling-wai-tai-ta, loc. cit. After the words quoted in the first paragraph it continues: «and there are some who bestow upon them (the elephants) embroidered
housings and golden mangers. Every day the elephants are taken into the presence of the king.
The king, his officers and the people all twist their hair into a knot, and wrap (themselves) in white 25
cotton cloth. They make coins of gold and silver. The country produces (出) finger-rings, camphor,
cat's-eyes and such like things; also pearls, elephants' tusks, amber of different colours and cotton
stuffs with coloured silk threads (色 絲 布)».

9) The yü-kan, t'öng-lo, and kan-lo are, so far as I am aware, unidentified. «K'un-lun
plum» may have been a fruit also met with in the Malay (K'un-lun) country. The kan-lo is said 30
in the Shǐ-ki to be the same as the kan-mau-sun (甘 茂 孫). See China Review, XIX, 193.
This does not help us, however.

10) Most of these flowers are indetermined, the names seem to be foreign. Instead of shö-
ts'i-sang the Sung-shǐ (489), which reproduces this paragraph, has shö-ts'i-fo (佛). Sang is the
Chinese name of the mulberry tree, but here the character is probably used phonetically.   35

11) The passage in brackets is taken from the Ling-wai-tai-ta, loc. cit. Chóu K'ü-feï,
Chau Ju-kua, Ma Tuan-lin and the author of the Sung-shǐ, all appear to have derived their
information concerning this mission from one and the same written source. Ma and the Sung-shǐ
(489,20—22) contain information not found in the works of the two earlier writers. The Sung-shǐ says
the principal envoy from Chu-lién was called So-li San-wön (娑 里 三 文); So-li, I take it, 40
represents the name Chola. Concerning the voyage of the mission to China, this envoy said:
«After leaving Chu-lién they had sailed for 77 days and nights, during which they passed the
island (or headland) of Na-wu-tan (那 勿 丹 山) and the island of So-li Si-lan (娑 里
西 蘭 山 Ceylon of the Cholas?), and came to the country of Chan-pin (占 賓 not identified,
but presumably in Pegu). Thence going 61 days and nights they passed the island of I-ma-lo-li 45
(伊 麻 羅 里 not identified), and came to the country of Ku-lo (古 羅 possibly on W.
coast Malay Peninsula, but see infra, p. 124, n. 25), in which there is a mountain called Ku-lo,
from which the country takes its name.

«Proceeding again 71 days and nights and passing the island of Kia-pa (加 八 山
not identified), the island of Chan (or Ku)-pu-lau (占 [or 古] 不 牢 Cham pulo) and the 50
island of Chóu-pau-lung (舟 寶 龍 not identified), they came to the country of San-fo-ts'i.

«Going again for 18 days and nights and having crossed (or passed by 度) the mouth of
the Man-shan river (? 蠻 山 水 口 in Kamboja?) and the T'ién-chu islands (天 竺 山

Pulo Aor?), they came to (至) the Pin-t'óu-lang headland (賓 頭 狼 山 Cape Padaran), from whence, looking eastward, the tomb of the Si-wang mu (西 王 母 塚) was about 100 *li* from the ship.

«Proceeding 20 days and nights and having passed by (度) Yang island (羊 山 Pulo
5 Gambir) and Kiu-sing island (九 星 山), they came to Pi-p'a island (琵 琶 洲) of Kuang-tung (Canton).

«From their home they had taken in all 1150 days to reach Kuang-chóu». See supra, p. 83, n. 1. Conf. China Review, XIX, 193.

As previously noted, great exaggeration is met with in all that has come down to us
10 concerning this mission. It is said by Ma Tuan-lin and the Sung-shǐ that the king of Chu-lién sent the Emperor of China, among other presents, 21000 ounces of pearls, 60 elephants' tusks, and 60 catties of frankincense. The envoys' gifts to the Emperor included 6600 ounces of pearls and 3300 catties of perfumes!

The ranking of the envoys of Chu-lién with those from K'iu-tzǐ, K'ucha in Eastern Tur-
15 kestan, a vassal state of China, shows the low estimate in which Chu-lién was held. In 1106 the Chu-lién vassalage to San-fo-ts'i was given by the Burmese envoys as a reason for asking greater privileges at the Chinese court than they had received. See supra, p. 23.

12) Quotation from Ling-wai-tai-ta, loc. cit. For further details concerning this mission, see Ma Tuan-lin (Hervey St Denis, Ethnographie, etc., II, 571—582), and Sung-shǐ,
20 489,22. These works mention tribute missions from Chu-lién in 1020 and 1033. In 1077 the «native produce» offered as tribute included pearls like peas (? 豌 豆 珠), a large wash-bowl of opaque glass, white «plum-blossom» camphor (白 梅 花 腦 see infra, Pt. II, Ch. I.), cotton, rhinoceros horns, jugs of frankincense, rose-water, golden lotus flowers (tropæolum majus, Linn.), putchuk, asa-fœtida, borax and cloves. The Emperor gave the envoys as a return
25 present for the king 81,800 strings of cash and 52,000 taels of silver.

13) This and the preceding paragraph are based upon the Ling-wai-tai-ta, 3,4, which reads about as follows: «Among the hundreds of countries in the West that are famous, the one which ranks the highest of all is Wang-shö-ch'öng, the Mid-India (Yin-tu) of the T'ién-chu country, which owes its great fame to being the birthplace of the Buddha.

30 «Tradition says that to the east of this country is the Hei-shui-yü river or «Black-water-muddy river« (黑 水 游 河 Irrawadi? see supra, pp. 26 and 59. n. 1) and a Sea (大 海). Still farther east beyond this are the Western Regions (西 域 Turkestan), the T'u-fan (吐 蕃 the Tibetans), Ta-li (Yün-nan) and Kiau-chǐ (Tongking). To the west of this country is the Eastern Ocean of the Ta-shǐ (Arabs), and still farther west than this are the realms of the Ta-shǐ. To the
35 south of (Mid-India) is an island called the kingdom of Si-lan (細 蘭 Ceylon), and its sea is called the Sea of Si-lan.

«In olden times the envoy Chang K'ién being in Ta-hia (Bactria) learnt that the land of Shön-tu (India) was 1000 *li* south-east of Ta-hia. He also learnt that the kingdom of Ta-li (S. W. Yün-nan) was not more than forty stages from Wang-shö ch'öng (Mid-India). Kia Tan's Huang-hua-
40 ssǐ-ta-ki says: 'From Annam there exists (land) communication with T'ién-chu (India), but as Ta-mo (Dharma, the first Buddhist patriarch in China) came by sail all the way to P'an-yü (Canton), we may draw the conclusion that this sea-route is the more practicable one to follow». See supra, p. 4 on Chang K'ién's mission, and T. W. Kingsmill, J. R. A. S., n. s. XIV, 74 et seqq.

45 Wang-shö-ch'öng, as used by Chóu K'ü-feǐ, is synonymous with Magadha. It is generally used in Chinese works to designate the city of Kuçāgārapura, the old capital of the kingdom of Magadha, and occupying, it was supposed, the exact center of that country. New Wang-shö ch'öng was Rājagṛha. Chavannes, Relig. éminents, 65, n. 8. See also supra, pp. 26 and 51, n. 1.

Kia Tan, a great geographer of the T'ang period, lived from about A. D. 730 to 805. He
50 was the author of a number of geographical and ethnographical books and of maps, one entitled «Chinese and Foreigners within the Seas» (海 內 華 夷) on a scale of 100 *li* to the inch. T'ang-shu, 58, and Mém. conc. les Chinois, XVI, 151. The work mentioned in the text has appa-

rently been lost, but what may be an extract from it has been preserved in the Tʻang shu, 43, where we find a number of itineraries and sailing directions to various parts of Asia. — A translation of Kia Tan's sailing directions from Canton to the Persian Gulf is given in the Introduction (supra, pp. 10—14). Pelliot, B. E. F. E. O., IV, 131 et seqq., has translated and studied with great care those relating to S. E. Asia, and Chavannes has translated and annotated, with his   5 usual learning, two itineraries of Kia Tan's referring to Central Asia, in his Documents sur les Tou-kioué occidentaux, 7—10.

14) Although Pʻöng-kʻié-lo suggests Bangala, Bengal, I am disposed to think it possible that the «kingdom of the Balhara (البهرا)» of mediaeval Arab writers is meant. Elliot, Hist. of India, I, 358, says «the Tápti on the south, and the Aravalli mountains on the north, may perhaps 10 represent an approximation to the real extent of the kingdom». The native products mentioned do not assist us in locating it; as to the name of the capital city, it remains unidentified. Tóu-lo is Sanskrit *tūla* «cotton».

15) This paragraph and all the subsequent passages marked with brackets are quotations from the Ling-wai-tai-ta, 3,5. Nan-ni-hua-lo or Southern Ni-hua-lo is not mentioned in any other 15 Chinese work, before or after Chóu and Chau. The fact that it was exposed to the raids of the light horsemen of the West and that it produced the best putchuk, incline me to believe it must have been in Sindh.

16) Fo in this case and in the next paragraph, is to be taken as meaning Brahma. Conf. supra p. 89.   20

17) The Ling-wai-tai-ta, after the words «offer flowers», has «the altars are also smeared with cow-dung».

18) Mohammedans were treated thus through caste prejudice, not to show them special honour.

19) *Su-lo*, literally «hard *lo*», and *ju-lo* — literally «milk *lo*», usually mean «butter» and «milk». There can be little doubt that, when used in connection with India or southern Asia, these 25 words should be taken in their usual acceptations. When used in reference to Mongol and Turkish countries, *ju-lo* has often a different meaning — «dried sour milk». See infra, Ch. XXXII.

20) «Light horsemen of the West» may be a reference to the early Moslim invaders of Sindh in the latter part of the seventh and beginning of the eighth century.

---

20.   30

BAGHDAD.

Ta-tsʻin (大 秦).

«The country of Ta-tsʻin», *also called Li-kién* (犂 靬), «is the general mart of the natives of the Western Heaven, the place where the foreign merchants of the Ta-shï assemble» [1].   35

«Their king is styled Ma-lo-fu» (麻 囉 弗);» *he rules in the city of An-tu* (安 都) [2]. «He wears a turban of silk with gold embroidered characters, and the throne he sits upon is covered with a silken rug» [3].

«They have walled cities» *and markets with wards and streets.* «In the king's residence» *they use crystal in making pillars, and* «plaster in guise of 40 tiles. Wall-hangings abound. The circuit (of the wall) is pierced with seven gates, each guarded by thirty men[4].

«Tribute bearers from other countries pay homage below the platform of the (palace) steps, whence they withdraw after having offered their con-
5 gratulations».

The inhabitants are tall and of a fine bright complexion, somewhat like the Chinese, which is the reason for their being called Ta-ts'in[5].

They have keepers of official records, and in writing they use Hu (胡) characters. They trim their hair and wear embroidered gowns. They also
10 *have small carts with white tops, flags, etc. (Along the roads) there is a shed (亭) every ten li, and every thirty li there is a beacon-tower (堠). There are many lions in this country that interfere with travellers and are likely to devour them unless they go in caravans of an hundred well-armed men[6].*

15 «Underneath the palace they have dug a tunnel through the ground communicating with the hall of worship (禮拜堂) at a distance of over a *li*. The king rarely goes out except to chant the liturgy (誦經) and worship (禮佛). On every seventh day he goes by way of the tunnel to the hall of worship for divine service (拜佛), being attended by a suite of over
20 fifty men. But few amongst the people know the king's face. If he goes out he rides horseback, shaded by an umbrella; the head of his horse is ornamented with gold, jade, pearls and other jewels[7].

«There is among the kings of the Ta-shï country he who is styled *Su-tan* (素丹); every year he deputes men to send in tribute, and, if trouble is
25 apprehended in the country, he orders the Ta-shï to use their military force to keep order[8].

«The food consists principally of cooked dishes, bread (餅) and meat. They do not drink wine; they make use of vessels of gold and silver, helping themselves to the contents with ladles. After meals they wash their hands in
30 golden bowls full of water.

«The native products comprise opaque glass, coral, native gold (or gold bullion, 生金), brocades (or kincobs, 花錦), sarsenets (縵布), red cornelian and pearls»[9]; also (the precious stone called) *hié-ki-si* (駭雞犀) or *túng-t'ién-si* (通天犀)[10].

35 *In the beginning of the* yen-hi *period of the Han (A. D. 158—167)*[11] *the ruler of this country sent an embassy which, from outside the frontier of Ji-nan (日南), came to offer rhinoceros (horns), elephants' (tusks), and tortoise-shell;—this being the first direct communication with China. As the*

presents comprised no other rarities, it may be suspected that the envoys kept them back.

During the t‘ai-k‘ang period of the Tsin (A. D. 280 — 289) tribute was again brought from there[12].

There is a saying that in the west of this country is the Jo-shui (弱 水) and the Liu-sha (流 沙), near the place where the Si-wang-mu (西 王 母) resides and almost where the sun goes down[13].

Tu Huan (杜 還) in the King-hing-ki (經 行 記) says: «The country of Fu-lin (拂 菻) is in the west of the Chan (苫) country; it is also called Ta-ts‘in. The inhabitants have red and white faces. The men wear plain clothes, but the women brocades set with pearls (珠 錦). They like to drink wine and eat dry cakes (乾 餅). They have many skilled artisans and are clever weavers of silk.

«The size of the country is a thousand li. The active army consists of over ten thousand men. It has to ward off the Ta-shï[14].

«In the Western Sea there is a market where a (silent) agreement exists between buyer and seller that if one comes the other goes. The seller first spreads out his goods; afterwards the (would be) purchaser spreads out the equivalent (he offers), which must lie by the side of the articles for sale till taken by the seller, when the objects purchased may be carried off. This is called the 'Devil (or Spirit) market' (鬼 市)»[15].

Notes.

1) The first part of this chapter is taken nearly literally from Chóu K'ü-feï's account of Ta-ts'in, 3,1. The work of this author, as stated in the Introduction (supra, p. 22.) appeared in A. D. 1178, and was the result of personal enquiries made by him on the subjects of which it treats, and nowise a compilation from previous works. It may be looked upon as containing chiefly contemporaneous matter. All other portions of this chapter are taken from the older Chinese historians; they are mentioned in the footnotes to this chapter.

To emphasize the additions made by Chau Ju-kua, all portions of this chapter occurring in previous records other than Chóu K'ü-feï's, are printed in italics. The first phrase of Chau Ju-kua's chapter on T'ién-chu (infra, p. 110) and another phrase in the same chapter (infra, p. 111) are the only passages of Chóu K'ü-feï's notes on Ta-ts'in omitted from this chapter.

The Ta-ts'in of the twelfth century, as represented in Chóu K'ü-feï's account, has all the characteristics of an ecclesiastical state. As in ancient times Ta-ts'in and Fu-lin may be looked upon as the representatives of the Christian world united under a spiritual chief, the Patriarch of Antioch, so the king of Ta-ts'in of the twelfth century must have been a patriarch, and, as is shown in a subsequent note, this king must have been the Nestorian patriarch of Baghdad, which city was indeed, at that time, the point of junction where all the great trade routes of Western Asia united. The words «also called Li-kién», added here by Chau, are taken from the Hóu Han-shu, 88 (see Hirth, China and the Roman Orient, 40 and 146), and refer to the Ta-ts'in of ancient times.

2) Since the Capital of Ta-ts'in is called An-tu (Antioch) in the Weï-shu, 102 (see Hirth, op. cit., 48 et seqq.), the so-called king of Ta-ts'in may have to be identified with the Patriarch

of Antioch, who was indeed considered the spiritual head of all the Christians in Asia, certainly before the schism in 498 A. D., when the adherents of Nestorius († 440) established their own church in Chaldæa. According to the T'ang-shu, 198 (see Hirth, op. cit., 55 and 60) the king of Fu-lin called Po-to-li (波 多 力 Canton dialect and probable old sound: Po-to-lik), sent
5 ambassadors to the Chinese court in 643 A. D. This name lends itself admirably as a transcription of the Syriac form for «patriarch», viz. batrik. In Chóu K'ü-feï's account, as copied by Chau Ju-kua, the king of Ta-ts'in in the twelfth century is styled (號 i. e., he is addressed by the title of) Ma-lo-fu (麻 曜 弗 Canton dialect: Ma-lo-fat, probable old sound Ma-lo-pat, or Ma-lo-ba, since fu [弗] may stand for bha in Sanskrit transcriptions, see Julien, Méthode pour
10 déchiffrer, 104, № 309). This again is an excellent transcription for Mar Aba, one of the titles by which the Nestorian patriarch could be addressed. Mar is a title of honour given to learned devotees among the Syrian Christians, somewhat like our «Venerable» (Ducange, Glossarium, etc., ed. L. Favre, s. v. Mar). Aba means «father». Mar-Aba may thus be translated by «Venerable Father». Its Latin and Greek equivalent was Patricius (πατρίκιος). (Assemani, Bibl. Orient.,
15 III B, 92: «Quem enim Graeci Latinique Patricium vocant, is dicitur Syriace Aba, et praefixo Mar, seu Domini titulo, Mar-Aba»). In the Syriac portion of the Nestorian inscription of Si-an-fu the patriarch Hannanjesus II, who died in 778 A. D. three years before the erection of the monument in 781, is referred to under the title Abad Abahotha Mar Hanan Isua Qatholiqa Patrirkis («Père des Pères, le Seigneur Hanan-Jésus, étant le Patriarche universel.» Pauthier, L'inscription de
20 Si-ngan-fou, Paris, 1858, 42). This does not exclude the possibility of all the patriarchs mentioned in Chinese records up to the time of Chóu K'ü-feï as kings of Ta-ts'in or Fu-lin being patriarchs of Antioch. Still we may entertain doubts as to whom the title should be applied in Chóu K'ü-feï's Ta-ts'in chapter, at the end of which it is stated that «T'ién-chu (India) is subordinate to Ta-ts'in» (天 竺 國 其 屬 也), and that the sacred water by which the waves of the sea
25 can be stilled is found there (see infra, p. 111). It would seem that Chau Ju-kua has built up his account of T'ién-chu on little more than this information, which in Chóu K'ü-feï's original merely refers to the Indian Christians, and not to India generally, by adding all possible notes referring to non-Christian India from older records. Since we are in the possession of ample evidence showing that the Indian Christians of the St. Thomas church were Nestorians and that
30 their chiefs were appointed by the Chaldæan patriarch in Baghdad (see Assemani, op. cit., 435, et seqq.: Christiani S. Thomae in India), it must seem strange that, according to Chóu K'ü-feï at some time preceding the appearance of his book in 1178, it was the «king of Ta-ts'in», if this means the Patriarch of Antioch, who appointed the chief of T'ién-chu, i. e. the Indian Christians, and that this statement seems to correspond with that of a Byzantine author, the archimandrite
35 Nilos Doxopatres, a notary in the service of the Patriarch of Constantinople, who wrote in 1143, for king Rogers II of Sicily, a short treatise on the patriarchal thrones (Krumbacher, Gesch. der byzantin. Litteratur, 2ᵈ ed., München, 1897, 415 et seqq.). Doxopatres says in unmistakable Greek that «the Patriarch of Antioch was in charge of all Asia and Anatolia, and even India, whither he had sent a 'katholikos' ordained by himself, styled the one of Romogyris, and also of
40 Persia and Babylon, called Baghdad at his time, and that he had under him altogether thirteen metropolitans». (See Varia Sacra Stephanile Moyne, Leiden, 1685, II, 211 et seqq.; cf. Renaudot, Ancient Accounts of India and China, London, 1733, 119). It seems to follow from this that, whatever the relations of the Nestorians in India were to their immediate chief on the patriarchal throne in Baghdad, the one of Antioch was looked upon as a still higher authority. Assemani
45 (III, 289) admits that the Melchite, Maronite and Jacobite Syrians gave their chiefs the title «Patriarch of Antioch», but he emphatically denies it for the Nestorians. For materials regarding this crux of patriarchal history, see Assemani, passim; W. Germann, Die Kirche der Thomas-christen, Gütersloh, 1877; Richter, Indische Missionsgeschichte, Gütersloh, 1900, where the Greek passage referred to is quoted on p. 163, note; and Charles Swanston, A memoir of the
50 Primitive Church of Malaya, or the Syrian Christians of the Apostle Thomas, etc., in J. R. A. S. London, I, 172—192, and II, 54—62 and 243—247; La Croze, Histoire du Christianisme des Indes, La Haye, 1758. Swanston says among other things: «Whatever credit may be thought

due to the current tradition of these Christians, that the Apostle Thomas planted the seeds of
the Gospel among them, so much may be considered established beyond contradiction, that
they existed in Travancór as a flourishing people, connected with the Syrian church, from
the first centuries of the Christian Era» (op. cit., II, 234); «their liturgy is that which was formerly
read in the churches of the Patriarch of Antioch, and their language is the Syriac» (237); «they   5
hold in the highest respect their Patriarch of Antioch, or Mosul, and make mention of him in
their prayer» (239). These relations between Chau Ju-kua's India and his Ta-ts'in were first
pointed out by Hirth, «Chao Ju-kua's Ethnography», in J. R. A. S., 1896, 496—499. Though
the Antiochian patriarch is referred to in these records, the main fact to us is the position
of the one of Baghdad as the immediate chief of the Indian Christians. It seems, therefore, that 10
Chóu K'ü-feï's Ta-ts'in is not the ancient Ta-ts'in as far as its territory is concerned, and that
Antioch or An-tu, though referred to by Chau Ju-kua as its capital on the ground of former
statements, cannot be the place «where the foreign merchants of the Ta-shï assemble». This
remark is much more likely to apply to Baghdad, in 1178 A. D. the seat of the Nestorian
patriarch. Here indeed was «the point of junction where all the great trade-routes of Western 15
Asia united» (von Kremer, Culturgesch. des Orients, II, 47), which in those days could not quite
so well be said of Antioch. See also Hirth, The Mystery of Fu-lin, in J. A. O. S., XXX, 1—31.

3) «He wears a turban of silk with gold embroidered characters». According to Assemani
III B, 389) the Nestorian patriarchs did not wear a mitre like other church dignitaries of this
rank, but an embroidered turban, called *biruna* («Biruna, hoc est, Cidaris, phrygio operé ornata, 20
qua caput tegitur, instar Amictus»). It appears, however, that scholars disagree as to the meaning
of this word *biruna*, which according to some must have been a kind of burnoose rather than a
turban, if not even a gown of considerable length. See infra, p. 107.

4) The first four words (in Chinese 有 城) may also be rendered «there is a wall
(around the city)». This reference to the use of plaster is not original with Chóu K'ü-feï, he found 25
it in the Kiu T'ang-shu, 198 (see Hirth, China and the Roman Orient, 53). The reference to the
use of crystal is taken from Hóu Han-shu, 118. (See Hirth, op. cit., 40, 44, 51). On the 'Seven
gates', cf. Le Strange, Eastern Caliphate, 30, 3I, his description of Baghdad.

5) Quotation from Hóu Han-shu, 118. See Hirth, op. cit., 40, 44, 50, 70, 78.

6) This paragraph is substantially a quotation from Weï-lio, 30, and Hóu Han-shu, 118. 30
See Hirth, op. cit., 70 and 40, 55, 58. The custom of wearing short hair is referred to in the
oldest Ta-ts'in texts. «Different from the custom both of the Greeks and the Egyptians, that of
the Hebrews was to wear their hair generally short, and to check its growth by the application
of scissors only». Kitto, Cyclopædia of Biblical Literature, s. v., 'Hair'.

7) Chóu K'ü-feï and our author make frequent use of Buddhist terms when speaking of 35
other religions. See supra, p. 73, note 1, p. 93, et passim.

Benjamin of Tudela, who visited Baghdad in the middle of the twelfth century, says of the
Caliph: «But in that Palace of the mightie king, there are buildings of an admirable greatnesse,
the Pillars whereof are of silver and gold, and the inner parts of the houses are over-laide
with these metals, and beautified with all kind of Precious stones and Pearles: out of the which 40
Palace he goeth forth once only in the yeere, on that festival day or Easter, which they call
Ramadan. And on that day, great multitudes of men from divers and remote Countries, flocke
together to see his face. And he is carried upon a Mule, attired in princely garments, intermingled
with gold and silver, having his head adorned with a Myter, shining with stones of incomparable
price: but he weareth a blacke Handkerchiefe upon the Myter, ... But he commeth forth of his 45
Palace to the great house (as they call it) of Prayer, built in the gate Bosra: for that is accounted
their greatest home of Prayer. ... All that whole yeere after he is conteyned within the Palace,
never to goe forth to any other place». And of the chief of the small Jewish community dwelling
in Baghdad, the «Chief of the Captivity», as he was called, he says: «But when he commeth forth
to visit the Great king, he is guarded with a great number of Horse-men, Jewes and gentiles 50
accompanying him, a Cryer going before him. ... But he is carried upon an Horse cloathed with
silken and embroydered garments, he adorneth his head with a Miter, upon the Miter he weareth
a white Shash, and upon the Shash a Chaine». Purchas, His Pilgrimes, VIII, 559—562. Conf.

M. N. Adler, The Itinerary of Benjamin of Tudela, London, 1907, 36 et seq. Such, it appears, was the style in which the minor rulers residing in Baghdad paid their state visits to the Caliph, who himself, as an Abbaside, wore a «black handkerchief upon his mitre». What we know about the official dress of the Nestorian patriarch seems to be quite compatible with Chóu K'ü-feï's
5 account. Each patriarch, as we may conclude from Mar Amr's lives of the Nestorian patriarchs (quoted below), was at his coronation endowed with a pallium (*biruna*) of some particular colour peculiar to his government. This pallium is not clearly referred to in Chau Ju-kua's text, who contracts into one word *san* (繖), umbrella, Chóu K'ü-feï's words: «protected by a blue (or green) umbrella provided with threefold eaves» (打三簷青繖). This blue (or green)
10 umbrella may have got into the text from a mistaken description of the sacred gown called *biruna*, the exact shape and use of which seems to be a matter in dispute. Assemani calls it a «pontifical gown» in one place and a «cidaris» in another. A Chaldæan archbishop, consulted on the meaning of the term, also gives four different explanations, the second of which seems to be the most likely to answer, viz. «*biruna* vocatur indumentum exterius perlongum et amplum personam
15 totam cooperiens, ad modum fere togae senatoriae aut purpurae cardinalitiae» (see Abbeloos and Lamy, Barhebraei Chronic. ecclesiast., I, 355, note 2); and since Assemani, in his last volume (III B, 683) distinguishes the *biruna* as a cidaris, i. e. a low turban, from the «paenula, quae pluvialis formam repraesentat», it may have been a kind of hood, or cape, used primarily for protection against rain, thus corresponding to the sacred gown called
20 *phaina* by the Jacobites and *maaphra* by the Nestorians. Assemani (op. cit., 674) describes the final act in the coronation of the Nestorian patriarch in such a way as to suggest that the two, the *maaphra* or *kaphila*, i. e. the rain cloak, and the *biruna*, i. e. the turban, have to be put on, before coronation can be pronounced to be complete. It seems that, whatever the two terms may mean, they practically belong to one another, which may have given rise to the confusion existing
25 in their interpretation. It is quite possible that Chóu K'ü-feï, who was a native of Wön-chóu and, when he wrote his book, held the post of Assistant Sub-Prefect in Kui-lin, the capital of Kuang-si, collected his notes in Canton, which place he had to pass on his way from his home to his official residence; and in Canton, as we know (see supra, pp. 14—16), there was then, and had been for centuries, a large foreign, mostly Mohammedan, settlement. Among these foreigners
30 there may have been natives of Baghdad familiar with Nestorian institutions in that city, if not some merchants, or business friends, who happened to be Christians themselves. One of these may have supplied the information regarding the patriarch, and from his description of the «pluviale» forming part of his official dress, the Chinese writer may have misunderstood what was originally a «rain cape, or cloak» to be an umbrella. Two years before the completion of Chóu K'ü-feï's
35 book, in 1176 A. D., the contemporary patriarch, by the name of Elias III, was elected and ordained at Madain, «pallio amictus pistacini coloris (see Gismondi, Maris Amri et Slibae De Patriarchis Nestorianorum Commentaria, II, 64). This vest, whatever it may have been, of pistachio-green colour, the colour of the patriarch's personal reign, may have something to do with Chóu K'ü-feï's *ts'ing*, i. e. «green», or «blue, umbrella», since that word may cover both
40 shades (see Hirth, Ancient Porcelain, 7 et seqq.).

If Elias III be meant by Chóu K'ü-feï's «king of Ta-ts'in», the tunnel leading from his palace (*cella*) to the hall of worship (*ecclesia*) might be considered his work. For, we have two passages testifying to his love of architectural enterprise. Mar Amr says (l. c.) that, after his ordination at Madain, he proceeded to the patriarchal residence in the Christian quarter of
45 Baghdad, and when he observed its being in a state of ruin began to rebuild it together with the church; that God favoured his ventures, and that by his exertions many benefices have been brought about («Inde ad cellam in aedibus Romaeorum positam profectus, eandemque dirutam contemplatus, illam reaedificare coepit unâ cum ecclesia: favitque eius conatibus Deus, operaque ipsius multa praestita sunt beneficia»). The other passage occurs in Barhebraeus' Chro-
50 nicon (Abbeloos and Lamy, III, 370), where he is referred to as having built up the ruins of the patriarchal residence and made it habitable («Ipse ruinas cellae catholici instauravit et habita-bilem fecit»). The two passages do not distinctly mention the subway, but it seems suggestive that just at this time both the palace, or cella, and the church of the patriarch were rebuilt. Jacobus

Golius (1596–1667) is quoted in Hottinger's Bibliotheca Orientalis, 62, as having referred to Elias III as «Patriarch of Antioch», but Assemani ridicules the idea, because he says, the title «Patriarch of Antioch» was never claimed by the Nestorians (see supra, p. 105, line 46).

8) Mahmud of Ghazni is wrongly reputed to have been the first sovereign prince to take the title of Sultan, in 1002 A. D. It was later on borne by Togrul beg and the succeeding Seldjuk princes. See de Guignes, Hist. des Huns, II, 162. In 1057 Togrul was made General of the Empire and Governor of all the Moslim by the Caliph. In 1072 the Sultan Malekshah was given by the Caliph the title of Amir el-Mumenin, which had only been borne by the Caliphs until then. On the other hand the Caliphs were confirmed in their title by the Sultans. Ibid. II, 197—198, 214.

In the time just preceding the year 1178, when Chóu K'ü-feï's work appeared, the Caliphs of Baghdad were politically powerless, though they continued to be the spiritual rulers of the Moslim world. The political masters of Baghdad itself were the Seldjuk Sultans, descendants of the great Malekshah. But even their power had begun to decline, and it seems doubtful which of the several rulers bearing the title of Sultan in Chóu K'ü-feï's time is referred to by that author. Possibly Saladin, who had captured Damascus and other Syrian cities, called himself 'Sultan' on his coins, and gave orders that in the mosque prayers the names of himself and the Caliph of Baghdad should be mentioned. When Elias III was elected Patriarch of the Nestorians, Mustadi was Caliph (see Mar Amr, op. cit., 64); the Seldjuk Sultans immediately preceding this period were Arslan and Togrul. See E. G. Browne, in J. R. A. S., 1902, 873—882.

Under the Seldjuk Sultans, the country was divided among numerous Emirs as feudal lords, who had to deliver an annual tribute to the Sultan and who, in times of war, had to fit out certain troops for service under the Sultan. Hence the remark that 'he orders the Ta-shï, etc.'. See von Kremer, Culturgesch. des Orients, I, 254.

9) In Chóu K'ü-feï's work there follow here the references to T'ién-chu being a dependency of Ta-ts'in and to the holy-water which quiets the waves; which our author has transposed to the beginning of his chapter on T'ién-chu, see infra, p. 110 line 30 and p. 111. lines 7—9.

10) Chóu K'ü-feï probably took this reference to the gem called hié-ki-si from the Hóu-Han-shu, 118, where it is found mentioned for the first time. If the hié-ki-si was a gem, it probably belonged to the same class as the yé-kuang-pi or 'jewel that shines at night', which is said to have been a product of Ta-ts'in. See Hirth, China and the Roman Orient, 79 and 242. See also infra. Pt. II. Ch. XLI. Note.

11) The date here given is apparently a misprint, the Hóu Han-shu gives the correct date, ninth year of the yen-hi period', i. e. 166 A. D. See on this famous mission from Marcus Aurelius Antoninus, Hirth, op. cit., 42 and 173. Cf. supra, p. 5.

12) Quotation from Tsin-shu, 97. See Hirth, op. cit., 45.

13) Quotation from Hóu Han-shu, 118. See Hirth, op. cit., 42—43, 291—293. The Weak-Water, as well as the other terms usually mentioned together with it, the Si-wang-mu, the Red Water (Ch'ï-shui) and the Flying Sands (Liu-sha), appear in very old Chinese legends, and, although it would be a fruitless task to seek to ascertain their actual whereabout (cf. F. W. Mayers, Chinese Readers Manual, Nos. 236, 330, 572), so much is certain, that these imaginary abodes of a fairy queen were, according to the ideas of the original legend writers, neither in T'iau-chï nor in Ta-ts'in. See also Hirth, Ancient History of China, 144—151.

14) Tu Huan, the author of the King-hing-ki, was made a prisoner by the Arabs in the battle of Taras in 751 A. D., and lived among them for ten years, and, when released, returned to Canton by sea. The King-hing-ki is an ethnographical work, fragments only of which have been preserved in the commentary of the T'ung-tién (通 典. Chs. 191—193), the author of which, Tu Yu (杜 佑), was his relative.

Tu Huan's account of Fu-lin throws a still better light on our identification of the country with Syria than the statements of the standard Chinese historians, because it was written by a Chinese author who had resided in Western Asia during a clearly definable period (751—762 A. D.), thus giving us an opportunity of comparing notes with information from contemporaneous western sources. Chan (苫 Canton dialect, Shim), in the west, (not north or north-west), of which Fu-lin is to be looked for, is a transcription of Sham, or ash-Shām, «that which is on the left hand (looking to the rising sun)», i. e., the northern country from Mecca, or Syria. At the time of Tu Huan's arrival in the West, it had just been the chief province of Merwan II, the last of the Caliphs of the house of Omaya, with its capital at Damascus. This city itself is also called Sham. Chau Ju-kua's text differs slightly from the original in the T'ung-tién. The latter says: «In the country

5 of Fu-lin there is the country of Chan (Sham), in the west screened off by (a range of) mountains several thousand *li* (in length)» (佛 菻 國 有 苫 國 西 隔 山 數 千 里). This seems to involve that Sham (Syria, or, in its most restricted sense, Damascus) was held to be part of the Fu-lin country. The fragment quoted in the T'ung-tién contains yet another characteristic addition omitted by Chau Ju-kua; it says that «when (the people of Fu-lin) are kept

10 as captives in the frontier states, they will rather accept death than change their national customs» (或 有 俘 在 諸 國 守 死 不 改 鄉 風). This is an improved translation suggested by G. M. H. Playfair («The Mystery of Ta-ts'in», in J. C. B. R. A. S., New Ser. XX, 78, referring to the corresponding extract from Ma Tuan-lin, given by Hirth in China and the Rom. Or., 83 and 116). Playfair applied this remark to the Israelites in exile, but there seems

15 to be no reason why Tu Huan should place on records facts of such remote antiquity as the Babylonian captivity. On the other hand he is sure to have come into contact with, or have heard of, the Syrian Christians living as captives among the Persians in Madain, or Ktesiphon, where Khosru I, after the fall of Antioch in 540 A. D., had built for them a second Antioch as an asylum for his Syrian slaves and a model of Greek civilization close to his Persian court

20 (Rawlinson, The Seventh Great Oriental Monarchy, 1876, 395, and Nöldeke, Geschichte der Perser und Araber zur Zeit der Sassaniden, Leiden, 1879, 165 and 329). These Syrian Christians had furnished the nucleus of a large foreign population on Persian ground, enjoying under their patriarchs rights amounting in ordinary times to those of an independent nation (see von Kremer, Culturgesch. des Orients, II, 174 et seqq.), while at other times they had to suffer the most

25 cruel persecutions, refusal to abandon the faith of their fathers being under Sassanide and Moslem rule often visited by torture and capital punishment. It is to those martyrs of Christian faith that Tu Huan refers, when he asserts that «the people of Fu-lin», i. e., the Christians, originally of Syria, living under their patriarchs as captives in Persia, «will rather accept death than change their national customs». A celebrated case of Christian martyrdom is recorded by

30 Mar Amr (op. cit., 37) as having occurred just a year after Tu Huan's arrival in 752 A. D.: «per id tempus martyrium fecit Israel medicus, cui Deus requiem concedat». Cf. Assemani, II, 432.

    Several of the notes placed on record in Tu Huan's fragment point to Syria as the country with which Fu-lin has to be identified. If it is said that the people drink wine, which he knew was forbidden to the Mahommedans; this may be accounted for by the term Fu-lin covering the

35 Christian population, mixed of native and Roman, or Greek elements. Skilled artisans and clever weavers of silk were notorious in Syria; so was an industry, not mentioned by Chau Ju-kua, but referred to in the original quotation of the T'ung-tién, the manufacture of glass, which it is said «has not its equal in the world (琉 璃 妙 者 天 下 莫 比).» Chau Ju-kua speaks of 10,000 men forming the army of Fu-lin, while the T'ung-tién text makes it to consist of a million.

40 The one figure is much too low, the other much too high for Syria under the Omaiads as well as the Byzantine empire. But both texts have the words: «they have to ward off the Ta-shï». This might tempt the defenders of the Constantinople theory to look upon it as an argument against Fu-lin being Syria. But we have to consider that Tu Huan does not view things from an historical point of view; he merely places on record what he had heard and seen on the spot. His

45 information is entirely contemporaneous, and refers to events immediately preceding and following the year 751, when the battle of Taras was fought. This was just the time when the Romans of Constantinople were much less molested by the Arabs than at any other period preceding, or following for at least a generation. The great disaster of 718 A. D., when the Arab fleet was entirely routed after a fruitless siege of thirteen months, owing to a combination of circumstances,

50 added to the murderous effect of Greek-fire, had discouraged the Arabs in their attacks for generations to come; and since in the sequel, especially during the middle of the century, both parties were fully occupied with domestic troubles, the Arabs with dynastic feuds, the Byzantines with iconoclastic controversies, there would have been scarcely any occaison for Tu Huan to say

that «the Romans of the Eastern Empire had to ward off the Ta-shï». We have, therefore, to look
for a different explanation of this statement. In 751, the year of Tu Huan's arrival in the West,
the term Ta-shï, from his point of view, applied to that portion of the Arabs who had just gained
that great victory over the Chinese under Kau Sién-chï, i. e. the Abbaside territory (see Chavannes,
Documents sur les Tou-kioué: Turcs Occidentaux, 297). In his account of the Ta-shï (T'ung-tién,   5
193,23) Tu Huan says: «the country of Chan (Sham, or Syria, of which Damascus was then the
capital) is on the western boundary of the Ta-shï» (苫 國 在 大 食 西 界), — which
seems to show that to him the Ta-shï were the Abbaside Arabs and that their western neighbours,
treated by him as a separate country, were the Syrians, then still fighting for their independence
here and there against the overwhelming numbers of the Abbaside armies, which had already 10
captured Damascus and driven the old Omaiad rulers out of the country. This view is supported
by Tu Huan's mentioning a city called by him A-kü-lo (亞 俱 羅) as the residence of the
king of the Ta-shï. This can be none other than the city of Kufa, the residence of Abu'l-'Abbas,
the Syriac name of which, according to Bar Hebraeus (Abbeloos and Lamy, III, 112: Cf.
Assemani, op. cit., III B, 715) was Akula. Tu Huan had no knowledge of Baghdad, the 15
foundation of which by the second Abbaside Caliph in 762 A. D. fell in the year of his return to
China by a trading vessel bound for Canton.

15) Sin T'ang-shu, 221, has taken some of its statements concerning Ta-ts'in from Tu
Huan's work, among others what he says of the people's fondness for wine and cakes, also the
passage concerning the «Devil market». See Hirth, China and the Roman Orient, 58, 60, 279, 283. 20
Ancient, mediaeval, and modern travellers mention such dumb trading in Asia and Africa.
Cosmas Indicopleustes, Christian topography, 52 (Hakl. Soc. edit.) speaks of it as practised
between the Ethiopians and the Barbarians—probably Somalis. Tavernier, Travels in India, II, 68
(Ball's edit.) refers to it as existing in his time in India, and Begbie (The Malayan Peninsula, 8)
says it is used among the aborigines of the Malay Peninsula. Cf. also what Chau Ju-kua says 25
(infra, Ch. XL) on the trade between the natives of the Philippines (Ma-i) and the Chinese.

21.

INDIA.

T'ién-chu (天 竺).

«The country of T'ién-chu is subordinate to the country of Ta-ts'in»; 30
its rulers are all selected by Ta-ts'in [1].

It is the custom of the people to plait their hair and to let it hang
down, but the temples and the crown of the head are covered with a silken
(帛) turban. In their dwellings they use plaster (石 灰) instead of tiles.
They have walled cities in which the people dwell.   35

The king dresses in brocaded silk, and his hair is wound into a spiral
knot on the crown of his head; the rest of the hair is cut short. When
holding his court in the morning he sits on a *töng* skin, — *töng* (毺) being
the name of an animal, — ornamented with representations of various objects
painted in red wax; and his courtiers make obeisance to him and pray for 40

his life. When he goes forth he rides on horseback, and his saddle and bridle are thickly set with dark gold (烏 金) and silver. His followers, three hundred in number, are armed with spears and swords.

His consort wears a gold embroidered scarlet dress with large sleeves.
5 Once a year she shows herself in public, when considerable bounty is given to the poor.

«In this country there is holy-water (聖 水) which can still the wind and waves. The foreign traders fill opaque glass bottles with it, and when they suddenly get in a rough sea they still it by sprinkling this water on it» [2].

10   It is said that «during the reign of Süan-wu of the Posterior Weï dynasty (A. D., 500—515), T'ién-chu sent envoys with a present of swift horses (駿 馬). It is said that their country produces (出) lions, sables, leopards, camels (橐), rhinoceros, elephants, tortoise-shell, gold, copper, iron, lead and tin, gold embroidered rugs (金 縷 織 成 金 剝), po-tié
15 (白 疊) and t'a-töng (毼 登). There is a stone like talc (雲 母), but of a reddish colour; when split it is as thin as a cicada's wing; when together the pieces look like silken gauze. There is the diamond (金 剛 石), which looks like fluor-spar (紫 石 英), but which will not melt, though exposed to the fire an hundred times». It can cut jade-stone [3].

20   There is sandal-wood (旃 檀) and other aromatic woods, sugar-cane, sugar (石 蜜) and all kinds of fruits. They trade yearly with Ta-ts'in and Fu-nan (扶 南). They use cowries as a medium of exchange. They are clever jugglers. They have bows and arrows, armour, spears, flying-ladders (飛 梯), saps (地 道), and also the contrivances called the «wooden-oxen»
25 and the «gliding-horses» (木 牛 流 馬); yet they are cowards in battle. They are good astronomers and calculators of the calendar (算 歷 or astrologers). They all study the Si-tan-chang-shu (悉 曇 章 書) . . . . . . [Note: A gap of seven characters occurs here]. They use the leaves of the peï-to (貝 多) as paper [4].

30   In the periods chöng-kuan (A. D. 627—650) and t'ién-shóu (690—692) of the T'ang (this country) sent envoys with tribute (to our Court). In the yung-hi period (of the Sung, A. D. 984—988) a priest, by name Lo-hu-na (囉 護 哪), arrived (in Ts'üan-chóu) by sea; he called himself a native of T'ién-chu. The foreign traders (番 商), considering that he was a foreign
35 priest (胡 僧), vied with each other in presenting him gold, silks, jewels and precious stones, but the priest had no use for them himself. He bought a piece of ground and built a Buddhist shrine (佛 剎) in the southern suburb of Ts'üan-chóu; it is the Pau-lin-yüan (寶 林 院) of the present day [5].

Notes.

1) The words in brackets are substantially a quotation from Chóu K'ü-feï's notes on Ta-ts'in. See supra p. 105. The rest of the paragraph seems original with our author. As in the account of Ta-ts'in, Chau Ju-kua has mixed up a good deal of information derived from earlier Chinese sources and applying to India (T'ién-chu) generally, with the India of the Ta-ts'in people, or 5 Christians, regarding whose dependency on the «king of Ta-ts'in» (i. e., the patriarch of Antioch or Baghdad) see supra p. 105. The term T'ién-chu, as here used, is not to be taken in all cases in the broad acceptation in which other Chinese writers use it, for our author has described the principal divisions of India in other chapters. It appears that Chau's T'ién-chu was the coast of Madras, at least so far as the first three paragraphs of this chapter are concerned; in the 10 rest of the chapter, derived nearly entirely from the T'ung-tién and other Chinese authorities, T'ién-chu must, I think, be understood in its broader meaning of India generally.

The manner in which the king, i. e., the head priest of the Christians, appointed by the king of Ta-ts'in, dressed his hair might be looked upon as a strange anomaly, considering his being deputed by the Syrian, or the Chaldaean, patriarch. But it appears that in India the 15 Christian clergy followed the native custom in this respect. Assemani (III B, 337) quotes Josephus Indus (15 century?, Assemani, ib., 439), who says «de Christianis Malabariae: Hi habent sacerdotes, levitas et hypodiaconos. Sacerdotes vero non ferunt tonsuram, sed nonnihil capillorum in summa parte capitis habent: quod et faciunt Saraceni, Persae, Indi, Tartari et Sinenses.»

It might also appear strange that the metropolitan of the Christian church was allowed to 20 have a wife at all; but the history of Nestorian patriarchs shows that opinions on the question of celibacy have changed a good deal. Certainly bishops could be married (Barhebraeus, op. cit., II, 64, 70, 80), and exceptions are even on record in the case of patriarchs, as in that of Babaeus (498—503 A. D.), who was married and had sons and who «sanxit, ut ecclesiae ministri universi nuberent, nemine aut presbyterorum aut diaconorum sine uxore manente: haberentque singuli 25 propriam uxorem palam et publice secundum legis praescriptum: nec quisquam in posterum caelibatum in saeculari conversationi coleret, ut vitatur nempe peccandi periculum» (Mar Amr, op. cit., II, 21; cf. Assemani, II, 408). One of the early bishops of India, known as Thomas Cana, some time about the year 800 A. D., is even credited with having had two wives, one of whom was held to be merely a concubine. Assemani (III B, 441 et seqq) fills several pages of 30 his erudition with the account of this legend. Of the modern Christians of the church of St. Thomas, Captain Ch. Swanston says (J. R. A. S., II, 241): «The celibacy of the priests is with them rather a custom than a dogma: they admit, not only that it is not required by Scripture, but also its evil tendency and consequences; and in later years, some of them were induced to marry by the influence and persuasion of the British authorities in Travancór, and a 35 marriage gift of four hundred rupees, presented by the sovereign of the country, to induce them to return to the ancient usage of their forefathers, and to enter the nuptial state. The feeling of the church is, however, against it.»

The Sung-shï, 490,3ᵇ says that sometime between A. D. 984 and 988, there came to the capital of China an Indian priest (婆羅門僧) called Yung-shï (永世) in company 40 with a Persian heretic called A-li-yen (阿里烟). Yung-shï said that his native land was called Li-tö (利得 Lāta of Masudi, was situated on the gulf of Cambay and was a part of the kingdom of the Balhara). The sovereign of his country bore the family name of Ya-lo-wu-tö (牙羅五得), his personal name was A-no-ni (阿喏你). His clothes were yellow, his cap was of gold and covered with all kinds of jewels. When he went forth he rode on an 45 elephant or in a small sedan-chair, preceded by a great throng of people and to the sound of conch shells and cymbals. When he visited the temples he made largess to the poor. His consort, whose name was Mahani (摩訶你), only appeared in public once a year, when she bestowed great bounty on the people.

The name of this Indian priest means «Time ever-lasting, eternity», and could never have 50 been borne by a Brahman or a Buddhist; it appears to me highly probably that Yung-shï was a

Malabar Christian, as may also have been the Persian «heretic» (外 道) who accompanied him on his journey to China.

2) Quotation from Chóu K'ü-feï, in his notes on Ta-ts'in (see supra, p. 108, note 9). The holy water here referred to must be that taken from the well Zemzem at Mecca. Ming-shï, in 5 its account of Mecca, says: «Behind the tomb of Ma-ha-ma (Mohammed) there is a well, the water of which is limpid and sweet. People who start on the sea voyage use to take along with them some water from this well, for it has the property of appeasing the waves in time of storm when sprinkled over the sea». Bretschneider, Med. Researches, II, 303. San-ts'ai-t'u-hui (Pién-i-tién, 68. Sec. T'ién-fang) attributes the same property to the water from the well of Ishmael (司 麻 10 烟), or Hagar's well, this is the well Zemzem, according to mohammedan tradition.

2) The portion of this paragraph in quotation marks is taken from Tu Yu's T'ung-tién (see supra, p. 108, note 14). Hóu Han-shu, 118,12ᵃ, mentions among the products of India elephants, rhinoceros, tortoise-shell, gold, silver, copper, iron, lead and tin, sugar (石 蜜), pepper, ginger, black salt, fine cloth, handsome rugs called t'a-töng — Liang-shu, 54,16ᵇ says the usual 15 exports from India were rhinoceros (horns), ivory, leopards (skins), marmot (? skins), tortoise-shell, huo-ts'i (火 齊), gold, silver, gold embroidered skin rugs, fine hemps (cloth ?), po-tié (muslin). fine fur garments and t'a-töng (rugs). «Huo-ts'i, it adds, is like talc, its colour is like dark gold, it is brilliant. When cleaved it is as thin as a cicada's wing; when put together the pieces look like silver gauze». Huo-ts'i appears to be a foreign word; the substance referred to 20 may be isinglass. According to Porter Smith, Contrib. mater. med., 129, it is lapis-lazuli.

4) This paragraph was compiled from a number of earlier Chinese writers, largely from T'ang-shu, 221ᴬ,17 et seqq. According to the Nan-fang-ts'au-mu-chuang, I, 4, shï-mi is cane-sugar. At the time that work was written, third century A. D., China got all her supply of sugar from Tongking and southern Indo-China, where the sugar-cane appears to have been indigenous. 25 See de Candolle, Origine des plantes cultivées, 122—127. It was cultivated also in India as early as the first or second century of our era, as we have seen by the reference made to it in the Hóu Han-shu in the previous note. By the sixth century its use must have been general in Central Asia, for Sui-shu, 83, mentions that sugar came from various countries of Central Asia and of the Sassanian empire. In the first half of the seventh century the cane was cultivated in 30 Central China, at Yang-chóu (揚 州 in Kiang-su), but the Chinese did not know the process of making sugar. Somewhere about A. D. 637 the Emperor T'ai-tsung sent a mission to Magadha (i. e., Central India) to learn the method of boiling sugar, and called the attention of his people to the superiority of the Chinese cane. T'ang-shu, 221ᴬ,19ᵇ.

At about the same time Hüan-tsang mentioned among the articles of food of the people 35 of India sha-t'ang (沙 糖 «granulated sugar») and shï-mi. He also stated that Gandhāra had much sugar-cane (甘 蔗) and produced (or exported 出) shï-mi. Si-yü-ki, 2,10ᵇ, 15ᵃ. — On sugar and sugar-cane in ancient India, see Lassen, Indische Alterthumsk., I, 317 et seqq.

Sui-shu, 83, makes mention of another kind of sugar, or product of sugar, called pan-mi 半 蜜). I can find no explanation of this term which, literally translated, means «half-honey». 40 Concerning the remarks about the trade relations of T'ién-chu, Hóu Han-shu, 118,10ᵇ already referred to its trade with Ta-ts'in, and Liang-shu, 54,17ᵃ stated that Central T'ién-chu had much sea-trade with Ta-ts'in, An-si (Parthia), Fu-nan, Jï-nan and Kiau-chï (i. e., Indo-China generally). Our author quotes from T'ang-shu, 221ᴬ,17ᵇ.

Cowries were not the only medium of exchange in India even in the first centuries of our 45 era. Hóu Han-shu, 118,10ᵇ states that the Indians used coins of gold and silver; the ratio was 10 to 1. Hüan-tsang says «in the commerce of the country gold and silver coins, cowries and small pearls are the media of exchange». Watters, On Yuan-chuang's Travels, I, 178.

The «wooden ox» and the «gliding horse» were, according to San-kuo-chï (Shu, 5,13,15), contrivances for facilitating the transport of provisions of armies, and were invented in the third 50 century by the great Chinese general Chu-ko Liang. Conf. Mayers, Chinese Reader's Manual, s. v. Chu-ko Liang. I can find no explanation of feï-t'i, literally «flying ladders», or of ti-tau literally «earth roads, saps».

*

Si-tan chang-shu appears to mean the «Siddhānta Book of Rules», and the work was probably one on astronomy. Alberuni says in his India (Sachau's translation, I, 153) «The book known among Muslims as Sindhind is called by them [the Hindus] Siddhāntā, i. e., straight, not crooked nor changing. By this name they call every standard book on astronomy, even such books as, according to our opinions, do not come up to the mark of our so-called *Zij*, i. e., hand-books of mathematical astronomy. They have five Siddhāntas». See also Lassen, Indische Alter-thumsk., IV, 621. On the usual, or orthodox, Buddhist sense of the word *si-tan*, i. e., a syllabary, see Watters, On Yuan-chwang's Travels, I, 155—159 and Eitel, Handbook, 152. The text is a quotation from T'ang-shu 221A,25[b], the characters missing in our text can be supplied from it. The passage reads as follows 善 步 曆 學 悉 曇 章 妄 曰 梵 天 法. «They are able astronomers and they study (the work called) *Si-tan-chang*, erroneously called (by the Chinese) *Fan t'ién-fa* (i. e., Indian Astronomy)».

The Hóu Han-shu, 118,12[a] and Liang-shu, 54,16[b] remarked on the Indians' cowardice and weakness.

Peï-to (in Sanskrit *patra*, «a leaf») are the leaves of the borassus flabelliformis. Yu-yang-tsa-tsu, 18,7[a] says there are three kinds of *peï-to* tree in Magadha (Central India), the largest is called *to-lo-p'o li-ch'a peï-to* (多 羅 婆 力 叉 貝 多) which is in Sanskrit *tāla vṛkṣa patra* «leaf of the tāla tree.»

5) The name of this priest, probably a transcription of Rāhula, has often been used by Buddhist monks; it was the name of the son of the Buddha Gautama. The term *hu*, rendered «foreign», is sometimes applied to Indians (see Pei-wön yün-fu, 70A s. v. 天 竺 胡), though usually used to designate the people of Western Asia.

Sung-shï, 490,3[b] has it that in the *yung-hi* period (A. D. 984—988, the same in which Lo-hu-na came to Ts'üan-chóu), Tzï-huan (辭 澣), a priest of Weï-chóu (衞 州), came back to China from the Western Regions with a foreign priest (胡 僧) by the name of Mi-tan-lo (密 坦 羅). They presented to the Emperor letters from the Prince of Northern India, and also from Na-lan-t'o (那 爛 陀), Prince of the Diamond Throne (金 剛 坐 王 i. e., Vajrāsana, Buddhgaya). *Mi-tan-lo* is a transcription of *Mitra*, a common termination of Indian Buddhist names.

22.

THE ARABS.

Ta-shï (大 食).

«The Ta-shï[1] are to the west and north (or north-west) of Ts'üan-chóu at a very great distance from it, so that the foreign ships (番 舶) find it difficult to make the voyage there direct. After these ships have left Ts'üan-chóu they come in some forty days to Lan-li (藍 里), where they trade. The following year they go to sea again, when with the aid of the regular wind (順 風) they take some sixty days to make the journey».

The products of the country are for the most part brought to San-fo-ts'i, where they are sold to merchants who forward them to China[2].

«This country of the Ta-shï is powerful and warlike. Its extent is very great, and its inhabitants are pre-eminent among all foreigners for their distinguished bearing».

«The climate throughout a large part of it is cold», snow falling to a depth of two or three feet; consequently rugs are much prized.

The capital of the country, called Mi-sü-li (蜜徐籬) (Note: Some make it to be Ma-lo-pa 麻囉拔), is an important centre for the trade of foreign peoples[3]. «The king wears a turban of silk brocade and foreign cotton stuff (buckram). On each new moon and full moon he puts on an eight-sided flat-topped headdress of pure gold, set with the most precious jewels in the world. His robe is of silk brocade and is bound around him with a jade girdle. On his feet he wears golden shoes. In his residence the pillars are of cornelian stone, the walls of lü-kan stone (綠甘) (Note: It is as transparent as crystal), the tiles of rock-crystal, the bricks of green stone (碌石 jasper?), and the mortar of huo stone (活石). The curtains and screens are of brocade with rich designs woven in all kinds of colour in silk and pure gold thread[4]».

The king's throne is set with pearls and precious stones, and the steps of the throne are covered with pure gold. The various vessels and utensils around the throne are of gold or silver, and precious pearls are knotted in the screen behind it. In great court ceremonies the king sits behind this screen, and on either side, protecting him, «the ministers of state surround him» bearing golden bucklers and helmets and armed with precious swords.

His other «officers are called T'ai-weï (太尉); each of them has the command of some twenty thousand horsemen. The horses are seven feet high and are shod with iron. His army is brave and excels in all military exercises».

The streets (of the capital) are more than fifty feet broad; in the middle is a roadway twenty feet broad and four feet high for the use of camels, horses, and oxen carrying goods about. On either side, for the convenience of pedestrians' business, there are sidewalks paved with green and black (or blueish black, 青黑) flagstones of surpassing beauty.

«The dwellings of the people are like those of the Chinese, with this difference that here thin flagstones (slates?) are used instead of tiles[5]».

The food consists of rice and other cereals; mutton stewed with fine strips of dough is considered a delicacy. The poor live on fish, vegetables and fruits only; sweet dishes are preferred to sour (實皆甜無酸). Wine is made out of the juice of grapes, and there is also the drink (called) ssï (思酥酒), a decoction of sugar and spices. By mixing of honey and spices they make a drink (called) *meï-ssï-ta-hua* (眉 思 打 華 酒), which is very heating [6].

Very rich persons use a measure (量) instead of scales in business transactions in gold or silver. «The markets» are noisy and bustling, and «are filled with great store of gold and silver damasks, brocades, and such like wares. The artisans have the true artistic spirit» (工 匠 技 術 咸 精 其 能).

The king, the officials and the people all serve (or revere 事) Heaven. They have also a Buddha by the name of Ma-hia-wu (麻 霞 勿) [7]. Every seven days they cut their hair and clip their finger nails. At the New Year for a whole month they fast and chant prayers (清 齋 念 經 一 月). Daily they pray to Heaven five times.

The peasants work their fields without fear of inundations or droughts; a sufficiency of water for irrigation is supplied by a river whose source is not known. During the season when no cultivation is in progress, the level of the river remains even with the banks; with the beginning of cultivation it rises day by day. Then it is that an official is appointed to watch the river and to await the highest water level, when he summons the people, who then plough and sow their fields. When they have had enough water, the river returns to its former level [8].

There is a great harbour (or anchorage 大 港) in this country, over two hundred feet deep, which opens to the south-east on the sea, and has branches (支) connecting with all quarters of the country (疏 達 於 諸 路) [9]. On either bank of the harbour (港) the people have their dwellings and here daily are held fairs (墟 市), where crowd (輻 湊) boats and wagons, all loaded with hemp, wheat, millet, beans, sugar, meal, oil, firewood, fowls, sheep, geese, ducks, fish, shrimps, date-cakes (棗 圈), grapes and other fruits.

The products of the country (of the Ta-shï) [10] consist in pearls, ivory, rhinoceros horns, frankincense, ambergris, putchuck, cloves, nutmegs, benzoin (*an-si hiang*), aloes, myrrh, dragon's-blood, asa-foetida, *wu-na-ts'i*, borax, opaque and transparent glass, *ch'ö-k'ü* shell, coral, cat's-eyes, gardenia flowers, rose-water, nut-galls, yellow wax, soft gold brocades, camel's-hair cloth, *tóu-lo* cottonades (兜 羅 綿) and foreign satins (異 緞).

The foreign traders (番 商) who deal in these merchandise, bring them to San-fo-ts'i and to Fo-lo-an to barter.

The following countries are dependencies of this country (of the Ta-shï):

Ma-lo-mo (麻 囉 抹) [11]   Nu-fa (奴 發)

Shï-ho (施 曷)   Ya-ssï-pau-hién (啞 四 包 閑)

5 Lo-ssï-meï (囉 施 美)
Mu-kü-lan (木 俱 蘭)
K'ié-li-ki (伽 力 吉)
P'i-no-yé (毗 喏 耶) [12]
5   I-lu (伊 祿)
10 Pai-ta (白 達)
Ssï-lién (思 蓮)
Pai-lién (白 蓮)
Tsi-ki (積 吉)
10   Kan-meï (甘 眉)

15 P'u-hua-lo (蒲 花 羅)
Ts'öng-pa (層 扳)
Pi-p'a-lo (弼 琶 囉)
Wu-pa (勿 扳)
Wöng-li (甕 籬)
20 Ki-shï (記 施)
Ma-kia (麻 嘉)
Pi-ssï-lo 弼 斯 羅)
Ki-tz'ï-ni (吉 瓷 尼)
Wu-ssï-li (勿 斯 离) [13].

This country (or people) was originally a branch of the Persians (波斯). In the *ta-yé* period of the Sui dynasty (A. D. 605—617) there lived a high-minded and wise man among the Persians who found deep down in a hole a stone bearing an inscription, and this he took for a good omen. So he
15 called the people together, took by force the things necessary (for arming men) and enrolled followers, who gradually increased in number till he became powerful enough to make himself king, and then he took possession of the western portion of Po-ssï.

Since the *yung-hui* period of the T'ang dynasty (A. D. 650—656) the
20 Ta-shï have come repeatedly to our Court to present tribute. Before the time of their king P'ön-ni-mo-huan (盆 泥 末 換 Beni Merwán) they were called «White-robed Ta-shï»; after A-p'o-lo-pa (阿 婆 羅 扳 Abu'l 'Abbás) they were called «Black-robed Ta-shï» [14].

In the fourth year of the *k'ién-tö* period of the reigning dynasty (A. D.
25 966) the bonze Hing-k'in (行 勤) journeyed to the Western Regions; on this occasion an (Imperial) letter to their king was granted to enlist his sympathy [15].

In the first year of the *k'ai-pau* period (A. D. 968) they sent envoys with tribute to our Court, and in the fourth year (A. D. 971) they sent presents
30 with Chan-ch'öng and Shö-p'o to Li Yü (李 煜) in Kiang-nan [16]. Yü did not venture to accept them, so the envoys submitted the matter to the Court, and an Order in Council was issued forbidding that tribute presents should henceforth be brought [17].

In the fourth year of the *shun-hua* period (A. D. 993) they sent tribute
35 through the Assistant Envoy Li-a-wu (李 亞 勿) who stated, at an audience granted him in the Ch'ung-chöng Audience Hall (of the Palace), that his country bordered on Ta-ts'in, and that it produced ivory and rhinoceros horns. The Emperor T'ai-tsung asked him how rhinoceros and elephants were

captured. He replied, «To capture elephants, we use decoy elephants to get so near them that we can catch them with a big lasso. To capture a rhinoceros, a man with a bow and arrow climbs a big tree, where he watches for the animal until he can shoot and kill it. The young (rhinoceros) are not shot as they can be caught».   5

The envoy was presented with a court dress, a hat and girdle, and, besides these, with as much gold as the tribute presents were worth [18].

In the third year of the *yung-hi* period (A. D. 986) envoys of the Ta-shï came to Court with a mission from the Pin-t'ung-lung country [19].

In the sixth year *hién-p'ing* (A. D. 1003) they sent Ma-ni and others 10 (麻 尼 等) with tribute of pearls and a request that return presents should not be made them. Although the Emperor Chön-tsung did not want to disregard their wish, when the envoys started on their homeward journey they were dismissed with extraordinary honours [20].

In the first year *king-tö* (A. D. 1004) the (Arab) envoy remained behind 15 at the capital, together with the envoys from San-fo-ts'i and P'u-kan, to celebrate the Feast of Lanterns, on which occasion they were treated to their heart's content with money and wine (賜 錢 縱 飲) [21].

In the fourth year (A. D. 1007) they accompanied a tribute mission from Chan-ch'öng, and were on this occassion entertained with most parti- 20 cular attention, and also allowed to visit the Buddhist and Tauist temples and the Imperial gardens and parks (苑 囿) [22].

During the *ta-chung siang-fu* period (A. D. 1008—1017), while the Emperor was absent in the eastern part of the Empire for sacrificial purposes, the chief T'o-p'o-li (陁 婆 離) expressed the wish to be allowed to 25 present his tribute presents in person (to the Emperor) on the T'ai-shan (where he had gone to sacrifice). He was allowed to do so [23].

In the fourth year (of the same period, i. e., 1011), while the Emperor had gone to Fön-yin (汾 陰) to make sacrifices, the envoy (T'o-p'o-li) came again, and was ordered by the Emperor to follow the Court [24].   30

According to an old tradition told in Kuang-chóu (Canton), there was a man from the Ta-shï country by the name of Wu-si-hu-lu-hua (無 西 忽 盧 華), who had attained to the age of an hundred and thirty years. He had double ear-beadings and an extraordinarily imposing aspect. He himself stated that long ago, impelled by his high regard for the civilization of the 35 Empire, he had embarked on a ship of the Ku-lo (古 邏) country and had made the journey to China. The Emperor presented him with a brocade gown and a silver girdle, to which he added a piece of silk [25].

In both the *yüan-yu* period (A. D. 1086 — 1094) and the *k'ai-hi* period (A. D. 1205—1208) the Ta-shï sent missions to Court with tribute[26].

A foreign trader (番 商) by the name of Shï-na-weï (施 那 幃), a Ta-shï by birth, established himself in the southern suburb of Ts'üan-chóu. Disdaining wealth, but charitable and filled with the spirit of his western home, he built a charnel house (叢 塚) in the south-western corner of the suburb (or outside the city in the south-west direction) as a last resting-place for the abandoned bodies (遺 骸) of foreign traders[27]. The Customs Inspector Lin Chï-k'i (林 之 奇) has recorded this fact[28].

Notes.

1) The name Ta-shï applied by the Chinese to the Arabs, and, as in the present work, to the Mohammedan world, is the name Tazi or Tay of western Asiatic writers. See Bretschneider, The knowledge possessed by the ancient Chinese of the Arabs and Arabian Colonies, 6. Among the earliest mentions of it in Chinese works is that of the pilgrim I-tsing, who, in the middle of the seventh century, speaks of the To-shï (多 氏) as interfering with travel on the road to Kapiça. Chavannes, Religieux éminents, 25. Another still earlier reference as far as facts are concerned, occurs in the T'ung-tién (193,22[b]) and the two T'ang-shu, where the first Arab embassy to the Chinese court is recorded under the year 651 A. D. In the Kiu T'ang-shu (198,28[b]) the king's name is given as Ta-shï, i. e. Ta-shï was his «tribal» name (其 姓 大 食 氏), his personal name being Han-mi-mo-mo-ni, probably a corruption for Emir-al-Mumenin, the title of the caliph, at that time Othman. According to the T'ang-shu (221 B, 19), the ambassadors «said themselves that their king belonged to the Ta-shï tribe» (自 言 王 大 食 氏). It appears from this that, whatever the origin of the Persian *tasi* may be, the king's tribal name, or his surname, was stated by some of his own subjects to be Ta-shï, though there may be a misunderstanding about that. The real meaning of the term, which appears as *Tazi* in Persian and Uïgúric (Vambéry, Kudatku bilik, 234), *Tadjik* or *Tazik* with the Armenians, Turks and Mongols, and *Tayi, Ta-ï, Tayoyè* with the Syrians according to d'Ohsson (Histoire des Mongols, I, 217, note), and which Dionysius, Patriarch of Antioch, in his history of the world (eighth century A. D.) refers to under the year 637 as *Taj* (*Tajos* vocat Dionysius, Assemani II, 103), is apparently quite uncertain, so much so that we could not even say with absolute confidence that they are all derived from the same root. Among the several forms in which the name appears *Tadjik*, or *Tazik*, is the most likely to be represented by the Chinese Ta-shï, pronounced Tai-shik in Canton. But Ta-i as the ancient sound of 大 食 is not quite impossible. The *shï* of Ta-shï being ranged with the group of characters anciently read *shik*, or *chik*, may be due to a guess made by the compilers of K'ang-hi's Dictionary. The reading *i*, though not the usual one, is certainly backed by old sound authorities (K'ang-hi, s. v. 食 ad finem: 羊 吏 切 音 異), so that Ta-shï may possibly stand for Ta-i. Bretschneider (Mediæval Researches, I, 268, note) says «that d'Ohsson is wrong in stating that the Mongols called the Mahommedans *Tadjik*; that, in early times [*query*: how early?] the Persians were called *Tadjik*, and even now-a-days this name is applied in Turkestan and Transoxiana to the aboriginal Iranian population there».

2) This and the preceding paragraph are partly taken from Chóu K'ü-feï (3,2). Conf. supra, p. 89, lines 3—6 and p. 120, n. 5; our author has attempted to edit the text of the Ling-wai-tai-ta, but with no success. Chóu says: «The name Ta-shï (大 食 者 諸 國) is a collective appellation for several countries. There are fully a thousand and more countries, but of those of which we know the names there are only these few.

«There is the country of Ma-li-pa (麻 離 拔 or 囉 拔); ships leaving Kuang-chóu during or after the eleventh moon (December) and sailing with a northerly wind, can make the country called Lan-li (藍 里 i. e., N. W. Sumatra) in forty days. Here they trade, buying sapan-wood, tin, and long white rattans. The following year, in winter, they set to sea again and, with a north-easterly wind favouring them, they make the voyage to this country of Ma-li-pa, (i. e., the Hadramaut coast of Arabia) in some sixty days.　　　　5

«The products (of Ma-li-pa) are frankincense, ambergris, pearls, opaque glass, rhinoceros horns, ivory, coral, putchuk, myrrh, dragon's-blood, asa-foetida, liquid storax, oak-galls and rose-water, to trade in all of which the countries of the Ta-shï resort to this place». See for the remainder of Chóu's description of Ma-li-pa, infra p. 121, note 11. The other countries of the Ta-shï mentioned by Chóu K'ü-feï are Ma-kia, Pai-ta, Ki-tz'ï-ni, Meï-lu-ku-tun and Wu-ssï-li; 10 his remarks on them are translated in subsequent notes to this work.

3) Mi-sü-li is the Mizraim of the Hebrews, our Egypt. The Arabic Misr, derived from the Hebrew, was applied by the Arabs to the capital of Egypt. In another chapter (XXXVI), derived in all likelihood from different sources, our author writers the name Wu-ssï-li (勿 斯 里 in Cantonese Mat-ssï-li). In the Yüan period the Chinese wrote the name Mi-ssï-ïr (迷 思 耳). 15 See Bretschneider, J. C. B. R. A. S., X, 295, and Mediaeval Researches, I, 141, II, 135. In another passage (Ch. XXXVI) our author calls the capital of Egypt Kié-yé, which is al-Ḳáhirah, the name given the new city founded in 973 A. D. The popular Arabic name of Cairo is Misr al-ḳáhirah. Chau evidently thought that Mi-sü-li and Ma-lo-pa were the same place. He got his more or less original information and that derived from Chóu K'ü-feï badly jumbled. Chóu's 20 notes only referred to Ma-li-pa.

4) This description of the king's dress and of his palace resembles what he tells us elsewhere of those of the king of Ta-ts'in. Conf. also infra, Ch. XXXVI. Lü-kan, Canton dialect luk-kōm, is apparently a transcription of Arabic and Persian rukhām, «marble», or «alabaster». Huo-shï, literally «live stone», may stand for hua-shï, 滑 石, soap-stone, of which it is an 25 equivalent, according to Geerts, Les produits de la nature Japonaise et Chinoise, 434 seq. Porter Smith, Contributions towards the materia medica, etc., of China, 205, distinguishes it as «steatite», which he says «differs from lardstone in containing magnesia, having the composition of a silicate of magnesia and alumina», and (130) he says of k'uai-huo-shï (塊 活 石) that it entered into the composition of some of the old Chinese pottery of the best kind». Cf. Julien, 30 Histoire et fabrication de la porcelaine Chinoise, 76, 256 et seqq.

5) This paragraph and also the preceding ones of this chapter, when in quotation marks, as well as lines 4—5 on p. 116, are substantially taken from the statements made to the Chinese court by Arabs who came there in the chöng-ho period of the Sung (A. D. 1111—1118). They did not mention the name of the capital of their country, hence our author's uncertainty 35 concerning it. See Sung-shï, 490,14. One is inclined to think that our author is describing some other city than Cairo, possibly Baghdad or Damascus; but it is more likely that this picture of the capital of the Ta-shï is, like many of those of Chau Ju-kua, a composite one.

6) Most of this paragraph is taken from Ling-wai-tai-ta; see infra, p. 121, n. 11. The drink called ssï is probably Persian sherbet, sharāb «a draught, drink, wine». Meï, ssï-ta and hua may 40 have to be distinguished, the two first as transcriptions, the latter as a generic term, meaning «flower wine», the term hua-ts'iu, 花 酒, being backed by a number of passages quoted in the Pién-tzï-leï-pién, 203,17. In another passage (infra, p. 127, n. 4) three kinds of drinks are mentioned, mi, sha and hua; it seems probable that we should likewise distinguish three here; meï, ssï-ta and hua. Both transcriptions represent the same original forms, whatever they may be. 45 Yu-yang-tsa-tsu, 4,2^b says that «in Po-ssï, Fu-lin and adjacent countries they ferment rice or seed of some kind in meat juice. When, after some days, it has become wine, it is an intoxicating drink».

7) In Cantonese Ma-ha-mat, the Prophet Mohammed. The fast referred to is, of course, that of Ramadan. The weekly cutting of hair and nails is a quotation from Ling-wai-tai-ta, 3,8^a. 50 See infra, Ch. XXX.

8) Confer what our author says here of the Nile with his other account of it in Ch XXX. Chóu K'ü-feï did not know of the Nile; our author, so far as we are aware, is the earliest Chinese author to refer to it.

9) This may be a reference to Kolzum on the Red Sea, the Clysma of late classical writers,
5 and to the canal re-opened by Amru somewhere about A. D. 642 between the Nile and the Red Sea, and which appears to have followed very closely the line of the Fresh-water Canal of the present day. After its re-opening by Amru it remained navigable for eighty years, when, choked with sand, it was again abandoned. Muir, Annals of the early Caliphate, 244. Another possible and more probable explanation is that it refers to Obollah and Basra, a district famous for its canals, which,
10 according to Ib̦n Haukal, exceeded 100,000 in number, and of these 20,000 were navigable for boats. Le Strange, Land of the Eastern Caliphate, 46.

10) The list of products here given includes the most important ones brought to China by the Arabs from various countries of the West; more detailed descriptions of them are given in Part II this work.

15 11) The last character is certainly an error, it should be *pa* (扳). In another passage (Pt. II, Ch. XXXVI) our author, however, writes the name Ma-lo-mo (馬羅楝). As shown in a previous note (supra, p. 25 note 3) the country referred to is Mirbāṭ (مرباط) on the Hadramaut coast of Arabia. Chóu K'ü-feï says of it (3,2, continuing the passage quoted supra, pp. 119—120): «The king of the country, the officers and the people all worship Heaven (i. e. are Moslims). The
20 gentry wear turbans of white silk falling down the back; they have designs in gold thread in them. Their clothes are made of white *yüé-no* stuff with golden characters in it, or else of brocades of sundry kinds. They wear red leather boots. They live in five-storied houses. They eat wheaten cakes, meat and milk. The poor eat fish and vegetables. The soil does not produce rice. The fruits they produce are more sweet than sour. They make wine from grapes. There is also the drink
25 (called) *ssï* (思酥酒) which is a decoction of sugar and spices. Mixing honey and spices they make drinks (called) *meï, ssï-ta, hua* (眉思打華), which are heating and stimulating. Their coins are of both gold and silver. (It is a place) where big ships and wealthy traders congregate (巨舶富商皆聚焉). In the third year *yüan-yu* of Chö-tsung (1088 A. D.) in the eleventh moon, people sent by the Ta-shï of Ma-lo-pa presented tribute to our Court. Now this
30 Ma-lo-pa is the same as Ma-li-pa» (麻離扳). Sung-shï makes sundry mentions of «the country of Ma-lo-pa of the Ta-shï». It records (17,3) the coming of the mission of 1088, spoken of by Chóu K'ü-feï, and also (17,13) that of missions from the same country in 1089 and in 1094.

12) Shï-ho is Shehr, another port on the Hadramaut coast, of considerable importance in mediaeval times; it is the Esher (or Soer) of Marco Polo, see Yule's, Marco Polo (2[d] edit.), II,
35 324, 439 and Heyd, Hist. du Commerce, II, 500. See also infra, Pt. II, Ch. XXV.

Nu-fa is Zufar, the modern Dhofar (ظفار), the Dufar of Polo, about 400 miles E. of Shehr. Yule, op. cit., II. 441—442, Heyd, op. cit., II, 615. Ming-shï, 326, calls it Tsu-fa-ïr (祖法兒).

Ya-ssï-pau-hién, in Amoy dialect A-su-pau-han, is Ispahan or Isfahan. In the Yüan period we find the name written I-ssï-fa-hang (亦思法杭). Bretschneider, J. C. B.
40 A. S., X, See also infra, Pt. II, Ch. IX.

Lo-shï-meï in Cantonese Lo-shï-mi, appears to be a truncated transcription of Khwārizm, the country south of the sea of Aral; Lo-shï-meï probably representing the sound *rizm*. See also infra, Pt. II, Ch. IX. It is called Ho-lı-si-mi-kia (貨利習彌迦) by Hüan-tsang (Julien, III, 283), and is probably first referred to (Ts'ien Han-shu, 96A, 176) as one of the dependencies of
45 K'ang-k'u (Sogdiana) under the name of Au-kién (奧鞬), the old sound of which characters, according to Yen Shï-ku, was Uk-ken, which may be connected with the name of the present city of Kuhne, (Old) Urgendj, the Gorgânîya of the Middle Ages. In the commentary on this passage (see Han-shu Si-yü-chuan-pu-chu, 1,31) Au-kién is identified with Hüan-tsang's Ho-li-si-mi-kia, and the abbreviated names (appearing in T'ang-shu, 221 B,5) of Huo-sün (火尋) and Kuo-li (過利),
50 which the T'ang-shu says correspond with the site of the ancient city of Au-kién The description of the T'ang-shu leaves but little doubt about the identification of all these names with Khwārizm.

Mu-kü-lan, in Cantonese Muk-kü-lan, is the Makrān province; there is another reference to it in Pt. II, Ch. XXIX.

K'ié-li-ki, in Cantonese K'é-li-kat, is presumably Kalhát, the Calatu of Marco Polo II, 448). It carried on a lively trade with India in mediaeval times. It was subject to the prince of Hormuz.   5

P'i-no-yé, in Amoy dialect P'i-lok-ya, is a transcription of Arabic Ifrikya, Africa, but applied by the Arabs to that part of it which included the present Tunis and Tripoli. See Hirth, Die Länder des Islam, 27, note 6 and infra, Pt. II, Ch. XXXI.

13) I-lu, appears to be the province of Irāk. There is no other reference to it.

Pai-ta is Baghdad, see infra, Ch. XXX.   10

Ssï-lién, may very likely be Siraf (سيراف) on the Persian Gulf, which in the ninth and tenth centuries was the starting-point of the Arab ships engaged in the Indian and Chinese trade. It may, however, be Shīrāz. Our author makes no other reference to it.

Pai-lién, the island of Bahrein in the Persian Gulf. This is the only reference to it.

Tsi-ki, in Cantonese Tsik-kat, possibly the port of Tiz on the Makrān coast and in 15 mediaeval times its chief commercial centre. See Holdich, The Gates of India, 298—301. The name does not occur elsewhere in this or other Chinese works of the time.

Kan-meï, in Cantonese Kŏm-mui, in Amoy dialect Kam-bi. The name suggests the Comoro islands. It does not occur in any other passage of this work. It is hardly likely to be Cambay, which our author refers to under the name of Kan-pa-i (supra, p. 88).   20

P'u-hua-lo, is Bokhara. See Bretschneider, J. C. B. R. A. S., X, 240.

Ts'öng-pa, probably the Zanzibar coast; see infra, Ch. XXIV.

Pi-p'a-lo, is the Berbera coast, see infra, Chs. XXV and XXVII.

Wu-pa, possibly Sohar (سحار) on the Persian Gulf; see infra, Ch. XXVI.

Wöng-li, is an error for Wöng-(or Yung-)man, Oman; see infra, Ch. XXVIII.   25

Ki-shï, is the island of Kish (Keis), in the Persian Gulf; see infra, Ch. XXIX.

Ma-kia, is Mecca; see infra, Ch. XXIII.

Pi-ssï-lo, is Basra, at the head of the Persian Gulf; see infra, Ch. XXXI.

Ki-tz'ï-ni possibly Ghazni; see infra, Ch. XXXII.

Wu-ssï-li, in Cantonese Mat-ssï-li, is Mosul or Misr; see infra, Chs. XXXIII and XXXVI. 30

14) This and the preceding paragraph are based on T'ang-shu, 221^b. See Bretschneider, Ancient Chinese and Arabs, 7,9. The Sung-shï, 490,16 quotes these two paragraphs textually. It seems extraordinary that the Chinese should have had such a very vague notion of the Prophet's history and of the rise of Arab power. The Omayyad Merwán II, the last Caliph of the house of Omayya, was killed in A. D. 750. Abu'l-Abbás, the first of the Abbaside Caliphs («Black-robed 35 Ta-shï»), was proclaimed Caliph the same year at Kufa. Mohammed's Call was in A. D. 609 or 610; this may be the event referred to in our text.

15) Sung-shï, 2,3, says that on this occasion 157 persons were sent forth by the Emperor to visit the Western regions, to each of whom was given 30,000 cash. In book 490,16, this paragraph of our text is reproduced with only slight changes.   40

16) Li Yü, Prince of the Southern T'ang, after making his submission to the first Emperor of the Sung in A. D. 972, rebelled three years later and held Nanking against the imperial forces under Ts'au Pin. The city was taken by storm and the principality incorporated in the Empire. Macgowan, History of China, 365—366. Mayers, Chinese Reader's Manual, 231.

17) Ta-shï continued, however, to come to the Court of the Sung. Sung-shï, 2, 3, and 4, 45 make mention of their presence there in 973, 974, 975, 976, etc. In 976, the Ta-shï seem to have formed an official mission, the only one recorded down to that of 1019. In connexion with the mission of 976, Sung-shï, 3,10^b says the Prince of the Ta-shï was called K'o-li-fu (珂黎彿 Caliph) and the envoy's name was P'u-hi-mi (蒲希密 or Pu-lo-hai 不囉海 in another passage (490,16^b), both forms transcribing probably Abu-Hamid). Sung-shï, 490,18^b mentions 50 a Li-a-wu, who in 1008 sent presents to Court; he is called «ship-master» (舶主). See infra, note 23. A mission under an Arab came from P'o-ni (Borneo) in 977. See, infra, p. 157.

18) The «Court Chronicle» of the Sung-shï does not mention any visit of the Ta-shï in 993, though there is one recorded in 994. A mission which came to the court in 993, is referred to in some detail in Sung-shï, 490,16ᵇ et seqq. The head of the mission was again the one mentioned before as P'u-hi-mi (Abu-Hamid), aliàs Pu-lo-hai. He is described as the master of
5 an Arab vessel, but being too old and sick to proceed to court himself, he sent his assistant captain Li-a-wu with his credentials, in which he addresses the Emperor on his own behalf, thanking him for past favours bestowed on him and the foreign trade at Canton, while explaining the reasons for his not submitting his tribute in person. Then again in 995 a tribute mission arrived under the «ship-master» P'u-ya-t'o-li (蒲押陁黎), who deputed P'u-
10 hi-mi (Abu-Hamid) again to offer his tribute at court. During the audience the emperor enquired about his country, when he stated, among other details, that «it was conterminous with Ta-ts'in, which, being a dependency, was now governed by his native country» (與大秦國相 鄰爲其統屬今本國所管之). Then follows the account of the elephant and rhinoceros hunting. It will be seen that Chau Ju-kua differs by two years as to the date
15 of the audience. In 988 P'u-ya-t'o-li came again as envoy from San-fo-ts'i.

19) Sung-shï, 5,24 records a visit to the Court of China of Ta-shï and people from Pin-t'ung-lung in the third year chï-tau (A. D. 997), but none in the third year yung-hi; the nién-hau only differing. See also Sung-shï, 490,15ᵇ and supra, p. 52, note 3.

20) Between the visit of 997 and that of 1003, Sung-shï, 6,8, records the coming in 999 of
20 «South-western barbarians, people of Chan-ch'öng and Ta-shï». The following year it notes (6,11) the coming of people from Ta-shï, Korea, and Kau-chóu (高州) aborigines. Concerning the mission of 1003, two references are made to it, in the first (7,2) it is simply stated that in the sixth year hién-p'ing San-fo-ts'i and the Ta-shï came with presents. In the second reference (490,18ᵇ) it is said that in the sixth year hién-p'ing the Ta-shï sent as envoys «P'o-lo-k'in, San-ma-ni and
25 others» (婆羅欽三摩尼等) with tribute. «Ma-ni and the others were received in audience in the Chung-ch'öng tién (hall), etc.». Bretschneider, Ancient Chinese and Arabs, 15, referring to this mission (he puts it in 1004, and gives the name of the envoy as Po-kin-lo-san-mo-ni), is of opinion that the last three sounds of this name indicate an allusion to the Arabian dynasty of the Samanides, who reigned till the beginning of the eleventh century in the East and
30 had their capital in Bokhara. Chavannes, Le Nestorianisme, 38, 40—41, says of the word Ma-(or Mo-)ni (摩尼 also written 末泥) that it was used solely to designate Mohamme-dans. He refers to this mission of 1003 as a proof that the Mani were Moslim. According to Broomhall, Islam in China, 95, n. 2, Mo-ni has been sometimes used, erroneously, by the Chinese to transcribe the word Mullah. He gives an example of this in the K'ien-lung inscription
35 of 1764 in the Peking mosque on the Ch'ang-an-ta-chiéh. Devéria, Musulmans et Manichéens chinois (Journ. Asiat., 1897, X, 477) looks upon the words P'o-lo-k'in-san-ma-ni as an Arabic name, such as Balkin Samâni, or Balkin-es-Samâni. But this seems improbable. Samâni is wrong, and Devéria confounded Sāmānī (سامانی) and Sam'ānī (سمعانی); furthermore Balkin cannot be an Arabic word.
40 21) Sung-shï, 490,18ᵇ referring to this mission, uses the same language as our author, but, instead of the last four characters used by Chau, it has 賜錢縱其宴飲.

22) Conf. Sung-shï, 7,14ᵇ and 490,18ᵇ.

23) According to Sung-shï, 7,19, T'o-p'o-li came to Court in 1008, with people from San-fo-ts'i and «south-western barbarians». In another passage (490,13ᵇ) it is said that in the third
45 year hién-p'ing (A. D. 1000) «the ship-master (舶主) T'o-p'o-li sent as his messenger Mu-ki-pi (穆吉鼻) with presents to the Emperor; when Mu-ki-pi went back the Emperor sent to T'o-p'o-li a letter and also vessels (of porcelain), clothes, a saddle and a horse....» In the tenth moon of the first year ta-chung siang-fu (A. D. 1008), while the Emperor was absent in the eastern part of the Empire for sacrificial purposes, T'o-p'o-li asked to be allowed to go
50 to the T'ai-shan to there offer his presents to the Emperor. He was allowed to do so. (The same year) the ship-master Li-a-wu (see supra, p. 117, line 35) sent a messenger Ma-(hia-)wu (麻勿 Mohammed) by name, who presented to the Emperor a jade — stone badge (玉圭) of great

beauty ... » These references are of great interest as showing the closeness of the commercial relations existing between the Arab traders and the Court of China. The Sung-shï contains frequent references to these Arab ship-owners and their visits to the court of the Sung emperors. T'o-p'o-li was apparently given a Chinese title on the occasion of his visit of 1008, for in 1011 he is called «General who has returned to virtue» (歸 德 將 軍). He was again at 5 Court in 1019. Similar titles were conferred on other Arabs on subsequent occasions.

24) Fën-yin, is the present Wan-ch'üan (萬 泉) in P'u-chóu-fu in southern Shan-si. Playfair, Cities and Towns, № 7901. Conf. Sung-shï, 8,1 and 490,19ᵃ, where the list of presents is given; T'o-p'o-li is there spoken of as «K'ui-tö tsiang-kün T'o-p'o-li».

25) Sung-shï, 490,19ᵃ reproduces this story with a slight variant; it begins by saying: 10 «In 1012 it was said in Kuang-chóu that the Ta-shï Wu-si-hu-lu-hua had lived to the age of 130», etc. It is also given in the Tung-si-yang-k'au, 4,5ᵃ; the hero of the story is there said to have come from Achcen in Sumatra (啞 齊), «which was formerly a Ta-shï country», from which we may infer that, in the Ming period, Ku-lo was supposed to have been on the Sumatra coast. Conf. supra, p. 76.   15

26) Sung-shï, 17,13, says that in 1094 people from Mau-li (貌 黎 a country otherwise unknown, but which may be the same as the Mo-lai of the T'ang period, i. e., Kulam-Malé), Ma-lo-pa (麻 囉 拔 or 跋 Mirbāṭ) and Arabs (Ta-shï) brought presents to Court. No visit is recorded during the k'ai-hi period (Sung-shï, 38,8—18).

27) Ts'üan-chóu-fu-chï, as quoted in T'u-shu-tsi-ch'öng (Sect. VI, Ch. 1045), says that on 20 the Ling-shan, or «Hill of souls», in the south-eastern part of Ts'üan-chóu were the Mohammedan tombs or the «tombs of the Medina-men» as they were called. We have shown in a preceding note (supra, p. 14, n. 4) that there is some evidence that Islam was brought to Ts'üan-chóu in the early part of the seventh century. T'u-shu-tsi-ch'öng (Sec. VI, Ch. 1500), quoting local chronicles, says that a mosque called the Ch'ing-ching-ssï, was built by Moslims (Hu-jön) during 25 the period 1131 to 1163.

28) Sung-shï, 334,10 gives a biography of Lin Chï-k'i; he is there called Customs Inspector of Min (Fu-kién). He died in 1176. He wrote a number of works, one called Tau-shan-ki-wön (道 山 記 聞) is possibly that referred to. See Hirth, Länder des Islam, 33.

23.

         30

MECCA.

Ma-kia (麻 嘉).

The country of Ma-kia is reached if one travels from the country of Ma-lo-pa for eighty days westward by land.

This is the place where the Buddha Ma-hia-wu (麻 霞 勿) was born. 35 In the House of the Buddha the walls are made of jade stone (or precious stones) of every colour. Every year, when the anniversary of the death of the Buddha comes round, the people from all the countries of the Ta-shï assemble here, when they vie with each other in bringing presents of gold, silver, jewels and precious stones. Then also is the House adorned anew with silk brocade.

Farther off there is the tomb of the Buddha. Continually by day and night there is at this place such a brilliant refulgence (霞 光) that no one can approach it; he who does loses his sight.

Whosoever in the hour of his death rubs his breast with dirt taken from this tomb, will, they say, be restored to life again by the power of the Buddha.

Note.

The journey from Mirbāṭ on the Hadramaut coast, through the Tehama (south-west coast of Arabia) to Mecca was the old trade-route of the Sabeans, it is presumably the one referred to in our text.

The whole of this chapter is taken from Chóu K'ü-feï (3,2[b]). He says: «There is the country of Ma-kia, which is reached if one journeys for eighty days and more westward by land from the country of Ma-li-pa. It is the place where the Buddha Ma-hia-wu (Mohammed) was born. In the House (居 方 丈) of the Buddha, the facings of the walls of the rooms are of precious stones (玉) of every colour. Every year, when the anniversary of the Buddha's death comes round, all the princes of the Ta-shï send people bearing presents of jewels, gold and silver, and they cover the House (方 丈 i. e., the Kaaba) with silk brocades. Yearly the (various) countries (of the Ta-shï) come here to visit the House and to offer prayers. Furthermore the high officials of these countries are not deterred by a journey of a myriad li; they all assemble to worship the House.

«Farther off (literally, «behind» 後) there is the tomb of the Buddha, where day and night there is such a brilliant refulgence that no one can approach it, those who do shut their eyes (合 眼) and run by. It is said that if a man is dying and takes some dirt from off this tomb and smears it on his breast, he is restored to life, so great is the power of this Buddha!»

Chóu K'ü-feï is, so far as I am aware, the first Chinese author who wrote of Mecca. The T'ang-shu (221[b],23) speaks of Mohammed (摩 訶 末) and of Medina (摩 地 那), of the Black Stone of the Kaaba, but not of Mecca. It gives, however, some interesting information about Islam which our author might with advantage have incorporated in his work. Among other things, it speaks of the five daily prayers to the «Spirit of Heaven» (天 神), and of the mosques, which it calls li-t'ang (禮 堂), and which can hold many hundreds of people. «Here every seven days the king from a high seat speaks to those below saying: 'Those who die fighting shall be born in Heaven; those who kill an enemy shall receive happiness».

The «House of the Buddha» of Chóu's text is not the Prophet's birthplace (Maulid el Naby) in Mecca, but the «House of Allah» (Bayt Ullah), better known as the Kaaba or «cube house»; the Chinese name (方 丈) has the same sense. In the Yüan and Ming periods Mecca was called «The Heavenly square» (天 方), an abbreviation of the earlier name.

Burton, Pilgrimage to El Medinah and Meccah, II, 278 says that the birthday of the Prophet (twelfth of the month Rabi' el Auwal) is celebrated in Mecca with great festivities, feasts, prayers and perusals of the Koran.

On the brilliant light which is said to emanate from the tomb of the Prophet, conf. what Barthema, who was in Medina in 1503, says of it in his travels (Purchas, His Pilgrimes, IX, 66). When visiting the tomb of the Prophet, the Elders who accompanied him and the Captain of his party suddenly cried out; «we asked what was the cause of that exclamation. The Elders answered: Saw you not the lightning which shone out of the Sepulchre of the Prophet Mahumet. Our Captaine answered, that he saw nothing; and we also being demanded, answered in like manner .... It is therefore to be understood, that none other shining came out of the Sepulchre, than a certaine flame which the Priests caused to come out of the place of the Tower spoken of here before, whereby they would have deceived us».

Burton, op. cit., I, 309, n. 311, n., says that there is a superstitious story connected with the tomb of the Prophet (Masjid El Nabawi or «Prophet's Mosque») in Medina, that when the eunuchs who have charge of the tomb enter the baldaquin to place over the tomb a new kiswah, they guard their eyes with veils against the supernatural splendours which pour from the tomb. These eunuchs say that anyone who ventures to approach the tomb would be at once blinded by　5 the supernatural light.

24.

ZANGUEBAR.

Ts'öng-pa (層拔).

The Ts'öng-pa country is on an island of the sea south of Hu-ch'a-la.　10 To the west it reaches to a great mountain[1].

The inhabitants are of Ta-shï stock and follow the Ta-shï religion. They wrap themselves in blue foreign cotton stuffs (纏青番布) and wear red leather shoes. Their daily food consists of meal, baked cakes (燒餅) and mutton[2].　15

There are many villages, and a succession of wooded hills and terraced rocks[3] (鄉村山林多障岫層疊).

The climate is warm, and there is no cold season.

The products of the country consist of elephants' tusks, native gold, ambergris and yellow sandal-wood.　20

Every year Hu-ch'a-la and the Ta-shï localities along the sea-coast send ships to this country with white cotton cloth, porcelain, copper, and red cotton[4] (紅吉貝) to trade.

Notes.

1) Ts'öng-pa, in Cantonese Tsang-pat, is Zange-bār or Zanzibar «the region of the Blacks» which, according to Masudi (Prairies d'or, III, 7), extended along the east coast of Africa «from the channel issuing from the upper Nile» (presumably the River Jubb) to the land of Sofala and of the Wakwak. Marco Polo regarded the coast of Zanzibar as belonging to a great island like Madagascar. Yule & Burnell, Glossary, 746. Masudi (op. cit., III, 31) included in the land of the Zanj the islands along their coast, including that of Kanbalu (presumably Pemba) in which he tells　30 us (op. cit., I, 232) there lived a population of Mohammedans and Zanj idolaters. See infra, Ch. XXXVIII. 2.

The mention of a great mountain on the western border of the Ts'öng-pa country is very interesting; can it be Kilimanjaro? The placing of Ts'öng-pa to the south of Guzerat is readily explained by the fact that junks going from Guzerat to the east coast of Africa would have to　35 sail a general southerly course. See supra, p. 79, line 26 et seqq.

2) These Ta-shï lived probably in some town, Quiloa perhaps, on the coast. Ibn Batuta, II, 192 says that Culua (Quiloa) was a great city whose inhabitants were for the most part Zanj of very dark complexion. Masudi (op. cit., III, 6, 30—31) says that the Zanj were of the same

stock as the Abyssinians, they had no religion, but each man worshipped whatsoever he pleased, a plant, an animal, a stone.

3) Masudi, op. cit., III, 7—8, says that the country of the Zanj was 700 parasang long and as many wide. It was «cut by valleys and mountains and sandy deserts».

4) Masudi, op. cit., III, 7—8, says the land of the Zanj abounded in elephants; also that the ivory was shipped to Oman and thence to India and China. See also infra. Pt. II. Chs. XXXVI, XXXVIII. Marco Polo (II, 404) says that on the island of Madagascar «they had many trees of red sanders of excellent quality; in fact, all their forests consist of it». See also infra, Pt. II, Ch. XII. Marco Polo, II, 416 says of Zenghibar: «the staple trade of the Island is in elephant's teeth, which are very abundant; and they have also much ambergris, as whales are plentiful». The reference to sandal-wood as a product of Ts῾öng-pa is interesting, it was probably brought there from Madagascar, which seems vaguely referred to in Ch. XXXVIII, 2.

Chinese porcelain of the Sung dynasty has been found in Zanzibar. Dr. S. W. Bushell says (North China Daily News, May 9, 1888): «Sir John Kirk during his residence as Consul-General at Zanzibar, made a collection of ancient Chinese céladon porcelain... Some of it was dug up, I believe from ruins, mixed with Chinese cash of the Sung dynasty ...» See also Hirth, J. A. O. S., XXX, 55—57 and S. W. Bushell. Description of Chinese pottery and porcelain, XVI.

Theo. Bent found among the ruins in the fort of Gibliah on the island of Bahrein, numerous fragments of «fine Nankin and Céladon china, attesting to the ubiquity and commerce of the former owners ...» Southern Arabia, 18.

Sung-shǐ, 490,20ᵇ—21ᵃ, contains a short description of a country called Ts῾öng-t῾an (層檀) which we are disposed to think is practically the same as the Ts῾öng-pa of our author, or some place in it, though the second character of the name is puzzling. It reads as follows: «Ts῾öng-t῾an is on the Southern Ocean. The town is twenty *li* from the sea-coast. In the fourth year *hi-ning* (A. D. 1071) it brought presents to our Court for the first time. Travelling by sea, and with a favourable wind (the monsoon), the envoy took a hundred and sixty days. He passed by Wu-sün (勿巡 presumably some place near Maskat), Ku-lin (古林 Quilon) and San-fo-ts῾ï (Palembang), and came to Kuang-chóu. The ruler of the country was named A-meï-lo A-meï-lan (亞美羅亞眉蘭 [Pers. *amîr-i-amîrân*]). They (the A-meï-lo) had ruled the country for five hundred years (during which time there had been) ten generations. The language sounds like that of the Arabs (Ta-shǐ). The climate (of Ts῾öng-t῾an) is warm all the year. The wealthy people wear turbans of *yüe-(no)* stuff and clothes of flowered brocade, or of *po-tié* cloth. They go forth riding elephants or on horseback. They have official salaries. According to their laws light offenses are punished with the bamboo, serious crimes with death.

«Of cereals, they have rice, millet and wheat. For food they eat fish. Of animals they have sheep (棉羊), goats, buffalo (沙牛), water-buffalo, camels, horses, rhinoceros and elephants. Of drugs they have putchuck, dragon's-blood, myrrh, borax, asa-foetida, frankincense. Of products, pearls, glass (*p῾o-li*), and three kinds of drinks called *mi* (密 Persian, *mei*, «wine») *sha* (沙 Arab-Persian, *sharāb*, *sherbet*) and *hua* (華 ?). In commercial transactions they use coins made by the Government only; three parts are of gold and copper in equal proportion, the fourth of silver. The people are forbidden coining them themselves.

«In the sixth year *yüan-föng* (A. D. 1083) the envoy Pau-shun-lang-tsiang Ts῾öng-k῾ié-ni (保順郎將層伽尼 the last three characters may mean «the Zanj») came again to Court. The Emperor Shön-tsung, considering the very great distance he had come, besides giving him the same presents which had been formerly bestowed on him, added thereto 2,000 ounces of silver».

25.

BERBERA COAST.

Pi-p'a-lo (弼 琶 囉).

The country of Pi-p'a-lo contains four cities (州); the other (places) are
all villages which are (constantly) at feud and fighting with each other[1].   5

The inhabitants pray to Heaven and not to the Buddha[2].

The land produces many camels and sheep, and the people feed
themselves with the flesh and milk of camels and with baked cakes (燒 餅)[3].

The (other) products are ambergris, big elephants' tusks and big rhinoceros horns. There are elephants' tusks which weigh over one hundred catties, 10
and rhinoceros horns of over ten catties weight.

The land is also rich in putchuck, liquid storax gum, myrrh, and tortoise
shell of extraordinary thickness, for which there is a great demand in other
countries[4].

«The country brings forth also the (so-called) «camel-crane» (駱 駝 鶴), 15
which measures from the ground to its crown from six to seven feet. It has
wings and can fly, but not to any great height»[5].

There is also (in this country) a wild animal called *tsu-la* (徂 蠟); it
resembles a camel in shape, an ox in size, and is of a yellow colour. Its fore
legs are five feet long, its hind legs only three feet. Its head is high up and 20
turned upwards. Its skin is an inch thick[6].

There is also (in this country) a kind of mule with brown, white and
black stripes around its body. These animals wander about the mountain
wilds; they are a variety of the camel (駱 駝 之 別 種 也). The inhabitants of this country, who are great huntsmen, hunt these animals with 25
poisoned arrows[7].

Notes.

1) Pi-p'a-lo, in Cantonese, Pat-pa-lo, which represents Par-pa-ra (see Hirth, Chinesische
Studien, I, 33), is Berbera, the Somali coast generally. The earliest mention of this country in
Chinese works is probably in the Yu-yang-tsa-tsu, 4,3[b], which was written in the middle of the 30
ninth century. It runs as follows: «The land of Pa-pa-li (撥 拔 力 Cantonese, Pat-pat-lik) is
in the south-western Ocean. They do not eat any cereals, but they eat meat; more frequently
even they prick a vein of one of their oxen, mix the blood with milk and eat it uncooked. They
have no clothes, but they wrap round their waists a sheep's skin which hangs down and covers
them. Their women are clear-skinned and well-behaved. The people of this country make their 35
own countrymen prisoners whom they sell to strangers at prices many times more than they would
fetch (at home). The products of the country are elephants' tusks and *a-mo* perfume (阿 末
香 Cantonese *o-mut*, Arabic 'anbar, i. e., ambergris).

«When Po-ssï (Persian) traders wish to enter this country, they form a caravan of several thousand men, and after having made (the natives) a present of strips of cloth (? 繰 布), all of them both young and old draw blood by pricking themselves and take an oath (刺 血 立 誓), after which they trade their goods.

5   «From of old (this country) has never been subject to any foreign power. In fighting they use elephant's tusks, ribs, and wild cattle's horns as spears, and they have corselets (甲 衣), and bows and arrows. They have twenty myriads of foot-soldiers. The Arabs are continually making raids on them». In a slightly abridged form, T'ang-shu, 222B,13b substantially reproduces the above. See Hirth, J. C. B. R. A. S., XXI, 219 and J. A. O. S. XXX, 47—51.

10   The four towns referred to were probably Berbera — the Barbara of western mediaeval writers, Zeila, which Ibn Batuta says was the capital of the country, Magadoxo, Ibn Batuta's Makdashan, and possibly Brawa. Ibn Batuta, op. cit., II, 180 says the Berbera country extended from Zeila to Magadoxo.

    2) Our author presumably refers only to the inhabitants of the four cities as being Moslims.

15   3) Ibn Batuta, op. cit., II, 180—181 says the people of Zeila and Magadoxo killed several hundred camels daily for food. He also refers to the wealth in sheep of the people of the latter place. See also what our author says of the people of Chung-li (infra, Ch. XXVII), which is also Somaliland.

    4) The Periplus, in the first century, mentions among the exports from the Berbera coast 20 myrrh, a little frankincense, tin, ivory, tortoise-shell, odoriferous gums and cinnamon. On the various products here mentioned, see infra, Ch. XXVII, and Pt. II.

    5) Quotation from Ling-wai-tai-ta, 3,6ª. The ostrich was first made known to the Chinese in the beginning of the second century of our era, when some were brought to the court of China from Parthia. The Chinese then called them An-si-tsio (安 息 雀 «Parthian bird»). See 25 Hóu-Han-shu, 88, and Hirth, China and Roman Orient, 39. In the Weï-shu, 102,12b, no name is given them, they are simply «big birds which resemble a camel, which feed on herbs and flesh and are able to eat fire». In the T'ang-shu, 221B,7ª it is said that this bird is commonly called «camel-bird» (駝 鳥) It is seven feet high, black of colour, its feet like those of the camel, it can travel three hundred li a day, and is able to eat iron.

30   The ostrich is called by the Persians ushturmurgh and by the Arabs teir al-djamal, both meaning «camel-bird». See Actes du Congrès Internat. Oriental., 1889, 21—22, and Bretschneider, Mediaeval travel., 87, n. 132.

    Chóu K'ü-feï (op. cit., 3,6) says the lo-t'o-hau (he uses the same name for the ostrich as our author) is found in K'un-lun-ts'öng-k'i — which, according to his views, apparently, embraced 35 all the east coast of Africa, but which he conceived to be a great island. See infra, Ch. XXXVIII, 2, note 1.

    6) Tsu-la, in Cantonese, ts'o-lap, is, of course, the girafe. The Chinese name is Persian zurnāpā, surnāpā (Meninski, but commonly ushturgāv, i. e. «camel-ox») «girafe», in Arabic zarāfa. Masudi, op. cit., III, 3, remarks that some people think the girafe is a variety of camel. He 40 adds, that it is very plentiful in the country of the Zanj — the Blacks.

    7) The zebra is found in parts of southern Abyssinia. In the Ming period we hear of the «spotted fu-lu» (花 福 祿) as found in the country of Brawa (不 剌 哇) near Magadoxo; Bretschneider, Ancient Chinese and Arabs, 27, conjectures that this was a species of zebra, the Hippotigris Burchelli, or Douw, the «Tiger-horse» of the ancients.

45   Duarte Barbosa, Coasts of East Africa, etc., 16, noted that the people of Magadoxo «use herbs with their arrows».

---

*

26.

SOHAR (?).

Wu-pa (勿 拔).

The country of Wu-pa is on the sea-coast and a land road leads hence to the Ta-shï. The king is of a dark brown complexion (紫 棠 色), he 5 wears a turban and a jacket. He follows both the religion and the rules (of daily life) of the Ta-shï.

Note.

The name Wu-pa does not occur in any other mediaeval Chinese work known to us. It appears possible that it is the same place referred to by Kia Tan as Wu-la (烏 剌) and 10 which, there is some reason to think, may have been Sohar. See supra, p. 14, n. 1. We are told (infra, p. 133) that Wöng-man, which is certainly Oman, was like Wu-pa in people and general conditions; this strengthens the belief that the two localities were in pretty close proximity to each other. Edrisi (Jaubert's trans., I, 152) speaking of Sohar says: «Formerly there came there traders from all parts of the world to bring the products of Yemen and export all kinds of things, and this 15 contributed to the prosperity of the country, which was besides rich in dates, figs, pomegranates, quinces and other fruits of superior quality. Expeditions to China were made from there; but all this state of things has come to an end» since the rise of the pirate nest on the island of Kish, which drove the trade of the Persian Gulf back to Aden.

27.   20

SOMALI COAST.

Chung-li (中 理).

The inhabitants of the Chung-li country go bareheaded and barefooted, they wrap themselves in cotton stuffs, but they dare not wear jackets, for the wearing of jackets and turbans is a privilege reserved to the ministers and 25 the king's courtiers. The king lives in a brick house covered with glazed tiles, but the people live in huts made of palm leaves and covered with grass-thatched roofs. Their daily food consists of baked flour cakes, sheep's and camel's milk. There are great numbers of cattle, sheep and camels[1].

Among the countries of the Ta-shï this is the only one which produces 30 frankincense[2].

There are many sorcerers among them who are able to change themselves into birds, beasts, or aquatic animals, and by these means keep the ignorant people in a state of terror. If some of them in trading with some foreign ship have a quarrel, the sorcerers pronounce a charm over the ship, so that it can neither go forward nor backward, and they only release the ship when it has settled the dispute. The government has formally forbidden this practice[3].

Every year countless numbers of birds of passage (飛 禽) alight in the desert parts of this country. When the sun rises, they suddenly disappear, so that one cannot find a trace of them. The people catch them with nets, and eat them; they are remarkably savoury. They are in season till the end of spring, but, as soon as summer comes, they disappear, to come back the following year.

When one of the inhabitants dies, and they are about to bury him in his coffin, his kinsfolk from near and far come to condole. Each person, flourishing a sword in his hand, goes in and asks the mourners the cause of the person's death. «If he was killed by the hand of man, each one says, we will revenge him on the murderer with these swords». Should the mourners reply that he was not killed by any one, but that he came to his end by the will of Heaven, they throw away their swords and break into violent wailing.

Every year there are driven on the coast a great many dead fish measuring two hundred feet in length and twenty feet through the body. The people do not eat the flesh of these fish, but they cut out their brains, marrow, and eyes, from which they get oil, often as much as three hundred odd *töng* (from a single fish). They mix this oil with lime to caulk their boats, and use it also in lamps. The poor people use the ribs of these fish to make rafters, the backbones for door leaves, and they cut off vertebrae to make mortars with[4].

There is a mountain (or island, 山) in this country which forms the boundary of Pi-p'a-lo. It is four thousand *li* around it — for the most part uninhabited. Dragon's-blood is procured from this mountain, also aloes (蘆 薈), and from the waters (around it) tortoise-shell and ambergris.

It is not known whence ambergris comes; it suddenly appears in lumps of from three to five or ten catties in weight, driven on the shore by the wind. The people of the country make haste to divide it up, or ships run across it at sea and fish it up[5].

Notes.

1) Chung-li, as a name of a country, does not occur in any other Chinese writer before or after Chau Ju-kua. There is no doubt, however, that the region to which it is applied is the Somali coast, but it included the island of Socotra. The name itself is not identified; it seems to point to the word Zing, Zang or Zenj, for the mediaeval Arab writers refer to this region as the «country of the Blacks» (Zanj). Ibn Batuta, II, 180 says, the country of the Blacks extended

from Zeila on the Berbera coast to Magadoxo. See also Masudi, op. cit., III, 6, and supra. The town in which the king of Chung-li lived may well have been Magadoxo.

2) The African frankincense, also called by the Ancients Peratic and Libyan frankincense, was found according to the Periplus (§ 11), near Cape Aromata (Ras Jardafun), and there only; the supply, it says, was most abundant, and it was of the very finest quality. See also infra, Pt. II.   5 Ch. II. Socotra produced, and still produces, frankincense. See Bent, Southern Arabia, 380, 381.

3) Ibn Batuta, IV, 227, says that the natives of the island of Barahnagar, which was between Bengal and Sumatra, used to raise storms by enchantment. Marco Polo (II, 399) speaks of the sorcery of the people of Socotra in nearly the same terms as Chau Ju-kua: «And you must know that in this Island there are the best enchanters in the world. It is true that 10 their Archbishop forbids the practice to the best of his ability; but 'tis all to no purpose, for they insist that their forefathers followed it, and so must they also. I will give you a sample of their enchantments. There, if a ship be sailing past with a fair wind and a strong, they will raise a contrary wind and compel her to turn back. In fact they make the wind blow as they list, and produce great tempests and disasters; and other such sorceries they perform, which it will be 15 better to say nothing about in our Book».

Friar Joanno dos Santos (A. D. 1597) says «In the Ile of Zanzibar dwelt one Chande, a great Sorcerer, which caused his Pangayo, which the Factor had taken against his will, to stand still as it were in defiance of the Winde, till the Factor had satisfied him, and then to fly forth the River after her fellowes at his words. He made that a Portugall which had angered him, 20 could never open his mouth to speake, but a Cocke crowed in his belly, till he had reconciled himselfe: with other like odious sorceries». See Purchas, His Pilgrimes, IX, 254.

Not twenty years ago Theo. Bent found that the Somalis were afraid of the witchcraft of the natives of Socotra. Theo. Bent, Southern Arabia, 361.

4) Eastern and Western mediaeval writers all speak of the vast numbers of whales in the 25 Indian Ocean and the Persian Gulf. Kazwini says that whales were often caught by the low tide in the channels near Basra. The people harpooned them and got much oil out of the brain, which they used for their lamps and smearing ships. Reinaud, Relations, I, 145—146. Marco Polo speaks of the capture of whales by the people of Socotra, and of the great abundance of whales and of capdols («oil-heads», spermaceti whales) off the Zanguebar coast (II, 399, 404).   30

Töng (㭷) is not known as a measure of capacity. It is usually the Sanskrit *tola*, a weight equal to 4 *mashas*. In our text the character must transcribe some other foreign word, Persian probably. Conf. supra, p. 69, n. 2. Edrisi, I, 95, 96, says: «All Chinese ships, big or little, which sail the sea of China, are solidly built of wood. The pieces bearing the one on the other are arranged in geometric figures, secured (against leaking) by palm fibres and caulked with 35 flour and whale oil . . . . This oily substance is famous in the Yemen, at Aden, on the coast of Fars, of Oman, and in the seas of India and China The people of these regions use this substance to caulk their ships». Conf. also Reinaud, Relations, I, 144—146.

All authors from the time of Nearchus (Arrian, Hist. Indica, §§ 29, 30) have spoken of the huts on the Makrān coast built with whale bones; although I find no references to this 40 custom having obtained on the Berbera or Somali coast, there is no reason to suppose that it did not. See Mc Crindle, Commerce and navigation of the Erythræan Sea, 196, 197.

5) The Periplus (§ 30) already mentions dragon's-blood as a product of the island of Dioskorides (Socotra), and it has continued one of the principal exports of the island ever since. See infra, Pt. II, Ch. IV. Socotra was famous from ancient times for its aloes which, according to 45 Edrisi (I, 47), was exported thence to the East and the West. Heyd, Hist. du Commerce, II, 563. Marco Polo (II, 399) speaks of the ambergris of the island. See infra, Pt. II, Ch. XXX and XLI, and Reinaud, Relations, I, 139. Also Duarte Barbosa, op. cit., 30.

The island of Socotra is very mountainous; Mount Haghier «rises in many jagged and stupendous peaks to the height of nearly 5,000 feet... The glory of Mount Haghier is undoubtedly 50 its dragon's-blood tree (Dracaenia cinnabari), found scattered at an elevation of about 1,000 feet and upwards over the greater part of Sokotra»... Theo. Bent, Southern Arabia, 378—379, 388.

28.

OMAN.

Yung (or Wöng-)man (甕 蠻).

The country of Yung-man resembles Wu-pa as regards inhabitants and
5 the products of the soil. The chief of the country wears a turban, wraps
himself in light silk, but wears no garments and goes barefooted. His servants
wear no headdress and go barefooted, but they wrap themselves in sarongs
(縵) so that the body is covered. They live on meal cakes, mutton, sheep's·
milk, fish and vegetables. The soil produces dates in large quantities. Along
10 the coast pearls are found, and in the mountains horse raising is carried on
on a large scale. The other countries which trade here purchase horses,
pearls and dates which they get in exchange for cloves, cardamom seeds and
camphor.

Note.

15   In the list of Arab states given in a previous chapter (supra, p. 117) the name of this
country is erroneously written Wöng-li. According to the Arab relations of the ninth century
(Reinaud, Relations, I, 13—15) the products of Oman and other countries were brought to
Siraf on the Fars coast and there loaded on ships which sailed to India. These ships touched at
Maskat in Oman for water and provisions, but apparently Maskat carried on no important direct
20 trade with the East at that time. A century later Masudi, op. cit., I, 281, speaks of the ships
of Siraf and Oman which sailed the seas of China, India, Sind, of the Zendj (Zanguebar), the
Yemen, of Kolzum and of Abyssinia, — but down to the twelfth century the centre of the Indian
and Chinese trade of the Persian Gulf was at Siraf, though it was already suffering at that time
from the pirates of Kish, who in the thirteenth century brought about its complete ruin. Then Ormuz
25 began its great career, and Aden took much of the trade of the Persian Gulf.
     In a subsequent chapter (infra, p. 137) our author states that Wöng-man and Kish
traded regularly with Basra.
     Ibn Batuta, op. cit., II, 374 says that the fleetest horses brought to India came from
the Yemen, Oman and Fars, and that Oman supplied the neighbouring countries with dates.
30 Marco Polo (II, 324) mentions Sohár (Soer) in Oman as one of the principal points from which
horses were brought to India. See also Heyd, Hist. du Commerce, II, 135.
     Masudi, op. cit., I, 328 says pearls were only found in the sea of Abyssinia, in Kharek,
Kotor, Oman, and Serendib. See infra, Pt. II, Ch. XXXIV.

29.

35

ISLAND OF KISH.

Ki-shï (記 施).

The country of Ki-shï is on a small island (嶼) in the sea, in sight of
the Ta-shï (coast), which is distant from it a half day's journey[1]. There are

very few towns (管 州) (in this region). When the king shows himself in
public, he rides a horse and has a black umbrella over him; he is accompanied by over an hundred retainers.

The people of the country are white and clean and eight feet tall. They
wear their hair loose under a turban eight feet long, one half of which hangs   5
down their back. Their clothing consists of a foreign-shaped jacket and an
outer wrap of light silken or woollen stuff, and red leather shoes. They make
use of gold and silver coins. Their food consists of wheaten cakes, mutton,
fish and dates. They do not eat rice. The country produces pearls and fine
horses.   10

Every year the Ta-shï send camels loaded with rose-water, gardenia
flowers, quicksilver, spelter, silver bullion, cinnabar (硃 砂), red dye plants
(紫 草), and fine cotton stuffs, which they put on board ships on arriving
in this country (本 國) to barter with other countries[2].

Notes.   15

1) Le Strange, Lands of the Eastern Caliphate, 257, says that the island of Kays, or, as
the Persians wrote the name, Kīsh, in the course of the twelfth century became the trade centre
of the Persian Gulf after the ruin of Sīrāf. «A great walled city was built in Kays island, where
water tanks had been constructed, and on the neighbouring sea-banks was the famous pearl
fishery. Ships from India and Arabia crowded the port, and all the island was full of palm   20
gardens ...... The island lay about four leagues from the coast, where the port of embarcation
was Huzū, to which, in the thirteenth century, a caravan road came down from Shīrāz through
Lāghir». A. W. Stiffe, Geog. Journal, VII, 644—649, says nine miles separate at the present time
the island from the Persian coast. The centre of old trade was on the north coast of the island.
See also Marco Polo, I, 64, II, 324 and Ibn Batuta, IV, 168. Chinese writers of the Yüan period 25
transcribed the name of the island K'ié-shï (怯 失). Bretschneider, Med. geography, II, 129.

2) The adjoining province of Fars was celebrated for the so-called attar of roses ('aṭar
or 'iṭr in Arabic signifies 'a perfume' or 'essence'), which, of divers qualities, was more especially made from the roses that grew in the plain round Jūr or Firūzābad. — Le Strange, op.
cit., 293. Marco Polo, II, 324, refers to the importance of the horse trade of Kish. Barbosa 30
mentions vermilion and quicksilver among the exports from Jeddah, Aden and Ormuz. Duarte
Barbosa, Coasts of East Africa, etc., 23, 27, 42. (Hakluyt Soc. edit.).

The «red dye plant» is madder. John Jourdain (1609) speaking of the trade of Aden says,
that the ships from India and Muscat carried back gum arabic, frankincense and myrrh, «and
an herbe which groweth here called fua or runa, which they carrie to the Indies to dye red   35
withall». See the Journal of John Jourdain (Hakl. Soc. edit.) 177. A century before Jourdain,
Varthema, speaking also of Aden, said: «yeerely from the Citie of Aden, depart fifteene or twentie
ships laden with Rubricke, which is brought out of Arabia Felix». فُوَّة fūwah is the Arabic
name for madder, rūnās, the Persian.

Kish carried on an important trade in slaves. Edrisi, I, 58 refers to the expeditions 40
which the Kish pirates sent to the Zanguebar coast on slave raids. Our author (infra, p. 137) says
it carried on trade with Basra.

30.

BAGHDAD.

___

Pai-ta (白 達).

«The country of Pai-ta is the great metropolis (一 都 會) of all the countries of the Ta-shï». Travelling by land from Ma-lo-pa one comes to it after about 130 days journey, passing on the way some fifty cities (州). This country is extremely powerful and large, and the number of its foot-soldiers and cavalry armed and equipped is very great[1].

«The king is a direct successor of the Buddha Ma-hia-wu», and the throne has, down to the present time, been transmitted through twenty-nine generations (代), covering a period of from six to seven hundred years[2]. «The other lands of the Ta-shï have waged war against each other, but none have dared to invade this country».

«When the king appears in public, a black umbrella is carried (over him); its handle is of gold and on the top is a jade lion with a golden moon on its back, shining like a star and visible from afar off»[3].

«The towns and markets are cut by well-made streets, and the people live lavishly. There is great store of precious things and of satins». There is little rice, fish and vegetables; the people «eat cakes, meat and su-lo[4] (酥 酪 butter).

«The products of the country are gold and silver, engraved glassware (liu-li) of the finest quality, white yüé-no cloth and liquid storax».

The inhabitants like to wear turbans and clothes of fine snow-white cotton (雪 布)». Every seven days they cut their hair and nails, and five times daily they pray to (or worship) Heaven (禮 拜 天)[5]; they profess the religion of the Ta-shï. As they (i. e., the Caliphs) are the descendants of the Buddha (i. e., the Prophet), the people of other countries come thither to do them honour.

Notes.

1) The phrases and parts of phrase in quotation marks in this chapter are from Ling-wai-tai-ta, 3,3ª. It is doubtful whether Po-ta (勃 達) of Tʻang-shu, 221B, 24ᵇ, is Baghdad, as in a subsequent passage in the same chapter it is said that the king of Po-ta, Mo-ho-sö-ssï received in A. D. 747 the title of a Chinese prince, together with five other petty kings, for Baghdad was only founded six years later, in 753. In the Yüan period the name was written Pau-ta (報 達), Pa-há-ta (八 哈 塔), and Pa-ki-ta (八 吉 打). See Bretschneider, Med. geogr., 287, and Med. travell., 67. Marco Polo must have taken his name for Baghdad — Baudas, from the Chinese.

Our author in another passage (supra, p. 124) gives the distance from Ma-lo-pa, i. e., Merbat on the Hadramaut coast of Arabia, to Mecca as eighty days' travel, he consequently allowed fifty days for the journey from Mecca to Baghdad. In another passage (infra, p. 138) he says that

Ki-tz'ï-ni, which there is some reason for identifying with Ghazni, was only a hundred and twenty stages from Ma-lo-pa. The probable explanation appears to be that his informant had travelled from Merbat to Baghdad, but had only the vaguest notion of Ki-tz'ï-ni. Confer this chapter with our author's chapter on Ta-ts'in (supra p. 102 seqq.).

    2) Since the remark about the number of generations during which the throne has been 5 transmitted does not occur in the Ling-wai-tai-ta, we may look upon it as a clue as to the time when Chau Ju-kua collected his information. In calculating the number of generations we cannot, of course, go beyond the Abbaside dynasty, because our text distinctly refers to a descendant of Mohammed as caliph of Baghdad. On the other hand the Arab, or Persian, traveller who supplied the information cannot have ignored the several caliphs who held the throne before 10 the Abbasides. From a genealogical point of view we have therefore to start from the one ancestor in whom the several dynasties, including the early rival chiefs of the Koreish tribe, united Mohammed the Prophet's ancestor Kusai, who represents the first generation in the following table derived from Lane-Poole's The Mohammedan Dynasties, 10—15, and Sir William Muir's The Life of Mahomet, 3ᵈ ed. p. XCV.   15

Generation 1 . . . . Ḳuṣai (fifth cent. A. D.)

2.	'Abd-Al-Dār	'Abd-Manāf		
3.	(headed a rival house of the Koreish tribe)	Hāshim		'Abd-Shams
4.		'Abd-al-Muṭṭalib		Omaiya
5.	'Abd-Allāh;	Abū-Ṭālib;	'Abbās	Omaiyad Dynasty 20
6.	Mohammed the Prophet		'Abd-Allāh	
7.	Fāṭimah = 'Alī		'Alī	
8.	Ḥasan	Ḥusain	Mohammed	
9.		1. Abu-'l-'Abbās;	2. Manṣūr	
10.		3. Mahdī		25
11.		4. Hādī; 5. Rashīd;	Manṣūr; Ibrāhīm·	
12.		6. Amīn; 7. Ma'mūn; 8. Mu'taṣim		
13.	Mohammed; 9. Wāthik;		10. Mutawakkil	
14.	12. Musta'īn; 14. Muhtadī;	11. Muntaṣir; 13. Mu'tazz;	15. Mu'tamid; Muwaffaḳ	
15.		Ibn-al-Mu'tazz	16. Mu'taḍid	30
16.	17. Muktafī	18. Muḳtadir	19. Ḳāhir	
17.	22. Mustakfī	20. Rāḍī; 21. Muttaḳi;	23. Muṭi'	
18.		25. Ḳādir;	24. Ṭà'ï	
19.		26. Ḳâ'im		
20.		Jāhirat-al-dīn		35
21.		27. Muḳtaḍī		
22.		28. Mustaẓhir		
23.	29. Mustarshid;	31. Muktafī		
24.	30. Rāshid;	32. Mustanjid		
25.		33. Mustaḍī		40
26.		34. Nāṣir		
27.		35. Ẓāhir		
28.		36. Mustanṣir		
29.		37. Musta'ṣim (1242—1258 A. D.)		

It appears that this is the only manner in which we may account for the twenty-nine generations referred to by Chau Ju-kua, whose informant ought to have spoken of twenty-four generations, and not twenty-nine, if he had looked upon the Prophet as the genealogical head. On the other hand the «six, or seven hundred years» of his text can only refer to the Prophet 5 himself, who died in 632 A. D. We may be allowed to look upon this passage as a clue helping us to fix the time of Chau Ju-kua's collecting his notes as falling between the years 1242 and 1258, the reign of the last Abbaside Caliph Musta'ṣim.

The only event Chau appears to have known of in the life of the Prophet is that mentioned previously in the vaguest terms (supra, p. 117) and which corresponds roughly with A. D. 610, the 10 date of Mohammed's Call. Six hundred years counted from that date (or even for that matter from 632, when the Prophet died) brings us down to the first half of the thirteenth century, which agrees with the previous conclusions.

3) Conf. supra, p. 103 our author's description of the ruler of Ta-ts'in. The «golden moon» on the top of the king's baldachin must have been a crescent, since, as an emblem, it would 15 otherwise have been taken for «a sun». The origin of the crescent among the Turks is wrapped in mystery, and this passage, (written before the year 1178), seems to support A. Müller's conjecture, who finds it mentioned by Mirkhond in connection with Sebuktegin, tenth century; see A. Müller, Der Islam im Morgen- und Abendland, Berlin, 1887, II, 72, note.

4) The Ling-wai-tai-ta differs slightly here; it says: «All the people eat cakes, meat and 20 *su-lo*, but rarely fish, vegetables or rice ..... What is called pliable opaque glass is a product of this country» (所謂軟琉璃者國所產也). I suppose annealed glass is referred to. Our author in the next paragraph refers to polished (ground, or engraved 碾花) opaque glass. The term *nién-hua* is not clear; I incline for «engraved». See infra, p. 138, and Pt. II, Ch. XXXII. On *su-lo* see p. 139 n. 1.

25   5) Heyd. Hist. du Commerce, II, 711 states that in the Middle Ages Damascus was particularly celebrated for its glass, as was also Kadesia near Baghdad, and other places in Irak.

The remark about cutting the finger nails and the daily prayers is a repetition of what he states in another passage, supra, p. 116 lines 9—10.

—

31.

BASRA.

—

Pi-ssï-lo (弼斯囉).

When the lord of the Pi-ssï-lo country shows himself in public, he is accompanied by more than a thousand mounted retainers in full armour of iron, the officers wearing coats of mail (連環鎖子甲). He receives the 35 orders of Pai-ta.

The people live on baked meal cakes, and mutton. Their almanack is tolerably correct, as regards the hot and cold seasons of the year, but they do not know of the new and full moon days (as holidays).

The products of the country are camels, sheep and dates. The Ki-shï 40 and Wöng-man countries send every year trading parties to this country.

Note.

Al-Basrah, the great commercial port of Baghdad and Mesopotamia, lay on the Arabian side of the estuary of Al-Baṣrah, in other words the Blind Tigris, and was about twelve miles, as the crow flies, from its bank. Muḳaddasi (10th century) says the town measured three miles across in its greatest width. The modern village of Zubayr now occupies the site of old Baṣra. 5 The city was founded in 638 A. D. in the reign of Omar. The city of Ubullah (the Apologos of the Greeks) was on the Tigris at the mouth of the canal of Ubullah (Nahr-al-Ubullah) which put it in communication with Baṣra. See Le Strange, J. R. A. S., 1895, 304, and Land of the Eastern Caliphate, 44.

Marco Polo (I, 64) speaks of the «great city of Bastra, surrounded by woods, in which 10 grow the best dates in the world». Ibn Batuta, II, 9 and IV, 376 speaks of the great abundance of dates at Basra. He says that a honey, called *sayalān* (سيلان), was made at Basra from dates.

Chóu K'ü-feï does not mention Basra, nor does any other Chinese author known to us either prior to our author or subsequently.

32.

15

GHAZNI (?).

Ki-tz'ï-ni (吉 慈 尼).

The Ki-tz'ï-ni country is reached from Ma-lo-pa in about an hundred and twenty stages. The country lies to the north-west, and is exceptionally cold, the winter's snow not melting until the spring. «This country is surrounded by high 20 mountains, and the city (or wall 城) is cut out in (the rocks of the) mountains. It is about two hundred *li* square and is surrounded by water. It has some two hundred mosques. The officials and the people all go to the mosques to pray, which they call *ch'u-mi*» (厨 幰), (Note: some write it *shu* 除).

«The people are, for the most part, well off, and live in houses five or 25 six storeys high. There is a great deal of camel and horse breeding». «The people eat cakes, meat, and *ju-lo* (乳 酪), but little fish and rice»; they also make use of a mixture of cow's milk and water as an habitual beverage [1].

The king's arms reach down to below his knees. He has an hundred chargers, every one full six feet high, also some dozen head of mules, three 30 (sic) feet high, which, on excursions, he rides alternately with the horses. His bow pulls several piculs, so that five or seven ordinary men cannot string it. When he is on horseback, he carries an iron mace weighing full fifty catties. The Ta-shï and all the people of the West fear him [2]. «The products of the soil are gold, silver, *yüé-no* cloth, gold brocade, camel's hair stuffs in all 35 colours (五 色 駞 毛 段), engraved opaque glass (碾 花 琉 璃), liquid storax, *wu-ming-i* (無 名 異) and *mo-so* stones» (摩 娑 石) [3].

Notes.

1) Quotation marks indicate passages taken from Ling-wai-tai-ta, 3,3[a],[b]. In the first paragraph the divergences between the two texts are important. The older one has: «As to the Ki-tz'ï-ni country it is entirely surrounded by high mountains. The mountains have been cut out and
5 made into a wall (鑿 山 爲 城) two hundred *li* square (方). It is surrounded by a great river (大 水)..... It has over a hundred mosques, one of which is over ten *li* square, etc.». The additions to this text made by our author are very difficult to explain. He says Ki-tz'ï-ni lay to the north-west — presumably of Ma-lo-pa, i. e., the port on the Hadramaut coast which he takes in other passages as a starting-point in estimating distances to Mecca and to Baghdad, but in
10 that direction no locality meeting the other requirements of his text is to be found. If the direction is to be taken from Baghdad, Kazvin, which has been suggested as the original of the Chinese name Ki-tz'ï-ni, is also out of the question, as it is north of Baghdad; furthermore, it is in a plain. Ghazni may be intended, if we assume that the direction was given as north-west from India. Yu-yang-tsa-tsu, 18,8[b] mentions Ghazni, under the name of K'ié-shö-na (伽 闍 那), as
15 producing asa-foetida. It says this country is also called «Northern India». See infra, Pt. II, Ch. XXIX Ghazni, it is true, was utterly destroyed in 1149, nearly thirty years before Chóu K'ü-feï composed his work, but that is a very slight objection. There is great paucity of information concerning Ghazni; among the best modern accounts of this country are the Reports on parts of the Ghilzi country and some of the tribes in the neighbourhood of Ghazni, etc. by Lieut[t]. J. S. Broadfoot
20 (Roy. Geog. Soc., Supplementary Papers, I), from which the following notes are taken. «The winter is most severe; frost continuing in the shade from September to April, and snow from December to the middle of March». «Elevated from 7,000 to 8,000 feet above the sea, the climate is severe. It freezes every evening in October, and the ice lasts till midday; in November it never thaws; in December the country is covered with three feet of snow, which melts in the
25 middle of March». «From Ghazni three distinct ranges are perceived, running north-east in one unbroken chain .... Within sixteen miles of the city are six passes». Concerning the inhabitants of the neighbourhood of Ghazni, he says that though poor «they live in little towers containing five or six families, and the country all round abounds in forts. The people raise horses, camels and cattle. With dried milk they prepare *kurut*, to make which, as well as cheese, butter-
30 milk and bread is the duty of the women». *Kurut* is not cheese, but dried *airan*, i. e , sour milk. The latter is condensed into pellets which are dried in the sun or fried in grease». See Vambéry, Das Türkenvolk, 209. This *kurut* is apparently identical with the Chinese *ju-lo* of our text. It is interesting to note that among the Mongols of the Koko-nor and the Tibetans, *kurut* is known as *chura*, which may be derived from the Chinese *ju-lo* — or *vice versa*
35 The word *lo* (酪) has several meanings. According to the K'ang-hi tz'ï-tién, two kinds, the dry and the wet *lo* (or *ju-lo*, lit., «milk lo»), have to be distinguished. The «dry» variety is described in the Yin-shan-chöng-yau (飮 膳 正 要), the work of a Court physician published in 1331, and quoted in the K'ang-hi-tz'ï-tién, in very much the same way as the kūrūt of the Turks.
40 In other passages of this work, *su-lo* and *ju-lo* are translated with their usual acceptation of «butter» and «milk». See supra, p. 98 and p. 102, n. 19.

2) Our author's yarn about the king of Ki-tz'ï-ni, may be founded on some stories still current in his time among Arab sailors who visited China, about Mahmud of Ghazni. I can think of no better explanation, unless it be that Alamut, the famous mountain citadel of the
45 Assassins in the twelfth century, which was near Kazvin, is the place referred to. The mention of bezoar stones as a product of Ki-tz'ï-ni points towards Ghazni, as Badakhshan, an adjacent country, was famous for these stones (Le Strange, Lands of the East. Caliphate, 436), and the she-camels of Kabul were held to be the best in Central Asia. Ibid., 349.

The last phrase of this paragraph is slightly different in Ling-wai-tai-ta; it reads: «The
50 people of the country go once in seven days to the halls (堂) to pray; this is called *shu-mi* (除 襪)». This is the Arabic word *jum'ah*, «assembly» (for prayer in the mosque on friday).

3) Besides being found in Badakshan, bezoar stones are reported by our author (infra, Ch.

XXXIV) to have come from Lu-meï (Rum, Asia Minor). See Tavernier's Travels in India (Ball's edit.), II, 146—151, and supra, p. 74, note 1. Linschoten, Voyage, II, 142 (Hakl. Soc. edit.) states that bezoar stones come from Khorasan. In the Malay Peninsula they are taken from monkeys or porcupines. Skeat, Malay Magic, 274. The best stone was from the stomach of a wild goat in the Persian province of Lar. See Yule and Burnell, Glossary, 68. On the identification 5 of the name mo-so, see Hirth, Die Länder des Islam, 45, note 4.

As to wu-ming-i, it has been shown by Hanbury, Science Papers, 223, to be the iron oxide known as limonite. The Pön-ts'au-tsi-kié (本 草 集 解), as quoted in the Tung-si-yang-k'au. IV, 8ᵃ says of it: «It is found in the Ta-shï countries on stones, and looks like black limestone. The foreign people heat it with oil (and make it into?) black granular stones (黳 石), 10 which they chew like a sweet (餳)». S. W. Bushell, Chinese Pottery and Porcelain, X and 67, n. 4, says, however, that wu-ming-i was cobalt blue.

33.

MOSUL.

Wu-ssï-li (勿 廝 離).   15

The country of Wu-ssï-li has many rocky mountains. In autumn there falls a heavy dew, which, under the action of the sun's rays, hardens into a substance like powdered sugar. This is gathered and is a sweet, pleasant tasting food with purifying and cooling properties; it is real kan-lu (甘 露)[1].

There is found in the mountains of this country a tree which grows 20 wild, and which the first year bears chestnuts (栗), called p'u-lu (蒲 蘆). The next year mo-shï (沒 石 子) grow on it. Asbestos cloth (火 浣 布) and coral are native products.

Note·

1) Taken from Ling-wai-tai-ta, 3,3ᵇ—4ᵃ, with only some slight verbal changes and the 25 addition of the words «called p'u-lu — and the change of «many famous mountains» (多 名 山) to «many rocky mountains» (多 石 山).

Wu-ssï-li, in Cantonese Mat-ssï-li, Al-Mawṣil, Mosul. In another chapter characters with the same sounds transcribe the name Misr, Egypt (supra, pp. 115, 120, n. 3 and infra, Ch. XXXVI). The reference to oak-galls point unmistakably to northern Syria.   30

Kan-lu is used in Buddhist Chinese to render Sanskrit amṛta, nectar. Muḳaddasi, in the tenth century, mentions the exportation of manna from Mosul. Our text does not say that manna was a product of Wu-ssï-li. Judging from the statement that it was «like powdered sugar», it must have been the Gaz or Alhagi manna (Persian and Arabic tar-augubīn, taranjabīn) the product of the Alhagi camelorum, Fisch., which is found in parts of Persia, Afghanistan and Baluchistan. See 35 P. Molesworth Sykes, Geo. Journal, XXVIII, 433. Oak manna, occurs in Kurdistan, it is found in the state of agglutinated tears. See Encyclop. Britan., XV, 493, s. v. Manna, and Heyd, Hist. du Commerce, II, 632.

On the subject of oak-galls (in Arabic ballūṭ 'oak', our author's p'u-lu), see infra, Pt. II. Ch. XX. Asbestos was not a product of Mosul, it was brought there probably from Badakshan. 40

See Le Strange, op. cit., 436—437. Likewise as to coral, our author can only mean that it was plentiful in the Mosul market.

Asbestos is first mentioned in the Hóu Han-shu, 116,27ᵃ under the name *huo-mau* (火 毳). See Hirth, China and the Roman Orient, 249—251. Asbestos, according to P'eï-
5 wön-yün-fu, 66ᴬ, 166, was described in the text known as Lié-tzï, but it was probably not known before the Han dynasty.

34.

RUM (ASIA MINOR).

Lu-meï (蘆 眉).

10   If one travels by land in a westerly direction for some three hundred stages from Ma-lo-pa, one reaches Lu-meï, also called Meï-lu-ku (眉 路 骨'). The city wall (城) is crooked, seven-fold, «and built of large smooth flat black stones, and each wall (城) is distant (from the adjoining one) a thousand paces». «There are over three hundred foreign towers (番 塔 mina-
15 rets), among which is one eight hundred feet high», which four horses abreast can be driven up. «It has three hundred and sixty rooms in it».

«The people all wear turbans which hang down on the neck, and their clothing is made of coloured woollen stuffs (色 毛 段). Their food consists of meat and meal (cakes). They use gold and silver coins». Forty thousand
20 families are employed weaving silk brocades (錦). The products of the country are byssus (? 鮫 綃), gold spangled *yüé-no* cloth (金 字 越 諾 布), bro-cades with alternating stripes of gold and silk, bezoar stones, *wu-ming-i*, rose-water, gardenia flowers, liquid storax, borax, and a superior quality of engraved opaque glassware. The people are fond of breeding camels, horses
25 and dogs.

Note.

There is but little doubt that our author's Lu-meï is the Rūm Bilād ar-Rūm, the 'Land of the Greeks' of the Arab geographers, Asia Minor; but where we are to look for Meï-lu-ku (or rather Meï-lu-ku-tun as the name is written by Chóu K'ü-feï) is quite another matter, as there
30 is nothing in the Chinese name or in the description of the place to help us to elucidate the question. One is inclined to look for it in Kūniyah (Iconium, Konieh) which was the capital of the Seljuk Sultanate of Rūm from 1077 to 1257, when it was captured by the Mongols. See Le Strange, op. cit., 140, 148. If we consider only the description of the city of Meï-lu-ku, we find some points of resemblance (the division of the city in seven parts, and the separation of these various
35 parts from each other) with Damascus. See von Kremer, Kulturgeschichte, etc., I, 127 et seqq. But Damascus was not in Rūm. The 'foreign tower' (minaret, mosque) eight handred feet high (!) with three hundred and sixty chambers in it, may refer to the Djāmi mosque of Damascus; the great impor-tance of the silk brocade industry of Meï-lu-ku points also to that great centre of Oriental trade.

In Chóu K'ü-feï's work (3,8ᵇ) the passage concerning this place reads as follows: «There
40 is the Meï-lu-ku-tun (眉 路 骨 惇) country. It is in (居) a seven-fold wall (or «city»).

From remote antiquity, they have used tiers of shining big black stones (黑光大石壘), and each wall is distant from the other a thousand paces (每城相去千步). There are foreign pagodas (minarets) over three hundred in number, among which is one eighty *chang* high; inside are three hundred and sixty rooms.

«All the people wear turbans covering the neck. When it is cold they use coloured 5 woollen stuffs (色毛段) for clothing. Their food consists of meat and bread. Gold and silver are used for coins. The substance called *kiau-siau* (鮫綃 byssus?), rose-water, gardenia flowers, bezoar stones, and borax are all products of this country».

It seems possible that Meï-lu-ku-tun may after all not be the name of any city, but a transcription of the Arabic word *mulḥidūn*, i. e., «Infidels», and that the Arab informant of Chóu 10 applied the name to Constantinople then the principal city of Rome, i. e., Lu-meï. One might see in the seven-fold wall, and in some other details, some vague reference to Rome and its seven hills. This would also explain the proximity of the country of Ssï-kia-li-yé (Sicily) to the frontier of Lu-meï, the customs of which are similar to those of Sicily. There seems little room for doubt that the description of our Chinese authors did not refer to any one country; it is a composite 15 picture, a jumble of sundry bits of information concerning the remote Mediterranean region. Conf. supra, pp. 115 and 120, n. 5, also infra, Ch. XXXVII.

The reference to byssus is important. Although this product — the threads of the pima squamosa, is found throughout the Mediterranean, it is more abundant near Smyrna than else- where. It was much prized for making fabrics by the Emperors of Byzantium, even after the intro- 20 duction of the silkworm into Europe. Conf. also infra, p. 153, lines 23—25.

35.

MURĀBIT, SOUTHERN COAST OF SPAIN.

Mu-lan-pʻi (木蘭皮).

«The country of Mu-lan-pʻi is to the west of the Ta-shï country. There 25 is a great sea, and to the west of this sea there are countless countries, but Mu-lan-pʻi is the one country which is visited by the big ships (巨艦) of the Ta-shï. Putting to sea from Tʻo-pan-ti (陀盤地) in the country of the Ta-shï, after sailing due west for full an hundred days, one reaches this country. A single one of these (big) ships of theirs carries several thousand 30 men, and on board they have stores (肆) of wine and provisions, as well as weaving looms (機杼). If one speaks of big ships, there are none so big as those of Mu-lan-pʻi» [1].

«The products of this country are extraordinary; the grains of wheat are three inches long, the melons six feet round», enough for a meal for 35 twenty or thirty men. The pomegranates weigh five catties, the peaches two catties, citrons (香圓) over twenty catties, salads (萵苣) weigh over ten catties and have leaves three or four feet long. «Rice and wheat are kept in silos (開地窖藏) for tens of years without spoiling. Among the native products are foreign sheep (胡羊), which are several feet high and have 40 tails as big as a fan. In the spring-time they slit open their bellies and take out some tens of catties of fat, after which they sew them up again, and the sheep live on; if the fat were not removed, (the animal) would swell up and die»[2].

5　　　«If one travels by land (from Mu-lan-p'i) two hundred days journey, the days are only six hours long. In autumn if the west wind arises, men and beasts must at once drink to keep alive, and if they are not quick enough about it they die of thirst»[3].

Notes.

10　　　1) The position assigned by Chóu K'ü-feï to the country of Mu-lan-p'i, as well as the similarity in sound of the name point to its being the kingdom of the Al-Murabiṭūn or Almoravide princes who reigned over Al-Maghreb and southern Spain from the latter part of the eleventh century to the middle of the twelfth. See Hirth, Die Länder des Islam, 48. T'o-pan-ti must, it seems, be the Dimiāth of the Arabs, or Damietta, on the eastern branch of the Nile near its
15　mouth. It was in the twelfth century an even more important seaport than Alexandria. This paragraph and the other portions of this article are taken from Ling-wai-tai-ta, 3,4. Our author omits at the end of this paragraph, the following remark of Chóu K'ü-feï: «At the present day when people say 'a Mu-lan ship', is it not simply saying that it is a big one?» — On these mammoth ships, see supra pp. 33—34.
20　　　2) Chóu K'ü-feï's statement of the marvellous products of this remote country, outdoes any of the fairy stories in the Shan-hai-king, but our author had to improve on his story. Chóu made the grains of wheat to be two inches long, Chau says they were three inches, then he adds to the list of marvels pomegranates, peaches, citrons and salads. The statement, first made by Chóu K'ü-feï that grain was preserved in silos is very interesting and, of course, correct. As to the big-
25　tailed sheep the only reason why he put them in Mu-lan-p'i is that they appeared to him to belong to this region of fancy. The Ethiopian broad-tailed sheep are mentioned by classical and mediaeval writers as found in Arabia, Kerman in Persia, and in parts of eastern Africa. Aelian, de Animal. nat., IV, 32 says in speaking of the sheep of the Indians: «The tails of the sheep reach down to their feet .... The shepherds cut also the tails of the rams, and having extracted
30　the fat, sew them up again so carefully that no trace of the incision is afterward to be seen». M° Crindle, Ancient India as described by Ktesias, 38. Herodotus (III, 113) speaks of the long-tailed sheep of Arabia and of the trucks put under them. He tells also of the broad-tailed variety, the tail a cubit across. The Chinese of the T'ang period had heard also of the trucks put under these sheeps' tails. «The Ta-shï have a foreign breed of sheep (hu yang) whose tails, covered
35　with fine wool, weigh from ten to twenty catties; the people have to put carts under them to hold them up». Fang-kuo-chï (方國志) as quoted in Tung-si-yang-k'au, 12,14ᵇ. Conf. also Marco Polo, I, 99, and Yule's note to same, I, 101, and Leo Africanus, Historie of Africa, III, 945 (Hakl. Soc. edit.), who says he saw in Egypt a ram with a tail weighing eighty pounds!
　　　3) In the Ling-wai-tai-ta this passage begins with the words: «There is a tradition in this
40　country (of Mu-lan-p'i) to the effect that ....» — The remote northern country where the days are only six hours long, is the Land of Darkness of which mediaeval Arab geographers and travellers told, see Ibn Batuta, II, 398—401. The killing wind must be the simoon (Arabic samūm) of the Sahara. These wonders found naturally place in the marvellous country of Mu-lan-p'i. San-ts'ai-t'u-hui (Pién-i-tién, 87,9.) quotes the two first paragraphs of this chapter,
45　but, instead of mentioning silos for grain, it has «they dig wells a thousand feet (deep), then (方) they find springs of water».

36.

MISR (EGYPT).

Wu-ssï-li (勿 斯 里).

The country of Wu-ssï-li is under the dominion of Pai-ta. The king is fair; he wears a turban, a jacket and black boots. When he shows himself in 5 public he is on horseback, and before him go three hundred led horses with saddles and bridles ornamented with gold and jewels. There go also ten tigers held with iron chains; an hundred men watch them, and fifty men hold the chains. There are also an hundred club-bearers and thirty hawk-bearers. Furthermore a thousand horsemen surround and guard him, and three 10 hundred body-slaves (新 奴) bear bucklers and swords. Two men carry the king's arms before him, and an hundred kettle-drummers follow him on horseback. The whole pageant is very grand[1].

The people live on cakes, and flesh; they eat no rice. Dry weather usually prevails. The government extends over sixteen provinces (州), with 15 a circumference (周 迴) of over sixty stages. When rain falls the people's farming (is not helped thereby, but on the contrary) is washed out and destroyed. There is a river (in this country) of very clear and sweet water, and the source whence springs this river is not known. If there is a year of drought, the rivers of all other countries get low, this river alone remains as 20 usual, with abundance of water for farming purposes, and the people avail themselves of it in their agriculture. Each succeeding year it is thus, and men of seventy or eighty years of age cannot recollect that it has rained[2].

An old tradition says that when Shï-su (十 宿), a descendant in the third generation of P'u-lo-hung (蒲 囉 吽), seized the government of this 25 country, he was afraid that the land would suffer from drought on account of there being no rain; so he chose a tract of land near the river on which he established three hundred and sixty villages, and all these villages had to grow wheat; and, so that the ensuing year the people of the whole country should be supplied with food for every day, each of these villages supplied it 30 for one day, and thus the three hundred and sixty villages supplied enough food for a year[3].

Furthermore there is a city (州) called Kié-yé (憇 野) on the bank of this river[4]. Every two or three years an old man comes out of the water of the river; his hair is black and short, his beard is hoary. He seats himself on 35 a rock in the water so that only half his body is visible. If he is thus seen taking up water in his hands, washing his face and cutting his nails, the strange being is recognized, and they go near him, kneel before him and say: «Will the present year bring the people happiness or misfortune?». The man says nothing, but if he laughs, then the year will be a plenteous one and sickness and plagues will not visit the people. If he frowns, then one may be sure that either in the present year, or in the next, they will suffer from famine or plague. The old man remains a long time seated before he dives down again[5].

In this river there are water-camels (水 駱 駝 cranes?), and water-horses (水 馬) which come up on the bank to eat the herbs, but they go back into the water as soon as they see a man[6].

Notes.

1) The contents of this chapter are not found in any other Chinese work that we know of anterior to our author. Chau in a previous passage (supra, p. 116) speaks of the capital of the Ta-shï by the name of Mi-sü-li (Misr). In that he followed the custom of the Arabs, who used the same name Miṣr for the country and its capital (e. g. Biblioth. geogr. Arab. II, p. 97,1. Yāḳūt IV, p. 554,6), but, using different modes of transcription, he shows he was ignorant of this fact.

2) Conf. supra, p. 116.

3) Shï-su is Joseph, the son of Jacob, the son of Isaac, the son of Abraham (P'u-lo-hung). Arab tradition says that the canal of the Fayum was dug by Joseph, and that he brought that region under cultivation; this latter fact is evidently the explanation of our author's story of the 360 villages founded by Joseph to supply Egypt with food. Edrisi, op. cit., I, 308—310 says that when the canal had been dug, Joseph said to the king: 'The public good demands that you should entrust me with one family for each district of Egypt'. The king consenting, Joseph ordered a village to be built for each of these families. There were eighty-five families; there were built as many villages. When the building was finished, Joseph gave to each village water sufficient to water its lands, but nothing more; then to each tribe he assigned drinking water sufficient even for the time of low water». Conf. Masudi, op. cit., II, 369, 384. This latter author says (II, 365—366) that when Joseph built the pyramids he built also a nilometer at Memphis. San-ts'ai-t'u-hui (Pién-i-tién, 86, Sec. T'ién-fang), mentions P'u-lo-hung «the Patriarch (祖 師) of the Ta-shï».

4) Kié-yé is Káhirah. The name of Al-ḳāhirah, «the Victorious» was given the new city founded in A. D. 973 by the general of the first Fatimite Caliph, Al-Mo'izz, who had conquered Egypt in 969. See supra, pp. 16 and 120, n. 3.

5) We have no explanation to offer of this story, nor can we find any similar one in any Arabic or western writers accessible to us.

6) Masudi, II, 394 is of opinion that the hippopotamus resembles somewhat a horse, except as regards the hoofs and tail and the greater breadth of the former's head. Leo Africanus, Historie of Africa, III, 949 speaks of both sea-horses and sea-oxen, which are found in the rivers of Niger and Nilus. His sea-horse is the hippopotamus, his sea-ox seems to be a rhinoceros. «The sea-oxe being covered with an exceeding hard skinne is shaped in all respects like unto the land oxe; save that in bignes it exceedeth not a calfe of sixe moneths olde».

37.

ALEXANDRIA.

O-kön-ʻto (遏 根 陀).

The country of O-kön-tʻo belongs to Wu-ssï-li (Egypt). According to tradition, in olden times a stranger (異 人), Tsu-ko-ni (徂 葛 尼) by 5 name, built on the shore of the sea a great tower under which the earth was dug out and two rooms were made, well connected (搏 結) and very well secreted. In one vault was grain, in the other were arms. The tower was two hundred *chang* high. Four horses abreast could ascend to two-thirds of its height. In the centre of the building was a great well 10 connecting with the big river[1].

To protect it from surprise by troops of other lands, the whole country guarded this tower that warded off the foes. In the upper and lower parts of it twenty thousand men could readily be stationed to guard, or to sally forth to fight. On the summit there was a wondrous great mirror; 15 if war-ships of other countries made a sudden attack, the mirror detected them beforehand, and the troops were ready in time for duty.

In recent years there came (to O-kön-tʻo) a foreigner, who asked to be given work in the guard-house of the tower; he was employed to sprinkle and sweep. For years no one entertained any suspicion of him, when suddenly 20 one day he found an opportunity to steal the mirror and throw it into the sea, after which he made off[2].

Notes.

1) O-kön-tʻo, in Cantonese, At-kan-tʻo, is clearly intended for a transcription of the name Iskanderiah, or Alexandria, and Tsu-ko-ni, in Cantonese Tsʻo-kot-ni is no less certainly Dhu-l- 25 ḳarnein, our Alexander of Macedon, the founder of Alexandria. See Hirth, Die Länder des Islam, 52, notes 3 and 5.

If we substitute *chʻi* ʻfoot', for *chang*, ʻten feet', the height of the Pharos of Alexandria would be approximately correctly stated. Edrisi (I, 298) says it was 300 cubits (of 27 inches) high. Abulfeda (II, Pt. 2, 144) gives its height as 180 cubits. Benjamin of Tudela says of 30 Alexandria: ʻBut the Citie it selfe is excellently built, as we have saide, upon the Pavement of the ground, and with Vaults and Arches under ground, through the hidden passages whereof, men may come into the Market places and not be seene: of the which some are a whole mile in length, as from the Gate Resid, unto the Gate leading unto the Sea, in which Gate a way was made and paved, unto the very Haven of the Citie of Alexandria, which is extended one mile 35 within the Sea, in which place a very high Tower was built, which the Inhabitants call Magraah, but the Arabians, Magar Alecsandria, that is, the Pharos of Alexandria: on the top of which Tower, it is reported that Alexander sometimes set a glittering Looking-glasse, in the which all the warlike Ships which sayled either out of Graecia, or from all the West into Egypt, to harme them, might be seene fiftie days journey by land, that is, above the space of five hundred leagues off». Purchas, His Pilgrimes, VIII, 589.

    2) Masudi, op. cit., II, 434—436 says that under the reign of the Omayyad Caliph Walid I, which was from A. D. 705 to 715, the king of Byzantium sent one of his favorite eunuchs 5 to Egypt on a secret mission. Led into the presence of el-Walid, he said that he had fled from the court of the Greek king to save his life, and that he wished to become a mussulman. This he did, and little by little he gained the confidence of the Caliph by disclosing to him the existence of hidden treasures in Damascus and other places in Syria. One day he told el-Walid that when Alexander had got possession of the property and the precious stones of Sheddad, son of Ad, or 10 of other Arab kings in Egypt and in Syria, he had built vaults and subterranean chambers, covered over with vaults and arches. In these he put all his treasures, ingots, coin and precious stones. Above these vaults he built the Pharos, which was not less than a thousand cubits high, and on the top of it he placed a mirror and a guard. As soon as an enemy appeared in the offing, the watchmen cried out to the neighbouring posts and, by means of signals, warned the 15 remotest ones. So the inhabitants were warned, ran to the defense of the city, and foiled the enemy's attempt. On hearing this the Caliph sent the eunuch with some soldiers who pulled down half of the tower and destroyed the mirror. The people of Alexandria and of the other cities saw the ruse, and that they would be its victims, and the eunuch, fearing lest the Caliph should soon hear of his perfidy, fled during the night and made off on a ship which he had got ready in 20 case of need. Edrisi, I, 298 says a fire burnt on the Pharos continually, but he does not mention the mirror. Cf. Yākūt, 263—4, who does not believe this tale.

    Conf. Abulfeda, II, Pt. 2, 144, who says the mirror was of «iron of China». Leo Africanus, Historie of Africa, III, 864 (Hakl. Soc. edit.), says it was a «steele-glasse by the hidden vertue of which glasse as many ships as passed by while the glasse was uncovered should imme- 25 diately be set on fire; but the said glasse being broken by the Mahumetans, the secret vertue thereof vanished».

38.

COUNTRIES IN THE SEA.

1. Andaman islands.

---

30 <center>Yen-t'o-man (晏 陀 蠻).</center>

When sailing from Lan-wu-li to Si-lan, if the wind is not fair, ships may be driven to a place called Yen-t'o-man. This is a group of two islands in the middle of the sea, one of them being large, the other small; the latter is quite uninhabited. The large one measures seventy *li* in circuit. The 35 natives on it are of a colour resembling black lacquer; they eat men alive, so that sailors dare not anchor on this coast[1].

This island does not contain so much as an inch of iron, for which reason the natives use (bits of) conch-shell (*ch'ö-k'ü*) with ground edges instead of knives. On this island is a sacred relic, (the so-called) «corpse on a bed 40 of rolling gold» (聖 跡 渾 金 床). This body has been there for genera-

10*

tions without decaying, and there is always a huge snake guarding it, on whose body hair has grown to the length of two feet. Nobody dares come near it. Near by is a spring (or well 井), the water of which overflows twice a year and runs into the sea; the gravel over which it passes, after it has been covered by this water, all turns into gold. The islanders offer sacrifice [5] to this spring. If copper, lead, iron, or tin is heated red hot and then put in this water, it is changed into gold[2].

There is an old story told of a trading-ship which got wrecked, and the sailors drifted on a bamboo raft to this island. Having heard of this sacred water, they secretly filled some bamboo tubes with it, then got on a raft, [10] and were driven by the current of the sea to the country of Nan-p'i, where they presented the water to the king of the country. Having tested its power, the king of Nan-p'i raised an army for the purpose of conquering that island; but before his fleet could arrive there, it met with a violent storm, the ships with all on board were thrown on the shore of this island, and all the men [15] were eaten up by the islanders. For on this island is the «Strange man of the golden bod» (金 床 異 人), which is silently guarded by the spirit, and no man may come near the place[3].

Notes.

1) Yen-t'o-man, in Cantonese, An-t'o-man. The Arab travellers of the ninth century were [20] the first to call these islands by this name. «Beyond (the Lendjebālus islands, i. e., the Nicobars) are two islands divided by a sea called Andāmūn. The natives of these isles devour men alive; their hue is black, their hair woolly; their countenance and eyes have something terrifying about them. Their feet are long; the foot of one of them is as much as a cubit long. They go naked, and have no boats». Reinaud, Relations, I, 8. Conf. Masudi, op. cit., I, 339. Nicolo Conti calls [25] the islands Andramania, and says it means 'the island of gold'. Ramusio, Navigationi, I, 339, D. See, however, Yule, Marco Polo, II, 292. Chóu K'ü-feï does not mention these islands; our author is apparently the first Chinese writer to do so.

2) I cannot find in any other work any reference to this treasure and to its $n\bar{a}ga$ guardian. There may be some connection between the story of the corpse and that noted by the author of [30] the Adjāib (tenth century) concerning Great Andaman. «At Great Andaman there is a temple of gold which contains a tomb, an object of veneration for the inhabitants; it is their great respect for this tomb which has led them to raise a golden temple over it. The inhabitants of both islands come there in pilgrimage, and they say that it is the tomb of Solomon, the son of David, — may God bless both of them. They add that that monarch had prayed to God to put his tomb in a [35] place where the men of his time could not go, and that God granting him that favour, had chosen their island to put it on. Devic, Merveilles de l'Inde, 134. See also Gerini, Researches, 379 et seqq.

The Arab relations of the ninth century mention silver mines near the Andaman islands. Reinaud, Relations, I, 9. Yule says Nicolo Conti speaks of 'a lake with peculiar virtues' as existing on the islands. See Encycl. Britan., IXth edit., II, 13. Ramusio's edition of Conti, the only [40] one I have seen, does not contain this passage. San-ts'ai-t'u-hui (Pien-i-tién, 107,30), reproduces textually this and the preceding paragraph, but adds nothing thereto.

3) Our author has evidently derived his information in this paragraph from an other source than that used in the second paragraph; the «sacred relic» being here called by a different name.

2. Islands of Pemba and Madagascar (?).

K'un-lun-ts'öng-k'i (崑 崙 層 期).

«This country is in the sea to the south-west. It is adjacent to a large island. There are usually (there, i. e., on the great island) great *p'öng* (鵬) 5 birds which so mask the sun in their flight that the shade on the sun-dial is shifted (飛 蔽 日 移 晷). If the great *p'öng* finds a wild camel it swallows it, and if one should chance to find a *p'öng's* feather, he can make a water-butt of it, after cutting off the hollow quill [1]».

«The products of the country are big elephants' tusks and rhinoceros horns».

10   In the West «there is an island in the sea on which there are many savages, with bodies as black as lacquer and with frizzed hair (蚪 髮). They are enticed by (offers of) food and then caught and carried off» for slaves to the Ta-shï countries, where they fetch a high price. They are used for gate-keepers (lit., to look after the gate-bolts). It is said that they do not long 15 for their kinsfolk [2].

Notes.

1) K'un-lun-ts'öng-k'i or 'The Zanj (or Blacks) from K'un-lun'. Considering the position assigned this island, near the island of the ruc (Madagascar), the use of the name Ts'öng for its inhabitants which we have previously seen (supra, p. 126, 130) was given to the blacks from the 20 Somali coast to the Mozanbique channel, considering further the similarity of sound between the name used by the Arabs of the time to designate the big island of Pemba, Kanbalu, we have little doubt that the Chinese name means the «Zanj of Kanbalu». Chóu K'ü-feï (for all of the first and second paragraphs, and half of the third are taken from his work, 3,6[a]) used probably the characters K'un-lun to transcribe the name Kanbalu, because he saw some connexion between these blacks 25 in the West, with the negritos inhabiting the Malay Peninsula and the islands of the Archipelago, who were known to the Chinese of his time as 'K'un-lun slaves'. See supra, p. 31, n. 2.

The bird *p'öng* is the *rukh*, or ruc of mediaeval writers; the story may have had its origin in the Indian legend of the *garuḍa*. The localization of the ruc in Madagascar was probably due to the presence there of the fossil eggs of the gigantic fossil Aepyornis. The ruc's quills are, 30 according to Sir John Kirk and Sir Henry Yule, the fronds of the rofia or raphia palm. See The Academy, March 22, 1884. According to Gabriel Ferrand (Journal Asiatique, 10ᵉ série, X, 551) they are the Malgash *langana*. The *langana* is a big bamboo, about 15 centimetres in diameter and 2 meters long, in which the knots have been perforated with the exception of the one at the end, so as to turn it into a water-vessel. The *langana* is used by a large number of tribes, and 35 particularly by the coast tribes (of Madagascar).

Marco Polo (II, 405) also says of the ruc that «it is so strong that it will seize an elephant in its talons and carry him high into the air, and drop him so that he is smashed to pieces; having so killed him the bird gryphon swoops down on him and eats him at leisure».

Chóu K'ü-feï's text has, after the remark about the ruc quills: «There are also camel-40 storks, which measure six to seven feet in height. They have wings and can fly, but not high. They can eat anything while it is burning hot, they can even eat red hot copper or iron». Chau Ju-kua, quite properly, put most of this phrase in his chapter on the Berbera-coast, where the ostriches properly belonged. Supra, p. 128.

2) In Chóu K'ü-fei's work, this island is not located, and after the words 'carried off', occurs the phrase: «thousands and tens of thousands of them are sold as foreign slaves (蕃奴)». Conf. supra, p. 31, n. 2. Edrisi, I, 58 says that the Arabs of Oman kidnapped children on the Zanguebar coast by offering them sweets. He also tells us (I, 61) that there was the Island of Monkeys some two days distant from the African coast. The inhabitants of the islands of Khartan 5 and Martan (Kurian-Murian Islands) captured the monkeys by ruse and sold them in the Yemen, where they were used as slaves. The people of Kish and of Socotra were great slave traders.

T'ang-shu, 222C,8ª, says that during the k'ai-yüan period (A. D. 713—742) there came a mission to China from Shï-li-fo-shï (Sumatra) which, among other things, presented two dwarf women and two women from Söng-ti (侏儒僧祇女各二), also singers and dancers. 10 It seems possible, considering the constant relations between the Arabs of Sumatra with those in the African trade, that these Söng-ti women were of the same race and country as the K'un-lun ts'öng-k'i of our author. There was, however, in the T'ang period, an island near the north-east point of Sumatra called Ko-ko-söng-chï (or ti), and Söng-ti in the present case may be an abbreviated form of that name. The T'ang-shu (loc. cit., 6ª) says the Shö-p'o country sent in 15 A. D. 613 as tribute to China «four Söng-chï slaves» (僧祇奴四). By a slight change of the second character the name may appear as Söng-k'i, 祇 without the dot underneath being homophonous with 期 as used by Chau Ju-kua.

---

3. Malay „Men of the Sea" (Orang-laut).

Sha-hua-kung (沙華公).   20

«The people of the country of Sha-hua-kung are in the habit of going out on the high seas for plunder, and sell their prisoners to Shö-p'o».

«Again in a south-easterly direction (from this country?) there are certain islands inhabited by savage robbers called Ma-lo-nu (麻囉奴). When traders are driven to this country, these savages assemble in large crowds 25 and, having caught the shipwrecked, roast them over a fire with large bamboo pinchers and eat them».

«The chiefs of these robbers bore their teeth and plate them with yellow gold. They use human skulls as vessels for drinking and eating. The farther one penetrates among these islands, the worse the robbers are».   30

Note.

The whole of this chapter is taken from Ling-wai-tai-ta, 3,5ᵇ. Our author has omitted some important remarks of Chóu. The latter begins by saying: «Sha-hua-kung is a country in (上) the south-eastern Sea». In the second paragraph, first line, after the word 'country', Chóu adds 'and near the Fo country' (近佛國), which, in view of the statement made in the 35 first paragraph that the pirates of Sha-hua-kung sell their prisoners in Shö-p'o (i. e., Java), we think must stand for Fo-shï (佛逝), the name used during the T'ang period to designate Eastern Sumatra, the San-fo-ts'i of the Sung period. Probably Chóu's authority wrote in the T'ang period, hence the use of the older name, fallen in disuse in his time. Pelliot, B. E. F. E. O., IV, 301 translated this passage of the Ling-wai-tai-ta differently; he read: «Further to the 40 south-east is the kingdom of Kin-fo, etc.» We have never met with this name in Chinese works, nor apparently had Pelliot, for he offers no explanation of it.

The name Ma-lo-nu is very like Maláyu, our Malay, but we are not aware that that name had already become an ethnical one in the twelfth century. The fashion of putting gold or brass studs in the front teeth and of covering them with gold plates is still adhered to among certain tribes in Borneo and Sumatra. See W. H. Furness, Home life of Borneo head-hunters, 157, and Marsden, History of Sumatra, 47.

4. The Amazons.

The countries of women (女 國).

«Still farther to the south-east (beyond Sha-hua-kung?) there is a country of women (女 國). (Here) the water constantly flows east, and once in several years it overflows, or flows out (泛 漲 或 流 出).

«In this country there are lotus seed (蓮 肉) over a foot in length, and peach stones two feet in length; the people who get them present them to the queen.

«In olden days, whenever a ship was wrecked by a tempest on these shores, the women would take the men home with them, but they were all dead within a few days. At last a cunning fellow who stole a boat at night, managed to get away at the risk of his life and told the story.

«The women of this country conceive by exposing themselves naked to the full force of the south wind, and so give birth to female children»[1].

In the Western Sea there is also a country of women where only three females go to every five males; the country is governed by a queen, and all the civil offices are in the hands of women, whereas the men perform military duties. Noble women have several males to wait upon them; but the men may not have female attendants. When a woman gives birth to a child, the latter takes its name from the mother. The climate is usually cold. The chase with bow and arrows is their chief occupation. They carry on barter with Ta-ts'in and T'ién-chu, in which they make several hundred per cent profit[2].

Notes.

1) Quotation from Ling-wai-tai-ta, 3,5[b]. The earliest reference in Chinese works to this fabulous country dates from the sixth century; the bonze Hui-shön is credited with it in the Liang shu, 54,28. He said the women went into the water in the second and third moons of the year and thereby conceived. See on the various countries of women, G. Schlegel, T'oung Pao, III and IV, and Hervey St. Denis, Ethnographie, I, 402—404. Pigafetta, First Voyage round the World, 154 (Hakl. Soc. edit.), says: «Our old pilot (taken on board at the island of Mallua) told us that in an island called Ocoloro, below Java Major, there are only women who become pregnant with the wind, and when they bring forth, if the child is a male, they kill it, and if a female, they bring it up; and if any man visit their island, whenever they are able to kill him, they do so».

Marsden, Hist. of Sumatra, 262, note, remarks: «Till within a few years the Lampoon people (island of Samanka, in the Straits of Sunda) believed the inhabitants of the island Engano to be all females, who were impregnated by the wind; like the mares in Virgil's Georgics. They styled them, in the Malay language, *Ana Saytan*, or imps of the devil». Col. Kenneth Mackay, Across Papua, 70, says that the natives of the Trobriand Islands off the east coast of New Guinea, 5 have a curious creation myth, according to which the first human beings were three maidens who conceived by the rain falling on them.

The legend of an island of women somewhere in the Malay archipelago was known to the Arabs in the tenth century, see Devic, Livre des merveilles de l'Inde, 20—29.

On the notion of the waters of the Ocean flowing downward, see supra, pp. 26, 75, 9. 10

2) The island in the Western Ocean inhabited by women and its relations with Fu-lin are mentioned by Hüan-tsang in his account of Persia, Beal, Records, II, 279, also in T'ang-shu, 221B,5a. Cf. Hirth, China and Roman Orient, 84, 200—202. Western mediaeval writers also refer to it; Marco Polo, places it some 500 miles south of the Mekran coast. See Yule, Marco Polo, II, 395—398, and Friar Jordanus, Marvels (Hakl. Soc. edit.), 44. 15

There were, according to the Chinese, other countries of women, in Tibet and Central Asia, see Rockhill, Land of the lamas, 339—341. The P'o-wu-chï (博物志), of the middle of the sixth century, mentions a country, or island, to the east of a place called Wu-tsü (沃沮), in the Great Ocean which was inhabited solely by women.

5. Besi (?). Sumatra. 20

Po-ssï (波斯).

«The country of Po-ssï is above the countries of the south-west. The inhabitants are of a very dark complexion and their hair is curly. They wrap around their bodies cotton cloth with green (or blue) flowers (or spots), and wear golden circlets on each arm. They have no walled cities. 25

«Their king holds his court in the morning, when he sits cross-legged on a divan covered with tiger skins. When withdrawing from his presence, his courtiers make their obeisance by kneeling down. When going out, the king sits in a hammock (軟 兜), or rides an elephant, followed by a body-guard of over an hundred men carrying swords and shouting. The people eat cakes 30 of flour, and meat; the food is put in earthenware vessels, from which they help themselves with their hands.

Note.

This is a quotation from Ling-wai-tai-ta, 3,6b. Our author has slightly changed the wording of the first phrase, which, in the original, reads «The country of Po-ssï is above (or «on» 35 上) the south-western Ocean». Po-ssï in Chinese mediaeval works is usually Persia, here it seems to be some country or tribe of south-eastern Asia, inhabited by Negritos; we might expect to find it in or near the Malay Peninsula. Gerini, Researches, 429, 670, 681—682, arrives at the conclusion that the Po-ssï of our text, is doubtless the same as de Barros' Lambrij, which adjoins Daya, which, in turn, adjoins Acheen. «The name itself, he says, may be Lambesi, i. e., 40 Besi or Basi — *lam* being merely the ordinary prefix meaning village — a petty state on the homonymous river on the west coast of Sumatra immediately below Achëh, upon which it borders».

6. Djabulsa, the Land of the setting sun.

Ch'a-pi-sha (茶 弼 沙).

The capital of the country of Ch'a-pi-sha is over a thousand *li* square. The king wears a military robe with a golden girdle. On his head he wears
5 a high golden cap (冠) and on his feet black boots. His courtiers wear clothes embroidered with pearls.

The country produces gold and precious stones in very great plenty. The people live in houses which have a much as seven storeys; on each storey lives a family.
10 This country is resplendent with light (光 明), for it is the place where the sun goes down. In the evening when the sun sets, the sound of it is infinitely more terrifying than that of thunder, so every day a thousand men are placed at the gates who, as the sun goes down, mingle with the sound of the (sinking) sun that of the blowing of horns and the beating of gongs and
15 drums. If they did not do this, the women with child would hear the sound of the sun and would die of fright.

Note.

The country referred to seems unquestionably to be the fabulous City of the West of the Arabs, called by them Djabulsa, Djabirso or Djaborso (جَابُرْس). Conf. Tabari, Annales, I, 68,
20 and M. J. de Goeje's note in Hirth, Die Länder des Islam, 64. The San-ts'ai-t'u-hui (Pién-i-tién, 87) has an illustration showing how the people of Sha-pi-ch'a (沙 弼 茶) salute the parting sun. The text refers to a legend according to which Tsu-ko-ni (Dhu-l-Karnein, Alexander of Macedonia) had visited this formerly uninhabited site, where he left an inscription saying that here was the place where the sun sets in the West.

---

25 ## 7. Sicily.

Ssï-kia-li-yé (斯 加 里 野).

The country of Ssï-kia-li-yé is near the frontier of Lu-meï. It is an island (嶼) of the sea, a thousand *li* in breadth. The clothing, customs and language (of the people) are the same as those of Lu-meï. This country has
30 a mountain with a cavern of great depth in it; when seen from afar it is smoke in the morning and fire in the evening; when seen at a short distance it is a madly roaring fire.

When the people of the country carry up on a pole a big stone weighing five hundred or a thousand catties and throw it down into the cavern, after a little while there is an explosion and (the stone) comes out in little pieces like pumice stone.

Once in every five years fire and stones break out and flow down as far as the sea-coast, and then go back again. The trees in the woods through which (this stream) flows are not burned, but the stones it meets in its course 5 are turned to ashes.

Note.

The Arabs called volcanoes عطمة 'aṭmah (from the Greek ἀτμή? Dozy); Mt. Etna was known to them as the *Jebel el-borkân* 'the blazing mountain'. Masudi, op. cit., III, 67. Our author is the first Chinese writer to mention Sicily and its volcano. Edrisi (II, 71) refers to Mt. Etna as 10 the «Mountain of fire» er Jebel-el-nār near Lebadj (Aci Reale) in Sicily. (Cf. also Yāḳūt, III, 407,2, 408,10).

The Arabs of Africa completed the conquest of Sicily in the latter part of the ninth century, and, although the island was taken from them by the Normans in the latter part of the eldventh century, the Moslims continued to form a large and influential part of the population. 15

Lu-meï, as here used, may very likely by the Eastern Empire, or perhaps even Rome.

---

8. Mogreb-el-aksa.

Mo-k'ié-la (默 伽 獵).

The king of Mo-k'ié-la reads every day the Scriptures and prays to Heaven. He wears a turban, clothes of wool (or camel's hair 毛 段) ornamented in 20 foreign fashion, and red leather boots. The religious observances (教 度) are the same as with the Ta-shï. Whenever the king goes forth, he rides a horse, and a copy of the Book of the Buddha of the Arabs is carried before him on the back of a camel. Over five hundred cities are under the rule (of Mo-k'ié-la), each with walls and markets. It has an hundred myriad of soldiers 25 who are all regularly mounted.

The people eat bread and meat; they have wheat but no rice, also cattle, sheep and camels, and fruits in very great variety. The sea (on the coast of Mo-k'ié-la) is two hundred feet deep, and the coral-tree is found in it.

Note.   30

Mo-k'ié-la, in Cantonese Mak-k'i-lap, must be the Dar el-Mogreb, or the Mogreb-el-aksa «the Far West» of the Arabs. Chóu K'ü-feï (supra, p. 24) is, apparently, the first Chinese author to mention this remote country by name, he ҫalls it Mo-k'ié (the character *la* has been inadvertently omitted in his work), but he knew only its name.

On the term 毛 段, Conf. supra, pp. 138, line 36, and 142, line 6, and on the coral-tree, 35 Pt. II, Ch. XXXI.

39.

BORNEO.

P'o-ni (渤尼 or 佛泥).

P'o-ni is to the south-east of Ts'üan-chóu; from Shö-p'o it is forty-five
days' journey; from San-fo-ts'i forty days' journey; from Chan-ch'öng and Ma-i
thirty days' journey in either case; all these distances are to be understood as
taken with a fair wind (i. e., with the north-east monsoon) [1].

In this country, the city walls are made of wooden boards and the city
contains over ten thousand inhabitants. Under its control there are fourteen
districts (or cities 州).

The king's residence is covered with *peï-to* (貝多) leaves [2]; the dwellings of the people with grass.

The king's mode of dressing is more or less like that of the Chinese.
When he does not wear clothes and goes barefooted, his upper arm is encircled
with a golden ring, his wrist with a golden silk band (金練), and his body is
wrapped in a piece of cotton cloth. He sits on a string bedstead (繩床
charpoy). When he goes out, they spread out a large piece of cloth unlined
(單) [3] on which he sits; a number of men bear it aloft; they call this a *juan-
nang* (院囊) [4]. He is followed by over five hundred men, those in front
carrying single and double edged swords and other weapons, those behind
golden dishes filled with camphor and betel-nuts. He has for his protection
over an hundred fighting boats, and when they have an engagement, they
carry swords and wear armour. The latter is cast of copper and shaped like
great tubes, into which they insert their bodies so as to protect the stomach
and the back.

Their household vessels are often made of gold. The country produces
no wheat; but hemp and rice, and they use *sha-hu* (沙糊) for grain;
furthermore, they have sheep, fowl and fish, but no silkworms. They use
the floss of the *ki-peï* (吉背) plant to make cloth. They draw the sap from
the heart of the *weï-pa* (尾巴), the *kia-möng* (加蒙), and cocoanut trees
to make wine [5].

The wives and daughters in rich families wear sarongs of fancy brocades,
and of «melted gold coloured silk» (銷金色帛). As marriage presents they
first give wine, then betel-nuts, then a finger ring, and after this a gift of
cotton cloth or a sum of gold or silver, to complete the marriage rite.

To bury their dead they have coffins und cerements, and they carry them to the hills on bamboo biers where they are left unheeded. When they commence ploughing in the second moon, they offer sacrifices to their spirits (祀), but when seven years have elapsed, they discontinue these sacrifices.

The seventh day of the twelfth moon is their New Year's day. The country is for the greater part hot. When the inhabitants give a feast, they make merry by beating drums, blowing flutes, striking gongs, and by singing and dancing. They make use of bamboo or *peï-to* leaves plaited together in lieu of dishes and cups, and throw them away when the meal is finished.

This country is close to the country of Ti-mön (底 門). There is a medicinal tree, the root of which is boiled into an ointment; the latter is taken internally and also rubbed all over the body, by this means sword wounds never prove fatal[6].

The country produces the following articles: camphor of four varieties, *meï-hua-nau* (梅 花 腦), *su-nau* (遠 腦), *kin-kiau-nau* (金 腳 腦), and *mi-nau* (米 腦), yellow wax, laka-wood-and tortoise-shell; and the foreign traders barter for these trade-gold and trade-silver, imitation silk brocades, brocades of Kién-yang (建 陽), variegated silk lustrings, variegated silk floss (茸), glass beads, glass bottles, tin, leaden sinkers for nets, ivory armlets, rouge, lacquered bowls and plates, and green porcelain[7].

Three days after a foreign ship has arrived at these shores, the king and his family, at the head of the court grandees, (Note: the king's attendants are styled *Ta-jön*, 大 人), go on board to enquire concerning the hardships of the journey. The ship's people cover the gang-plank with silk brocade, receive them reverently, treat them to all kinds of wine, and distribute among them, according to rank, presents of gold and silver vessels, mats with cloth borders and umbrellas[8]. When the ship's people have moored and gone on shore, it is customary, before they touch upon the question of bartering, for the traders to offer to the king daily gifts of Chinese food and liquors: it is for this reason that when vessels go to P'o-ni (佛 泥), they must take with them one or two good cooks. On the full moon and new moon days they must also attend at the king's levee[9], and all this for about a month or so, after which they request the king and the grandees of his suite to fix with them the prices of their goods; this being done, drums are beaten, in order to announce to all the people near and far that permission to trade with them has been granted. Clandestine trading previous to the prices being fixed is punishable. It is customary to treat the traders with great regard; for, if any of them commits a capital offense, he is let off with a fine and is not killed.

On the day when the vessel is about to sail for home, the king also gives out wine and has a buffalo killed by way of a farewell feast[10], and makes return gifts of camphor and foreign cotton cloth, corresponding to the value of the presents received from the ship's people. The ship, however, must wait to sail till the festival in honour of the Buddha on the day of the full moon of the sixth moon[11] is passed, when it may leave the anchorage; for, otherwise, its will meet with bad weather on its journey.

Their god (lit., Buddha) has no image in human shape (佛 無 他 像); his dwelling consists of a reed-covered building of several storeys, shaped like a pagoda; below there is a small shrine protecting two pearls; this is called the «Sacred Buddha» (聖 佛)[12]. The natives say that the two pearls were at the outset quite small, but that they have by degrees grown till they are of the size of a thumb (nail). On the god's feast the king in person offers flowers and fruits for three days, when all the inhabitants, both men and women, attend.

In the second year of the period *t'ai-p'ing hing-kuo* (A. D. 977), this country sent as envoys P'u A-li (蒲 亞 利 Abu Ali), and others, to present as tribute to our Court camphor, tortoise-shell, ivory, and sandal-wood. The official document they submitted to the Throne was covered by a number of wrappers, the paper was like tree-bark, but thin, smooth and glossy, and of a greenish tint, several feet long and over an inch in thickness; when rolled up, it was just as much as one could hold in the hand. The characters written upon it were fine and small, and were to be read horizontally. Their meaning was translated into Chinese as follows: «The King of P'o-ni bows his head to the ground in obeisance, and prays that his Imperial Majesty may live ten thousand times ten thousand times a million years», and it was further said in that document that, as in their annual tribute voyages, they were apt to be driven by the winds to Chan-ch'öng, they therefore requested that Chan-ch'öng be instructed by His Majesty not to detain them hereafter. Their envoys were lodged at the Li-pin-yüan (禮 賓 院), and were sent back with honour[13].

In the fifth year *yüan-föng* (A. D. 1082) they sent a further mission with tribute[14].

The inhabitants of the ocean islands of

Si-lung (西 龍)
Kung-shï-miau (宮 什 廟)
Jï-li-hu (日 麗 胡)
Lu-man (蘆 蔓)

T'óu-su (頭 蘇)

Wu-li-ma (勿 里 馬)

Tan-yü (膽 逾), and

Ma-jö (馬 喏)[15]

traffic in small boats; their style of dressing and their diet are identical with 5
those of P'o-ni; they produce *shöng-hiang* (gharu-wood), laka-wood, yellow
wax, and tortoise-shell; and (the foreign) traders barter for these com-
modities white porcelain, wine, rice, coarse salt, white silk piece goods and
trade-gold.

Notes.   10

1) The earliest mention of Borneo in Chinese literature dates from the latter part of the
ninth century, when it occurs in the Man-shu (蠻 書), 6,5 under the form P'o-ni (浡 泥).
Pelliot, B. E. F. E. O., IV, 287, 296. The two forms of the name used by our author are both
pronounced in Cantonese Put-ni, i. e., Bṛni, Borneo. See also Groeneveldt, Notes, 101 et seqq.
Gerini, Researches, 512 et seqq., is «perfectly sure» P'o-ni is Pāni or Pānei on the Barumun 15
or Pāni River, east coast of Sumatra, in about 2°20'—2°30' N. lat. The information given
by Chau Ju-kua strengthens the identification of P'o-ni with Borneo. He says it was near
Ti-mön (island of Timor, and south of Ma-i — unquestionably Luzon. He speaks of neighbouring
islands, not one of which can possibly have been near Sumatra, and some, at least, of which appear
to have been in the Celebes. Certain other facts — even the story of the two pearls, all point 20
to Borneo, and not one to Sumatra. — It is true that in a previous passage (supra, p. 76)
our author states that P'o-ni was 15 days sailing N.-W. of Shö-p'o, while in this chapter he says
it is 45 days journey from Shö-p'o, but this may partly be accounted for by reference to previous
remarks (supra, p. 58) on Chinese errors in compass directions at sea, and the course sailed,
whether straight or coast-wise, should also be taken into consideration.   25

2) Nipa palm (*weï-pa*) leaves probably, not palmyra palm (*peï-to*).

3) This character stands for 禪. On the suppression of radicals in Sung books, see Hirth,
J. A. O. S., XXX, 27.

4) In some editions of this work the first character of this word is written 軟. A *juan-
nang* is a litter or hammock; the word itself appears to be foreign. See supra, pp. 47, 50, 72. 30

5) *Sha-hu* is sago, see supra, p. 84. *Weï-pa*, in Cantonese *mi-pa* is the nipa palm. See supra,
p. 84. *Kia-möng*, in Cantonese *ka-mung*, is evidently the gomuti palm, the sap of which is the
ordinary substance from which toddy is made. See Crawfurd, Hist. Indian Archipelago, I,
397—399. We do not know what native word is transcribed by *kia-möng*.

6) The island of Timor. In a previous passage (supra, p. 83), giving a list of the depen- 35
dences of Java, the name is written Ti-wu, in Cantonese Ti-mat. In the Ming period the name was
written Ch'ï-mön (遲 悶) and Ki-li-ti-mön (吉 里 地 門). See Groeneveldt, Notes, 116.
On the medecine for wounds, conf. supra, p. 63, line 32,

7) On these products of Borneo, see infra, Pt. II. Kién-yang is a town in Kién-ning-fu,
Fu-kién. «Variegated silk floss». The character *jung* is probably for 絨 also pronounced 40
jung. Confer the terms *kié-jung* (結 茸) and *siu-jung* (繡 茸), P'eï-wön-yün-fu, 2,71.
«Green porcelain», is our céladon porcelain; it was principally manufactured at Lung-ch'üen in
Chö-kiang province, and was an important article of export in Chinese trade in mediaeval
times. See Hirth, Ancient Chinese porcelain, 29, 38—69. Conf. Pigafetta, First Voyage round
the World. (Hakl. Soc. edit.) 117.   45

8) «Mats with cloth borders», 祿 席. The first character is identical with 緣, according
to K'ang-hi-tzï-tién, and we find mentioned in P'eï-wön-yün-fu, 110A, 162, as a term used during
the Sung dynasty, «mats having a brocaded hem», 錦 緣 席. — On the subject of mats, see
infra, Pt. II. Ch. XXIV.

9) It is customary in China for hidg officials to receive the visits of their subordinates on the first and fifteenth of each moon, and these days are the ordinary holidays of the people, on which they make visits.

10) 祖 席 the first character stands for 徂 «to go to», «to travel». Peï-wön-yün-fu, 46,98 gives several quotations of analogous terms; e. g., 祖 餞 «a farewell dinner to a parting friend» also «a viaticum».

11) The feast of Kuan-yin, the patron of sailors, see supra, p. 69. Buddhism was not unknown in Borneo in mediaeval times. though the date of its appearance there is uncertain. See Lassen, Indische Altherthumsk. IV, 532. Crawfurd, J. R. G. S., XXIII, 83.

12) Can these pearls be the same Pigafetta speaks of in his Narrative? «They say that the king of Burné (Brunei, W. Coest of Borneo) has two pearls as large as a hen's eggs, and so perfectly round that if placed on a smooth table they cannot be made to stand still». See First Voyage round the World by Magellan (Hakl. Soc. edit.), 117, 120. 他 像 «human shape», according to the Fang-yen glossary in K'ang-hsi tzï-tién. The statue is placed in contrast with the pearls.

13) The full text of this letter of the ruler of Borneo is given in Sung-shï, 489,18. The king's name is there said to be Hiang-ta (向 打) and that of the envoy P'u Lu-sié (蒲 盧 歇). The king said in his letter to the Emperor of China concerning this envoy: «Recently there was a trader, P'u Lu-sié by name, whose ship arrived at the mouth of my river; I sent a man to invite him to my place, and then he told me he came from China. The people of my country were much pleased at this, and, preparing a ship, asked this stranger to guide them to the Court ....» See Groeneveldt, Notes, 109. It appears from this that it is to the enterprising Arab traders of Canton, or Ts'üan-chóu, that belongs the credit of opening relations between China and Borneo.

14) Sung-shï, 489,19a gives the name of the king of Borneo as Si-li-ma-jö (錫 理 麻 若) which may be Sri Maharaja or Maradja. The mission sailed back from Ts'üan-chóu.

15) These islands must probably be looked for in the Celebes and Moluccas; there is nothing to indicate how the nineteen characters which give their names should be grouped. The division here adopted is purely tentative. The first name may be Serang or Ceram, the third Gilolo. Wu-li-ma may be the same as the Wu-li (巫 里) of Yüan-shï, 162 which Groeneveldt, Notes, 27, thought might be Bali, but this seems doubtful. — Tan-yü suggests Ternate, and Ma-jö Mahono, but none of these islands produce any kind of gharu-wood.

40.

PHILIPPINE ISLANDS.

Ma-i (麻 逸).

The country of Ma-i is to the north of P'o-ni[1]. Over a thousand families are settled together along both banks of a creek (or, gully 溪). The natives cover themselves with a sheet of cotton cloth (披 布 如 被), or hide the lower part of the body with a sarong (lit., «loin-cloth» 腰 布).

There are bronze images of gods (佛), of unknown origin, scattered about in the grassy wilderness[2]. Pirates seldom come to this country.

When trading ships enter the anchorage, they stop in front of the officials place, for that is the place for bartering of the country. After a ship has been boarded, the natives mix freely with the ship's folk. The chiefs are in the habit of using white umbrellas, for which reason the traders offer them as gifts.

The custom of the trade is for the savage traders to assemble in crowds and carry the goods away with them in baskets; and, even if one cannot at first know them, and can but slowly distinguish the men who remove the goods, there will yet be no loss. The savage traders will after this carry these goods on to other islands for barter, and, as a rule, it takes them as much as eight or nine months till they return, when they repay the traders on shipboard with what they have obtained (for the goods). Some, however, do not return within the proper term, for which reason vessels trading with Ma-i are the latest in reaching home.

The following places belong to this country: San-sü («Three islands»), Pai-p'u-yen (白 蒲 延), P'u-li-lu (蒲 里 嚕) Li-kin-tung (里 金 東), Liu-sin (流 新) and Li-han (里 漢)[3].

The products of the country consist of yellow wax, cotton, pearls, tortoise-shell, medicinal betel-nuts (藥 檳 榔) and yü-ta cloth (于 達 布)[4]; and (the foreign) traders barter for these porcelain, trade-gold, iron censers, lead, coloured glass beads, and iron needles.

Notes.

1) According to Blumentritt, Versuch einer Ethnographie der Philippinen, 65. Mait, meaning «the country of the Blacks», was the name of the island of Mindoro. See B. Laufer, Relations of the Chinese to the Philippine Islands, 251—252. Considering that our author says that the Babuyan islands off the N. coast of Luzon, and Polillo island off the E. coast are a part of Ma-i, it seems fair to assume that the latter name is used by him as applying to Mindoro and Luzon at all events, if not to the whole Philippine group.

The name of Ma-i was first heard of in China in A. D. 982 when some traders from that country brought valuable merchandise to Canton. Hervey St. Denis, Ethnographie, II, 502.

2) When Magellan discovered the Philippines, he found the people worshipping idols. Referring to Çebu, Pigafetta says: «These idols are made of wood, they are concave or hollowed out behind, and the feet turned upwards; they have a large face, with four large teeth like those of a wild boar, and they are all painted». First Voyage round the World, (Hakl. Soc. edit.), 96. The images referred to by our author were probably of a like description. In the seventeenth century Spanish writers mention the idols of the Negritos of the Philippines and their many gods. W. A. Reed, Negritos of Zambales, 26.

3) On San-sü, see infra, p. 161. Pai-p'u-yen are the Babuyan islands, off the N. coast of Luzon. P'u-li-lu is Polillo island, off the E. coast of Luzon. The other three names are not identified, but Li-kin-tung may be Lingayen, an important port on the W. coast of Luzon, Liu-sin may be Luzon, and Li-han the island of Lubang — but this is pure guessing.

4) Yü-ta cloth is probably the cloth made from the ramie fiber (Boehmeria nivea), or the abacá, the manila-hemp fiber of the Musa textilis, L. On the term «trade-gold», see supra p. 82.

41.

ISLANDS OF CALAMIÁN, BUSUANGA, PALAWAN.

(Philippine Islands).

––––

San-sü (三 嶼).

The San-sü, (or «Three Islands»), belong to Ma-i; their names are Kia-ma-yen (加 麻 延), Pa-lau-yu (巴 姥 酉), and Pa-ki-nung (巴 吉 弄), and each has its own tribes (種) scattered over the islands. When ships arrive there, the natives come out to trade with them; the generic name (of these islands) is San-sü [1].

Their local customs are about the same as those of Ma-i. Each tribe consists of about a thousand families. The country contains many lofty ridges, and ranges of cliffs rise steep as the walls of a house.

The natives build wattled huts perched in lofty and dangerous spots, and, since the hills contain no springs, the women may be seen carrying on their heads two or three jars one above the other in which they fetch water from the streams, and with their burdens mount the hills with the same ease as if they were walking on level ground.

In the remotest valleys there lives another tribe called Hai-tan (海 膽) [2]. They are small in stature and their eyes are round and yellow (brown), they have curly hair and their teeth show (between their lips). They nest in tree tops. Sometimes parties of three of five lurk in the jungle, from whence they shoot arrows on passers-by without being seen, and many have fallen victims to them. If thrown a porcelain bowl, they will stoop and pick it up and go away leaping and shouting for joy.

Whenever foreign traders arrive at any of the settlements, they live on board ship before venturing to go on shore, their ships being moored in midstream, announcing their presence to the natives by beating drums. Upon this the savage traders race for the ship in small boats, carrying cotton, yellow wax, native cloth, cocoanut-heart mats, which they offer for barter. If the prices (of goods they may wish to purchase) cannot be agreed upon, the chief of the (local) traders (賈 豪) must go in person, in order to come to an understanding, which being reached the natives are offered presents of silk umbrellas, porcelain, and rattan baskets; but the foreigners still retain on board one or two (natives) as hostages. After that they go on shore to traffic,

*

11

which being ended they return the hostages. A ship will not remain at anchor longer than three or four days, after which it proceeds to another place; for the savage settlements along the coast of San-sü are not connected by a common jurisdiction (i. e., are all independent 不 相 統 屬).

The coast faces south-west, and during the south-west monsoon the surge dashes against the shore, and the rollers rush in so rapidly that vessels cannot anchor there. It is for this reason that those who trade to San-sü generally prepare for the return trip during the fourth or fifth moon (i. e., in May or June).

The following articles are exchanged in barter: porcelain, black damask and various other silks, (glass?) beads of all colours, leaden sinkers for nets, and tin.

Pʻu-li-lu is connected (聯 屬) with San-sü, but its settlements are more populous; most of the people are of a cruel disposition and given to robbery. The sea thereabout is full of bare ribs of rock with jagged teeth like blasted trees, their points and edges sharper than swords and lances; when ships pass by they tack out in time in order to steer clear of them; from here come coral-trees, the *tsʻing-lang-kan* (青 琅 玕) and the *shan-hu* (珊 瑚) varieties; but they are very difficult to get[3].

The local customs and commercial usages are the same as in San-sü.

Notes.

1) Kia-ma-yen is probably Calamián, the largest of the Calamianes group of islands, N. E. of Palawan; Pa-lau-yu may be Palawan, and Pa-ki-nung, it would seem, should be Busuanga Island. Laufer, op. sup. cit., 252, note 1, identifies Pa-lau-yu with Penon de Corón, near the E. end of Busuanga, and famous as one of the places where edible bird's nests are gathered.

2) The Aëta (*Aigta* or *Inagta*, appears to be the original form of the word, de Quatrefages, Distribution des Négritos, 5), the negrito aboriginals of the Philippines; they still occupy the most mountainous and inaccessible parts of Luzon.

3) See infra, Pt. II, Ch. XXXI.

42.

NORTHERN FORMOSA.

Liu-kʻiu (流 求).

The country of Liu-kʻiu is some five or six days' sail east of Tsʻüan-chóu[1]. The king's family name is Huan-ssï (歡 斯), but the natives style him *Kʻo-lau* (可 老). The king's residence is called Pʻo-lo-tʻan-tung (波 羅

檀 洞); it has a threefold mound and a palisade surrounded by running water and protected by thorn hedges, and the eaves of the palace building have many figures of birds and beasts carved upon them[2].

Both sexes bind their hair with white hempen cord and coil it up in a
5 knot at the back of the head; and they make clothes of different patterns from hempen cloth and (ornamented with) feathers[3].

They plait hats of rattan and decorate them with feathers. Their soldiers are armed with weapons of every kind, such as knives, pikes, bows and arrows, and swords; they use drums, and make buff-coats of bears' and
10 leopards' skins.

The carriages (車) in which (the chiefs) drive are chased with the images of wild beasts, and only several tens of men walk in front and behind[4]. They have no regular tax revenue, but when occasion arises, a duty in the nature of an equal impost (on all classes) is levied.

15 They do not understand the solar and lunar divisions of the year, but simply record time by observing the phases of the moon[5].

Fathers and sons sleep together on the same couch. They evaporate sea water in the sun to make salt, and they brew rice barm into spirits. Whenever they happen to have any extraordinary delicacy, they first offer it to
20 their principal men (or Worthies 先 進 尊 者).

Of meats they have bears and wolves, a great many pigs, and domestic fowls; but no cattle, sheep, donkeys nor horses[6]. The soil of this country is rich and loamy. After burning the grass (i. e., the stubble of the last crop), they flood the land and merely hoe it up a few inches deep.

25 There are no goods of any special importance to be got there; the people are, moreover, given to robbery, for which reason traders do not go there; but the natives, from time to time, take whatever they can get together in the way of yellow wax, native gold, buffalo tails and jerked leopard meat to San-sü for sale[7].

30 By its side are the countries of P'i-shö-yé (毗 舍 耶) and T'an-ma-yen (談 馬 顏)[8].

Notes.

1) There is no doubt that the country here called Liu-k'iu is Formosa, the indications furnished by our author are quite conclusive on this point. The name Liu-k'iu was used by the
35 Chinese—prior the sixteenth century—to designate all the islands from the coast of Fu-kién to Japan. Hervey St. Denis, Ethnographie, I, 414. Our author has taken nearly textually all this chapter — with the exception of the two last paragraphs—from Sui-shu, 81,10–13, which relates to the period extending from A. D. 581 to 617. It states (81,18ª) that in A. D. 605, a certain skipper, called Ho-man (何 蠻), and some others, (reported or noted) that every spring and
40 autumn, when the sky was clear and there was no wind, when looking eastward one distinguished

something resembling smoke or mist, but they did not know how many thousand *li* away it was. In 607 the Emperor having ordered Chu Kuan (朱 寬) to go to sea to seek for strange places, he took Ho-man with him and sailed to Liu-k'iu. A year or so afterwards the Chinese sent an expedition to Liu-k'iu, which, judging by the course it sailed, was the Formosan coast E. of the Pescadores. This expedition captured and sacked the king's capital and carried off the population. 5 After this relations with this country came to an end. See Hervey St. Denis, Ethnographie, I, 422—424, and G. Schlegel, T'oung-pao, VI, 174 et seqq.

2) Sui-shu, loc. cit , says the king was styled *Ko-la-tóu* (渴 刺 兜) or *Ko tz'ï-* (刺) *tóu* «it is not known, it remarks, whence (his family) comes, but it has ruled over the country for several generations». The people also called the ruler *K'o-lau-yang* (可 老 羊) and his consort 10 *To-pa-ch'a* (多 拔 茶). The local headmen were called *Niau-liau* (鳥 了).

The character *tung* (洞) after the name of the king's residence, and which commonly means «ravine», is clearly to be understood here as meaning «a village», in which sense our author uses the character (written 峒) in his chapter on Haï-nan in speaking of the villages of the aborigines. Sui-shu, 81,11ᵃ says of Liu-k'iu «each village has its own little chief» (洞 有 15 小 王). Each *tung* comprised a certain number of hamlets (村), ruled by local headmen.

In modern Kuang-tung a *tung* (洞) is equivalent to a *ta-hiang* (大 鄕), a community of villages, or parish, as a subdivision of a *ssï*, or township, which again is a subdivision of a territory in charge of a district magistrate. See Hirth, China Review, II. 1873, 158.

3) Sui-shu, 81,12ᵃ, remarks that the people have deep-set eyes and long noses, somewhat 20 like the people of Western Asia (Hu). The men pull out their moustaches, the hair on their temples and wherever it grows on their bodies. The women tattoo insects and snakes on their hands. This last custom, we may add, is still observed in the Liu-k'iu islands; some of the natives of Formosa tattoo their faces.

4) This is presumably our author's interpretation of the unintelligible phrase in Sui-shu 25 (81,11ᵇ) which says: «The prince rides a *mu-shóu* (lit. 'wooden animal') (王 乘 木 獸) and ..... «the princelings ride a *wu* (lit. 'a low table') carved to look like an animal (小 王 乘 机 鏤 爲 獸 形)».

5) Sui-shu, 81,12ᵃ says: «By looking at the waxing and waning of the moon they reckon the divisions of the seasons (時 節). They await the drying-up of (certain) medicinal plants to 30 reckon a year (候 草 藥 枯 以 爲 年 歲)».

6) «Of meats (肉) they have bears, etc.». This is a quotation from Sui-shu (81,12ᵇ) giving the products of Liu-k'iu. The addition of the word *jóu* «meat» is clearly an error on the part of our author or the editor of his work.

7) This reference to a regular trade existing between Formosa and the Philippine islands 35 is extremely interesting. Were it not that our author calls the Pescadores by the name of P'öng-hu, one would be disposed to think that he was referring to this latter group of islands, which in the Yüan period were called San-sü. See Yüan-shï, 210,15.

8) On P'i-shö-yé, or Southern Formosa, see infra, p. 165. T'an-ma-yen, in Cantonese Tam-ba-gan, may be Botol Tobago island off the S. coast of Formosa. 40

From the fact that our author takes practically all his information concerning Northern Formosa from the Sui-shu, and from his remark that traders did not in his time visit that part of the island, it seems fair to assume that intercourse was not kept up after the Chinese discovery of the island in A. D. 607. See however, C. Imbault Huart, L'ile Formose, 4, who is of a contrary opinion, but Ma Tuan-lin (Hervey St. Denis, Ethnographie, I, 424) says distinctly, that since 45 the time of the Sui there was no intercourse with Liu-k'iu. The Liu-k'iu-kuo-chï (琉 球 國 志) 15,10ᵇ–11ᵃ agrees with this. The first mission to China from Liu-k'iu proper was in the fifth year of Hung-wu of the Ming (A. D. 1372).

43.

SOUTHERN FORMOSA.

P'i-shö-yé (毗 舍 耶).

The language of P'i-shö-yé cannot be understood, and traders do not
5 resort to the country. The people go naked and are in a state of primitive
savagery like beasts.

In the district of Ts'üan-chóu there is an island in the sea by the name
of P'öng-hu (彭 湖); it belongs to the jurisdiction of Tsin-kiang-hién (晉
江 縣); now the country referred to is so near to this island that smoke on
10 it may be discerned[1].

The savages come to make raids and, as their coming cannot be fore-
seen, many of our people have fallen victims to their cannibalism, a great
grief to the people!

During the period *shun-hi* (A. D. 1174—1190) their chiefs were in
15 the habit of assembling parties of several hundreds to make sudden attacks
on the villages of Shui-au (水 澳) and Weï-t'óu (圍頭) in Ts'üan-chóu-fu,
where they gave free course to their savage instincts, slaying men without
number and women too, after they had raped them[2].

They were fond of iron vessels, spoons, and chopsticks; one could get rid
20 of them by closing the entrance door, from which they would only wrench
the iron knocker and go away. By throwing away spoons or chopsticks they
could be got to stoop down to pick them up, and thus fall behind some paces.

The officials' soldiers used to lay hold of them in this manner: when
the savages got sight of a horseman in mail, they struggled to strip off his
25 armour, when, in their headlong rush, they met their death without being
sensible of the danger.

When attacking an enemy, they are armed with javelins to which are
attached ropes of over an hundred feet in length, in order to recover them
after each throw; for they put such value on the iron of which these weapons
30 are made, that they cannot bear to lose them.

They do not sail in junks or boats, but lash bamboo into rafts, which
can be folded up like screens, so, when hard pressed, a number of them can
lift them up and escape by swimming off with them[3].

Notes.

35   1) In the preceding chapter our author says that P'i-shö-yé is beside (旁) Liu-k'iu. He
now states, that from the Pescadores (P'öng-hu) smoke could be seen in the country of the

P'i-shö-yé, consequently it was the south-western coast of Formosa. Tsin-kiang-hién is Ts'üan-chóu-fu. See Playfair, Cities and Towns, № 1087.

Térrien de Lacouperie, China before the Chinese, 127, was the first to identify the P'i-shö-yé with the Visaya or Bisaya of the Philippines. More recently B. Laufer, in his Relations of the Chinese to the Philippine Islands, 253—255, has on «culture-historical considerations» 5 greatly strengthened the evidence, previously based solely on phonetic coincidence. Laufer, however, thinks the text of Sung-shï, 491,1 — which is an abstract of our author's account of the P'i-shö-yé, refers to only one raid on the China coast, by a band of Visayans who had failed in a descent on the Formosan coast, and had been driven to attack that of China. In this, however, he is wrong, for both our author and Sung-shï state that during the period A. D. 1174—1190 10 these raids on the Fu-kién coast were of frequent occurrence. The P'i-shö-yé were consequently established along the south-western coast of Formosa at that time, but it seems probable that they were of Philippine origin. This belief is further strengthened by the statement of our author in the preceding chapter that the people of Liu-k'iu, the Formosans immediately to the north of the P'i-shö-yé, had regular trade relations with the Philippines (San-sü). It must be noted that 15 the raiders came to China on rafts, not in boats as they would have done had they come directly from the Philippines.

Although phonetic coincidence is but poor evidence on which to base identifications, never-theless it is interesting to note that there is still a branch of the Pepohuan Formosans called the Pazehhe tribe living scattered over the Taihoku plain and in the Kelung and Tamsui districts 20 of Formosa. The name resembles somewhat P'i-shö-yé. See J. W. Davidson, Island of Formosa, 581, C. Imbault Huart, op. cit., 256 et seqq., and R. Torii, Aboriginal Tribes of Eastern Formosa (Hansei Zasshi, XII, № 10), 43.

2) Weï-t'óu exists at the present day, it is situated on the spit of land to the east of and opposite Quemoy island in Chang-chóu Bay. It seems likely that these raids by the Formosans 25 continued for some time. In 1211, according to the Ts'üan-chóu-fu-chï, the foreign traders residing in Ts'üan-chóu petitioned the Throne to be allowed to put the city walls in thorough repair with funds to be raised by subscription among themselves. The Japanese pirates also made frequent descents on the Fu-kién coast at this time.

3) Ma Tuan-lin, Wön-hién-tung-k'au, 347,4, reproduces this chapter of our author. See 30 also Hervey St. Denis, Ethnographie, I, 425.

44.

KOREA.

Sin-lo (新 羅).

«The country of Sin-lo is inhabited by a race which descends from 35 Pién-han» (弁 韓)[1]. This country rises opposite to the sea entrance to Ts'üan-chóu, but, from the popular superstition concerning what geomancers call the «relation between north and south» (陰 陽 家 子 午), traders journeying thither must first go to Ssï-ming (四 明), and then put out to sea again; others say that the water current of Ts'üan-chóu gradually lessens, which 40 renders is necessary to pass by way of Ssï-ming[2].

There are two great clans called the Kin (金) and the P'o (朴). During the *wu-tö* period of the T'ang dynasty (A. D. 618 — 627) Chön Kin (眞 金 or the true Kin) was appointed Prince of Lo (or Yo)-lang (樂 浪 郡 王); his descendants have always been princes (君)[3].

During the period *k'ai-yau* (A. D. 681 — 682) they sent a mission to ask for the T'ang Ceremonial and their request was complied with[4].

Their houses, utensils and implements, their mode of dressing and their methods of administration are more or less copies of what we have in China.

In their government the people are ruled by severe laws, for which reason offences are of rare occurrence; and the idea of theft is so foreign to the people that they do not even pick up things dropped on the road[5].

When contracting marriage, they do not send presents. The people can write, and are fond of learning; even the menial classes are given to studious pursuits; in the villages they have colleges, called «public halls» (局 堂) in the inscriptions over their doors. In these their unmarried sons and younger brothers are placed in order to study literature and to practice archery. They have a triennial examination for the degree of *K'ü-jön*, also the examination for the degree of *Tsin-shï*, with the several faculties, as «Exact Sciences», etc. On account of all this the country is styled *Kün-tzï-kuo* (君 子 國 «the Country of Gentlemen»)[6].

The soil of the country is well adapted to the growing of rice, and there are (no) camels or buffalo. They use no cash, but merely barter with rice. Their household vessels and other implements are all made of copper, and they have two kinds of music called the *k'u* (庫 樂) music and the *hiang* (鄉 樂) music[7].

During the period *k'ai-yüan* (A. D. 713—742) Hing Shóu (邢 璹) was sent on a mission of condolence (to the Sin-lo Court)[8]. During the periods *t'ung-kuang* (A. D. 923—926) and *ch'ang-hing* (A. D. 930—934) of the Five Dynasties, tribute missions were sent to the Court of China to perfect the ceremonial; and under the present (Sung) dynasty, in the second year *kién-lung* (A. D. 961), they sent tribute; this was repeated in the second year of *king-kuo* (A. D. 977).

The people of this country believe in the theory of the male and female principles, and in good and evil spirits, and are very superstitious. When Chinese envoys arrive, they must first select a lucky day before they can properly receive the Imperial commands; and, whenever such a message has been received, an address of thanks is written by them to the Emperor, which is not devoid of elegance in style.

The products of the country are ginseng, quicksilver, musk, pine-seeds, hazel-nuts, haliotis shells (石決明), pine-cones, libanotis root (防風), *pai-fu-tzï* (白附子), *fu-ling* (茯苓), cotton cloth of all sizes, *mau-shï* (毛施) cloth, bronze temple bells (銅磬), porcelain, straw mats, and writing brushes made of rats' hair (鼠毛)[9]. Trading ships barter in exchange for these articles coloured silk piece-goods, calendars, and books (建本文字)[10].

Notes.

1) Quotation from T'ang-shu, 220,13[b]. The kingdom of Sin-lo (in Korean Shinra) occupied the eastern and south-eastern portions of the Korean peninsula, from Fusan to the Tumen river, thus extending over most of present northern Korea. This kingdom appears to have been founded in the middle of the first century B. C.; the first mention of the name in Chinese histories appears to date from the Weï period (A. D. 220—264), when it was written Sin-lu (新盧). In the fifth century it occurs under the form Ssï-lo (斯羅). Liang-shu, 54,25[a]. In 934 Sin-lo was absorbed into the newly founded united Korean dynasty of Kau-li (高麗), by which name it was called during the Sung dynasty. Sung-shï, 487,1—20. See Hervey St. Denis, Ethnographie, I, 298 et seqq., J. Ross, History of Corea, 147—195, W. E. Griffis, Corea, 32, 45 et seqq.

The Arab traders of the ninth century, though they knew something of Korea, do not appear to have been there. Suleyman says of it: «Towards the sea China is bounded by the islands of Sïla (Al-Sïla); they are white people, who live in peace with the sovereign of China, and who pretend that if they did not send him presents, the sky would not send down rain on their land. However, none of our countrymen have visited them, so as to be able to tell of them. White pheasants are found in that country». Reinaud, Relations, I, 60.

Masudi (Prairies d'or, I, 346), differs slightly with this. «Beyond China, he says, there is towards the sea no known kingdom or country which has been described, except the territory of es-Sila and the islands which depend on it. It rarely happens that a foreigner who has gone there from Irak or any other country, leaves it afterwards, so healthful is the climate, so clear the water, so fertile the soil, so abundant all things». Cf. Ibn Khordâdhbeh, (de Goeje edit.,) 51, 132.

2) Ssï-ming-chóu in Shang-yü-hién in Chö-kiang. Playfair, Cities and Towns, № 6655. Sung-shï, 487,20 says that after leaving Ting-hai (定海) of Ming-chóu (明州 i. e., Ning-po) with a good wind the sea is reached in three days. Five days later Mo-shan (墨山 Nimrod islands, off extreme S. W. coast of Korea) is made, and the frontier (of Korea) entered. After Mo-shan, passing islands and islets by tortuous rocky channels, the junk sailing swifty arrives in seven days at the Li-chöng-kiang (禮成江 Ta-dong-gang). The river flows between two mountains and rushes down through a rocky gorge called Ki-shui-mön (急水門 «the gate of hurrying waters»), a very dangerous point. Three days hence and the landing point is reached, where there is a house (館) called the Pi-lan-ting (碧瀾亭). From this point the land-route leads by a rough and uneven path over hills and through vales for over 40 *li* to the capital of the kingdom (Pyöng-yang)».

Ssï-ming is the name of a hill near Ning-po which gave its name to the entire neighbourhood, especially the coast facing the east. Yü-ti-ki-shöng, 11,6. The name may be said to stand for Ning-po, as it does in the term Ssï-ming-kung-so, well-known in Shanghai as the «Ning-po joss-house.»

3) T'ang-shu, 220,14[a] says: «the king's family name is Kin, the family name of the nobles is P'o. The common people have no clan names but only surnames».

Lo (or Yo)-lang, in Korean Ak-rang (the present Pyöng-yang), was a Chinese colony since B. C. 108, and remained subject to foreigners until near the fourth century. Maurice Courant, La Corée jusqu'au IXe siècle, 3.

4) The T'ang Ceremonial or T'ang-li (唐禮). The full title of this work has not been preserved, it was probably Hién-k'ing-li-shu (顯慶禮書). It was published during the

chöng-kuan period (A. D. 627—650) and served as the basis for the Ta-T'ang K'ai-yüan-li (大 唐 開 元 禮) in 150 chapters, published in A. D. 713—742, and described in the Shï-k'u-ts'üan-shu-ts'ung-mu, 82,₂. The material from which both these works were compiled is to be found in Tu-Yu's T'ung-tién, and in the Li-chï (禮 志) division of the T'ang-shu.
5 The phrase of our text is taken from T'ang-shu, 220,15[b].

5) Sung-shï, 487,20[a] says «Their forms of punishment are neither barbarous nor cruel; open rebels and those who curse their parents are beheaded, all other criminals are punished with the heavy bamboo on the ribs. Those who have been condemned to death in the provinces are sent to the capital, where, every year in the eighth moon, there is a revision of criminal
10 cases; capital crimes are commuted to deportation to an island, and other sentences are reduced or pardons granted».

6) The Shan-hai-king mentions a «Country of Gentlemen» where the people wore modest clothing and carried swords, and who were of an amiable disposition and not given to litigation. Liu An († B. C. 122) in his Huai-nan-tzï refers to a «Country of Gentlemen in the East». Pei-
15 wön-yün-fu, 102A,24. Our author bases presumably his application of this name to Korea on the use made of it by Hing Shóu during his mission to Korea in A. D. 737 referred to further on (infra, n. 8) and which is related in T'ang-shu, 220,16[a].

7) The information contained in this paragraph, and the previous remarks about exam-inations, etc., are derived from the statements made in A. D. 1015 by the Korean envoy Kuo-
20 Yüan (郭 元). He said there were neither sheep, hares, camels, buffalo nor donkeys. We have corrected our author's text accordingly. He said there were two kinds of music called *k'u* and *hiang*. In a subsequent passage (20[a]) Sung-shï states that there were two styles of music in Korea, the right and the left style; the right style is called *T'ang-yo* (唐 樂) or «Chinese music», the left *hiang-yo* (鄉 樂) or «village music» is their old music. Conf. infra, p. 171, line 10, Kuo-
25 Yüan said that his countrymen did not use cash, but only stuffs and rice for purposes of barter. Sung-shï, 487,17 et seqq. under date A. D. 1164, says that in Korea rice and cloth were used to barter with, for, though there was copper in the country, they had not known how to cast cash, and had hoarded in their storehouses that which came from China. After the *ts'ung-ning* period (A. D. 1102—1106) they learnt how to cast cash, and they had three denominations.

30 8) It was in A. D. 737 that Hing Shóu was sent on a mission of condolence to Korea on the death of Hing-kuang (興 光), king of Sin-lo. When the deceased king's son Ch'öng-k'ing (承 慶) ascended the throne, the envoy was instructed to state in the name of the Emperor that Sin-lo was styled the «Country of Gentlemen», because its people understood poetry and literature, and that, as Hing Shóu was deeply versed in literary matters, He had chosen him as
35 His envoy so that he might discuss with them the meaning of the Classics, and impress them with the mental superiority of the Great Country.

9) On the *fang-föng* or libanotis root, see Bretschneider, Botanicum Sinicum, III, 76—79. *Pai-fu-tzï* (the second character is usually written 附) is an official root, resembling closely that of the Aconitum. Bretschneider, op. cit., 257—258, and Porter Smith, Materia medica,
40 s. v., Aroideæ. *Fu-ling* a funguslike substance used medicinally by the Chinese. It is the Pachyma Cocos, Fries, or China-root. It is found also in North America, where it is called «Indian Bread». Bretschneider, op. cit., 532—536. «Serge» is the usual rendering for *mau-shï*. Sung-shï, 487,18[b], under date A. D. 1164 says that Korea «is cold and mountainous, the soil is good for pines (松) and juniper (栢); it produces rice (秔), millet (黍), hemp and wheat, but no
45 *shu* (秫 a glutinous variety of Setaria italica, Kth.). They make wine from rice. Silkworms are rare, and a piece of silk (繰) is worth over ten ounces of silver. Clothes are made of hempen cloth. There are several hundred Chinese, mostly from Fu-kién province, living in the capital (Pyöng-yang), who have come there on trading junks».

10) It may be that these four characters should be translated «books printed at Foochow».

45.

JAPAN.

Wo (倭).

The country of Wo is to the north-east of Tsʻüan-(chóu). It is at present called Jï-pön (日 本), which name has arisen from the fact that this 5 country is situated near the place where the sun rises. Some people say that they changed the old name because they disliked it[1].

The country extends for several thousand *li* in all directions. In the south and west you come to the sea, in the north and east the country is bounded by big hills; beyond the hills is the country of the Hairy men (毛 人)[2]. 10

The country is divided into five *Ki* (畿), seven *Tau* (道), three islands (島), 3772 communes (鄉), and 414 posting-stations (驛), and its population amounts to fully 883,000 male adults (丁)[3].

Since the country is full of hills and forests and without good arable lands, the inhabitants have a liking for the various kinds of sea food[4].   15

Many of them tattoo their bodies, and they call themselves descendants of Tʻai Po (泰 伯)[5]. It is also said[6] that from remote antiquity they have sent envoys to China who styled themselves *Ta-fu* (大 夫), and, just as in olden times when the descendants of Shau-kʻang of the Hia dynasty were invested with the rule of Kui-ki (會 稽) they cut their hair and tattooed 20 their bodies in order to ward off the harmful attacks of dragon-monsters, so the present people of Wo tattoo their bodies, in order to drive away the beasts of the sea when they dive under water for fishing purposes.

From a calculation of the way thither, (Wo) lies due east from Kui-ki. The climate resembles that of China[7].   25

The king's surname (姓) is *Wang* (王), and this has been so without change for the last seventy generations at least. Civil and military offices are hereditary[8].

Men's dresses consist of strips of cloth worn crosswise, tied, not sewn, together. Women's dresses are like bed sheets, with an opening to run the 30 head through, a whole suit consisting as a rule of two or three pieces of cloth. Both sexes wear their hair unbraided and go barefooted[9].

They have the Chinese standard works, such as the Five Classics and the Collection of poetry by Pai Lo-tʻién (白 樂 天 文 集), all of which are obtained from China[10].   35

The country yields all kinds of cereals, but little wheat. For purposes of exchange they use copper cash bearing the inscription *Kién-yüan-ta-pau* (乾元大寶). They have water-buffalo, donkeys, sheep, (but neither) rhinoceros (nor) elephants, also gold and silver, fine silks and fancy cotton cloth [11].

5   The country produces quantities of cryptomeria trees (杉木) and *lo* trees (羅木), reaching to heights of upwards of fourteen or fifteen *chang*, and fully four feet in diameter. The natives split them into planks, which they transport in large junks to our port of Ts'üan-chóu for sale. The people of Ts'üan-chóu rarely go to this country [12].

10   As regards music, they have the Chinese and the Korean notation (部). They have swords, shields (楯), bows, and arrows which have iron points, but they cannot shoot far with their bows, the reason being that in this country the people are not accustomed to fighting [13].

In their houses separate rooms are used as bed-rooms by father and 15 mother and by the different brothers [14].

When taking their meals, they use dish-stands and dishes (俎豆) [15]. When contracting marriage, they do not make presents of money [16].

For the dead they have coffins (棺), but no coffin-cases (椁). Their tombs consist of simple earthen tumuli. At the beginning of their time of 20 mourning they lament and wail and eat no meat, but when the burial is over, the whole family takes a bath to wash away ill-luck from their bodies [17].

Whenever important affairs are to be entered upon, they scorch bones in order to foretell whether they will turn out luckily or otherwise [18].

They do not know the division of the year with its four seasons, but 25 reckon the year from harvest to harvest [19]. The people attain to great age, frequently to about eighty or ninety years [20].

Women are neither licentious nor jealous. There is no litigation, but when some one is found guilty of a crime, serious cases are punished by the extirpation of the culprit's family, light offenses by the enslaving (沒) of his 30 wife and children [21].

Gold and silver are used in paying taxes to the government; these metals are found in Yüé-chóu (粵州) in the east of this country, and in another island [22].

This county has had intercourse with China since the later Han dynasty 35 (A. D. 25—221), and it has sent envoys with tribute to our Court during the Weï, Sung, Sui and T'ang dynasties. During the first year *yung-hi* of the present dynasty (A. D. 984) a Japanese bonze, by name Tiau-jan (奝然) [23], came across the sea to China with five or six of his disciples and offered presents of more than ten pieces of copper (bronze) ware of most delicate workmanship. The Emperor T'ai-tsung gave orders that he should have an audience and that he should be lodged at the T'ai-p'ing-hing-kuo temple (太平興國寺); he bestowed on him a purple priest's robe and treated him with great kindness. On hearing from him that their kings formed an unin- 5 terrupted line of rulers, all of the same family name, and that the high offices in the country were hereditary, the Emperor sighed, and said to his ministers Sung K'i (宋琪) and Li Fang (李昉)[24]: «These are merely island barbarians, and they have a line of monarchs for such a long time, and even their officials form an uninterrupted hereditary succession; this is indeed the Way 10 of the Ancients»!

Thus it came about that the barbarians of a single island caused the Emperor T'ai-tsung to sigh. Cannot these customs be a survival of the spirit inherited from T'ai Po, who «used the doctrines of our Great Land to change barbarians»?[25]   15

Notes.

1) The name Wo—in Japanese Wa, or perhaps Wani, was probably the name of the ruling tribe or family from which the sovereigns of Japan were at one time taken. Wani appears not unfrequently, as a proper name in the Kojiki and Nihongi. W. G. Aston, Early Japanese History, 40, 41. The Arabs of the ninth century appear to have known of Japan under the name of 20 Wāqwāq, transcribing the Japanese words Wa koku «kingdom of Wa» Van der Lith & Devic Livre des merveilles de l'Inde, 295 et seqq.; also Ibn Khordâdbeh, 50. According to T'ang-shu, 145,18[b] the name Jï-pön — in Japanese Nippon, was first used in A. D. 670. See also T'ang-shu, 220,18[b].

The character Wo means «dwarf», and the Chinese have frequently called Japan Wo-jön- 25 kuo (倭人國), «kingdom of dwarfs», and Wo-nu-kuo (倭奴國) «kingdom of dwarf slaves». See e. g, Sung-shï, 491, and Yüan-shï, 101. It was only in 1895 that, at the urgent request of the Japanese Government, an Imperal Rescript was issued by the Chinese Emperor prohibiting the use of this term in China.

2) This refers to an early period of Japanese history, probably in the seventh century, when 30 the Ainu still possessed the northern portion of the island of Hondo. We find mention of «Hairy men» in as old a work as the Shan-hai-king, but it is not possible that they were the Ainu, the «Hairy men» of our text. The earliest mention we have found in Chinese works of the use of the correct name of the Ainu, Hia-i (蝦夷), occurs in T'ang-shu, 145,18[b], where it is said that in A. D. 632 the Wo came to Court and with them were Ainu (蝦蛦人) who lived on an island 35 in the Ocean. Their envoy had hair four feet long. They wore earrings and had arrows stuck in their hair. A gourd was hung up, and at a distance of some tens of feet they hit it with their arrows every time.

3) The Japanese bonze Tiau-jan— in Japanese Chōnen, who visited the Court of the Sung in A. D. 984, is the authority for this statement. Sung-shï, 491,7. He also gave the population of 40 Japan as 883,329 male adults. The division of Japan into five Home Provinces (五畿內) in Japanese Go-kinai, consisting of the Kyoto, Nara and Asaka districts, seven Provinces — in Japanese Do, and two islands — Tsushima and Iki,—was made in the third century of our era by the Empress Jingo, after her Korean expedition, and in imitation of the Korean system. The Emperor Mommu (696—707) increased the number of provinces to 66 by subdividing the older ones. See 45 Tsin-shu, 97,7 and Chamberlain, Things Japanese (fifth edit.), 211. Hiang, in Japanese go, here

rendered «commune», was, in Japan, a group of hamlets. The «posting-stations», called *yeki* in Japanese, were established along all the highroads throughout the Empire. Sui-shu, 81,15 notes that females were more numerous than males in Japan, so likewise does the T'ang-shu, 220,17[a].

4) See San-kuo-chï (Weï-chï), 30,24[a]. Our author quotes, however, Tsin-shu, 97,4[a].

5) Quotation from Tsin-shu, 97,4[a]. See also Liang-shu, 54,25, and conf. Hóu Han-shu, 145,12[b]. On T'ai Po, see Mayers. Chin. Reader's Manual, 263, s. v., Wu T'ai Peh. See also Legge, Chinese Classics, I, 71.

6) In Tsin-shu, 97,4. See also San-kuo-chï (Weï-chï), 30,25. Hóu Han-shu, 115,13[a] says: «In the second year *chung-yüan* (A. D. 57), in the reign of Kuang-wu, the Wo-nu country sent an envoy with tribute. He styled himself *Ta-fu* (In Japanese *Daibu*). He came from the extreme southern part of the Wo country» (Satsuma?). On tattooing in early Japan, conf. Aston, Nihongi, I, 200, 305, and Munro, Prehistoric Japan, 256—260.

7) Kui-ki is, roughly speaking, the present province of Chö-kiang. The first phrase is quoted from Tsin-shu, 97,4[a]. Conf. Hóu Han-shu, 115,12[b]:

Down to the middle of the eighth century intercourse between China and Japan appears to have mostly been carried on, at least by the official envoys, by a circuitous sea-route which, starting from Satsuma — for the Chinese down to the days in which our author wrote, do not appear to have gone beyond the island of Kyūshū — led to Hakata in Chikuzen, then to Ikishima, Tsushima and the coast of Korea, from whence the coast was followed all the way to Chökiang or Fu-kién. In A. D. 761 a mission was sent for the first time directly from Kyūshū to Ning-po. T'ang-shu, 220A,19[a].

The San-kuo-chï (Weï-chï), 30,24 describes the earlier route between China and Japan; unfortunately many of the names mentioned are still, we believe, unidentified. See Aston, Trans. Asiat. Soc. Japan, XVI, 57. Liang-shu, 54,28[b], describes practically the same route, but with less detail, though in clearer terms. It says in substance that Wo is distant from Kui-ki (i. e., Chö-kiang) over 12,000 *li*, in a general easterly direction by way of Tai-fang (near Pyöng-yang in Korea). The extreme point of this route by way of Tai-fang is in Wo. «The stages of this sea-route are successively, the Han country (i. e., northern Korea), then east, then south for 7,000 *li* and more. (Then) one crosses a sea which is over 1,000 *li* broad and is called the Han-hai (i. e., Sea of Japan). Then one comes to the Iki country (一 支 Ikishima). Thence again across the sea for over 1,000 *li* to the Mo-lu country (末 盧 國 Matsura, but probably Hakata in Chikuzen). Then south-east overland 500 li to the I-tu country (伊 都 or 怡 土 Ido in Chikuzen?). Thence going south-east 100 *li* one comes to the Nu country (奴 國 probably in Naka, Chikuzen). Going thence east 100 *li* one comes to the Pu-mi country (不 彌 國 Kasaga, Chikuzen). Proceeding thence south by water (possibly partly descending the Chikugo gawa) for 20 days one comes to Shö-ma (設 馬 國, not 投 as in text, Satsuma). Thence ten days by water (and) a month overland, and one comes to the country of Yé-ma-t'ai (邪 馬 臺 Yamato), where the Prince of Wo has his residence». Some modern Japanese historians are of opinion that the Yamato here mentioned was in S. E. Kyūshū, presumably in the present Hyūga; its rulers were probably thought by the Chinese — who had never been farther in Japan — to be the rulers of the Empire. See, however, Aston's remarks on this point, loc. cit.

8) Hóu Han-shu, 115,12[b] says: «Wo comprises over one hundred principalities (國) ..... more than thirty of them have had intercourse with China. All the principalities are styled Wang (國 皆 稱 王); they succeed each other generation after generation. The Great Wang of Wo lives in the Yé-ma-t'ai principality (Yamato)». Sui-shu, 81,13[b], says «Wo is divided into thirty principalities and they all call themselves Wang (Japanese *Miko*) or Prince» (皆 自 稱 王)·

T'ang-shu, 220,17[b] says that around the principal island of Wo there are some fifty islands, each one of which calls itself «principality» (國). In 984 the Japanese bonze Tiau-jan (Chōnen) told the Emheror T'ai-tsung of the Sung that the sovereign of his country was called Wang (國 王 以 王 爲 姓) and that at the present time there had been a succession of sixty-four generations of Wangs in direct descent. Civil and military offices were hereditary. Sung-shï, 491,5[a].

9) This is the description of the dress of the Japanese in the first or second century of our era; our author quotes here from Hóu Han-shu, 115,12[b]—13[a]. Conf. San-kuo-chï (Weï-chï), 30,25[b], Tsin-shu, 97,4 and T'ang-shu, 220,18[a].

10) This paragraph is taken from Tiau-jan's (Chōnen's) statement in 984, mentioned previously. «We have, he said, in our country the Five Classics, also the Buddhist Canonical   5 works, and Pai Kü-yi's poetry (白居易集) in 17 books, all of which have been obtained from China». Sung-shï, 491,4[b]. On Pai Lo-t'ien's works, see Pfizmaier, Der Chinesische Dichter Pe Lo-t'ien, and Mayers, Chin. Read. Manual, 170.

11) The bonze Chōnen said: «The soil produces the five kinds of cereals, but little wheat. For purposes of barter (or exchange) we use copper cash bearing the inscription *Kién-wön (yüan)*   10 *ta-pau* (乾文(元)大寶). We have water-buffalo, donkeys and sheep in abundance, also rhinoceros and elephants. The native product is much silk, from which we weave a fine, soft silk, most pleasant to wear». Sung-shï, loc. cit. The correct superscription of these coins is *Kién-yüan-ta-pau*, in Japanese *Ken-gen tai-ho*. Both our author and Sung-shï write the second character erroneously *wön*. This coin, which was in use in the second year of Tentoku (A. D. 958),   15 was the last of the antique coins issued in Japan. No coins were made by Government during the six hundred and odd years which separate the period of Tentoku from the fifteenth year of Tensho (A. D. 1587). N. G. Munro, Coins of Japan, 75, 79. The earliest mention of coin in Japan appears to be in the year 486 A. D. Copper coins were first made in Japan in A. D. 708. Aston, Nihonji, I, 360, 391, II, 414.   20

The text of Chōnen's statement concerning Japan contained in the Sung-shï was presumably taken from an original in which there were a number of undoubted clerical errors, as for example, in the superscription of the coins of Japan, and in the phrase 西別島出白銀, which should unquestionably read 西對島出白銀. We are justified, therefore, in thinking that the text used by Chau Ju-kua and the author of Sung-shï, and which makes Chōnen   25 say that there were rhinoceros and elephants in Japan, was corrupt also in this case, and that he really told T'ai-tsung the simple truth, that there were neither rhinoceros nor elephants in Japan.

12) So far as we can learn there is no tree in Japan called *lo*. It is possible that *lo* is a truncated form of *so-lo* (娑羅 Shorea robusta), though we do not believe that this tree grows in Japan. It may, however, be the Chinese horse-chestnut (Aesculus chinensis, Bge.), which is also   30 called *so-lo* (as in text, though more commonly 桫欏). T'u-shu-tsi-ch'öng (XX, 314, p. 11), quoting the Ko-ku-yau-lun (格古要論, completed in A. D. 1387, see Hirth, Ancient Chinese porcelain, 13), says that *lo* wood (欏木) comes from the Hu-kuang provinces and Nan-an-fu (南安府 Kiang-si), where a hill called Wan-yang-shan produces it. Its wood is white with yellow streaks, and coarsely veined, though not unpleasant to the eye. This kind is called *Wo-lo*   35 (倭欏 i. e., Japanese *lo*), of which many trees are not veined. Another variety, rather tough, with straight fine streaks is called *ts'au-lo* (草欏) and is popularly known as *t'u-mu* (楡木). See also K'ang-hi-tzï-tién, s. v. Lo (欏). Giles, Chin. Engl. Dictionary, 746, identifies the *ts'au-lo* with the horse-chestnut (Aesculus chinensis). The *lo* mentioned by our author was probably some kind of pine tree, but it seems impossible to identify it. This paragraph   40 of our text is practically the only original contribution of our author in the chapter on Japan.

13) The first phrase of this paragraph is taken from the bonze Chōnen's statement, quoted previously. The substance of the second phrase is taken from Tsin-shu, 97,4[a]. Conf also Hóu Han-shu, 115,12[b] and San-kuo-chï (Weï-chï), 30,25[b]. Chinese music, called *kure gaku*, is said to have been introduced into Japan from Korea in A. D. 612. Aston, Nihongi, II, 144—376.   45

14) Quotation from Hóu Han-shu, 115,13[a]. See also San-kuo-chï (Weï-chï), 30,15[b], and Tsin-shu, 97,4[a].

15) Quotation from Hóu Han-shu, 115,13[a] except that for *tsu-tóu* it has *pién-tóu* (籩豆). Tsin-shu, 97,4[a] uses the word *tsu-tóu*. Conf. San-kuo-chï (Weï-chï), 30,25[b] and Sui-shu, 81,15[a].

16) Quotation from Tsin-shu, 97,4[a]. Conf. Sui-shu, 81,15[b]. «Shinto never had a marriage   50 ceremony». Aston, Shinto, 249.

17) Quotation from Tsin-shu, 97,4[a] or Liang-shu, 54,26[a]. Conf. Hóu Han-shu, 115,13[a] and San-kuo-chï (Weï-chï) 30,25[b]. See Aston, Shinto, 252.

18) Quotation from Hóu Han-shu, 115,13ᵃ. See also San-kuo-chĭ (Weï-chĭ), 30,26ᵃ. Aston, Shinto, 339 says: «The greater, or official, divination consists in drawing conclusions according to certain conventional rules from the cracks which appear in a deer's shoulder-blade when exposed to fire».

5   19) San-kuo-chĭ (Weï-chĭ) 30,26ᵃ, quoting the Weï-lio, says: «They (the Japanese) do not usually know the true year and the four seasons. They simply reckon as a year from the spring cultivation of the fields to the autumn in-gathering». Aston, Trans. Asiat. Soc. Japan, XVI. 59, remarks on this passage: «It is not quite clear what is meant by this. It may mean simply that the Japanese reckoned their year from the spring or autumn equinox and not from the New 10 Year, and it may not have been intended to imply that their year consisted of only six months. Another writer says that the Was reckoned their year from autumn to autumn ...» This latter view is that of Tsin-shu, 97,4ᵇ which our author quotes from. Some native etymologists connect *toshi*, the Japanese word for «year» with the harvest and with *tcru* «to take».

20) Quotation from Tsin-shu, 97,4ᵇ. See also Hóu Han-shu, 118,13ᵃ; San-kuo-chĭ (Weï-chĭ), 15 30,26ᵃ, and Liang-shu, 54,26ᵃ.

21) Hóu Han-shu, 115,13ᵃ. San-kuo-chĭ (Weï-chĭ), 30,26ᵃ. Tsin-shu, 97,4ᵇ.

22) It was again the bonze Chōnen who told this to the Chinese in 984. The text, both in our author and in Sung-shĭ, is certainly corrupt here in two places. The character *yüé* in Yüé-chóu is clearly an error for *au* (奧 in Japanese *ō*), as Ōshu (奧 州) was the part of Japan where 20 gold was first discovered, in A. E. 749. Ōshu is now divided into several provinces, but it is probable that the Handa mine in the province of Iwashiro is the one referred to by Chōnen. The other error is, as pointed out on page 174, note 11, writing «another island», instead of *«Tui-tau»* (對 島) in Japanese Tsushima, on which island silver was found in A. D. 675, and where mines were worked for a long period subsequently.

25   23) Tiau-jan, in Japanese. Chōnen (posthumous title, *Kozi daisi*), belonged to the great Fujiwara clan. He was a priest of Nara. Our author has incorporated into this chapter all the information which the Sung-shĭ states he gave the Emperor Tʻai-tsung.

24) The biography of Sung Kʻi is in Sung-shĭ, 264,12; that of Li Fang, in Sung-shĭ, 265,1. Mencius, Bk. III, Pt. I, Ch. IV, 12 (Legge, Chinese Classics, II, 129) said: «I have heard 30 of men using the doctrines of our great land to change barbarians, but I have never yet heard of any being changed by barbarians».

46.

ISLAND OF HAINAN.

Hai-nan (海 南).

35   Hai-nan is the Chu-ai (朱 崖) and Tan-ïr (儋 耳) of tho Han period. When the Emperor Wu-ti (B. C. 140—86) had made the conquest of Southern Yüé (粵), he sent a mission from Sü-wön across the sea to reconnoitre the country; as a consequence the two prefectures (郡) of Chu-ai and Tan-ïr were established. His successor Chau-ti (B. C. 86—73) dropped Tan-ïr 40 and incorporated it in Chu-ai. On the advice of Kia Küan-chĭ (賈 捐 之), the Emperor abandoned Chu-ai, and it was only again occupied under the Liang (A. D. 502—527) and the Sui (A. D. 589—618) dynasties[1].

In the first year of the *chöng-kuan* period of the T'ang dynasty (A. D. 627), the country (of Hai-nan) was divided into three departaments (州), Ai (崖), Tan (儋), and Chön (振), and they were attached to the province of Ling-nan (嶺 南 道). In the fifth year (A. D. 631), K'iung shan (瓊 山) in Ai was made a prefecture (*kün*), and Wan-an-hién (萬 安 縣) was raised 5 to departmental rank (*chóu*), identical with the military districts (軍) or *kün* of the present day; while Tan and Chön were then as now the military districts of Ki-yang (吉 陽) and Ch'ang-hua (昌 化)[2].

In the fifth year of the *chön-yüan* period (A. D. 789), K'iung was made the seat of a military prefecture (督 府), which it still remains.   10

K'iung-(chóu) lies some 360 *li* from the place (called) Ti-kio-ch'ang (遞 角 場) in Sü-wön on the main-coast, and the passage to it can be made with a fair wind in half a day. The mid-channel is called San-ho-liu (三 合 溜); when this has been passed, if there is neither wind nor sea, the sailors can congratulate themselves with raised hands on their good luck[3]. 15

Ki-yang lies at the extreme (southern) end of the coast (of Hai-nan), and there is no land beyond it, but outside there are two islets, Wu-li (烏 里) and Su-ki-lang (蘇 吉 浪). Chan-ch'öng faces it to the south, and to the west it looks towards Chön-la. To the east (of Hai-nan) are the «Thousand *li* banks» (千 里 長 沙) and the «Myriad *li* rocks» (萬 里 石 床), and 20 (beyond them) is the boundless ocean, where the sea and the sky blend their colours, and the passing ships sail only by means of the south-pointing needle —if it be closely watched by day and night—for life or death depends on the slightest fraction of error[4].

The island (of Hai-nan) is divided into four prefectures (*kün*), eleven 25 departments (*hién*) in all, being attached to the western circuit (路) of Kuang-nan (廣 南). They lie around the Li-mu mountain (黎 母 山) where the wild Li (黎 獠) have their huts (蟠 踞). The Li are divided into Savage Li and Semi-civilized Li. Although they have much fallow land, there is not raised enough rice to supply food for the people; to get their fill 30 they have to make soup of tubers, taro, and different kinds of grain; this is the reason for the trade in sweet-scented woods (carried on by the Li)[5].

The products of the country are gharu-wood, *p'öng-lai* gharu-wood, *chö-ku-pan-hiang* (gharu-wood) (鷓 鴣 斑 香), *tsién-hiang* (gharu-wood), *shöng-hiang* (gharu-wood), cloves, betel-nuts, cocoanuts, cotton (*ki-peï*), hemp 35 (苧 麻), paper-mulberry bark, red and white rattan, flowered silk sarongs (花 縵), and curtains embroidered by the Li (黎 幙), green cassia-wood, rose-wood, *hai-meï-chï* (海 梅 脂), *k'iung ch'ï-ts'ai* (瓊 枝 菜), *hai-ts'i*

(海 漆), long pepper (蓽 撥), galangal root (高 艮 薑), fish glue (魚 鰾), yellow wax, and fossil crabs (石 蟹). Most of these products come from the mountain villages of the Li and are exchanged with the Chinese for salt, iron, fish, and rice; the latter sell them to traders (on the coast)[6].

5 The junks which come hither from Ts'üan-chóu to trade, are laden with samshu, rice, flour, silks, lacquer, and china ware. They sail from Ts'üan-chóu at the end of the year, or in the first month of the year, so as to return thither in the fifth or sixth month (i. e., June to August); but, if they want cargoes of fresh betel-nuts, they must sail earlier, so as to get back in the 10 fourth month (i. e., April-May).

K'iung-chóu is situated to the north-east of the Li-mu mountain. The prefectural capital is the same as Ai-chóu of antiquity. During the *chöng-ho* period (1111—1118) it was made the headquarters of a military brigade (節 鎮), with the Tsing-hai (靖 海) regiment as garrison. It borders on 15 the sea, and is not very hilly. As to the climate, it is rainy in autumn, dry in spring, not too hot in summer, not too cold in winter. Typhoons (颶 風) are frequent in the fifth and sixth months (i. e., June to August), and if one of these is accompanied by a rainbow, the latter is called «storm (or typhoon) mother» (颶 母)[7].

20 According to the 'Records of the Sui dynasty' (隋 志) the people (of K'iung chóu?) were of a frivolous but cruel nature. They did their hair up in a mallet-shaped knot, and wore clothes made of grasses (卉 裳). They kept records by means of notches in pieces of wood, were laborious cultivators, but of uncouth manners. Father and son followed different vocations. Important 25 persons cast bronze into big drums and hung them up in their houses; when one of them beat his drum to call his people (同 類), and if they hastened to gather around him in great numbers, he was known as a *tu-lau* (都 老)[8]. The people wore silk clothes (人 着 細 緶), and made pots out of clay, and household vessels of calabashes. As they had no yeast, they fermented 30 their wine with pomegranate flowers.

At the present time their upper garments differ not from those of the Chinese, the nether clothing of the men is a cotton sarong (縵) and that of the women a plaited skirt (裙). They make their living by spinning cotton. They still use earthenware pots, and occasionally calabashes to ladle water; 35 in brewing wine they use tubers and grain for ferment (以 變 色). Although there are no wealthy people among them, nevertheless, as they are a thrifty people, there are no poor and one sees no beggars in bad years.

When Ting, Duke of Tsin (丁 晉 公), was degraded to the rank of

Prefectural Finance Commissioner (州 司 戶) he taught the people (of K'iung-chóu) to read books and to compose (著 文)[9]. During the *k'ing-li* period (1041—1049) Earl Sung Kuan-chï (宋 貫 之) built the prefectural college, which was renovated in the *köng-wu* year of the *kia-ting* period (1210) by Earl Chau Ju-hia (趙 汝 厦), on which occasion tablets to the manes of Dukes Su Tung-po (蘇 東 坡) and Hu Tan-an (胡 澹 庵) were erected on the east and west sides of the Lecture hall, and on the tablet of the hall was written «*ming tau*» (明 道 «Understanding and Method» or «Enlighteners of the Way»)[10].

In Hai-k'óu (海 口) there is a «Temple of the two Fu-po of the Han dynasty» (漢 兩 伏 波 廟), where the manes of Lu Po-tö (路 博 德) and Ma Yüan (馬 援) are worshipped. Those who pass by on the sea must pray here, and no one may pursue his journey before learning his luck from the *peï-kiau* tablets (环 珓)[11].

Five towns, K'iung shan (瓊 山), Ch'öng-mai (澄 邁), Lin-kau (臨 高), Wön-ch'ang (文 昌) and Lo-hui (樂 會), are subordinate to this district (of K'iung-chóu), and in each of them there is a Maritime Customs Collector (市 舶)[12].

The junks which trade there are divided into three classes: the first is called *po* (舶), the second *pau-t'óu* (包 頭), the third *tan* (蜑)[13]. When a junk arrives, a Customs Inspector (津 務) reports the fact to the District Magistrate (州), who then sends an officer to gauge the tonnage and determine the regulation duty. Officials of all ranks, as well as the soldiers, look to this (duty) for their maintenance.

After a journey of 236 *li* farther west the military district (軍 治) of Ch'ang-hua (昌 化) is reached.

Ch'ang-hua is situated to the north-west of the Li-mu mountain, and is the same as the ancient Tan-chóu[14]. The city walls are fourteen feet high and measure 220 paces (*p'u*) around. According to ancient records the city was built by the noblewoman Tan-ïr (儋 耳 夫 人); she made the goblins (鬼) work for her, and they with baskets and shovels completed the whole work in a single night.

According to another version the people of this country were called Tan-ïr (i. e., «pendant ears») because their ears hung down on their shoulders. Although at the present time no children are born in Ch'ang-hua with long ears, nevertheless the Li, as devout Buddhists, put big rings in their ears, making them to reach down to the shoulders[15].

The country is free from epidemics (i. e., malaria) and marshes. As the climate is absolutely different to that of China, all flowers bud early in the year and have already ceased blooming in the spring, only the water-lily blooms from the fourth or fifth month (i. e., May to June) to the end of the twelfth month, and the plum and chrysanthemum follow it immediately.

The people are simple, honest, and frugal folk. The women do not wear silk gauzes (羅綺), nor do they whiten their faces nor blacken their eyebrows (as Chinese women do). They follow the orthodox (Chinese) fashions in their marriage and funeral ceremonies. No one of the common people suffers from hunger or cold (i. e., there are no indigents).

The College was originally situated in the south-eastern section of the city; it was later on transferred to the western, but in the *shau-hing* period (1131—1163) it was again transferred to the eastern. The Memoir (記) concerning it was written by Duke Li Kuang (李公光), Assistant Prime Minister (參政)[16].

Fifteen *li* from the Departmental Capital there is a place called Tan-ch'ang (蜑場). When Chau Ting, who was canonized as Duke Chung-kién (忠簡趙公鼎), was degraded to the rank of Magistrate in Ki-yang[17], he passed this place, where all the springs had gone dry during a great drought in midsummer; and here, on digging a well, water was found at a depth of a few feet. (This well) has not dried up to the present day, and it is called the Siang-ts'üan or «The Minister's spring» (相泉); it is also well known as the Pai-ma-tsing-ts'üan or «White horse well spring» (白馬井泉); it has wonderfully good water, and trading junks supply themselves from it for the voyage home.

There is a shrine called the Ling-tsi-miau (靈濟廟) inside the Chön-an gate (鎮安門), which is dedicated to the worship of the noble-woman Tan-ïr (儋耳夫人). During the *shau-hing* period (1131—1163) she was raised to the rank of an official deity under the appellation of Hién-ying Fu-jön (顯應夫人 «the Noblewoman not invoked in vain»). When the Li villages (峒) away from the coast (i. e., in the mountains) get much loot in a raid on the Tan district, they believe they have solely to thank the power of the Fu-jön.

Some 50 *li* west of the city there is, in a big laguna on an islet of the sea, a rocky peak shaped like a lion, which the people call «the Lion god» (獅子神). The fact is that there is here one of the temples consecrated to the manes of Marquess Chön Li (貞利侯)[18], where trading junks pray for good wind. The district has three cities, I-lun (宜倫), Ch'ang-hua, and Kan-ön (感恩)[19].

After a journey of 340 *li* in a southerly direction, one reaches the

border of the military district of Ki-yang (吉 陽 軍), which is situated to
the south-west of the Li-mu mountain. The capital, a second-class prefecture
(郡 冶 州), is founded on the site of the (older city of) Ki-yang-hién [20].

Although the different districts of K'iung(-chóu, i. e., Hai-nan) might
be reached by land, they are nevertheless so cut off from the Capital by the 5
villages of the wild Li, that one must go by sea to get to them. That is what
Hu Tan-an (胡 澹 庵) meant when he said: «Again I passed a great billowy
danger» (再 涉 鯨 波 險) [21].

To the south of the district city (of Ki-yang) is the post-station of Hai-
k'óu (海 口 驛), below which traders moor their junks. There is a small 10
pavilion in front of this place for the reception of travellers.

The country is a narrow strip (along the foot of the Li-mu mountain); it
is sparsely peopled. The climate is not normal, for the spring is usually
excessively dry, while, when the summer is already passed, then comes the
rain (涉 夏 方 雨).   15

They cultivate the land without either manuring or weeding it. Wood-
choppers, herdsmen, fishermen and huntsmen must go about carrying bows
and arrows, as they are always falling in with Li savages. The women do not
occupy themselves with raising silkworms and making silk, but they weave
with cotton (ki-pëi) flowered coverlets, and sarongs in the Li patterns. The 20
men have no occupation, and live simply from hand to mouth. They all believe
in spirits, and have neither medical science nor medicines. When some one is
ill, they slaughter a bullock, then, with beating of drums and music, they make
an offering of it (祀), and this they call «making good luck»; furthermore no
one is allowed to pass by the door (of the sick person). In their mortuary 25
ceremonies they have music [22].

The country is full of lofty peaks and picturesque mountain scenery (岡
峻 嶺 峰 巒), so it has come about that among the scholars of the district
many have made reputations (as able poets) (秀 拔 故 郡 之 士 人 間
有 能 自 立 者) [23].   30

The College is situated in the north-eastern part of the district capital.
Thirteen li from the city there is a rock with a surface which is as flat as the
palm of the hand, without any human labour having been used to make it so.
It is some tens of feet in circumference so that visitors can sit on it;
(here) there is a grove of thick, luxuriant trees, and a cool, clear brooklet 35
ripples by. At this spot the Marquess of Chóu (周 侯) built a reed hut, and
over the entrance he put this superscription «untroubled enjoyment» (清 賞).

The villages of the semi-civilized Li are few and far between, their

dwelling-places being from five to seven *li* apart. The wild Li who formed over an hundred villages, from time to time made raids (upon the country of the Chinese settlers). The Marquess of Chóu sent a head-man of the semi-civilized Li on a mission to them to get them to make an arrange-
5 ment for holding a weekly market (寅 酉 二 日)²⁴; after this they came on foot with their goods on their backs and shoulders, or else floated down on rafts to trade with the Chinese settlers. The district (of Ki-yang-kün) was divided into two districts (*hién*), Ki-yang and Ning-yüan (甯 遠), which, in the *chöng-ho* period (1111—1118), were united into one, Ning-yüan-hién.
10   A hundred and twenty *li* to the east, one reaches the border of the military district of Wan-an (萬 安 軍). The Wan-an military district is north-east of the Li-mu mountain. It was founded in the fifth year of the *chöng-kuan* period of the T'ang dynasty (A. D. 631) under the name of Wan-an-chóu (州), and divided into three districts (*hién*) called Wan-an, Fu-yün (富 雲) and Po-liau
15 (博 遼). In the beginning of the *t'ién-pau* period (742) it was changed from a department or *chóu*, to a *kün* (郡) or prefecture. In the second year of the *chï-tö* period (757) its name was changed to that of Wan-ts'üan (萬 全), and in the beginning of the *k'ién-yüan* period (758) it was once more made a department.
20   During the present (Sung) dynasty the two districts (*hién*) of Fu-yün and Po-liau were done away with, and Wan-an-hién was called Wan-ning (萬 甯); but in the sixth year *hi-ning* (1073) it (i. e., the whole district) was made a military district (*kün*), and the name of Wan-ning was changed to Ling-shui (陵 水); at the present time they are both included (in the one dis-
25 trict or *hién*)²⁵.
     The Chinese settlers of this district live mixed with the Li and the Tan (蜑)²⁶. They are plain and uncouth in their habits, but so law-abiding and disliking robbery and theft that people can let their cattle and sheep roam about unguarded without fear of their being wrongfully claimed.
30   Their dwellings are mostly of reeds and bamboo, and seldom have tiled roofs. Women of all ages occupy themselves with weaving cotton, but they do not make patterns on it. The sick take no medicine. They put their faith in sorcery (巫), and devils, (to whom) they sacrifice an ox, praying for happi-ness and aid. After the establishment of the first drug shops by Huang Hóu-
35 shön (黄 侯 申)²⁷, they gradually came to see the advantage of taking medi-cine. In the eastern part of the city is the Po-chu Tu-kang-miau or «Temple of the ship-captain Tu-kang» (舶 主 都 綱 廟)²⁸. Whosoever with profound faith prays here for an omen (卜), gets a reply. Passing ships

make an offering here before proceeding (farther). The annual and triennial examinations for literary degrees for the three prefectures (of Ch'ang-hua, Ki-yang and Wan-chóu) are all held, with those for K'iung-chóu, (at this place).

The native tribes of the four prefectures of the island of Hai-nan are 5 called Li (黎). The Li-mu mountain of the island is recognizable at night by its cheering glitter (祥光), which is visible in all the four adjacent prefectures. According to a passage in the Tsin-shu (or History of the Tsin (晉) dynasty) referring to the divisions of the land, (this) division, which is under the influence of the *wu-nü* star (婺女), is said to be under the light of the 10 stars Li-niu (黎牛) and Wu-nü (婺女), which are (collectively) called Li-wu (黎婺), the sound of which has been corrupted to Li-mu (黎母, the name of the mountain) [29].

The dwelling places of the native tribes (蠻) are situated around this mountain, whose summit rises to an extraordinarily great height, for it is 15 generally wrapped in fog. The Li themselves only rarely see it, save on clear autumn days, when its azure peak is visible, floating as it were in space (浮插半空) [30]. There is a spring on this mountain which bubbles up to form five streams, one of which flows to (the town of) Ch'ang-hua, one to Ki-yang, one to Wan-an, two to K'iung-chóu, one of which becomes a big creek (溪) 20 and, with 36 rapids (in its course), flows down to the village of Chang-liau (長寮村) in Ch'öng-mai-hién (澄邁縣), the other becomes a small creek which, with 24 rapids (in its course), runs to the village of Chu-yün (硃運村) in Lo-hui-hién (樂會縣). These two streams flow into each other and become the San-ho-shui (三合水), which goes to 25 K'iung-shan-hién.

(Those of the aborigines) who live in the remotest parts of the province are called *Shöng-Li* (i. e., 'Wild Li'), those who live nearer (to the Chinese) are called *Shóu-Li* (i. e., 'Tame Li'), and these latter are under the control of the nearest one of the four Military districts (軍). The villages (峒) of the 30 Li grow daily, so it is not possible to know their populousness. Neither do they remain under one chief, but usually each village has its own head-man who must belong to either the Wang (王), the Fu (符), the Chang (張) or the Li (李) family. Persons of the same family name may inter-marry. Frequently Chinese criminals seek refuge among the Li. The males wear their hair 35 twisted in a knot, they go barefooted and stick silver, copper or pewter pins in their hair. The women wear copper rings and ear-pendants which hang down to their shoulders. Young girls when they reach marriageable age have their cheeks finely tattooed; this is called «embroidering the face» (繡面), and, when the tattooing is completed, the relatives and friends assemble to offer congratulations. Female slaves do not «embroider» their faces[31].

The women's work is spinning and weaving, for which purpose they
5 buy Chinese coloured silk stuffs, draw out the coloured threads and weave these with tree-cotton (木 棉) into single curtains (單 幕); they also make excellent cloth of (both kinds of) cotton.

They sacrifice to the gods oxen, dogs, fowls, and pigs, often as many as an hundred (at a time). As there is neither salt nor iron, fish, nor shrimps
10 (in their country), they barter for them with the neighbouring Chinese settlers with gharu-wood, unbleached cotton cloth, tree-cotton, and hemp (麻 皮), for they do not make use of coined money.

Their dwellings have bamboo frames; the ground floor is occupied by their live-stock, the inhabitants live in the upper part. The men carry usually
15 a long wooden-handled knife (肥) and a long bow (弰 弓); they do not take a step without them. They delight in taking revenge and killing (their ene-mies), they call this «seizing» (捉 劫). In the case of a relative being killed, they lay hold of and fetter some member of the family of the (dead man's) enemy or of his village, and, for a fetter, they use a piece of lichee-wood six
20 feet long and in shape like a foot-pestle (碓). Then they demand of the prisoner, before they will release him, either a cow, wine, silver, or a pitcher (缾), to «ransom his life» as they call it[32].

On the conclusion of a marriage contract they break an arrow in two as a proof of good faith. The festivals are held with beating of drums,
25 dances and singing. When a person dies they always kill an ox as a sacrifice[33].

Among the native products of this country the *ch'ön-shui* and *p'öng-lai* (varieties of gharu-wood) take the first rank in the Hiang-p'u (香 譜)[34]. The mountains are covered with areca and cocoanut palms; there are also
30 ponies, kingfishers' feathers, and yellow wax[35]. It often happens that traders from Min (i. e., Fu-kién), driven on the coast by storms and having lost everything in the wreck of their junks, have gone into the Li country to make a living by tilling the soil[36]. When Chinese officials or people are travelling to the native villages, they can expect perfect security when they stop in the
35 houses of (these Chinese inland-settlers).

Military posts of the four departments (州) of Hai-nan keep guard outside the (territory of the) Tame Li in the four quarters (四 隅), along a line of a thousand *li*. There is a road like a connecting ring (between the posts). A person wishing to take a trip through this country could not do so in less than a month[37].

When Ma Fu-po (馬 伏 波) had pacified Hai-nan, he ordered potters to make some earthenware vessels (器), the larger of which held several piculs of rice, the smaller from five to two or three bushels. Then he invited 5 (the natives), even from the most remote villages, who had made their submission, and he gave (these vessels) to them at their choice. By this means he was enabled to form an idea of the accessibility, or otherwise, of their nests and caves (巢 穴). The Wild Li took the small jars of two or three bushels, and when asked the reason, replied that they had all come down 10 from steep cliffs and the (forks of) trees (緣 木) and that they could not take the big ones, because they feared that they would not be able to carry them home. By this (the General) learnt that their villages and caves (峒 穴) were deep in the interior, in precipitous and inaccessible places[38].

Among (the Chinese) population of the four prefectures the clan name 15 of Li (黎) is very common, because this clan is descended from the Li. At the present time there are many descended from the Li who bear the surname of Wang (王). In the first year of the *shun-hi* period (1174) the head-man of the wild Li of the Wu-chï-shan (五 指 山), Wang Chung-k'i (王 仲 期) by name, gathered together the neighbouring Li villages, eighty in 20 number with a population of 1820 adult males (丁), for the purpose of making their submission to Chinese rule. When Chung-k'i and the various head-men, Wang Chung-wön (王 仲 文) and others, in all eighty-one men, repaired to K'iung (-chóu) to present themselves, they bound themselves, by an oath taken in the Hién-ying-miau (顯 應 廟), by stone-rubbing and blood-drinking (研 25 石 歃 血), to give up misdoing and to desist from rapine and acts of violence. The Prefect of K'iung-chóu arranged drawings of their outward appearance and of their clothing which were submitted to the Viceroy (經 略 司)[39]. (According to these drawings) those of the natives who wore their hair in a knot (or knob) and uncovered, wrapped the lower part of the knot with 30 red silk, or wrapped the hair entirely in coloured silk, or else they wore little flaring ornamented bamboo hats (小 花 笠), but all of them wore two silver combs (銀 篦) stuck in their hair. Some of them wore a short embroidered skirt[40]. Wang Chung-k'i was further distinguishable by a blue turban (巾) and a long red silk brocade gown, bound round with a girdle. He 35 himself said that this was a brocade gown which one of his ancestors, during the *süan-ho* period (1119—1126), had received from the Emperor for having ceded a piece of land to the Chinese Government[41].

The products of Hai-nan are also found in foreign lands; the difference
is in their quality. The *tsién* and *ch'ön* (gharu-wood) from K'iung (i. e. Hai-
nan) far surpass those from foreign lands by the quality and strength of their
perfume; those from Chan-ch'öng and Chön-la are not to be compared with
5 them. On the other hand, the yellow wax of Hai-nan is not to be compared
with that of San-fo-ts'i, it is even inferior to that of San-sü. The other products are mostly like those of foreign lands, with the exception of betel-nuts
and cotton (吉 貝), which are extraordinarily plentiful; the Ts'üan-chóu
traders look principally to the latter as a profitable article[42].

10   Notes.

1) In the two texts we possess of the Chu-fan-chï, the account of Hai-nan appears as an
appendix to Part II. Nan Yüé or Southern Yüé, was the southern portion of the kingdom of Yüé,
and corresponded approximately with the present province of Kuang-tung. Sü-wön, a note in the
text says, «is the present prefecture (Hién) of Sü-wön in the Leï-chóu peninsula». For fuller notes
15 on this chapter of our author, see Hirth, Die Insel Hainan nach Chao Ju-kua. Only such notes as
are necessary for a good understanding of the text have been added in the present work. See also
Ts'ién-Han-shu, 6,20^b.

2) «Province (Tau) of Ling-an». It corresponded roughly with the present Kuang-tung, a
portion of Kuang-si and of Tung-king. On Ch'ang-hua, in Cantonese Ch'öong-fa, see infra, p. 178.
20 Substantially all the information in this and the first paragraph is found in Ling-wai-tai-ta, 1,16.

3) B. C. Henry, Ling-nam, 332, speaking of Hainan straits, says that it «is the most
dangerous point on the route; the rocks and the currents are so treacherous and the channel
so intricate, that no ship will go through in the night. These difficulties of the passage are
increased by the state of the tides, which ebb and flow through the straits but once in twenty
25 four hours».

Chóu K'ü-feï says of it: «The Great Sea which is south-west of Hainan is called the Sea
of Kiau-chï (交 阯 洋). In it is the San-ho-liu («the Triple-joint-currents»). The waves
break here violently, dividing into three currents; one flows south and is the sea which forms the
highway to foreign lands; one flows northward and is the sea of Kuang-tung, Fu-kién and Chö-
30 kiang. One flows eastward and enters the Boundless Place (無 際 所), which is called the
Great Eastern Ocean Sea.

«Ships in the southern trade, both going and coming, must run through the San-ho-liu. If
they have the wind, in a moment they are through it. But if on getting into the dangerous
place, there is no wind, the ship cannot get out and is wrecked in the three currents». Ling-wai-
35 tai-ta, 1,13^b.

4) Ling-wai-tai-ta, I, 13^b—14^a says: «It is said that in the Great Eastern Ocean Sea there
is a long bank of sand and rocks some myriads of *li* in length, it marks the *Weï-lü*, the gulf
leading to Hades (尾 閭 所 洩 淪 入 九 幽). In olden times there was an ocean
going junk which was driven by a great westerly wind to within hearing distance of the roar of
40 the waters (falling into) the *Weï-lü* of the Great Eastern Ocean. No land was to be seen. Suddenly
there arose a strong easterly wind and (the junk) escaped (its doom)». Conf. supra, pp. 26, 75, 79, n. 2.

Groeneveldt, Notes, 25, translating the narrative of Shï Pi's (史 弼) expedition to
Java in 1292 (Yüan-shï, 162,12^b—13), refers to the fleet — which started from Ts'üan-chóu, sailing
through the Sea of the Seven Islands (七 洲 洋 the Sea of the Paracels Islands) and the Long
45 Reef (萬 里 石 塘 Macclesfield Banks), and passing the land of Kiau-chï and Champa, etc.
This identification is, I think, correct. Our author's Wan-li-shï-ch'uang is certainly the same, and
ch'uang (床) may well be an error for *t'ang* (塘), the two characters are somewhat alike. The
«long bank of sand and rocks» (長 砂 石 塘) of the Ling-wai-tai-ta can hardly be
the same.

5) During the Sung dynasty most of the present provinces of Kuang-tung and Kuang-si formed one province called Kuang-nan, divided into an eastern and western Circuit or Lu.

On the Li-mu mountains and the Hainan aborigines, or Li, see pp. 182—183, and infra, note 30.

6) On these different varieties of gharu-wood, see infra, Pt. II. Ch. XI. Haï-meï-chï, literally «Sea-plum gum» may be the same as the la-meï (蠟梅), Chimonanthus fragrans, Porter Smith, Chin. Materia medica, 60. O-meï-shan-chï, as cited in T'u-shu-tsi-ch'öng, XX, 206, describes a hai-meï growing on Mt. Omi, as a shrub about three feet high with fruit like the Chinese cherry (Cerasus pseudo-cerasus).

K'iung-chï-ts'ai is said by Pön-ts'au-kang-mu, 28,23, to be identical with the shï-hua-ts'ai, or agar-agar, an edible sea-weed much used in China. Hai-ts'i, literally «sea-varnish», is, I believe, unidentified. Shï-hié or «stone-crabs» are mentioned in the List of medicines exported from Hankow, etc. (Imp. Marit. Customs. II. Special Series, № 8), 37 as «Fossil crabs. Macrophthalmus Latreilli and Portunus leucodea.» Ling-wai-tai-ta, 7,15 says they are found along the whole coast of Hainan and that they are exactly like the big sea-crab or siu-mo (蝤蛑). It is used, it adds, as a medicine in eye complaints.

7) Ling-piau-lü-i (嶺表錄異) written by Liu Sün (劉恂) during the T'ang dynasty says (1,1ᵃ), that a kü-föng is a terrible wind which destroys houses, trees, etc. Sometimes there is none for two or three years, while at times there may be three in a single year. This appears to be the real typhoon. Certain works quoted in the T'ai-wan-fu-chï, however, distinguish between the kü-föng and the t'ai-föng, the former being less disastrous than the latter. See Hirth, «The word Typhoon», J. R. G. S., 1880, pp. 6—7 of reprint.

8) See Sui-shu, 31,15, of which this paragraph of our text is an abstract. In regard to the bronze drums Sui-shu says that as soon as they had cast a big bronze drum they hung it up in their courtyard, put out wine and invited their people to come. Some of the well-to-do sons and daughters made big hair-pins of gold or silver, and proclaimed the fact by beating their drum, then they stored them away. Such wealthy people were known as «bronze drum and hair-pin people» (銅鼓釵). They also beat their drums to call their clan together to avenge the death of one of their number. Those who had drums were called Tu-lau. In the days of the Han the great chief of the Man savages (蠻夷) was called Lau-fu-ch'ön (老夫臣), the Li continued thereafter to call their elders (or persons of high standing, 尊) tau-lau (倒老), a word which by phonetic decay has become tu-lau.

On the subject of the bronze drums, the invention of which is ascribed by the Chinese to the General Ma Yüan (regarding whom see infra, note 11), see F. Hirth, Chinesische Ansichten über Bronzetrommeln, 1904.

9) Ting Tsin-kung was born in Su-chóu in the latter part of the tenth century; his name was Ting Weï (丁謂). He rendered distinguished services to the state in various capacities, and was made Duke of Tsin in 1022. Later on, having become implicated in an intrigue with the eunuch Leï Yün-kung, he was degraded and banished. Three years of his exile he lived in a village in Hainan and five more on the Leï-chóu peninsula. He died in 1033. Sung-shï, 283,8, et seqq., and Hirth, Die Insel Hainan, 15, note 2.

10) Sung Kuan-chï, also called Sung-hién (宋咸) was born about the beginning of the eleventh century; so far as known he did not visit Hainan. The great biographical work called Wan-sing-t'ung-pu, mentions a Sung Shóu-chï (宋守之) as having promoted literary studies in Hainan. The name given in the text should presumably be corrected accordingly.

Chau Ju-hia was an ancestor of our author (see Hirth in J. R. A. S. 1896, 77—81). He wrote several works, one entitled K'iung-kuan-t'u-king (瓊管圖經) which, to judge from the title, must have been an illustrated description of the island of Hainan. The date here mentioned in our text, 1210, is the latest found in Chau Ju-kua's work.

Su Tung-p'o, or «Su of the eastern slope», is the popular name of Su Shï (蘇軾) one of the greatest poets of China. A. D. 1036—1101. In 1069 he entered official life. In 1072 he was dismissed to Huang-chóu for having lampooned in verse a couple of Censors. Here he built himself a hut on the eastern slope (tung-p'o) of a hill, and afterwards took these two words as his fancy, or literary, name. In 1086 he was restored to favour, but in 1094 he was banished, first to Hui-chóu in Kuang-tung, and afterwards to Hainan. In 1101 he was recalled to Court, but died the same year. See Sung-shï, 338, particularly p. 12, and Giles, Biographical Dictionary, 680.

Hu Tan-an or Hu Ts'üan (胡 銓) was born in Kiang-si about the beginning of the
5 twelfth century. He rose to high office at Court and used all his influence to oppose the policy of Ts'in K'ui, which was in favour of a division of the Empire with the Kin Tartars. Hu Ts'üan was degraded and exiled, in the first place to Kuang-si, and later on to Hainan, where he remained for eight years in a small official office. On the death of Ts'in K'ui in 1156, he was recalled to Court, and held the highest offices of state till his death in 1169. Hirth, Die Insel Hainan,
10 17, note 2.

11) Hai-k'óu, in Cantonese Hoi-how, is the port of K'iung-chóu-fu, which is three miles distant from it. Hoihow is now the principal port of the island.

Lu Po-tö, was the General of the Emperor Wu-ti of the Han dynasty, who in 120 B. C. conquered the kingdom of Nan-yüé, i. e., the present two Kuang provinces and Tongking. He
15 received the title of Fu-po-tsiang-kün or «General Queller of the waves» on account of his victories along the sea-coast and on the sea. Ts'ién-Han-shu, 55,17. Mayers, Chin. reader's Man., 138.

Ma Yüan, the greatest Chinese General of the first century of our era. In A. D. 41, when already more than seventy years of age, he commanded an army sent to Tongking to suppress
20 an insurrection. After successfully terminating his military operations he fixed the southern border of China in the present Annam by erecting five bronze pillars, at each of which he established Chinese garrisons. The title of Fu-po-tsiang-kün, formerly given to Lu Po-tö, was revived for him. Hóu-Han-shu, 54. Mayers, op. cit., 149. See also infra, p. 184, and infra, note 38.

The peï-kiau tablets were two pieces of jade or of wood, convex on one side, flat on
25 the other, which were used for divination. They were thrown down before the altar, if both fell with the flat side up, the omen was bad; if they fell with different sides up it portended good luck.

12) These five towns still bear the same names, which in Cantonese are K'ing-shan, Ch'ing-mai, Lam-kō, Man-ch'öong and Lok-üi.

30   13) Po is the ocean-going junk used in the foreign trade by Chinese and Arabs. See supra, pp. 27, 34, n. 2. Pau-t'óu is the same as the present t'óu-möng (頭 艋), a small junk with open framework in the bows, and known in Canton as «West Coast boat». Tan, literally «egg-boat», the boat peculiar to the Tanka or boat-people of Canton. See Notes & Queries on China and Japan, 1,28,107. On the present Li Aborigines of K'iung-shan, see China Review, XIX, 383—394.

35   14) Ch'ang-hua, in Cantonese Ch'öong-fa, is on the west coast of Hainan in Lat. 19°12′.

15) This paragraph is practically a paraphrase of Ling-wai-tai-ta, 10,8ᵇ. See also Ts'ién-Han-shu, 6,20ᵇ, which is probably the authority on which our author relies. On the Tan-ïr Fu-jön, see supra, p. 179.

16) Li Kuang, an official of the beginning of the twelfth century, died in 1156. Through
40 political intrigues he was degraded from his high office of Assistant Prime Minister and exiled to Hainan where he held a small office. Sung-shï, 363,1 et seqq.

17) Chau Ting was born in the latter part of the eleventh century in Shan-si. He attained high metropolitan honours under the Emperor Kau-tsung. Later on he was degraded for his opposition to the weak policy of Ts'in-k'ui (秦 檜) with the Kin Tartars, who were rapidly overrunning
45 China. He was then sent in an insignificant capacity to a place in Fu-kién, and later on to Hainan, whence he continued to admonish the Emperor. He died in exile in 1147. For his fidelity to his sovereign he was canonized by the Emperor Hiau-tsung (1163—1190) and given the title Chung-kién or «Loyal and true» — the same which was also given by the same Emperor to Hu Tan-an mentioned previously (supra, note 10). Chau Ting was a voluminous writer. See for his
50 biography, Sung-shï, 360,11 et seqq.

18) A temple bearing this name is mentioned in the 1672 edition of the «Description of Hainan» (K'iung-chóu-fu-chï).

19) I-lun may be the present Pak-lai on Pak-lai Bay, south of Ch'ang-hua. Kan-ön, in Cantonese Kom-yan, still bears this name. It is south of Ch'ang-hua, and near Uen-mun Bay on the S. W. coast of the island.

20) Ki-yang is, I take it, the present Ngai-chóu on Po-ping Bay on the extreme southern coast of Hainan.   5

21) This paragraph is substantially taken from Ling-wai-tai-ta, 1,16.

22) Ling-wai-tai-ta, 2,8[a] says of the Li: «When a relative dies they sacrifice an ox, but they do not cry or have a funeral festival, they only eat raw beef. As to the burial, a man goes ahead of the coffin-bearers throwing eggs on the ground, and wherever one falls without breaking it is considered a lucky place for the interment». Conf. infra, 213.   10

23) The idea appears to be that the wild, picturesque scenery of this part of Hainan has been a source of happy inspiration to the Chinese scholars who have lived in this district. The characters *siu-pa* are understood as abbreviated forms of *siu-ts'ai* (秀才) «bachelors of arts», and *pa-kung* (拔貢) «senior bachelors». A literal rendering of this phrase would be «there are *siu-ts'ai* and *pa-kung*, so of the scholars of this district there are those who have been able 15 to establish themselves (as able literary men)».

24) *Yin* is the third of the Twelve Branches, and *yu* the tenth; in other words there were two market days in every twelve.

25) The town is still called Ling-shui; it is a Hién or District town.

26) These Tan or Tan-ka were of the same tribe as the boat-people of Canton.   20

27) Nothing is known to us of this person, not even the period in which he lived.

28) K'iung-chóu-fu-chï (as cited in T'u-shu-tsi-ch'öng, VI, 1380,7), mentions a temple called Chau-ying-miau, 35 *li* N. W. from Wan-chóu. The divinity there worshipped bore the name of «Captain» or «Po-chu». In 1370 he was raised to official rank under the name of Sin-tsö-hai-kiang. It was forbidden to offer pork in sacrifice to it. This temple was popularly known as 25 the Fan-shön-miau or «Temple of the Foreign god» (番神廟). Captain Tu-kang, here worshipped, was probably a Moslim skipper.

29) The passage referred to in the Tsin-shu is in Ch. 11,23[a]. Conf. also Sui-shu, 31,13[b]. On the star Wu-nü, see G. Schlegel, Ouranographie Chinoise, 203. The derivation of the name of the Li-mu-shan here given is fanciful. Mayers, Historical Sketch of the Island of Hainan (J. N. 30 C. B. R. A. S., new Series VII), 6, note, states on good authority that the aborigines had a tradition that the mother of their race dwelt on this mountain; hence the name, which means «Li mother mountain».

30) R. Swinhoe, Exploring visit to Hainan (J. N. C. B. R. A. S., new Series VII), 57, estimated the highest peak of the Li-mu-shan range as not exceeding 7,000 feet. Henry, Ling-Nam, 35 478, placed the height of the Li-mu-shan at about 5,500 feet. He refers to the fleecy veil of clouds which hung most of the time over the summit. Ling-wai-tai-ta, 1,8—9, from which this paragraph of our text is substantially taken, says: «In the autumn the sky is clear and the peak is visible, a (spot of) azure floating in space, while below are masses of fog». It then goes on to say that on the summit of the mountain, cut off from the rest of the world by impassible gorges and guarded 40 by tigers and other wild beasts, live recluses; «can it be, Chóu K'ü-feï adds, that they are of the family of the old men's village of the Astor pool?» (菊花潭老人村之類耶). Ma Tuan-lin quotes all that Chóu K'ü-feï wrote on Hainan, giving as his authority Fan Shï-hu (i. e., Fan Ch'öng-ta, middle of twelfth century). Hervey St. Denis, Ethnographie, II, 400—401. Wylie, Notes on Chinese literature, 218 mentions a collection of odes of the Sung dynasty 45 entitled Kü-t'an-shï (菊潭詩) or «Odes of the Astor pool».

31) The customs and dress of the Li of the present day do not differ very materially from what they were in the twelfth century. See R. Swinhoe, op. cit., 26—27. Henry, op. cit., 382—383, 410 et seqq., and an article in the North China Daily News (Shanghai), of Sept. 3, 1902 entitled The Lois or Aborigines of Hainan; also China Review, XIX, 383—394.   50

Chóu K'ü-feï (Ling-wai-tai-ta, 2,11[b]), whom our author substantially quotes for the last part of this paragraph, says in effect that «there being many good-looking women among the Li

women, foreigners in olden times used to steal them. So the chaste ones at least took to smearing
their faces with mud to hide their charms, and later on tattooing was resorted to for the same
purpose. When a girl reaches marriageable age the family sets out wine and invites the relatives.
Then an old woman prickes out with a needle patterns of flowering plants and flying moths and
5 puts in the colour in kingfisher blue; the work is very fine and well done». At the present day the
designs tattooed on the faces of the Li appear to be lines and dots, like those of the Formosans.
See Henry, op. cit., 383.

32) Ling-wai-tai-ta, 2,₈, from which this paragraph is substantially taken, says that the
Li knives were two feet long, with handles of horn over a foot long. The Li also wore helmets
10 of rattan. Referring to the Li bow, the same work (6,6ᵇ) says that they were of wood or bamboo,
and the string of rattan. They were shorter than the Japanese bow, though like it. The arrow was
not feathered. Conf. Swinhoe, J. N. C. B. R. A. S., new Series VII, 79. The Ling-wai-tai-ta,
speaking of the revengeful spirit of the Li, says they call killing a person in revenge «tso-yau»
(作 拗), meaning, like the cho-yau of our text, «seizing, mancipation (?)».
15 The same work also notes that «for the most part, the Li are ignorant and superstitious.
When a stranger comes to see them, they do not meet him at once, but first examine him through
some peephole. If he is of pleasing presence and not a dangerous looking person, they send a
slave to spread a mat for him to sit on, and after a little while the master himself comes out and
meets him. After a short conversation he has wine served, but in the first place he tries the
20 visitor with some bad-tasting herbs (惡 穢), and if he patiently eats of them without hesitating,
the host is pleased, and follows up the wine with beef. But if the guest refuses (to eat the herbs)
he is sent back to his people».

The Li of the present day all carry heavy wood-knives in small baskets, long and narrow,
attached to the waist behind. In these they also carry their flint and steel and a few other neces-
25 sary articles.

33) Taken from Ling-wai-tai-ta, 2,₈ᵃ.

34) Hiang-p'u or «List of perfumes». This title has been given to several works on the
subject of aromatic substances. One was written in the early part of the twelfth century by Hung Chu
(洪 芻). Sung-shï, 205,₂₂, mentions this work, which it says is in 5 chapters, and also one
30 by Shön Li (沉 立). Still another work with this title was written during the Sung dynasty
by Yé T'ing-kui (葉 廷 珪). See Bretschneider, Botanicon Sinicum, I, 149, № 153.

35) See Ling-wai-tai-ta, 2,₈ᵃ, which also mentions sapan-wood (su-mu) among the products of
Hainan.

36) Ling-wai-tai-ta, 2,₇ᵃ says that «living among the semi-civilized Li (Shóu-Li) are many
35 desperadoes (姦 民) from the Hu-kuang and Fu-kién provinces, a cruel, thieving lot who,
though to all outward appearances obeying the officials, are in league with the Wild Li (Shöng-
Li) to plunder the country».

37) Quotation from Ling-wai-tai-ta, 1,₁₆ᵃ.

38) Ma Fu-po is the Ma Yüan mentioned previously p. 178. The text states that these
40 earthenware jars could hold several piculs of water (水). This must be a clerical error for rice
(米), as water is not measured by the picul or bushel.

39) The Wu-chï-shan or «Five-finger mountain», is south-west from the Li-mu-shan
proper. Henry, op. cit., 478 estimated its height as about 1,000 feet more than the Li-mu-shan,
or about 6,500 feet. There is also a Ts'i-chï-shan or «Seven-finger mountain» in this Hainan
45 central massif. With the exception of the first and the last phrases of this paragraph, all the
rest is a quotation from Ling-wai-tai-ta, 2,₇ᵇ. On the form of oath here mentioned, see Hirth,
Die Insel Hainan, 29, note 5.

40) This description of the costume and head-dresses of the Li occurs, in substantially
the same words, in Ling-wai-tai-ta, 2,₈ᵃᵇ, but it is not said that the description is based on the
50 pictures of the Li. King-lio-ssï was one of the titles, corresponding to the present «Governor
General», or «Viceroy», used during the T'ang and Sung dynasties.

41) Instead of this reference to Wang Chung-ki's dress, Ling-wai-tai-ta, 2,₈ᵇ, has «formerly in the hi-ning period (A. D. 1068—1078) Wang Tsu-tau (王 祖 道), head-man of the

(pacified) Li villages was given official Chinese robes. At the present time his descendants (lit., grand-children) wear an additional garment consisting of a long silk brocade gown (錦 袍) with a girdle and silver buckle. They say they do so because their ancestor received the like from the Emperor».

Concerning the dress of the women among the Li, Ling-wai-tai-ta, 2,8[b] says: «The married 5 women wear their hair in a high knot (or knob 髻), tattoo their faces, and wear copper earrings which hang down to the shoulder. Their clothing consists of a plaited skirt of cotton stuff of bright colours. Though they have neither trowsers nor jacket, the skirt they wear is of several thicknesses, for they make their skirts with four flounces (圍) sewn together; they put it on by the feet (not over the head), and tie it at the waist». 10

42) On these various products, see infra, Pt. II.

PART II

1.

CAMPHOR (腦子).

Nau-tzï, or camphor, comes from P'o-ni, called according to some Fo-ni (佛 尼); it also comes from the country of Pin-su (賓 窣)[1].

5 The common report that it is also found in San-fo-ts'i is an error; the fact is merely this — that, owing to this country being an important thoroughfare for the traffic of all foreign nations, the produce of all other countries is intercepted and kept in store there for the trade of foreign ships.

The camphor-tree is like the pine-tree (杉); it grows in the depths of 10 the hills and the remotest valleys. So long as branches and trunk continue unhurt, the tree will contain the gum even for hundreds and thousands of years; otherwise it will evaporate.

When the natives go into the hills in order to gather the camphor, they go in troops of several tens of men; they are provided with clothes made 15 of tree bark (or fibre) and with supplies of *sha-hu* (沙 糊 sago) for food. They go in different directions, and whenever they find any camphor-trees, they fell them with their hatchets, and mark as many as ten or more; they then cut these into lengths and divide them among themselves equally, after which each one cuts his share into boards; these again they notch along the 20 sides and cross-wise so as to produce chinks, and the camphor collecting in these is got out by forcing a wedge into them[2].

The camphor which forms crystals is called «plum flower camphor» (梅花 腦), because it resembles the plum flower; an inferior quality is called «gold foot camphor» (金 脚 腦); broken bits are called «rice camphor» 25 (米 腦); when these are mixed up with splinters, it is called «grey camphor» (蒼 腦); after all the camphor has been removed from the wood, it is called «camphor chips» (腦 札). Nowadays people break these chips into small bits and mix them with sawdust, which mixture they place in a vessel of porcelain, covered by another vessel, the openings being hermetically closed; 30 when baked in hot ashes, the vapour formed by the mixture condenses and

13

forms lumps, which are called «collected camphor» (聚 腦); it is used for women's head ornaments and the like purposes[3]. There is furthermore an oily sort of camphor called «camphor oil» (腦 油), which is of a strong and pungent aroma; it answers for moistening incense, or mixing with oil[4].

Notes.   5

1) Fo-ni and P'o-ni, both pronounced in Cantonese Fat-ni and Put-ni, transcribe respectively Brṇi, Borneo, and apply more particularly to the west coast of that island. See supra, pp. 155, 156. Pin-su, in Cantonese Pan-ts'üt, the latter form representing the sound Pansor, is the Pansur or Fansur of mediaeval Arab and western writers, the Barus of later writers. Barus is the name of the principal mart of this commodity in Sumatra, and the word has been affixed by traders to 10 discriminate it from the camphor of Japan. See Reinaud, Relations, I, 7, Masudi, Prairies d'or, I, 338, Ibn Batuta, Voyages, IV, 241, and especially Yule, Marco Polo, II, 282, 285—288. Also Crawfurd, Hist. Malay Archipelago, I, 515—517.

Liang-shu, 54,14[a], mentions among the products of Lang-ya-siu (狼 牙 脩) (which may be Tennasserim or the Kra district on the Malay Peninsula) p'o-lü-hiang (婆 律 香), 15 and T'ang-pön-ts'au (Pön-ts'au-kang-mu, 34,56) says that «in olden times p'o-lü-hiang came from P'o-lü». We are inclined, however, to believe that p'o-lü is a truncated transcription of Sanskrit karpūra, and does not represent Bārūs, as Gerini (Researches, 427) and Pelliot (B. E. F. E. O., IV 341) are disposed to think. Hüan-tsang, Si-yu-ki, 10, speaks of kié-pu-lo (羯 布 羅) as a product of Madura.   20

Yu-yang-tsa-tsu, 18,7[b], says «The tree which produces the «lung-nau perfume» (龍 腦 香) comes from P'o-li (婆 利 Perak, or thereabout), where it is called ku-pu-p'o-lü (固 不 婆 律 kapur). It also comes from Po-ssï (Persia, i. e., it was brought to China by Persian ships). The tree is from eighty to ninety feet high, and some six or seven (feet) in circumference. The leaves are round and white on the back. It has no flowers. The tree is either 25 «fat» (肥) or «lean» (瘦). Lean trees produce the p'o-lü-kau (or «balm» 膏). One authority says that lean trees produce lung-nau (our «baroos camphor»), and the fat ones p'o-lü-kau (camphor balm). If one cuts into the heart of the tree and splits it open, the oil (lit. grease) flows out freely from the butt (端). The drug can be got also by chopping up the wood and putting the pieces in a pit. There are other methods of extracting it». Conf. Marsden's remarks in note 2. 30

2) Marsden, History of Sumatra, 121, says: «The natives, from long experience, know whether any (camphor) is contained within, by striking it (i. e., the tree) with a stick. In that case, they cut it down and split it with wedges into small pieces, finding the camphire in the interstices in the state of a concrete crystallization. Some have asserted that it is from the old trees alone that this substance is procured, and that in the young trees it is in a fluid state, called meenia capoor, 35 or camphire oil; but this, I have good authority to pronounce a mistake. The same kind of tree that produces the fluid, does not produce the dry, transparent, and flaky substance, nor ever would .... The traders distinguish usually three different degrees of quality in it, by the names of head, belly and foot, according to its purity and whiteness, which depend upon its being more or less free from particles of the wood, and other heterogeneous matter, that mix with it in 40 collecting, after the first large pieces are picked out. Some add a fourth sort, of extraordinary fineness, of which a few pounds only are imported to Canton in the year, and sell there at the rate of two thousand dollars the pecul».

3) In a previous passage (supra, p. 156), our author mentions four varieties of camphor as coming from Borneo; one of these he calls su-nau; it may be the same as the ts'ang-nau here 45 mentioned. See Gerini, Researches, 432 et seqq.

Yu-yang-tsa-tsu, 1,3[a], mentions some extraordinarily fragrant camphor which was brought to the Emperor of China Hüan-tsung (in A. D. 756) as tribute from Kiau-chï or Tongking. It was called lau-lung-nau (老 龍 腦), and also, apparently, jui-lung-nau (瑞 龍 腦). This may be «the fourth sort» mentioned by Marsden in the preceding note, though no longer known by the name given it in the T'ang dynasty.

Nearly all the camphor used in China is procured from the Laurus camphora, L., called *chang* (樟). Nan-yüé-pi-ki (of the eighteenth century), 5,10, says that *lung-nau* (baroos camphor)
5 comes from Fo-ta-ni (佛打泥 Patani?). The Cantonese mix it with *chang-nau* (i. e., camphor from the Laurus camphora) which comes from Shau-chóu (韶州 in Kuang-tung); hence its name of *shau-nau*. In northern China camphor is usually called *ch'au-nau* (湖腦) from Ch'au-chóu, also in Kuang-tung, and not far distant from Shau-chóu. This latter name *ch'au-nau* must be the correct form. See also Bretschneider, Botanicon Sinicum, 346 (J. C. B. R. A. S., XXV).
10 Linschoten, Voyage to the East Indies, II, 118 (Hakl. Soc. edit.) remarks that one pound of Borneo camphor was worth one hundred pounds of Chin-cheu (i. e., Chinese) camphor.

4) Marsden, op. cit., 123 says: «The camphire oil is a valuable domestic medicine, and much used by the Sumatrans .... It is rather a liquid and volatile resin, distilling from one species of the camphire tree, without any oleaginous quality».
15 Our author states (supra, p. 67) that camphor was also a product of Tan-ma-ling, of Java (p. 77), and of Ling-ya-ssï-kia (p. 68) Chóu K'ü-feï adds Chu-lién. See supra, p. 100, n. 8.

2.

FRANKINCENSE (乳香).

Ju-hiang («milk incense»), or *hün-lu-hiang* (薰陸香)[1], comes from (出)
20 the three Ta-shï countries of Ma-lo-pa, Shï-ho, and Nu-fa, from the depths of the remotest mountain valleys. The tree which yields this drug may, on the whole, be compared to the *sung* (松 pine). Its trunk is notched with a hatchet, upon which the resin flows out, and when hardened, turns into incense, which is gathered and made into lumps. It is transported on elephants to the Ta-shï
25 (on the coast); the Ta-shï load it upon their ships for barter against other goods in San-fo-ts'i; and it is for this reason that the incense is commonly collected at San-fo-ts'i[2].

When the foreign merchants come to that place to trade, the Customs authorities, according to the relative strength of its fragrance, distinguish
30 thirteen classes of incense. Of these, the very best is called *kién-hiang* (揀香), or «picked incense»: it is round and of the size of the end of a finger; it is commonly called *ti-ju* (滴乳) or «dripping milk»[3]. The second quality is called *p'ing-ju* (缾乳) or «potted milk», and its colour is inferior to that of the «picked incense». The next quality is called *p'ing-hiang* (缾香)
35 or «potted incense», so called, they say, owing to its being prized so much at the time of gathering, that it is placed in pots (*p'ing* 缾). In this *p'ing-hiang* (variety of frankincense) there are three grades, superior, medium, and inferior. The next quality is called *tai-hiang* (袋香) or «bag incense»;

13*

thus called, they say, because at the time of gathering, it is merely put into
bags; it is also divided into three qualities, like the *p'ing-hiang*.

The next kind is the *ju-t'a* (乳 楊); it consists of incense mixed
with gravel.

The next kind is the *heï-t'a* (黑 楊), because its colour is black. The 5
next kind is the *shui-shï-heï-t'a* (水 濕 黑 楊), because it consists of
incense which has been «water-damaged», the aroma turned, and the colour
spoiled while on board ship.

Mixed incense of various qualities and consisting of broken pieces is
called *chö-siau* (斫 削 «cut-up»); when passed through a sieve and made 10
into dust, it is called *ch'an-mo* (纏 末 «powder»). The above are the various
varieties of frankincense.

Notes.

1) *Ju-hiang* or «milk incense»; this, the common name for olibanum or frankincense in
China, was given it from its appearance. The Arabic name of incense *luban* means likewise 15
«milk». Marco Polo calls it «white incense». The second name *hün-lu* (in Cantonese *fan-luk*,
old sound *hun-luk*) is unquestionably derived from the Arabic *kundur* (كندر), or the Indian form
kundu or *kundura*. Turkish-osm. *günlük*, «frankincense, olibanum», Radloff, Wörterbuch d. Türk-
Dialecte, vol. II, col. 1636, may be derived from the Chinese. Conf. Hirth, J. A. O. S., XXX, 23.
The older Chinese works only use the word *hün-lu* to designate frankincense, but there is some 20
confusion in their use of the term, benzoin and other drugs being frequently confounded with the
true olibanum. See Bretschneider, Botanicon Sinicum, III, 460—462, and Ancient Chinese and
Arabs, 19; also Hirth, China and the Roman Orient, 266—268. Pön-ts'au, 34,45[b] gives its
«foreign names» as *mo-lö* (摩 勒), *tu-lu* (杜 嚕) and *k'ié-to-lo*, (伽 多 羅, erroneously
written *to-k'ié-lo*). *Tu-lu* is probably Sanskrit *turu(shka)*, the Indian incense, and *k'ié-to-lo* is 25
khādira, the Acacia catechu.

2) Ma-lo-pa or Merbat, Shï-ho or Shehr and Nu-fa or Dufar, were the three ports of the
Hadramaut coast of Arabia, the «Land of Frankincense». See supra, pp. 116 and 121, n. 11.

Nan-fang-ts'au-mu-chuang (third century A. D.) 2,1[b], says «*hün-lu* incense comes from the
sea-coast in Ta-ts'in. It is a big tree (which furnishes it), the branches and leaves are just like 30
those of an old pine (松). It grows in the sand. The flowers (lit. buds) are full-blown in summer,
(when) the sap of the tree flows onto the sand, where it is gathered». Sui-shu, 83,16[a] mentions
hün-lu-hiang among the products of Po-ssï (Persia), meaning probably that it was brought to
China on Persian ships. Hüan-tsang stated that in the country of O-ch'a-li (in Southern
India, near Malwa) grew the *hün-lu-hiang* tree, the leaves of which resembled those of the 35
t'ang-li (棠 梨 pyrus). This is presumably the Boswellia thurifera, Colebrooke, whereas the
Arabian olibanum is produced by the Boswellia Carterii, Birdw. See Bretschneider, Botanicon
Sinicum, II, 303, III, 460. See also Linschoten, op. cit., II, 99.

Marco Polo, II, 441, says «Dufar is a great and noble and fine city, and lies 500 miles
to the north-west of Esher (i. e., es-Shehr) .... Much white incense is produced here, and I will 40
tell you how it grows. The trees are like small fir-trees; these are notched with a knife in several
places, and from these notches the incense is exuded. Sometimes also it flows from the tree without any notch; this is by reason of the great heat of the sun there.» See also Yule's exhaustive
note on the above in his Marco Polo, II, 442—447. Theodore Bent, Exploration of the Frankincense country, Southern Arabia (Geo. Journal VI, 109—134, says (p. 119): «Near Cape Risut a 45
large tract of country is covered with frankincense trees, with their bright green leaves like ash
trees, their small green flowers, and their insignificant fruit .... The best is obtained at spots called
Hoye and Haski, about four days journey inland from Mirbat .... The second in quality comes

from near Cape Risut, and also a little further west at a place called Chiseri». «To the south of Mount Haghier (in Sokotra) one comes across valleys entirely full of frankincense-trees. The best quality is called *leban lakt*, and the second quality *leban resimi*.» Theo. Bent, Southern Arabia, 234, 252, 380. Our author knew of the African frankincense (supra, p. 130) as well as of the Arabian.

5   3) Also called *ju-t'óu-hiang* (乳頭香) or «nipple incense» by mediaeval Chinese writers. Bretschneider, Botanicon Sinicum, III, 460.

3.

MYRRH (沒藥).

Mo-yau comes from the country of Ma-lo-mo (麻囉抹) of the Ta-shï.
10 The tree resembles in height and size the pine-tree (松) of China; its bark is one or two inches thick. At the time of gathering the incense they first dig a hole in the ground at the foot of the tree, and then split open the bark with a hatchet, upon which the juice runs down into the hole during fully ten days, when it is removed.

15   Note.

The Chinese name for myrrh, meaning «*mo* medicine or drug» is a transcription of the Arabic name *murr* — through the Cantonese *mut*. See Bretschneider, Ancient Chinese and Arabs, 20, note 4; and Hirth, J. C. B. R. A. S., XXI, 220. Pön-ts'au, 34,49, quotes no authorities on this subject earlier than the Sung.

20   Ma-lo-mo is clearly an error for Ma-lo-pa or Merbat, the Hadramaut coast of Arabia. This error has been noticed in a previous passage, supra, p. 121, n. 11. Our author has stated in his description of the Berbera coast (Pi-p'a-lo) that that country produced much myrrh (supra, p. 128). At the present time the best myrrh comes from the Somali country near Harar. The myrrh which is got from the hills about Shugra and Sureea to the east of Aden (which must have been included 25 in Merbat as Chinese understood it) is of an inferior quality. See Encyclopædia Britannica (9th edit.) XVII, 121. Theo. Bent, Southern Arabia, 254, says myrrh in large quantities grows in the Gara mountains of the Hadramaut. Hanbury, Science Papers, 378—380, says myrrh comes from the Ghizan district on the east coast of the Red Sea, from the coast of Southern Arabia, east of Aden, from the Somali country, south and west of Cape Gardafui, and from the 30 country between Tajura and Shoa. See also Linschoten, op. cit., II, 99.

     The *mo* mentioned in the Yu-yang-tsa-tsu (18,10b) as being called *a-tz'ï* (阿縒 the last character being also read *so, tso* and *tsok*) in Fu-lin, is the myrtle, the Aramean name of which is *asa*, the original of *a-tz'ï*. Hirth, J. A. O. S, XXX, 21.

4.

35   # DRAGON'S-BLOOD (血碣).

Hüé-kié comes also from the Ta-shï countries. This tree is somewhat like the myrrh-tree, except that its leaves are rather different in size from those of the latter; the manner of gathering is also the same. There is a variety of tree which is as smooth as the face of a mirror; these are old trees, their juice flows spontaneously, without their being tapped by the hatchet; this is the best quality. Incense which contains an admixture of bits of wood is made of the juice of the lakawood-tree (降眞香), and is commonly called «imitation dragon's-blood» (假血碣).   5

Note.

In his description of Chung-li, i. e., the Somali coast including the island of Socotra, our author says (supra, p. 131) that dragon's-blood, aloes, tortoise-shell and ambergris were procured from this island or the adjacent waters. The Periplus of the Erythraean Sea (§ 30) mentions it as a product of the island of Dioskorides (Socotra) under the name of «Indian cinnabar» (κιννά-   10 βαρι τὸ λεγόμενον Ἰνδικόν), «which is gathered as it exudes in drops (tears) from the tree.» The Arabs called it *ḳâtir* (القاطر), and this name, occurring in Yakut's description of Socotra (ed. Wüstenfeld, III, 102,3), may be the original of *hüé-kié*, pronounced *hüt-k'it* in Cantonese. This Socotran dragon's-blood is the «drop dragon's-blood» of commerce, the spontaneous exudation of a leguminous tree, Pterocarpus draco, which grows at elevations between 800 and 2,000 feet 15 above sea-level. See also Theo. Bent, Southern Arabia, 379, 388.

The ordinary *hüé-kié* used in China is the produce of a large species of rattan growing on the north and north-east coasts of Sumatra, with some parts of Borneo, and principally manufactured at Jambi, Palembang and Banjermassin. Crawfurd, Hist. Indian Archipelago, III, 240.

The P'ön-ts'au (34,50–51) calls dragon's-blood *k'i-lin-kié* (騏驎碣 «*k'i-lin* blood»). 20 The Nan-yüé-chï (南越志), it adds, says that «it is the sap of the *tzï-kung*-tree (紫鉚). The test of its purity is that it is like wax when bit into.» This is a confusion with stick-lac, and traceable to T'ang period writers. Giles, Dictionary, s. v., 血 Hsüeh, says that dragon's-blood is yielded by the *k'o-liu* (渴留 Daemonorops draco). Bretschneider and Porter Smith are of opinion that the Chinese drug is furnished by the Pterocarpus draco. Bretschneider, 25 Ancient Chinese and Arabs, 21, note 6. See also Encyclop. Britann. VII, 389.

5.

SWEET BENZOIN (金顏香).

Kin-yen-hiang comes, in its best and standard quality, from Chön-la; the Ta-shï kind is of inferior quality. The statement that this incense is 30 found in San-fo-ts'i must be understood as meaning that it is imported thither from the Ta-shï and merely transshipped at that place by merchants for importation to China.

This incense is the juice of a tree; there is a pale yellow coloured kind, and another of a black colour. That which, on being broken open, shows a 35 snow-white colour, is the best; that which contains gravel is of inferior quality. Its aroma is so strong that it may be used in combination with all other perfumes. It is largely used for mixing by those who wear sachets of ambergris and other perfumes of delicate aroma. Foreigners also prepare from it, with (other) perfumes, a mixture with which they rub their bodies.   40

Note.

Kin-yen hiang or «golden coloured incense». From the description given of it in the second paragraph, and the remark that the finest quality of it came from Kamboja (Chön-la), I think there can be no doubt that «sweet» benzoin is meant, the «benioin de boninas» of Linschoten, op. cit.,
5 II, 97, while the *an-si-hiang* mentioned subsequently (infra, p. 202) as a product of Eastern Sumatra (San-fo-ts'i) is the «benioin amendoado» of the same writer. It was known to the Arabs as *laban Djawi* or «incense of Java (Sumatra), but did not become known in Europe before the middle of the fifteenth century. Heyd, Hist. du Commerce, II, 580. See also Ibn Batuta, Voyages, IV, 240. Possibly *kin-yen-hiang* was the name specially given the Kambojan variety of the drug.
10 　　　The Styrax Benzoin is a native of Sumatra and Java, and was introduced into Siam, Borneo, etc. «Siam benzoin is generally regarded as the best, and of it two varieties are distinguished. The finest quality is Siam benzoin «in tear», it being in small flattened drops, from the size of an almond kernel downward. «Lump» Siam benzoin consists of agglutinated masses of such tears, or of tears imbedded in a darker coloured resinous matrix. Tear benzoin varies in
15 colour from a pale yellow to a reddish-brown colour, and lump benzoin has a conglomerate-like structure from the dissemination of almond-shaped tears throughout the substance. .... Sumatra benzoin occurs in larger rectangular masses of a greyish tint, with few large tears in it, but containing small white opaque pieces, with chips of wood and other impurities, in a translucent matrix». Encyclop. Britann. (9th edit.), III, 581.
20 　　　«The Ta-shï kind is of inferior quality» means, I take it, that the incense brought to China by the Arabs from their various trading-stations by way of Palembang in Sumatra, was inferior to that which was brought direct to China from Kamboja.
　　　Tung-si-yang-k'au, 3,17ᵃ, refers among the products of Palembang to *kin-yin-hiang* (金 銀 香) or «gold and silver incense», which seems, from the few words of description there
25 given of it — and quoted from the Hua-i-k'au (華 夷 考) — to be the same as the *kin-yen-hiang*. It is true that on this same page we find mention of *an-si-hiang*, but the description of this drug there given only strengthens the probability of these two products being the two varieties of benzoin mentioned by Linschoten and other travellers. In another passage, Tung-si-yang-k'au, 3,9ᵇ, mentions *kin-yen-hiang* as a product of Kamboja and describes it on the
30 authority of the I-t'ung-chï (一 統 志), which in turn quotes textually our text.

6.

DAMMAR (篤 耨 香).

Tu-nau-hiang comes from the country of Chön-la: it is the exudation of a tree which resembles the pine (杉) and juniper (檜) family in shape; but
35 the gum (香) lies concealed in the bark. When the tree is old, it runs out spontaneously, as a white and vitreous resin, for which reason it does not melt, though the summer heat may be at its height; this is called *tu-nau*.

　　　If, in the summer months, the trunk of the tree is scorched by a fire kept burning around it, this will cause the fluid resin to flow out freely
40 again; it may be gathered during the winter, when it hardens; for this variety of incense is liquid in the summer, and hardens during the winter; it is called «*heï* (or black) *tu-nau*». The natives fill gourds (瓢 *p'iau*) with it,

and the shippers afterwards transfer it into porcelain vessels. The flavour of this incense is pure and lasting; the black variety easily melts and leaks through the gourd; but by breaking the gourd and exposing it to the fire, one may obtain something similar to the original substance. This is the article now called *tu-nau-p'iau* or «gourd dammar».   5

Note.

The Chinese word *tu-nau* transcribes the Malay *damar*. In the fifteenth century Ying-yai-shöng-lan the form *ta-ma-ïr* occurs (打 麻 兒). Crawfurd, Hist. Indian Archipelago, I, 455, says: «In almost every country of the Indian islands there are trees which afford *damar*. Rumphius enumerates four varieties. These produce different sorts of the rosin, which take 10 their names in commercial language from their colour or consistency. One is called *Damar-batu* in Malay, or *Damar-selo* in Javanese, which means the stony rosin, and another in common use *Damar-putch*, or white rosin ..... Damar is used for all the purposes to which we apply pitch, but chiefly in paying the bottoms of ships and vessels».

Marsden, Hist. of Sumatra, 128, says that white dammar is a species of turpentine, 15 yielded by a tree growing in Lampoon called *cruyen*, the wood of which is white and porous. It differs from the common sort, or *dammar battoo*, in being soft and whitish, having the consistence, and somewhat the appearance of putty.» See also Yule and Burnell, Glossary, 228.

7.

LIQUID STORAX (蘇 合 香 油).   20

Su-ho-hiang-yu comes from the countries of the Ta-shï. Its aroma and taste are, on the whole, similar to those of *tu-nau* (dammar). Richness and freedom from sediment are the first requisites in a good sample.

Foreigners commonly use it to rub their bodies with, and the natives of Fu-kién use it in like fashion when afflicted with paralysis (大 風). It is 25 mixed with *juan-hiang* (軟 香 or «incenses of delicate aroma»), and may be used in medicine.

Note.

The present day *su-ho-hiang-yu* or «sweet oil of storax», or *su-ho-yu* «storax oil», which occurs in commerce in China, is a product of the Liquidambar orientalis, L., of Asia Minor. The 30 storax of the ancients, which became known to the Chinese in the early part of the Christian era as a product of Ta-ts'in, and the name of which στύραξ, they may have mutilated into *su-ho*, was a solid gum, and appears to have been a product of the Styrax officinalis, which is still common in Syria. Sui-shu, 83,16ᵃ mentions *su-ho* as a product of Po-ssï (Persia). Apparently the storax sent to China in those early days was very largely adulterated, for Liang-shu, 54,17ᵃ, (covering the first half 35 of the sixth century), says that in Western Asia (Ta-ts'in) «storax (*su-ho*) is made by mixing and boiling the juice of various fragrant trees and that it is not a natural product. It is further said that the inhabitants of Ta-ts'in gather the *su-ho* (plant, or parts of it), squeeze out its juice, and thus make a balm or ointment (香 膏); they then sell this drug to the traders of other countries;

it thus goes through many hands before reaching China, and when arriving here, it is not so very fragrant.» See Hirth, China and Roman Orient, 41, 47, 263—266.

D. Hanbury, Science Papers, 143, has conclusively shown that the drug now used in China is imported into Bombay from Aden, the Persian Gulf and the Red Sea, being probably
5 brought thither from Alexandria. He has also established by comparison its identity with the substance known as Liquid Storax, obtained from the Liquidambar orientalis, L., in Asia Minor. Bretschneider, Botanicon Sinicum, III, 465.

The Hiang-p'u, a Treatise on perfumes of the eleventh century, makes the remark that *su-ho-yu* is a kind of *tu-nau-hiang* or dammar. Bretschneider, op. cit., 464. The Su-ch'ön-liang-fang
10 (蘇 沈 艮 方), also of the eleventh century, says (1,13ᵇ): «The *su-ho-hiang* of the present day is like hard wood, of a dark red colour. There is also *su-ho-yu* which is like birdlime.» This *su-ho-hiang* may well have been the classical or solid storax.

Our author, in the first part of his work, mentions liquid storax as a product of Baghdad, Asia Minor (Lu-meï, Rum) and of Ki-tz'ï-ni (Ghazni). The Huan-yü-chï (寰 宇 志 of the
15 tenth century) says that *su-ho-yu* was produced in An-nan and San-fo-ts'i. Bretschneider, Bot. Sinic., III, 464. It is likely that this was the resin of the Liquidambar altingiana, Bl. of Java, called in Malay *rasamala*. Pön-ts'au, 34,54, gives the Sanskrit name of *su-ho-yu* as *turushka* (咄 魯 瑟 劒), which, according to Monier Williams, Sansk. Engl. Dict., is Indian olibanum. See supra, p. 196, n. 1.
20 The expression *ta-föng* is actually used in the province of Fu-kién as a term for paralysis of either the body or limbs.

8.

BENZOIN (安 息 香).

An-si-hiang comes from the country of San-fo-ts'i; it is the resin of a
25 tree. It resembles the edible part of a walnut in shape and colour, but it is not fit to burn as incense; however, it brings out other scents, for which reason there is a demand for it for mixing purposes.

The T'ung-tién (通 典), speaking of the Western Barbarians, says that the country of An-si has sent tribute to China during the periods *t'ién-ho*
30 of the Chóu (A. D. 566—572) and *ta-yé* of the Sui dynasty (A. D. 605—617). It may be conjectured that the name is derived from this (country) and that the article was imported by way of San-fo-ts'i.

Note.

Our author's doubts about the country of origin of this incense and his failure to explain its
35 name, are common to other Chinese writers. See Bretschneider, Ancient Chinese and Arabs, 19, note 2. Bot. Sinic., III, 465—467. An-si, which, in the second and third centuries of our era, was the Chinese designation of Parthia, was transferred, after the overthrow of the Arsacides, to the new Persian kingdom of the Sassanide dynasty. Hirth, China and Roman Orient, 198. During the Chóu and Sui dynasties (A. D. 557—618) An-si may therefore be held to be identical with
40 Persia. Sui-shu, 83,16 says that «the kingdom of Ts'au (漕), which was the same as the Ki-pin (罽 賓) of the Han dynasty, had (whether as a product or brought there from other countries is not clear) *an-si-hiang, ts'ing-mu* (putchuck, our author's *mu-hiang*) and other aromatic substances.» The same work, in the section on K'iu-tz'ï (龜 茲 Kuchar in Chinese Turkestan),

83,11[b], mentions *an-si-hiang* among its products. I fancy it only means that *an-si-hiang* reached China by way or K'iu-tz'ï. It is evident none reached China in Chau's time.

Yu-yang-tsa-tsu, 18,7[b] says: «The *an-si-hiang* tree comes from Po-ssï (Persia). In Po-ssï it is called the *pi-sié* tree (辟邪樹 or «destroying evil tree»). It is thirty feet high; the bark is yellowish black. The leaves have four angles (角); they do not shrivel up in winter. 5 In the second moon it blossoms; the flower is yellowish, the heart of the flower is greenish. It has no fruit. When the bark of the tree is cut, its gum (膠) is like syrup (飴); it is called *an-si-hiang*. In the sixth and seventh moons it hardens, when it can be burned, propitiating the gods and dispelling all evil».

The I-t'ung-chï (of the Ming), as quoted in Tung-si-yang-k'au, 1,11, says that the tree 10 which produces *an-si-hiang* is like the *k'u-lién* (苦楝 Melia azedarach, L.) but straighter; the leaves are like those of the *yang-t'au* (羊桃 Carambola tree) but broader. The sap which supplies the incense is in the heart of the tree. Pön-ts'au, 34,53[a], says «formerly it came from Persia, but now An-nan, San-fo-ts'i and all foreign countries have it.»

Marsden, Hist. of Sumatra, 123, says: «Benjamin or benzoin (caminyan) .... is produced 15 by a tree which grows in great abundance in the northern parts of the island (of Sumatra), particularly in the Batta country, and met with, though rarely, to the southward of the line.»

Crawfurd, Hist. Indian Archipelago, I, 518, remarks that «Borneo and Sumatra are the only countries which produce it (i. e., benzoin), and the territory of Borneo proper in the one, and that of the Battas in the other, the only portions of them .... It has but one name, or at 20 least only one which is current. This is a native term, and is at full length *Kăminyan*, or abbreviated *Minyan*». The Pön-ts'au-kang-mu, 34,52, gives as the «foreign» name of *an-si-hiang* 拙貝羅 *kü-peï-lo*, which seems to be a corrupt transcription either of Sanskrit *khădira* or of *kundura*, catechu or Indian frankincense. See supra, p. 196, n. 1.

Both Duarte Barbosa (op. cit., 185) and Linschoten (II, 96—98) distinguish two varieties 25 of benzoin, one which does not smell except when in the fire, and the other with a strong scent. Barbosa adds that it is with this latter variety that «the good and genuine storax is made in the Levant, before extracting from it the oil, which in the Levant is extracted from it». Linschoten calls the scented variety «benioin de boninas» or benzoin of the flowers; it is of blackish colour; the other variety is «benioin amendoado» or «benzoin of almonds», because it is mixed with pieces 30 of white benzoin, like pieces of almonds among the black. «The benzoin from Sumatra and Java, he adds, is not as good as that from Siam and by Malacca.»

9.

GARDENIA FLOWERS (梔子花).

The *chï-tzï-hua* comes from the two countries of Ya-pa-hién (啞巴 35 閑) and Lo-shï-meï of the Ta-shï. It resembles the safflower (紅花) in appearance, but it is of a light brown (or purple) colour. Its scent is penetrating and lasting. The natives gather the flowers, dry them in the sun, and place them in bottles of opaque glass. Flowers of carnation colour are rare.

What in Buddhist books is called *tan-po* (簷蔔) is the same as this. 40

Note.

On the Gardenia florida or becho-nuts, see Hanbury, Science Papers, 241 et seqq., and Bretschneider, Bot. Sinic., III, 500—503. Although our author only refers to its use as a perfume, it was, however, largely used as a dye. Ya-pa-hién (or as it is written supra, p. 116 Ya-ssï-pau-hién) is Isfahan, and Lo-shï-meï probably stands for Khwārizm. Supra, p. 134, our author refers to the trade in gardenia flowers from the Persian coast through the island of Kish. He also says (supra, p. 141) that it was a product of Asia Minor (Lu-meï).

Ling-wai-tai-ta, 7,3—4 says: «The foreign gardenia (蕃 梔 子) comes from the land of the Arabs. It is what is called in the Buddhist books *tan-po* (薝 蔔). The Sea foreigners (海 蕃) dry it like dyer's safflower. At the present day when one wants to be scented as if with ambergris, one uses foreign gardenia, which is even more penetrating. There is a white flower just like the gardenia but five-petaled. People say that (the *chï-tzï*) brought from Si-chu (西 竺 possibly an error for 西 天 竺 «Western India») is (real) *tan-po*, but I apprehend that this is not correct.»

Yu-yang-tsa-tsu, 18,3[b] says of this product: «*Chï-tzï* flowers with six petals are rare, but, according to T'au Chön-po (陶 貞 白 or Tau Hung-king 陶 弘 景 A. D. 451—536, the author of an important work on materia medica; see Giles, Biograph. Dictionary, 718—719), only six-petaled *chï-tzï* flowers can properly be called by that name. If one cuts off a six-petaled flower and slits open the calyx in seven places, the perfume is very powerful. It is said that it is the *chan-po* of the Western Regions.» The text has 薝 *yen*, which stands for 薝 *tan* or *chan,* the change of radicals being frequent in old texts. Hirth, J. A. O. S., XXX, 27. *Chan-po*, in Cantonese *cham-pak* or *chan-po-kia* (瞻 博 迦), is Sanskrit *champaka*, the champac tree, Michelia Champaca.

<hr>

10.

ROSE-WATER (薔 薇 水).

Ts'iang-weï-shui is the dew of flowers in the country of the Ta-shï. In the time of the Five Dynasties (A. D. 907—960) the foreign envoy P'u-ko-san (蒲 謌 散 Abu-l-Hassan?), brought as tribute fifteen bottles, after which time importation became rare. Nowadays a common substitute is manufactured by gathering the flowers, which are steeped in water and steamed, in order to extract the essence.

Rose-water is much counterfeited and adulterated; to test its genuineness, the substance should be placed in glass bottles and shaken about for a while, then, if it is full of bubbles moving up and down, the substance is genuine. The flower (from which it is made) is not identical with the Chinese rose (薔 薇).

Note.

Rose-water is also known in China as *ts'iang-weï-lu* or «rose-dew». In a preceding passage (supra, p. 134) Chau refers to the trade through the island of Kish in rose-water. The adjacent province of Fars was celebrated for its rose-water, which, says Ibn Haukal, was exported to all parts of the world. The city of Shapur and its valley produced, according to Mukaddasi, ten different kinds of perfumed oils, which were exported far and wide over the Eastern world. Le Strange, Lands of the Eastern Caliphate, 293. Edrisi, op. cit., I, 394, speaks of the rose-water of Djur in Fars as being particularly pure. In another passage (supra, p. 141) our author mentions rose-water among the products of Asia Minor (Lu-meï).

Rose-water, *gulāb* in Persian, is not to be confounded with the «essence of roses» *'atr* in   5 Persian, our attar of roses, which is an essential oil obtained from the petals of the flower, the chief seat for the manufacture of which is at Ghāzipur on the Ganges. «The attar is obtained after the rose-water is made, by setting it out during the night and till sunrise in the morning in large open vessels exposed to the air, and then skimming off the essential oil which floats at the top». Yule and Burnell, Glossary, 494. The «common substitute» of which our author speaks 10 seems to have been prepared in much the same way as the attar. We are told, however, that the Arabs and Persians did not know of attar of roses, it was a discovery of Princess Nurdjihan, wife of Jehangir. L. Langlès, Recherches sur la découverte de l'essence de rose, 1804.

The Chinese rose is the Rosa indica, Lour. According to the Pön-ts'au the people in southern China prepared a fragrant water from the petals of the *ts'iang-wĕ* flowers. Bret- 15 schneider, Bot. Sinic., III, 303. See also Duarte Barbosa, op. cit., 188.

11.

GHARU-WOOD (沉 香).

Ch'ön-hiang comes from different places. That coming from Chön-la is the best; the second quality is that of Chan-ch'öng, and the poorest qualities 20 are those of San-fo-ts'i and Shö-p'o. It is customary to distinguish between «Upper Coast» and «Lower Coast» countries; Chön-la and Chan-ch'öng are called «Upper Coast»; Ta-shï, San-fo-ts'i and Shö-p'o are called «Lower Coast» [1].

This incense is, as a rule, considered superior in quality if it comes 25 from a living tree; and inferior, if from a decayed one. The hard and black kind is considered superior, the yellow (or brown) inferior. The shape of this incense varies widely, and several varieties have, accordingly, to be distinguished; one looks like a rhinoceros horn (*si-kio*), and is called *si-kio-ch'ön* (犀 角 沉 «rhinoceros horn gharu-wood»); another which resembles the beak 30 of a swallow (*yen-k'óu*), is called *yen-k'óu-ch'ön* (燕 口 沉); another kind, resembling aconite roots (*fu-tzï*) is called *fu-tzï-ch'ön* (附 子 沉); another kind resembles a shuttle (*so*) and is called *so-ch'ön* (梭 沉). If the graining be well marked and the veins close together, it is called *höng-ko-ch'ön* (橫 隔 沉) [2].   35

But, on the whole, when judging of the quality, more importance is attached to fragrance than to appearance. Furthermore, the common opinion that it is a product of P'o-ni (渤 泥 Borneo) is a fallacy [3].

Some authorities assert that *shöng-kié-ch'ön* or «fresh» (生 結) gharu is pruned off the tree with a knife while still growing, whereas *shóu-chʻön*, or «ripe» (熟) gharu, drops from the tree of itself[4]. The produce of the Lower Coast is called *fan-chʻön* (番 沉 «foreign gharu-wood»). Its smell catches the breath and its taste is bitter and pungent. As it is used for curing chills,

5 it is also called *yau-chʻön* (藥 沉 «medicinal gharu-wood»). Hai-nan also produces gharu-wood of a pure and lasting fragrance; it is called *pʻöng-lai-hiang* (蓬 來 香)[5].

Notes.

1) *Chʻön-hiang* means literally «sinking-incense»; it is thus called because it sinks in

10 water. Its name in Malay and Javanese is *kalambak* or *kalambah*, but it is also known in those languages by that of *gharu* or *kayu gharu*, gharu-wood, a corruption of the Sanskrit *agaru*, which in turn is the original from which the Portuguese formed the name of *pao d'aguila*, whence the French *bois d'aigle* and our «*eagle-wood*». The name, «aloes-wood» or «aloes», which is also given it in the Bible and by Arab and other mediaeval writers, is likewise derived from the

15 Sanskrit form. The French «bois de *calambour*» is derived from the Malay name *kalambak*.

On the division of countries into «Upper Coast» and «Lower Coast» countries, conf. supra, p. 79, lines 37—40. Ta-shï is here to be understood as the Arab colonies in Sumatra, and the lower part of the Malay Peninsula. See also quotation from Ling-wai-tai-ta in Note 2.

2) Nan-fang-tsʻau-mu-chuang, the earliest Chinese work in which I have found gharu

20 described, says (2,3) «The *mi-hiang* (蜜 香) tree of Kiau-chï has a trunk like the *kü-liu* (柜 柳 a kind of elm), its flowers are white and abundant. Its leaves are like those of the orange (橘). If one wants to get the aromatic substance, it must first be cut into (伐), the following year its root, stem, branches and joints are each of a different colour. The (parts of the) heart of the wood and of the joints (節), which are hard and black, and which sink in water, are

25 *chʻön-hiang*; those which float on the surface of water are *ki-ku-hiang* (鷄 骨 香 «chicken bone perfume»); its root is called *huang-shóu-hiang* (黃 熟 香), its trunk is *chan-hiang* (棧 香), its small branches which are hard and unbroken are *tsʻing-kui-hiang* (靑 桂 香 «green cassia perfume»); the knots in the root which are light and of large size are *ma-tʻi-hiang* (馬 蹄 香 «horse-hoof perfume»). The flowers have no perfume. When the fruit has ripened

30 it is aromatic and is known as *ki-shö-hiang* (鷄 舌 香 «chicken-tongue perfume»). It is certainly a most wonderful wood!» On the true nature of *ki-shö-hiang*, see infra, p. 210.

The same work (2,6) says the kind of paper called *mi-hiang-chï* is made from the bark and leaves of a *mi-hiang* tree. It is somewhat of a yellow clay colour and has markings in it like fish-roe. It is strongly perfumed, strong and tough, though soft. Soaking in water does not disinte-

35 grate it.» In A. D. 284 a mission from Ta-tsʻin presented 30,000 rolls of it to the Emperor of China. The mission had, of course, landed in Tongking, and had purchased the paper there as an acceptable present. See Hirth, China and Roman Orient, 272, 275. A paper known by the same name was, at a later date, made in the province of Kuang-tung at Lo-chóu (羅 州) from the bark of a tree called *chan-hiang* (棧 香). See Ling-piau-lü-i (written in the Tʻang dynasty), 2,6[b].

40 Ling-wai-tai-ta, 7,1 says: «The best *chʻön-hiang* comes from Chön-la (Kamboja), the second best from Chan-chʻöng (Tongking). The Chön-la kind is the hardest, that from Töng-liu-meï (Ligor possibly, in Malay Peninsula; see supra, p. 57) the most aromatic. The San-fo-tsʻi product is called «Lower Coast incense», that from Pʻo-lo-man (婆 羅 蠻 probably an error for Fo-lo-an, see supra, p. 69) is far superior to the Lower Coast incense.»

45 Ibn Batuta, Voyages, IV, 242 says the best quality of lign-aloes was that of Kākulah and Kamarah (the Khmer country, Kamboja). The Arabs knew also the lign-aloes of Chan-chʻöng (their Sanf), which they called Sanfi. See Heyd, Hist. du Commerce, II, 581, 584.

According to Loureiro, Flor. Cochin., 327, gharu is a product of the Alöexylon agallochum (the Aquilaria agalocha, Roxb.), Bretschneider, Bot. Sinic., III, 459. W. W. Skeat, Malay magic 206—210, (quoting Journal Roy. Asiat. Soc., Straits Branch, № 18, 359—361) says: «The gharu-tree is a tall forest tree, sometimes reaching the size of fifteen feet in diameter. The bark is of a silvery gray colour, and the foliage close and dense, of a dark hue. The Malay name for the tree is *tabak* ... Gharu, the diseased heart-wood of the *tabak*, is found in trees of all sizes, even in trees of one foot in diameter, thus showing that the disease attacks the tree at an early 5 stage. The gharu is found in pockets, and may sometimes be discovered by the veins which run to these pockets .... The tree is generally cut down and left to rot, which exposes the gharu in about six months .... There are great differences in the quality of gharu, and great care is taken in classifying them. It requires a skilled man to distinguish between some of the varieties». Eight varieties are then given with their distinctive peculiarities. The first — which is the *ch'ön-hiang* of 10 the Chinese, is called in Malay *chandan*. The *tsién* (or *chan*)-*hiang* referred to in another passage (infra p. 206) is the Malay *tandok* (or *tandak*). The other varieties of gharu mentioned by the Chinese are more difficult to identify with the Malay ones. The classification varies greatly in different Chinese works, thus the Nan-yüé-pi-ki (南越筆記) by Li T'iau-yüan, the eighteenth century editor of Chau Ju-kua's work, mentions (14,2°) fifteen varieties, most of the 15 names being quite different from those used by older writers. Pön-ts'au, 34,₂₆—₂₉, describes twenty odd varieties of gharu-wood.

3) In the first part of this work, our author says that gharu-wood of one kind or another is procured in the following countries: Kiau-chï, Chan-ch'öng, Chön-la, Töng-liu-meï, San-fo-ts'i, Tan-ma-ling, Ling-ya-ssï-kia, Fo-lo-an, the islands east of Borneo, and Hainan. In Chan-ch'öng (Annam), 20 he tells us (supra, p. 48) there was levied a special tax on persons engaged in hunting for gharu.

4) This definition of the difference between «raw» and «ripe» gharu appears — in the light of the information supplied from Malay sources (supra, n. 2.)—to be correct; it is however, very difficult to follow our author in his explanations concerning the various varieties of this product.

5) Kiau-chï also produced *p'öng-lai* gharu (see supra, p. 46). Ling-wai-tai-ta, 7,1—2 says that 25 *p'öng-lai* gharu-wood is also known as *ch'ön-shui-hiang* or «sinking in water incense». Perfect nodules are rare, they are like little bamboo hats (小笠) or big mushrooms. If they float on water, they have lost their fragrance and are worth but little. This *ch'ön-shui* is used in medecine. There is also a good variety of *p'öng-lai-hiang* called *chö-ku-pan-hiang* (鷓鴣斑香) because it is spotted like a partridge's breast. Its perfume is weak but agreeable. There is also a 30 *p'öng-lai-tsién-hiang* which comes from Hainan.

11ᵃ.

TSIÉN-HIANG GHARU-WOOD (箋香).

Tsién-hiang is an inferior quality of gharu-wood, being similar to (*ch'ön-hiang*) in fragrance and taste, but fibrous and not very solid, whence it is 35 considered inferior to the *ch'ön-hiang*, though better than the «ripe *su*» (熟速) variety.

Note.

Nan-fang-ts'au-mu-chuang (loc. cit.) says that *chan-hiang* (棧香) is the product of the trunk of the tree; this is probably the same as the *tsién-hiang*. Ling-wai-tai-ta, 7,2, says 40 that *tsién-hiang* comes from Hainan; it flows from the tree in liquid form and coagulates in a mass like needles. *P'öng-lai-tsién-hiang* coagulates in a flat plate-shaped mass. The small fragments off the edges of this variety are known as *hié-k'o-hiang* (蟹殼香 «crab-shell incense»). The *kuang-hiang* (光香 «brilliant incense») which comes from «north of the Sea» (海北 Southern China?) and Kiau-chï is identical with *tsién-hiang*. The *shóu-su* variety is 45 mentioned in the next paragraph.

11ᵇ.

SU AND CHAN GHARU-WOOD (速 暫 香).

Shöng (or fresh)-*su* (生 速) comes from Chön-la and Chan-ch'öng, but *shóu* (or ripe)-*su* (熟 速) has various sources. The Chön-la kind is the best; 5 the second class is the one from Chan-ch'öng, and the lowest that of Shö-p'o. We call *shöng-su* that kind which is obtained from the wood of the tree cut down for the express purpose (of getting it), and *shóu-su* the incense remaining in the rotten wood of a tree which has fallen down. The fragrance and taste of *shöng-su* are lasting, those of *shóu-su* are apt to have a singed 10 smell; for this reason the *shöng* kind is superior to the *shóu*.

A still inferior incense is called *chan* (暫). Its source of origin is the same as that of *shóu-su;* but we call the incense which has fallen off the tree from its own accord *shóu-su*, and that which consists partly of wood *chan;* it is partly *shöng*, partly *shóu*. Traders slice the wood with a knife, 15 in order to obtain the incense, of which the better pieces are selécted to be mixed with *shóu-su*, in which state it reaches the market; nor can purchasers distinguish it from the genuine article (i. e., *shóu-su-hiang*).

11ᶜ.

HUANG-SHÓU-HIANG GHARU-WOOD
20 (黃 熟 香).

Huang-shóu-hiang comes from several countries, but the Chön-la variety is the best. It is so called because it is yellow (*huang*) and ripe (*shóu*). It is called *huang-shóu-t'ung* (黃 熟 桶) if its surface is hard, while the inside is decayed, and if it is barrel (*t'ung*)-shaped. When it contains *tsién-hiang* 25 and is black throughout, and when its aroma is particularly good, it is called *kia-tsién-huang-shóu* (夾 箋 黃 熟); this is the best quality of this variety of gharu[1].

Note.

1) Nan-yüé-pi-ki, 14,3 says, speaking of Hainan *huang-shóu-hiang*, that it is divided into 30 *kio-ch'ön* (角 沉) and *huang-ch'ön* (黃 沉); there is furthermore a kind of soft *huang-ch'ön* called *la-ch'ön* (蠟 沉 «wax-gharu»). *Kia-tsién-huang-shóu* means literally «yellow-ripe-containing-*tsién*-gharu».

11ᵈ.

SHÖNG-HIANG GHARU-WOOD (生 香).

Shöng-hiang comes from Chan-ch'öng and Chön-la; it is also found throughout Hai-nan. Its price is cheaper than that of black *kio-ch'ön* (烏 [角 沉])[1]. 5

The incense is procured from the lopped off young branches. If the incense is fresh (生) in the wood, it is called *shöng-hiang*.

If the bark (over the gharu) has grown three-tenths (of an inch) in thickness, (the gharu) is called *chan-hiang* (暫 香); if it is five-tenths (of an inch) thick, it is *tsién-hiang* (箋 香); when a full inch thick, then it is 10 *ch'ön-hiang* (沉 香)[2].

Notes.

1) A character or two are missing in the text after the word «black» (*wu*); but there can be no doubt that this blank should be filled by the characters *kio-ch'ön*, as the only kind of gharu called «black» is the *kio-ch'ön* variety. Supra, p. 158, our author says that *shöng-hiang* 15 was a product of the islands lying to the east of P'o-ni, presumably the Celebes; he was misinformed.

2) In other words the quality of the gharu improves with the thickness of the bark (皮) over the gharu — *ch'ön-hiang*, the best quality, being found in the heart of the wood.

12.

SANDAL-WOOD (檀 香). 20

T'an-hiang comes from the two countries of Ta-kang (打 綱) and Ti-wu (底 勿); it is also found in San-fo-ts'i. The tree resembles the lichee of China, even the leaves are like it. The natives fell the tree and dry it in the shade. Its aroma is pure and strong and apt to evaporate; in burning it surpasses all other incenses. A variety of yellow colour is called *huang-t'an* 25 (黃 檀); a red-brown variety is called *tzï-t'an* (紫 檀); a light and brittle kind is called *sha-t'an* (沙 檀). The aroma of these varieties is about the same.

The best quality is that derived from old trees, when the bark is thin and the full proportion of fragrance is contained in it. The second quality 30 contains only seven or eight tenths of fragrance. The poorest quality is called *tién-sing-hiang* (點 星 香). Pieces of sandal-wood which have dropped down like rain are called *p'o-lóu-hiang* (破 漏 香), or «scented (wood) broken off and dropped down.» The root of the tree is called *hiang-t'óu* (香 頭) or «incense head.» 35

Note.

In Chinese Buddhist works sandal-wood is called *chan* (or *chön*)-*t'an* (栴 [or 真] 檀), transcribing the Sanskrit word *chandana; t'an*, the name now in general use in China, is a truncated form of that first used. Weï-shu, 102,18[b] mentions «white *chön-t'an* (白 真 檀) as a product

5 of Pa-lai (拔 賴) in Southern India. Ta-kang and Ti-wu are mentioned among the dependencies of Java. Ta-kang, which our author says (supra, p. 84) was an island, remains unidentified; Schlegel has suggested (see supra, p. 86) that Ta-kang is the old name of Samarang. Ti-wu, in Cantonese Tai-mat, is the island of Timor, elsewhere called Ti-mön. In the first part of his work our author has told us that sandal-wood was also a product of T'ién-chu (western coast of India),

10 and of the Malay Peninsula, and that Ts'öng-pa (Zanguebar) produced yellow sandal-wood. On this latter point, see supra, p. 127, n. 4.

The Ku-kin-chu (古 今 注 2,2) mentions red sandal-wood, which it calls *tzï-t'an* and *tzï-meï-mu* (紫 梅 木), as a product of Fu-nan (Siam). Conf. Pön-ts'au-kang-mu, 34,35–36[a], which quotes the T'u-king-pön-ts'au to the effect that a *t'an* tree, but with odorless wood, grew

15 in the valleys of the Yang-tzï and of the Huai-ho.

Crawfurd, Hist. Indian Archipelago, I, 519, says, regarding sandal-wood, that «from Java and Madura eastward it is scattered in small quantities throughout the different islands, improving in quality and quantity as we move to the east, until we reach Timur, where the best and largest supply occurs. In the language of Timur sandal-wood is called *Aikamenil*, and in that of

20 Amboyna *Ayasru*. In the western countries, where it either does not exist at all, or exists in small quantities and of bad quality, it is universally known by the Sanskrit name *Chandana*.» In another passage (III, 421) he says «the sandal-wood of the Indian Islands is considered inferior to that of Malabar.»

13.

25
CLOVES (丁 香).

Ting-hiang come from the countries of the Ta-shï and from Shö-p'o. They are called *ting-hiang* or «nail-incense» because they resemble in shape the Chinese character *ting* (丁, «a nail»). They have the property of removing bad smells from the mouth, and high officials at Court put cloves into their

30 mouths when they have to lay matters before the Emperor. The large ones are called *ting-hiang-mu* (丁 香 母), and this is the same as *ki-shö-hiang* (雞 舌 香), though some say that *ki-shö-hiang* is the stone of the Persian date (千 年 棗).

Note.

35   In the first part of this work, Chau has stated (supra, pp. 77, 84) that cloves were a product of Eastern Java and of its dependencies, the same region which produced sandal-wood, in other words the Moluccas. He refers also to the trade in cloves in Ceylon and in Malabar, whither they were brought by foreign traders (*Fan-shang*). Our author was, therefore, better informed on this subject than Marco Polo who, though stating in one passage (II, 254) that they were a

40 product of Java, adds in another (II, 289) that they grew also on the island of Necuveran (Nicobar Islands). Ibn Batuta, Voyages, IV, 243, confounded the cinnamon and the nutmeg-tree

with cloves. De Candolle, Origine des plantes cultivées, 128, thinks that cloves, a product of the Caryophyllus aromaticus, Linné, are indigenous to the Molucca Islands. See Heyd, Hist. du Commerce, II, 603—607, and Crawfurd, History Malay Archipel., I, 494.

In the Chinese Customs Tariff of the present day we find *mu-ting-hiang*, «mother-cloves», answering to the *ting-hiang-mu* of our text. The Su-ch'ön-liang-fang (蘇沉艮方) [1,9], [5] says that *ki-shö-hiang* («chicken-tongue incense») is *ting-hiang-mu*, but, it adds, «at the present day the name is likewise applied to a substance found in *ju-hiang* (frankincense), and which is of the size of a *shan-chu-yü* (山茱萸 Cornus officinalis); when cut out it is like a persimmon seed; it is tasteless.» According to the Pön-ts'au-kang-mu (34,32[a]) *ki-shö-hiang* is the female, and *ting-hiang* the male, clove. The Nan-fang-ts'au-mu-chuang (2,3, and supra p. 205, note 2) says [10] that *ki-shö-hiang* is the ripe and aromatic fruit of the *mi-hiang*, or eagle-wood tree, of China.

The Chinese name here given the date, *ts'ién-nién-tsau*, or «thousand year *tsau*», was evidently used on account of the stony hardness of the dates on reaching China, and on account of their resemblance to the *tsau* or common jujube (Zizyphus vulgaris, Lam.), which is indigenous to China. Yu-yang-tsa-tsu, 18,9[a], the earliest work we have seen describing the date, [15] calls it *Po-ssï-tsau*, i. c., «Persian *tsau*», and says that in Persian it is called *k'u-mang* (窟莽 Arabic, *khurmā*). In the T'ang-shu, 221[B],13[a], we find the name written *hu-mang* (鶻莽), and the Pön-ts'au, 31,21[b], gives also the form *k'u-lu-ma* (苦魯麻). See also Ling-piau-lü-i, 2,4[b].

14.

NUTMEGS (肉荳蔻).

[20]

Jóu-tóu-k'óu are brought from the foreign tribes in the depths of the islands of Huang-ma-chu and Niu-lun (牛崙). The tree resembles the Chinese juniper (栢), and attains a height of upwards of an hundred feet. Its trunk and branches, with the foliage, present the appearance of a large shady roof under which forty or fifty men may find protection. When the blossoms open [25] in the spring they are taken off and dried in the sun; this is the article now known as *tóu-k'óu-hua* (荳蔻花). The fruit (nut) resembles the *feï-tzï* (榧子) nut; when the shell is removed the pulp can be kept a long time, if preserved in ashes (灰). According to the Pön-ts'au its properties are warming.

[30]

Note.

Huang-ma-chu and Niu-lun were dependencies of Java (supra, p. 83), presumably in the Moluccas, in which islands the nutmeg (Myristica fragrans) is indigenous. De Candolle, Origine des plantes cultivées, 336, Crawfurd, op. cit., I, 505. Heyd, Hist. du Commerce, II, 644, says the original home of the nutmeg-tree is still doubtful. [35]

In the early part of the eighth century Ch'ön Ts'ang-k'i (陳藏器), in his Pön-ts'au-shï-i (本草拾遺), was the first Chinese author to describe *jóu-tóu-k'óu*, which he states was brought to China from foreign countries, where it was called *kia-kü-lö* (迦拘勒), probably intended for *ḳāḳulah* (قاقلة), which is the Arabic name for cardamom. Bretschneider, Bot. Sinic., III, 123, 124. The nutmeg-tree must have been imported from its original habitat [40] into the province of Kuang-tung somewhere between the time of Ch'ön Ts'ang-k'i and the end of the eleventh century, for we find it mentioned in Su Sung's (蘇頌) work, entitled T'u-king-pön-ts'au (圖經本草), that the tree was cultivated in Ling-nan. «The buds and flowers, he says, grow in the spring; the fruit resembles the cardamom, but it is round and smaller, the shell darker brown, sticking closer to the pulp and thinner than that of the cardamom. The pulp has an acrid taste. The crop is gathered in the sixth moon.» He gives an illustration of a nutmeg, which he calls «Cantonese nutmeg». Su died in A. D. 1101, according to Sung-shĭ, 340,30.

Tóu-k̒oú-hua is mace, the arillus of the nutmeg. Crawfurd, op. cit., I, 506. The *feï-tzĭ* is
5 now the hazel nut (torreya nucifera); it seems that the name was applied to that nut at the time our author wrote. Bretschneider, Bot. Sinic., III, 429, and Hanbury, Science papers, 233.

We translate *hui* by «ashes» and not «lime» on the strength of a passage in the Chöng-leï pön-ts̒au (證 類 本 草), 9,32, in which Leï-kung (雷 公 fifth century A. D.) says with regard to the nutmeg: «when it is to be used glutinous rice is powdered and soaked in boiling
10 water, after which the nut is wrapped in it and baked in hot ashes until the rice coating has turned brown. The rice is then removed and the nut is fit for use. The use of copper vessels is to be avoided.» The correct translation may be, however, «lime», for Crawfurd (op. cit., I, 509) says that in the process of curing nutmegs they are «dipped twice or thrice in lime-water, or rather a thick mixture of lime and water, made of fine shells, which is supposed to secure them
15 from the depredations of insects and worms.» The Pön-ts̒au referred to, the chief botanical work of the Sung dynasty, was compiled in A. D. 1108. See Bretschneider, Botanicon Sinicum, I, 47.

15.

LAKA-WOOD (降 眞 香).

Kiang-chön-hiang comes from San-fo-ts̒i, Shö-p̒o and P̒öng-föng; it
20 is also found in all the districts of Kuang-tung and Kuang-si[1]. Its aroma is strong and penetrating; it counteracts bad smells. All the people of Ts̒üan-chóu, no matter whether a household be rich or poor, burn this incense at the end of the year, as if (they were making) a Sacrifice to Heaven[2].

Its price is very cheap. The product of San-fo-ts̒i is considered the best
25 on account of the purity and strength of its fragrance. This wood is also called *tzĭ-t̒öng-hiang* (紫 籐 香) or «red vine incense»[3].

Notes.

1) P̒öng-föng, Pahang, on the east coast of the Malay Peninsula. In the first part of this work the author states that laka-wood was a product of Sumatra, Tan-ma-ling (Kwantan), Fo-
30 lo-an (Beranang), Shö-p̒o (Java), the Celebes (?), and Borneo.

Tung-si-yang-k̒au, 3,13[a],17[a] uses the name *kiang-hiang*, and says it was a product of Patani (大 泥), and Palembang. The Pön-ts̒au, 34.36, says it is also called *ki-ku-hiang*, which, in another passage (supra, p. 205, line 25), is given as the name of a kind of gharu-wood.

2) The «Sacrifice to Heaven», or *fan-ch̒ai* (燔 柴 lit. «burning fuel»), was not performed
35 by the people at large, but by the Sovereign. See Legge, Li Ki, II, 202. The simile does not appear a happy one; it can only mean that, in view of the cheapness of this odoriferous wood, every one celebrated the coming of the New Year in the same way as the Emperors did with the *fan-ch̒ai*.

3) In another passage (supra, p. 198) our author states that the sap of the laka-wood tree
40 was used to make an «imitation dragon's-blood».

16.

MUSK-WOOD (麝 香 木).

Shö-hiang-mu comes from Chan-ch'öng and Chön-la. It is a tree which from age falls down and sinks into the ground, where it decays; this is the best variety. As its fragrance has a slight resemblance to that of musk, the 5 wood is called «musk-wood». When fresh cut, it is of a strong and unpleasant odour; this is the inferior quality. The people of Ts'üan-chóu use this wood a good deal for making furniture resembling that made of rose-wood (花 梨 木)

Note. 10

We have been unable to identify this product, nor have we found any mention of it in other Chinese works. The Tung-si-yang-k'au, 3,10[b] mentions this product as coming from Kamboja, but has nothing to say concerning it, except that the I-t'ung-chï says it has the odour of musk. The Pön-ts'au does not refer to it.

17.　　　　　　　　　　　　　　　　　　　　15

JACK-FRUIT (波 羅 蜜).

The *po-lo-mi* is of the size of a pumpkin; its outer skin is covered with nodules like the hair on a Buddha's head. Its colour is green while growing, and turns yellow when ripe. The pulp, when cut out of the fruit, is of extreme sweetness. The tree resembles a banian, and the flowers grow in 20 clusters (叢). When the flowers fall and the fruit sets, only one develops, the rest shrivel up. The *po-lo-mi* comes from Su-ki-tan; it is also found at the Nam-hoi Temple (南 海 廟) in Canton.

Note.

This fruit is the product of the Artocarpus integrifolia; the origin of our name for it, *jack*, 25 is the Malayālam name of the fruit, *chakka*. Its Sanskrit names are *pānasa, phalasa*, and *kantaka-phala*. Yule and Burnell, Glossary, 335. Crawfurd, Hist. Indian Archipel., I, 422. De Can-dolle, op. cit., 239, thinks it is indigenous to the Western Ghats—possibly Malabar. The fruit was at first called *p'o-na-so* by the Chinese, which is the Sanskrit name *pānasa*. The Sui-shu, 82,7[b] is, I be-lieve, the earliest Chinese work to mention this fruit. Among the products peculiar to Chön-la (Kam- 30 boja) it speaks of «the *p'o-na-so* (婆那娑) tree which had no flowers, and whose leaves were like the *shï* (櫞 Diospyros kaki) and whose fruit was like a pumpkin (*tung-kua*). «Later on it received the name of *po-lo-mi*, which, the Chinese say, was given it on its introduction into Canton in the sixth century by a native of «the country of Po-lo» (波 羅), whence the name of the fruit. Po-lo, according to T'ang-shu, 222[B], was S. W. of Kamboja (Chï-t'u), and Wön-hién-tung-k'au, 35 331. Sect. P'o-li, identifies it with P'o-li, which is supposed to have been in the Malay Peninsula. Conf. supra, pp. 83, 85, n. 4, 96.

Yu-yang-tsa-tsu, 18,8[b], has the following on the jack-fruit: «The *P'o-na-so* (婆那娑) tree grows (出) in Po-ssï (Persia); it also grows in Fu-lin, where it is called *a-p'u-to* (阿 部 亶 or *a-sa-to* 阿 薩 亶 according to Pön-ts'au). The tree grows to 50 or 60 feet high. The bark is blueish-green. The leaves are very shiny, they do not wither in winter or
5 summer. The fruit does not come out of the flower, but proceeds from the stem of the tree, and is as large as a pumpkin. It has a husk enveloping it, and on the husk are spines (刺). The pulp is sweet and edible. The pips (inside the pulp) are as big as jujubes, and one fruit has a number of them. They have stems (枚). Inside the pips there is a kernel like a chestnut and yellow, which is excellent eating when roasted.» See also Hirth, J. A. O. S., XXX, 24.
10   P'ing-chóu-k'o-t'an, 2,5[a] says: «In front of the Nan-hai-miau (in Canton) there is a big tree. The ripe fruit is like a pumpkin, when opened its sections (房) are like bananas. The natives call it *po-lo-mi*. When properly prepared (lit. steeped) it is good to eat (漬 之 可 食).»

The Nan-hai (Nam-hoi in Cantonese)-miau in Canton is supposed to have been founded at the end of the sixth century A. D. The two jack-fruit trees in it were said to have been
15 planted during the Liang dynasty (A. D. 502—557), and are supposed to have been the ancestors of all the jack-fruit trees in the neighbourhood. See Kuang-tung-sin-yü (published in 1700), 6,7, and 25,28, et seqq. At the present time the jack-fruit is found all over Kuang-tung, Hainan and southern Formosa. The image of the first propagator of the jack-fruit in China — the native of the kingdom of Po-lo referred to previously — is worshipped down to the present day in the Nam-hoi
20 temple, where jack-fruit trees are still grown. Notes and Queries on China and Japan, II, 169, 191, III, 14.

Concerning the origin of the Chinese name *po-lo-mi* for this fruit, Thos. Watters, Essays on the Chinese language, 437, is inclined to think it a mixed term, *po-lo* may be Sanskrit for *phala* fruit, and *mi* may be the Chinese word for honey. This explanation appears to us a fairly
25 satisfactory one.

The T'ang-shu, 221A,17[b], mentions that in the twenty-first year of the *chöng-kuan* period (A. D. 647) a mission from Magadha (Central India) which came to the Chinese court, presented the Emperor with a *po-lo* (波 羅) tree. This tree, it is said, resembled a *pai-yang* tree (白 楊 Populus alba, L.). *Po-lo* is, as noted previously, the Sanskrit word for «fruit» — but it seems
30 possible that this particular one may have been a *po-lo-mi* or jack-fruit tree, if not a pine-apple.

18.

ARECA-NUTS (檳 榔).

The *pin-lang* comes from several foreign countries, also from the four districts of Hai-nan; it is likewise found in Kiau-chï. The tree resembles the
35 coir-palm (椶 櫚) [1].

«The fruit grows on the leaves, fastened to them in clusters, as on willow twigs. When gathered in the spring it is called *juan-pin-lang* (軟 檳 榔 or «soft areca-nuts») and is commonly known as *pin-lang-sién* (檳 榔 鮮 or «fresh areca-nuts»); it is then good to chew. When gathered in
40 the summer or the autumn and dried it is called *mi-pin-lang* (米 檳 榔

or «rice areca-nuts»). Preserved in salt it is called *yen-pin-lang* (鹽檳榔 or «salted areca-nuts»). Small and pointed nuts are called *ki-sin-pin-lang* (雞心檳榔 or «chicken heart areca-nuts»), large and flat ones *ta-fu-tzï* (大腹子 or «big bellies»).»[2]

When chewed, these nuts have the effect of preventing eructation. In San-fo-ts'i they make wine out of the juice.

«The Customs at Canton and Ts'üan-chóu derive an annual revenue of several tens of thousands of strings of cash from the trade carried on in this product» by foreign ships. But most of the product comes from Hai-nan. The «fresh nuts» and the «salted nuts» come from there, whereas the *ki-sin* and the *ta-fu-tzï* varieties come mostly from Ma-i.

Notes.

1) *Pin-lang* is a transcription of the Malay name of the areca-palm (Areca catcchu, L.) *pinang*. Nan-fang-ts'au-mu-chuang, 3,1[b], says that it comes from Lin-i (林邑 Southern Indo-China) and that it is also called *pin-mön-yau-tsién* (賓門藥餞) or «*pin-mön* medicinal comfit». De Candolle, op. cit., 344 thinks it may be indigenous to the Malay Peninsula. Our author mentions betel-nuts in the first part of his work as a product of Coromandel, of Hainan and of the Philippine islands (Ma-i). He calls (supra, p. 160) the betel-nuts brought from the last named place *yau-pin-lang* or «medicinal areca-nuts». He mentions (supra, pp. 60, 78) wine made with areca-nuts as in use in Sumatra (San-fo-ts'i) and Java.

2) This paragraph, as also that part of the last paragraph in quotation marks, are taken from Ling-wai-tai-ta, 8,3. The Pön-ts'au, 31,14–19, says the *ta-fu-tzi* is also called *chu-pin-lang*, «pig betel-nut».

19.

COCOANUT (椰子).

«The *yé-tzï*, as regards the trunk and leaves, closely resembles the coir-palm and the areca-palm. The fruit grows in the leaves in bunches of several nuts of the size of a vessel holding five pints (升). It is the biggest of fruits, with the sole exception of the jack-fruit. When cut the outer skin is at first green and tender, but after some time it turns yellow, and when kept a long time the skin shrivels and dries up. The nut shell contained in the outer skin can be made into vessels; the pulp inside the shell is of a jade-like white, and of an agreeable taste, resembling that of cow's milk. The juice (酒) inside the pulp is very clear and fragrant when fresh, but when stale it turns muddy, and is no longer drinkable.» In the states of Nan-p'i they make wine out of the juice of its flower mixed with syrup.

Note.

The whole of this section, except the last phrase, is quoted from Ling-wai-tai-ta, 8,4. De Candolle, op. cit., 345—350 discusses the question of the original habitat of the cocoanut. He is disposed to place it in the Indian Archipelago. It appears to have been already known in China in the second century before our era. Nan-fang-ts'au-mu-chuang, 3,2, refers to the toddy made from it in Indo-China (Lin-i and Nan-yüé) and to its intoxicating property. The cocoanut, it adds, is commonly called *Yüé-wang-t'óu* (越 王 頭 «head of the king of Yüé»), because in olden times there was a feud between the king of Lin-i and the king of Nan-yüé, and the former sent an assassin who killed the king and cut off his head, which the king of Lin-i had hung on a tree. After a while it changed into a cocoanut, when the king in anger had it cut down and made into a slop-bowl (飲 器). The people of the South, the author adds to clinch the story, still follow this custom of making slop-bowls out of cocoanuts. See also Ling-piau-lü-i, 2,6[b] (T'ang dynasty). On the subject of liquors used in southern Asia, the Pön-ts'au, 31,20, refers to a number, among them to one made in Tun-sun (in the Malay Peninsula probably) with the juice of the flowers of a tree like a pomegranate. In a previous passage (supra, p. 89) our author says that in Ku-lin (Quilon) «they made a liquor with a mixture of honey (or syrup) with cocoanuts and the juice of a flower, which they let ferment;» perhaps it was similar to that mentioned in the Pön-ts'au.

20.

OAK-GALLS (沒 石 子).

Mo-shï-tzï come from Wu-ssï-li (勿 厮 離 Mosul) in the Ta-shï country. The tree resembles the camphor-tree, it blossoms once a year and bears a fruit similar to the Chinese acorn (茅 栗), and called *sha-mo-lü* (沙 沒 律), or *p'u-lu* (蒲 蘆), and which is edible. The following year it grows what is called *ma-ch'a* (麻 茶), which is the same as *mo-shï-tzï*. The year following appear again *sha-mo-lü*, and the *mo-shï-tzï* grow in alternate years, so it is a valuable article. What a wonderful thing to see one root produce different fruits!

Note.

The Yu-yang-tsa-tsu, 18,8[a], appears to be the earliest Chinese work to describe in some detail oak-galls. It says: «*Wu-shï-tzï* (無 石 子) come from Po-ssï (Persia), and in Persian they are called *mo-tsö* (摩 賊). The tree is sixty to seventy feet high, and eight or nine feet in circumference. The leaves are like peach leaves but larger. In the third moon its flowers open, they are white and reddish in the center. The seed is round like a pill, at first green, but when ripe a yellowish white. Those with holes in them have been pierced by insects, the perfect nuts are without holes in the skin; these are used to make medicine. One year the tree produces *wu-shï-tzï*, the following it produces *po-lü-tzï* (跋 屢 子) of the size of the finger tip and three inches long. On the upper end there is a cup (壳) in which is the kernel, like a chestnut, of brown colour and which is edible.»

Our author derives most of his information from Ling-wai-tai-ta, 3,4[a], only adding the Persian names of the oak, *balut*, (*p'u-lu*) and *shah-balut* or royal oak, in Chinese *sha-mo-lü*. Wu-shï-tzï, mo-shï-tzï, mo-tsö and ma-ch'a, all represent the Persian *māzū*, the word for oak-galls.

Thos. Watters, Essays on the Chinese language, 349. See also supra, p. 140. Weï-shu, 102,12ª,
and Sui-shu, 83,16ª mention *wu-shĭ-tzĭ* as one of the products of Po-ssï (Persia).

Duarte Barbosa, in the beginning of the fifteenth century, speaking of the trade of
Malacca, says that among the articles its merchants dealt with were *magican*, «which are gall-
nuts, which they bring from the Levant to Cambay, by way of Mekkah, and they are worth a   5
great deal in China and Java». Description of the Coasts of East Africa and Malabar, 191 (Hakl.
Soc. edit.). See also Heyd, Hist. du Commerce, II, 644.

There is some doubt whether *mau-li*, which we have translated by «acorn», should not be
rendered by «chestnut»; this confusion exists among the Chinese. See Porter Smith, Contributions, 60 and Bretschneider, Botanicon Sinicum, II, 320.   10

21.

EBONY (烏 樠 子).

Wu-mön-tzĭ resembles the coir-palm (棕 櫚); it is an erect tree of
olive-green colour, growing to a height of an hundred feet and more, with a
thick green and highly luxuriant foliage. Its wood is as hard as iron and 15
lends itself to the manufacture of woodware, being glossy like lacquered
ware, for which reason it is generally considered a precious wood (珍 木).

Note.

Ku-kin-chu, 3,1, says: «*I-mu* (翳 木) or *wo-i-mu* (殹 翳 木) comes from
Tongking (Kiau-chóu). Its colour is black, and it is veined. It is also called *wu-wön-*(Canton. *mön*) 20
mu (烏 文 木 «black-veined-wood»).

Pön-ts'au-kang-mu, 35ᴮ,37, says that the name *wu-mön-mu* and *wu-wön-mu* are identical
with *wu-mu* (烏 木), the name used at the present day to designate ebony. This disposes of
Schlegel's doubts, who (T'oung Pao. Ser II, Vol. II, 127) says *wu-man-mu* (烏 樠 木)
stands for «Black fir-tree» and signifies «Arenga saccharifera.»   25

Nan-yüé-pi-ki, 13,6 says that «*wu-mu* is a product of Kiung-chóu (in Hainan) and of the
islands. It is much used among the natives to make chopsticks of. The *Kuang-chĭ* (廣 志)
says there comes from Hainan a kind of *wu-mu* called *kio-wu* (角 烏), which is uniformly
black throughout and is very brittle. There is also a variety called *ch'a-wu* (茶 烏), which is
(brought to China) by foreign ships and which is so dense that it sinks in water. There are a 30
great many varieties of (this kind of) *wu-mu*, all of which are good for making canes and tables.
None is real unless it sinks in water.» In Amoy dialect *wu-mön-tzĭ* is pronounced *o-ban-tzĭ*, and
this word no doubt corresponds to the Persian *ābnūs* (ἔβενος) «ebony», from which the Spanish
abenuz and our *ebony* are derived. The Persian *ābnūs* is also, apparently, the *bonus* of Marco
Polo, of which he says there were vast forests in Champa (the Chan-ch'öng of the Chinese). Yule, 35
Marco Polo, II, 250, 252.

The explanation of this wood being designated by the same term in old Chinese works
and by the Persians must be that, either the Chinese received their first supplies of it through
Persian traders, or the word is indigenous to one of the Indo-Chinese districts where the
tree grows, and that it had travelled to the east and west with the article. This last expla- 40
nation would somewhat modify the traditional etymology of the names for ebony known to the
ancient Greeks, Hebrews and Latins. Ebony, it should be remembered, is the wood of various
species of trees of the genus Diospyros and the natural order Ebenaceæ. The Nan-yüé-pi-ki, in
the passage quoted above, shows that the Chinese are aware of this fact.

22.

SAPAN-WOOD (蘇木).

Su-mu comes from the country of Chön-la. The tree resembles the pine and juniper. The leaves are like those of the *tung-ts'ing* tree (冬青). Its
5 habitat is in the uncultivated parts of the hilly country, where the people are allowed to cut it. When the bark is removed and the wood dried in the sun, it is of a deep red colour and may be used in dying purple. It is popularly known as *wa-mu* (窊木).

Note.

10   The wood of the Caesalpinia sappan. It was known to the Arabs as *bakkam*, and as Brazil-wood in Western mediaeval commerce. Its name in Malay is *supang*, which is the original of the Chinese *su-mu*, or rather of the earlier form *su-fang*, concerning which Nan-fang ts'au-mu-chuang, 2,4, says: «The *su-fang* (蘇枋) belongs to the *huai* (槐 sophora) variety. The flowers have black seeds. The tree grows in Chan-ch'öng (Annam). The men of the south (of
15 China) make a deep red dye by steeping it in Ta-yü (大庾) water, which (has the property of) making the colour particularly deep.» The word *su-fang* is said by some Chinese writers to be the name of an island. Pön-ts'au, 35ᴮ,35ᵇ. Conf. Yule, Marco Polo, II, 369, where *sappan* is derived from *Japan*, an impossible derivation, as the name *Ji-pön* (Japan) was first used in A. D. 670.

       In connexion with dye stuffs, it is interesting to note that already in the sixth century, or
20 very early in the seventh, the true indigo or Indigofera tinctoria, L. was known to the Chinese as a product of the Persian (Sassanian) province of Ts'au (漕); it was called in Chinese *ts'ing-tai* (青黛). Sui-shu, 83. Sect. Ts'au. See Bretschneider, J. C. B. R. A. S., XXV, 214.

       The term *tung-ts'ing* here used is a descriptive and comprehensive one («winter-green») applied to certain evergreen oleaceous trees which harbour the wax-insect. Porter Smith,
25 Materia medica, 229, Hanbury, Science papers, 67. It is the Ligustrum lucidum, Bretschneider, Bot. Sinic., III, 513–517. *Wa-mu* may be an abbreviation for *Wa-li-mu* or «wood of Wa-li». Wa-li is mentioned by our author (supra, p. 54) as a dependency of Chön-la.

―――――――

23.

COTTON (吉貝).

30   «The *ki-peï* tree resembles a small mulberry-tree, with a hibiscus-like (芙蓉) flower furnishing a floss half an inch and more in length, very much like goose-down, and containing some dozens of seeds. In the south the people remove the seed from the floss by means of iron chopsticks, upon which the floss is taken in the hand and spun without troubling about
35 twisting together the thread. Of the cloth (布) woven therefrom there are several qualities», the most durable and the strongest is called *tóu-lo-mién*

(兜羅綿); the second quality is called *fan-pu* or «foreign cloth» (番布); the third «tree-cotton» or *mu-mién* (木棉); the fourth *ki-pu* (吉布). These textures are sometimes dyed in various colours and brightened with strange patterns. The pieces measure up to five or six feet in breadth.

Note.

All the first part of this article is substantially a quotation from Ling-wai-tai-ta, 6,12—13, the only change made by our author being that Chóu K'ü-feï compares cotton to willow-down (柳綿).

Oriental or herbaceous cotton (Gossypium herbaceum, Linn.), which de Candolle, op. cit., 323, thinks is indigenous to Sindh, and which was called *karpāsa* in Sanskrit, was in general use throughout India in the Vedic times. The Greeks first learnt of it by the expedition of Alexander; they retained its Indian name, calling it χάρπασος. By the end of the first century of our era cotton, both raw and manufactured, formed one of the staples of trade between the ports on the western coast of India, Egypt, and the Greek world. See Mc Crindle, 52, 64, 108, 113, and Strabo, XV, I, 20, 21. Cotton was introduced into Nineveh about 700 B. C.; it was called «wool-tree». Proc. Soc. Bibl. Archeol., Dec. 1909, 339.

It would seem that cotton and cotton fabrics first reached China from Central Asia, for the earliest name given them in Chinese, *po-*(or *pai-*)*tié*, is certainly borrowed from one of the Turki languages. The two characters composing the name *po-tié* (帛疊 or 白氎) furnish no sense in Chinese, and the use of different but homophonous characters to write it, point to its being a foreign word. The nearest equivalent seems to be the Jagatai Turki word for cotton *pakhta* (باقتن). See Radloff, Wörterbuch d. Türk-Dialecte, IV, 1138. Conf. Gerini, Researches, 243, n. 2.

Strangely enough the earliest recorded use of the word *po-tié* which has come down to us relates to a country lying to the south-west of China, and it is applied to a hempen fabric. Hóu-Han-shu, 116,18[b] says that the Ai-lau aborigines (then in Yün-nan) manufactured *po-tié*, which a later history (Weï-shu, 101,23[b]) tells us was a textile fabric of hemp, which was called in their language *lan-kan*. We have to come down to the sixth century of our era to find a reference to cotton in Turkestan. Liang-shu, 54,31[b], says that «in K'au-chang (Turfan) there grew in great abundance a plant the fruit of which resembled a silk cocoon. In the cocoon is a silky substance like fine hemp (細纑) which is called *po-tié-tzï* (白疊子). The natives weave it into a cloth which is soft and white, and which they send to the markets (of China).»

Its use was not so general in Turkestan in the sixth century but that we find in Yen-ki in Eastern Turkestan the people using silk cocoons as wadding for clothes. Weï-shu, 102,7[b].

The pilgrim Fa-hién, who travelled in India in the beginning of the fifth century, calls the cotton fabrics of the country *po-tié* in the only passage of his Fo-kuo-ki in which he refers to them (26,27 of Legge's edit., 79 of his translation). Conf. also, China Review, XIX, 192.

A century later occurs the first use of a new term for cotton, *ku-peï* (古貝) or *ki-peï* (吉貝), which is the Malay word *kapas* (the Sanskrit *karpāsa*), still in use throughout the Indian Archipelago, from Macassar to Sumatra, to designate Gossypium herbaceum. This reference occurs in Liang-shu, 54,15[a], where it is said of the people of P'o-li (婆利 north coast of Sumatra or Southern Malay Peninsula?): «the people of this country wear *ki-peï* as a breech-clout (帊) or to make sarongs (都縵).» In the third year of the *p'u-t'ung* period (A. D. 523) a mission from this country to the court of the Liang brought, among other presents, some *ki-peï*, and probably introduced the use of the term; as to the material itself, the Chinese did not perceive, apparently, that it was the same as *po-tié*. Conf. Nan-shï, 78,2[a].

The great traveller Hüan-tsang in the early part of the seventh century, describing the dress of the people of India, says they wore clothing of *kiau-shï-yé* (憍奢邪) — which he also chinesefies into *ch'au-hia* (朝霞 literally «blush of the Court»), both terms transcribing Sanskrit *kausheya* «silken stuff» — and also clothing of *tié-pu* (氎布 «cloth of (po-)tié»). He makes nowhere mention of the term *karpāsa*, nor does he use the Chinese *ku-peï* or *ki-peï*. See

Watters, On Yuan-chwang's travels, I, 147, 287. The original meaning of the word *po-tié*, it would seem from Hüan-tsang's use of a mutilated form of it, had already been lost in his time.

It would appear that the identity of *po-tié* and *ki-peï* was not realized till some time later; it was, at all events, when the T'ang-shu was written, for it says ($222^C,2^a$), in referring to this
5 same P'o-li country (in Siam or Sumatra): «The *ku-peï* plant is found in P'o-li. The flowers are gathered and cloth (布) made from them; the coarse kinds (we) call (*ku*)-*peï* (貝), the fine ones (*po-*) *tié* (疊毛)». It seems probable that *po-tié* was given as a name to the lighter Sumatran cotton fabrics because they resembled in texture those from India and Persia, to which the name had long been exclusively applied. The Pön-ts'au, $36,69^b$, says *ki-peï* was also called *ku-chung* (古 終),
10 pronounced *ku-tüng* in the Foochow dialect, probably from Arabic *kutun*. Mayers, Notes and Queries, II, 95.

With the simultaneous use of two distinct terms, *po-tié* and *ki-peï*, to designate the same material, it becomes very difficult to distinguish the various cotton fabrics mentioned in Chinese works. Thus T'ang-shu, $221^C,1^a$ says that the king of Huan-wang (Annam) wore clothes of *po-tié-ku-peï*, and
15 his consort's were of *ch'au-hia-ku-peï*, *ch'au-hia* the Indian word *kausheya* «silken stuff», being here transferred to a cotton fabric. The confusion still existed in the twelfth century, for Ling-wai-tai-ta, 6,13, says: «the people of the Laos country (南 詔) wore an extraordinarily fine and beautifully white (cotton fabric) called *ch'au-hia*». Another instance of the confusion in the Chinese cotton terminology is furnished by T'ang-shu ($222^C,4^b$) in its notice of Java (Ho-ling), where the word for
20 cotton is *kapas*; it says: «they make *po-tié-pu* and *ch'au-hia-pu*.» In another passage of the same work ($222^C,6^a$) it speaks of *ch'au-hia-tié*; and, in reference to the cotton of K'au-chang (Turfan), it reproduces ($221^A,6^a$) substantially the earlier statement of Liang-shu given previously, without any suspicion, apparently, that the *po-tié* of that country was the same as the *ki-peï* of the South. «There is in Kau-ch'ang, it says, a plant called *po-tié* (白 疊), the flowers of which are gathered and can be
25 woven into cloth (布)».

In the Sung period the use of the word *ki-peï* was at last extended to Indian cotton fabrics, and a new term introduced (not occurring, however, in Ling-wai-tai-ta or any other work earlier than our author's), *tóu-lo-mién* (兜 羅 綿), composed of the Sanskrit word *tūla* «cotton», and of *mién* «soft, downy», a word which appears to have been applied to certain cotton stuffs of
30 Western Asiatic manufacture as far back as the Weï period, when we find *kin-mién* (錦 綿) or *kin-tié* (錦 疊) used to designate brocaded cotton stuffs. Weï-shu, 102,3,10,12.

At the time at which our author wrote there were, therefore, four foreign terms in use in China for cotton fabrics, *po-tié*, *ch'au-hia*, *ki-peï* and *tóu-lo*, and two purely Chinese terms, *pu* (布), which in the earliest Chinese works designated hempen cloth, and *mién* (綿) or
35 *mién-pu* (棉 布). It appears likely that the word *mién* was more particularly applied to certain fabrics made from the «tree-cotton» (Gossypium arboreum, Linn.), which our author states in the first part of his work was cultivated in Tongking, Hai-nan and probably Siam, and which is still cultivated in the Indian Archipelago and in India.

The word *mién* (棉), now in general use in China to designate the cotton shrub, and
40 *mién-hua* (綿 花) «cotton» were unknown to the Chinese of the Sung dynasty. They would appear to have been coined after the introduction of cotton cultivation and spinning into China (Kiang-su) in the fourteenth century. Already in the twelfth century the cotton of Hai-nan was woven into cloth in various localities of Kuang-tung adjacent to that island. Ling-wai-tai-ta, 6,13, mentions Leï-chóu, Hua-chóu and Lién-chóu (雷 化 廉 州) as manufacturing cotton cloth
45 both beautifully fine and white, which was called *man-ki-peï* (慢 吉 貝) or «soft *ki-peï*,» and also a coarser and yellowish coloured kind called *ts'u-ki-peï* (粗 吉 貝) or «coarse *ki-peï*.» As an article of clothing it was only used in Kuang-tung and Hai-nan by well-to-do people who preferred it to silk and linen. It was a woman, Huang Tau-p'o (黃 道 婆), a native of Hai-nan, who introduced cotton spinning into Kiang-nan. Mayers, Chin. reader's Man., 71.
50 In the latter part of the twelfth century, as we have seen in the first part of this work, China got most of her cotton, both raw and manufactured, from Hai-nan and Indo-China, but Java, Borneo, India, Persia, the Philippines, and even Asia Minor, supplied her with certain

cotton fabrics. These stuffs were either white or dyed various colours, also dotted, striped, mixed silk and cotton stuffs, brocaded, or gold-spangled. Chintzes came to China from Annam, India and Persia, and damasks from Java.

One fabric of which our author, as well as Chóu Kʻü-feï, speaks, cannot as yet be identified. It is *yüé-no-pu* (越 諾 布), a manufacture of the Coromandel coast, of Baghdad, of Asia 5 Minor, and of Ghazni (Ki-tzʻï-ni). It would seem to have been a light cotton gauze, or muslin, and was of two kinds, pure white, and spangled with gold. The word *yüé-no* is not otherwise known in Chinese literature, except possibly as the name of a country — Bukhara, or neighbourhood — from which, on one occasion at least, dwarfs were brought to the court of China. Tʻang-shu, 221B,1b. Edrisi (I, 185) speaks of the cotton stuffs made in Cabul and which were exported 10 to China, Khorasan and Sindh.

On the subject of cotton in the Middle Ages, see Heyd, Histoire du Commerce, II, 611—614, 693—710, and Hirth, J. C. B. R. A. S., XXI, 230 et seqq.

24.

MATS (椰 心 簟).　　　　　　　　15

The mats called *yé-sin-tién* come from Tan-jung-wu-lo. The foreign traders carry them to San-fo-tsʻi, Ling-ya-mön and Shö-pʻo for trade. They also come from the island of Pʻu-li-lu in the San-sü. They are made from a plant resembling the rattan in shape and more than ten feet in length with a longitudinally striped and smooth surface without knots, which is called *yé-sin-* 20 *tsʻau* (椰 心 草). The women in those foreign parts gather (this vine), peel it and weave it into mats. They are sometimes dyed with red and black checkered patterns, when they are called «figured mats» or *hua-tién* (花 簟) They are warm in the winter and cool in the summer, and are very convenient to carry about. The mats coming from San-fo-tsʻi are the best, those 25 coming from the San-sü being of the poorest quality.

Note.

Tan-jung-wu-lo is mentioned by our author (supra, p. 84) as a dependency of Sukitan or Java. Ling-ya-mön is the island of Lingga (see supra, p. 60). Pʻu-li-lu is the island of Polillo off the east coast of Luzon. The mats made in the Philippines are still famous, though perhaps not 30 so fine as those of Formosan manufacture, which are locally called *i-nan-tsʻau* (宜 男 草). The Peï-wön-yün-fu, 58,52, mentions *liu-sin-tién* (柳 心 簟 lit., «willow-heart mats»), and the Tung-si-yang-kʻau 4,3ª refers to *tsiau-sin-tién* (蕉 心 簟 lit., «banana-heart mats») as a product of Ma-liu (Malacca), and (3,4b), among the products of Hia-kiang in Java, to *tʻöng-hua-tién* (籐 花 簟 lit., «rattan figured mats»). The *yé-sin-tién*, lit., «cocoanut-heart mats» of 35 our author are not mentioned elsewhere.

25.

PUTCHUCK (木香).

Mu-hiang comes from the country of Ma-lo-mo of the Ta-shï; it is also found in Shï-ho and Nu-fa. The plant resembles the Chinese *ssï-kua* (絲瓜 Luffa cylindrica, Roem.). The winter months is the time for gathering the root, which is chopped into pieces of one or two inches in length and sundried. Pieces like a chicken bone are of the best quality.

Note.

Ma-lo-mo is Merbat, Shï-ho is Shehr, and Nu-fa is Zufar, the modern Dhofar, all on the Hadramaut coast of Arabia. See supra, p. 116. Our author also states (supra, p. 128) that *mu-hiang* came from the Somali coast (Pi-p'a-lo); but the best quality of the drug came, he says (supra, p. 98) from Nan-ni-hua-lo, which we think must be identified with Sindh, or a section of that region. Our author is wrong in stating that this product was found in Hadramaut and on the Somali coast. It is a native of Kashmere and was an important export from the ports of Sindh, when the author of the Periplus wrote, and probably ages before his time, as it was well known to the Hebrews who called it *ketzioth* (קציעה, *cassia*), which, we presume, is derived from its Sanskrit name, *kushtha*, which is the original of the Greek χόστος, and the Latin *costus*. In Malay it is called *pucho*, which may be the origin of our *putchuk*, or our term may be derived from *putchok*, by which name this root is known in Calcutta. Putchuck is the root of the Aucklandia costus, Royle. Hamilton, New Account of the East Indies (1744), I, 127, says: «The Wood Ligna dulcis grows only in this country (i. e., Sindh). It is rather a Weed than a Wood, and nothing of it is useful but the Root called Putchock, or, Radix dulcis. I never heard it is used in Physic, but it is a good Ingredient in the Composition of Perfumes. There are great Quantities exported for Surat, and from thence to China.»

The earliest mention we have found in Chinese works of this drug is in the Weï-shu, 102,12ᵃ, and the Sui-shu ,83,16ᵇ, where mention is made among the products of Po-ssï (Persia) of *ts'ing-mu-hiang* (青木香 lit., «green-wood incense»). The name *mu-hiang* occurs, however, in a Chinese Materia medica of the fifth century, Ming-i-pié-lu by T'au Hung-king, as a plant growing in western Yün-nan, and which was also called *mi-hiang* (蜜香). But already at that time the Chinese product was no longer used, and *ts'ing-mu-hiang* was brought to China from abroad by foreign ships, it being said that it came from Ta-ts'in. Bretschneider, Bot. Sinic., III, 111. It would seem, therefore, that the name *mu-hiang* was at first applied by the Chinese to a native product, probably because it was 'wood perfume'. In Chinese Buddhist books it is called *kü-sö-t'o* (矩瑟佗), Sanskrit *kushtha*. Bretschneider, loc.cit., 112. See also Yule, Marco Polo, II, 387.

26.

CARDAMOMS (白荳蔻).

Pai-tóu-k'óu come from Chön-la, Shö-p'o and other foreign countries; but Chön-la produces them in the largest quantity. The plant resembles the *ssï-kua* (絲瓜), and the seed a grape; it is a creeping plant fond of deep valleys (山谷). It blossoms in the spring and ripens in the summer. The people are allowed to gather it without hindrance.

Note.

The *pai-tóu-k'óu* is the Amomum cardamomum, Linn., the 'round' or 'cluster cardamom', a native plant of Kamboja, Siam and Java. The Javanese name *kapulaga*, appears to be the only one in use in the Indian Archipelago. Crawfurd, Hist. Indian Archipelago, I, 514.

The earliest mention of the *pai-tóu-k'óu* or «white *tóu-k'óu*» in Chinese works occurs in 5 the eighth century. Ch'ön Ts'ang-ki (supra, p. 210, line 36) says that it was a product of K'ié-ku-lo (伽古羅 possibly Kia Tan's Ko-ku-lo, east coast Malay Peninsula) and is there called *to-ku* (多骨). In another passage (supra, p. 210) the same author gives the native name of the nutmeg as *ka-kü-lo*, which Bretschneider points out is probably *kākula*, the Arabic name for cardamom. Yu-yang-tsa-tsu, 18,10 reproduces this phrase from Ch'ön Ts'ang-k'i. 10 It says: «*Pai-tóu-k'óu* comes from K'ié-ku-lo, where it is called *to-ku*. In shape it is like the banana (tree). The leaves are like those of the *tu-jo* (杜若) eight or nine feet long; they do not wither in winter or summer. The flowers are light yellow. The seeds form clusters like grapes. When the seeds first appear they are light green, when ripe they turn white; they are gathered in the seventh moon.» 15

Already in the eleventh century, the cardamom was grown in Kuang-tung and Kuang-si, but it was inferior in quality to that brought from abroad. Bretschneider, Bot. Sinic., III, 120—123.

Ling-wai-tai-ta, 8,13[b], says that the *pai-tóu-k'óu* comes from the foreigners of the South, while the herbaceous (草) or *ts'au-tóu-k'óu* comes from the mountainous districts of Yung- 20 chóu (邑州 the present Nan-ning-fu in Kuang-si). «There is also the flower of the *tóu-k'óu* which is very much prized …. The people of the South pick the flowers, steep them in plum juice and dry them. They are very tasty ….» The flower of the *tóu-k'óu* is described in Nanfang-ts'au-mu chuang, 1,2[b]. It is there said that it stops flatulency and dispels phlegm, it has also the property of increasing the strength of wine. In A. D. 281 a basket of these flowers was 25 brought the Emperor from Tongking. He found out by experimenting with them that they really possessed the properties attributed to them. Tung-si-yang-k'au, 3,5[a] mentions red (赤) *pai-tóu-k'óu* among the products of Hia-kiang in Java.

27.

PEPPER (胡椒). 30

Hu-tsiau comes from the following places in Shö-p'o: Su-ki·tan, Ta·pan, Pai-hua-yüan, Ma-tung, and Jung-ya-lu; but the pepper coming from Sin-t'o (新梔) is the best; the Ta-pan variety takes the second place.

Pepper grows in the uncultivated wilds, and the villages in the country ….. the Chinese grape. The natives grow it on frames made of bamboo 35 or other wood ….. the flower opens, and in the fourth moon the fruit forms[1].

The flower resembles a *föng-weï* (鳳尾 or a «phoenix-tail»), and is blue (and) red in colour. The grains are gathered in the fifth moon, dried in the sun, and stored in godowns, whence they are withdrawn in the 40 following year, carts drawn by oxen being used to transport them to the market. The grain cannot stand the sun, but stands rain; therefore crops are but poor after dry weather, whereas heavy rainfalls may double the ordinary yield of the harvest.

5   (Note. Some say that most of the pepper comes from the country of Wu-li-pa (無 離 扱), in Nan-p'i, and that the produce bought by the foreign traders in Shö-p'o comes from Wu-li-pa)[2].

Notes.

1) The term *tsiau* was applied by the Chinese in the classical period to Zanthoxylon, of
10 which more than a dozen species are known in China. Bretschneider, Bot. Sinic., II,
323. *Hu-tsiau*, our Piper nigrum, literally 'Western Asian *tsiau*' is first mentioned, it would appear, in the Hóu-Han-shu, 118,12[b], where it figures as a product of T'ién-chu (India). Later on it occurs in the Weï-shu, 102,12[a] and the Sui-shu 83,16[a], as a product of Po-ssï (i. e., it was brought to China by Persian traders from India); they also mention *pi-po* (畢 撥), in Sanskrit
15 *pippali*, or «long pepper».

    Yu-yang-tsa-tsu, 18,9[b] says: «*Hu-tsiau* comes from Mo-k'ié-to (i. e., Magadha, or Central India), where it is called *mo-li-chĭ* (眛 履 支 Sanskrit *marīcha*). The plant is a creeper, at first very flexible. The leaves are an inch and a half long, they grow on stems two by two, on either side of the stem. They open at dawn and close up at night, rolling up when closed. The
20 seeds are between the leaves; in shape they are like the *tsiau* (Chinese pepper). When they are good they have a pungent taste. They are picked in the sixth moon (August-September). At the present day people in China who eat meat cooked in foreign style (胡 盤 肉 食) all make use of it.»

    Of the long pepper, the same work (18,10[a]) says that it comes from Magadha, where it is
25 called *pi-po-li* (畢 撥 黎), and that in the country of Fu-lin it is called *a-li-ho-t'o* (阿 黎 訶 咜). On the localities here mentioned and the pepper trade, see more particularly, supra, pp. 70, 78, 83, and on the great profits of the pepper trade in our author's time, supra, p. 78. Crawfurd, op. cit., I, 482 et seq. says that to enable the vine to bear first it must be trained on some tree or pole. There are two crops which, in point of time, are, extremely irre-
30 gular, and in some situations run into each other in such a manner that the reaping is pursued nearly throughout the year. The mutilated paragraph in our text is made clear by this remark.

    Crawfurd, Hist. Indian Archipelago, III, 358, says that pepper is principally obtained on the north-eastern coast of the Archipelago, at Patani, Tringanu and Kalentan; in the straits on the island of Lingen, also at Achin, Tikao, Bencoolen, Padang and the country of the Lam-
35 pongs. That of Penang and the west coast of Sumatra is the best.

    2) This paragraph is printed in the text in the form of a foot-note. It is due presumably to the editor Li T'iau-yüan, as the name Wu-li-pa — in Cantonese Mo-li-pat, — is not used by our author, for whom the Malabar country was Nan-p'i. It is just possible that the dependency of Nan-p'i which appears in his work (supra, pp. 88, 90, n. 8) under the name of Ma-li-mo (in Amoy
40 dialect Ma-li-bwat) is Malabar. Even then he does not speak of pepper being a product of Nan-p'i, presumably because nearly, if not all, the pepper trade of China in his days was with the Indian Archipelago.

    It is noteworthy that Chóu K'ü-feï is the first Chinese author to mention pepper as a product of the Indian Archipelago; the Arab traders of the ninth and tenth centuries speak
45 only of the pepper of India. Ibn Khordadbeh knew that pepper was produced in Ceylon, but his information went no farther; the one source of supply was, for him, Malabar. As showing the great importance of the Chinese pepper trade in Marco Polo's time, that traveller tells us (II, 186), that he «heard it stated by one of the Great Kaan's officers of customs that the quantity of pepper

introduced daily for consumption into the city of Kinsay amounted to 43 loads, each load being equal to 223 lbs.» And in another passage (II, 217) he says «And I assure you that for one shipload of pepper that goes to Alexandria or elsewhere, destined for Christendom, there come a hundred such, aye and more too, to this haven of Zaytun». Duarte Barbosa, op. cit., 206, mentions also the great quantity of pepper used in China. See on the pepper trade in the Middle 5 Ages, Heyd, Hist. du Commerce, II, 658.

28.

CUBEBS (蓽 澄 茄).

Pi-töng-k'ié come from a plant of creeping habits, which blossoms in the spring and bears fruit in the summer, resembling the *k'ién-niu-tzï* (牽 10 牛 子), with a white flower and black seeds, which are packed up after being dried in the sun. It is grown in Su-ki-tan in Shö-p'o.

Note.

Pön-ts'au-kang-mu, 32,12, says that *pi-töng-k'ié* is a foreign word, and that the form *pi-ling-k'ié* (毗 陵 茄) also occurs. It adds that it belongs to the same family as *hu-tsiau*. 15

The cubeb (Piper cubeba), called in Javanese *kumukus*, and in Malay *lada barekor* or «pepper with a tail», is, like the common black pepper, the product of a vine, a native of Java, and grows there only. Crawfurd, Hist. Indian Archipelago, I, 465. See also Hanbury, Science papers, 246 et seq.

K'ién-niu-tzï is Pharbitis triloba, according Bretschneider, Bot. Sinic., II, 89, 193. It is 20 Ipomoea hederacea or Pharbitis Nil, according to Porter Smith, Materia medica, 170.

29.

ASA-FOETIDA (阿 魏).

A-weï comes from the country of Mu-kü-lan (木 俱 蘭) in the Ta-shï country. The tree is not a very high or large one, but the resin exudes freely 25 from its bark. The natives wind a piece of string round a twig, remove its tip, and cover it with a bamboo tube which fills with resin. This bamboo tube is broken up in the winter, when the resin is gathered and packed in skin bags.

Some say that this resin is so poisonous that people do not dare to 30 come near it themselves, but, when the drug has to be gathered, tie up a sheep at the foot of the tree and shoot arrows at it from a distance. The poison of the resin then drops upon the sheep, which dies of it, and its decayed flesh turns into asa-foetida. I do not know which of the two accounts is correct; meanwhile they are both placed here on record.   35

Note.

Asa-foetida is a gum-resin, the product of the Narthex asa-foetida of Falconer. It was principally collected in the Persian province of Lāristān — which confined on the Mekrān — our author's Mu-kü-lan. It is also found near Kandahār. See Bretschneider Mediæval Researches, 5 I. 85. In Sanskrit it is called *hingu*. Pön-ts'au-kang-mu, 34,61—62, gives the Persian name as *a-yü-(tsié)*, and the Indian as *hün-k'ü* (薰渠), and *hing-yü* (形虞).

The earliest mention I have found of this drug occurs in Sui-shu, 83,16[b] where «*a-weï* medicine» is mentioned among the products of the kingdom of Ts'au (漕) which, it says, is the same as the Ki-pin (罽賓 Cabul) of the Han period. *A-weï* is a foreign word, derived pre-10 sumably from the Sanskrit or Persian name of the drug.

The next mention of the drug occurs in Hüan-tsang's Si-yü-ki (12,1. Julien, Pélerins Bouddhistes, II, 187), where he gives its Sanskrit name *hing-k'ü* (興瞿草), and says that it is found in the country of Ts'au-kü-ta (漕矩吒 the Ts'au of Sui-shu), the capital of which he notes is Ho-si-na (霍鸖悉那 Ghazni).

15 Yu-yang-tsa-tsu, 18,8[b], says «*A-weï* comes from K'ié-shö-na (伽闍那 Ghazni), which is also called Northern India. In K'ié-shö-na it is called *hing-yü* (形虞). It also comes from Po-ssï (Persia), where it is called *a-yü-tsié* (阿虞截 Persian *angŭzad, angŭza*). It grows to 80 or 90 feet (!). The bark is a yellowish green. The leaves come out in the third moon; they are like a rat's ear in shape. It has neither blossoms nor fruit. When a branch is cut off, the sap 20 flows like syrup and for a long time. When it coagulates, it is called *a-weï*. Wan (彎) the monk from Fu-lin, agrees with T'i-p'o (提婆 Deva) the monk from Mo-k'ié-to (Magadha, or Central India) in saying that *a-weï* is formed by the joining together of particles of the sap each of the size of a grain of rice or a bean.»

30.

ALOES (蘆薈).

25 *Lu-weï* comes from the land of Nu-fa of the Ta-shï country. It is derived from a vegetable product, which looks like the tail of a king-crab. The natives gather it and pound it with implements made of jadestone, after which it is boiled into an ointment and packed in skin bags, and this is 30 called *lu-weï*.

Note.

Our author states (supra, p. 131) that *lu-weï* was a product of an island off the Somali coast, which must be the island of Socotra, whence it was probably taken to Nu-fa on the Hadramaut coast for exportation. The name *lu-weï* seems to be Persian *alwā*, the name given the Socotran 35 aloes (Aloe Socotrina, Lam.). Yule and Burnell, Glossary, 10. See also Thos. Watters, Essays, 332.

The Socotran product must have disappeared from the Chinese market after our author wrote, for in the Ming dynasty the substance which went by the name of *lu-weï*, but which was also called *nu-hui* (奴會), *no-hui* (訥會) and *siang-tan* (象胆 «elephant's gall») was, 40 as it is now, catechu, a product of the Acacia catechu (Sanskrit *khādira*, see supra. p. 196, n. 1). See Pön-ts'au-kang-mu, 34,63[b]—64, and Bretschneider, Ancient Chinese and Arabs, 20, note 5.

Edrisi (1, 47), speaking of the aloes of Socotra, says: «In the month of July the leaves are gathered; the juice is then extracted and dried in the sun, and in the month of August it is packed in skin bags.»

Theo. Bent, speaking of the collecting of the aloe-juice at the present day in Socotra, says (Southern Arabia, 381): «The aloe-gatherers dig a hole in the ground and line it with a skin. Then they pile old leaves, points outward, all round till the pressure makes the juice exude .... The drops are knocked off into bags. The drops which come off unbroken are the most valued, and called *edah amsello*.... It is exported in skins....» He also notes that the juice, 5 when first extracted is called in Socotran *taïf diho* (or *riho*), the latter word meaning «water».

31.

CORAL-TREE (珊 瑚 樹).

The *shan-hu-shu* comes from the country of P'i-no-yé of the Ta-shï. The tree grows in the deepest parts of the sea; its colour is at first white; as the 10 buds form and the twigs put forth, after rather more than a year, the colour gradually turns yellow, and the branches begin to interlace. The greatest height it attains is three or four feet, and large specimens are a foot in circumference.

The natives, in fishing for it, first make use of a grappling-iron of five 15 prongs fastened to a silk rope; it is kept under water by leaden sinkers, the whole apparatus being thrown into the sea. When the root has been detached, the rope is made fast to the boat and the tree is hauled on board by means of a windlass. They are not always sure to get the (whole) tree, though probably they will get a branch. At first covered with a slimy coating, it dries up 20 and hardens when exposed to the air, and then assumes a dull carnation colour. The higher the tree, the more valuable it is. If the proper time for fishing is missed, it will be destroyed by worms.

Note.

The earliest mention of coral in Chinese literature seems to be in Hóu-Han-shu, 118,10[a], 25 where it occurs as a product of the Roman Orient (Ta-ts'in). T'ang-shu, 221B,12[b], describes the coral fisheries in the 'Coral islands' (珊 瑚 洲), presumably in the Red Sea, in much the same terms as our author, who may have derived much of his information on the subject from this source. See Hirth, China and Roman Orient, 41, 59 and 246.

In the first part of this work, our author says that coral was found (on the market) of 30 Wu-ssï-li (Mosul), and was fished on the coast of Mo-k'ié-la (el-Mogreb, substantially the same as the P'i-no-yé here mentioned (see supra, p. 122, line 6), and also on the coast of Polillo island in the Philippines. At these last named fisheries two varieties of coral were found, the one known as *shan-hu*, the other as *ts'ing* (blue or green) *lang-kan*. The term *lang-kan* occurs in Shu-king, Pt. III, Bk. I, Ch. X, 81 (Legge's, Chinese Classics, III, Pt. I, 127), but no satisfactory explanation 35 is given of it. Hóu-Han-shu and Weï-lio mention both *shan-hu* and *lang-kan* among the products of Ta-ts'in. Hirth, China and Roman Orient, 41, 73.

32.

OPAQUE GLASS (琉璃).

Liu-li comes from several of the countries of the Ta-shï. The method followed in melting it is the same as that of China, that is to say, it is made
5 by burning oxide of lead (鈆), nitrate of potash (硝), and gypsum (石膏). To these materials the Ta-shï add southern borax (南鵬砂), which causes the glass to be elastic without being brittle (滋潤不烈), and indifferent to temperature, so that one may put it in water for a long time without spoiling it. It is, therefore, more valuable than the Chinese product.

10   Note.

        Liu-li, or as it was first written, *pi-liu* 璧珋) and *pi-liu-li* (璧流離), is a very early transcription of the Sanskrit word *vaidūrya*, or the Pali *veluriya*, which probably meant lapis-lazuli or rock-crystal. It occurs in the Shuo-wön (說文 published A. D. 100), and also in the Ts'ién-Han-shu, 96ᴬ,11, where it is said to be a product of Ki-pin (Cabul). Tuan Yü-ts'ai, the fa-
15 mous eighteenth century editor of the Shuo-wön says in his Shuo-wön kié-tzï-chu (說文解字注 s. v., 瑠), «the three characters (*pi, liu, li*) form a Hu (胡 Western Asian) word, just as *sün-yü-k'i* (珣玗琪) form an I (夷 Eastern Asian Barbarian) word .... Indian books (梵書 Chinese Buddhist Classics) speak of *feï-liu-li* (吠瑠璃), the sound *feï* approxi-mating that of *pi* .... Present day commentators of the Han-shu have omitted the character *pi*,
20 students wrongly holding the character *pi* by itself and *liu-li* to designate two separate and district things ....» See also Hirth, China and Roman Orient, 230.
        The Arab-Persian *bullūr*, the Greek βήρυλλος, Latin *beryllos*, our beryl, are traced likewise to the word *vaidūrya*. Yule and Burnell, Glossary, 67.
        While originally designating a precious stone it appears likely that, from the first, the
25 word *liu-li* was applied to coloured glass which was imported from India, Egypt or Phoenicia. It occurs, with the sense of a precious stone, in Hóu-Han-shu, 116,19ᵃ, and as a native product of the Ai-lau country — the present Yünnan — being there mentioned with rock-crystal, amber, etc. Pliny, Nat. Hist., XXXVI, 26, 66 says that no glass was to be compared with that made in India, and its superiority was due to the fact that it was made from broken crystals; but we find
30 that the *liu-li* from the Roman Orient, that is to say Egypt as well as Syria, was most prized in China; even in the twelfth century the *liu-li* from Baghdad was held to surpass all others.
        The Weï-lio, speaking of the period between A. D. 220—264, states that glass of ten colours was found in Ta-ts'in. These colours were carnation, white, black, green, yellow, blue, purple, azure, red and red-brown. Hirth, China and Roman Orient, 73.
35   The manufacture of *liu-li* was introduced into China in the latter part of the fourth century A. D. In the reign of Shï-tsu of the Weï there came to the capital (which was the present Ta-t'ung-fu in northern Shan-si), men from the land of the Ta-yüé-chï (大月氏) in Northern India, who said they knew how to fuse certain minerals together and to make *liu-li* of any colour. They dug in the hills and got together what they required and fused it in the
40 city. The finished product was more brilliant and beautiful than that which came from the West, so dazzlingly radiant was it that, when they took it to the Palace, all the people standing there-about were filled with fear, thinking there was something supernatural about the radiance. After this *liu-li* became cheap in China and no one prized it particularly. See Weï-shu, 102,15—16.
        Yen Shï-ku (顏師古 a seventh century commentator of the Han-shu), referring to the
45 mention of *liu-li* in Ts'ién-Han-shu says that it was the custom in his time (in China), when making what was called *liu-li*, to use all (the ten kinds of coloured *liu-li* known in the West?) and to melt

                                                                                                    15*

them down to a liquid state (皆 銷 冶 石 汁), to which certain chemicals were added (加 以 衆 藥). The glass (thus manufactured) was, however, filled with air-holes (lit., hollow 虛), and brittle, not the clear, true, genuine thing. Ts'ién-Han-shu, 96A,11ᵃ.

At an early date, but much later than that when the word *liu-li* first appeared, we find another word in Chinese literature used to designate the ordinary, transparent glass. This word 5 *po-li* (玻 璃 or 瓈), and sometimes *pi-po-li* (碧 玻 離), appears to have been copied on the word *liu-li* and *pi-liu-li*. So far as we can find out, the earliest record of the word is in the dictionary called Yü-pién (玉 篇), which dates from the fifth century A. D. It is there explained as meaning «a precious stone» (玉). It seems possible that the word was coined in the fifth century after the manufacture of glass had been introduced into China, and it had 10 become necessary to differentiate this common glass from the more valuable coloured and cut kinds. It transcribes, in a contracted form, the Sanskrit word *sphaṭika*, one of the seven precious substances (*sapta ratna*), and originally meaning rock-crystal. In Chinese Buddhist works *sphaṭika* is usually transcribed *p'o-chï-kia* (婆 致 迦), but Hüan-tsang (Si-yü-ki, 8,25ᵇ, *et passim*) uses the contracted from *po-chï* (頗 胝). 15

Chang Yüé (張 說 seventh century A. D.) says in his Liang-ssï-kung-ki (梁 四 公 記) «The big sea-going junks of Fu-nan that come from Western India sell mirrors of *pi-po-li* (碧 玻 璃 鏡) which are clear and transparent on the surface and throughout their mass (內 外 皎 潔). Objects of all kinds placed before them are reflected to the sight without one's seeing the mirror itself. These plates are a foot and a half 20 in diameter and weigh forty catties.» T'u-shu-tsi-ch'öng, 32,227, Ki-shï, 4.

In A. D. 643 we read (T'ang-shu, 221B,13ᵃ) of a king of Fu-lin sending red (赤) *po-li* as a present to the Emperor of China. As late as 742, the same work (221B,7ᵇ) chronicles the fact that a prince of Tokharestan sent «red *pi-po-li*» (紅 碧 玻 瓈 «red glass» or «red transparent glass») as a present to Court. 25

Chóu K'ü-feï and our author both speak of the superior quality of the coloured and opaque glass ware (*liu-li*) made in the countries of Islam, which was «cut into patterns» or «engraved» (碾 花), and annealed (軟). Baghdad led in this industry, but Asia Minor, Ki-tz'ï-ni (it included probably Cabul, the Ki-pin of the Han period, whence *liu-li* was first brought to China), and other places sent specimens of it to China which were greatly prized. 30

Transparent glass (*po-li*) is mentioned by Chau as a product of Ceylon and of the Coromandel coast. It was perhaps from the former country that the Fu-nan traders, mentioned previously, got the big glass mirrors they brought to China, for it appears, from what our author states, that it was extensively used there for decorative purposes, and was probably made in sheets, or lenses, as he speaks of glass screens which surrounded the throne of the king of Ceylon. 35

Glass beads of sundry colours and glass bottles (presumably very small ones for carrying perfumes or for such like purposes), both of opaque glass, were used as regular trade articles in the dealings between the Chinese and Arab traders of the period and the natives of Borneo and the Philippine islands. See supra, pp. 156, 162.

Edrisi is the only Arab writer we know of who mentions the manufacture of glass in 40 China; he says (I, 100) that at Djankou (Khanfu, Hang-chóu) «they worked in Chinese glass.»

33.

CAT'S-EYES (貓 兒 睛).

Mau-ïr-tsing are of the size of the end of the thumb, that is, they are but small stones. They are brilliant, smooth, and transparent like the eyes of 45 a cat, for which reason they are called «cat's-eyes». They come from the country of Nan-pʻi. In this country there is a river, called the Tan-shui-kiang (淡 水 江), where several streams unite into one. There, in the depths of the hills, pebbles are washed down by the heavy rains and collect there. The officials go there in small boats and dredge them out of the water. Round 5 and brilliant specimens are called «cat's-eyes». Some people say that they are the reflection of stars shining on the surface of the earth and hardened there by magic influence.

Note.

«The cat's-eye is one of the jewels of which the Singhalese are especially proud, from a 10 belief that it is only found in their island; but in this I apprehend they are misinformed, as specimens of equal merit have been brought from Quilon and Cochin on the southern coast of Hindustan». Tennent, Ceylon, I, 37.

In the first part of his work (supra, p. 73) our author says that cat's eyes were also found in Ceylon. The present article is substantially a repetition of what he has said in his chapter on 15 Nan-pʻi (Malabar), supra, pp. 88, 90, n. 7. It would appear from the passage of the Pʻing-chóu-kʻo-tʻan there quoted that in the eleventh century the use of this jewel in China was confined to the Moslim traders of Canton.

Linschoten, Voyage to the East Indies (Hakl. Soc. edit.) II, 141 says that cat's-eyes come from Cambaia, «but the best out of Seylon and Pegu .... the Indians esteeme much of 20 them, specially the Chinos, and thether they are caryed, better esteemed, and sold there then any other stones.»

34.

PEARLS (眞 珠).

The *chön-chu*, or «real pearls», which come from certain islands in the 25 land of the Ta-shï are the best. They also come from the two countries of Si-nan (西 難) and Kién-pi. Pearls are even found in Kuang-si and Hu-peï, but less brilliant than those of the Ta-shï and of Kién-pi[1].

Whenever pearls are fished for they make use of thirty or forty boats, with crews of several dozens of men (to each). Pearl-fishers, with ropes fastened around 30 their bodies, their ears and noses stopped with yellow wax, are let down into the water about 200 or 300 feet or more, the ropes being fastened on board. When a man makes a sign by shaking the rope, he is pulled up. Before this is done, however, a soft quilt is made as hot as possible in boiling water, in order to throw over the diver the moment he comes out, lest he should be 35 seized with a fit of ague and die. They may fall in with huge fishes, dragons, and other sea monsters and have their stomachs ripped open or a limb broken by collision with their dorsal fins[2]. When the people on board notice even as much as a drop of blood on the surface of the water, this is a sign to them that the diver has been swallowed by a fish. Cases occur in which the pearl-fisher makes a signal with his rope and the man holding it on board is not able to pull him up; then the whole crew pull with all their strength, and bring him up with his feet bitten off by a monster.

What the pearl-fishers call «pearl's-mother» (珠 母)[3] is under the con- 5
trol of the foreign officials, who keep a register in which the finds of shells are entered under the names of the fishermen, in the order in which they occur. The shells are then placed in a pit. After rather more than a month the shell will be found to have decayed, when the pearls may be removed, cleaned, and divided between (the government and) the pearl-fishers. 10

As a general rule a pearl is considered valuable if it is perfectly round; the test for its absolute roundness is, that it will not cease rolling about all day when put on a plate. Foreign traders (coming into China) are in the habit of concealing pearls in the lining of their clothes and in the handles of their umbrellas, thus evading the duties leviable upon them. 15

Notes.

1) The substance of this article is taken from Ling-wai-tai-ta, 7,6. The word *chön-chu*, literally 'real pearl', is possibly connected with Turkish *jänchü*. In the Old Turkish inscriptions we have *jänchü-ügüz* as the equivalent of Chinese *chön-chu-ho* «Pearl river». Hirth, Nachworte zur Inschrift des Tonjukuk (in Radloff's, Alttürk. Inschrift. d. Mongolei, 2. Folge, p. 80). *Jinzü* and 20
inzü, «a pearl» occur in A. Vambéry's, Etymolog. Wörterb., 33. Conf. also Russian *shemchug*, the standard word for «pearl». The term Kuang-si referred to as covering a district containing pearl fisheries probably stands for Kuang-nan-si-lu, the official designation under the Sung dynasty of the Western Kuang province, of which Lién-chóu-fu with its celebrated fisheries on certain islands of the sea south of Pakhoi was then a dependency. «Kuang-si» as an official 25
designation of that province, it appears, dates from the Yüan period. The pearl fisheries along the coast of Lién-chóu-fu did not yield sufficient profit to justify their being continued after the sixteenth century. They have become famous in literature by the story of a disinterested magistrate of Ho-p'u, i. e. Lién-chóu-fu, who in the second century A. D. distinguished himself by the just administration of his offic ewith its pearl fisheries. See F. W. Mayers, in Notes and Queries 30
on China and Japan, I, 1, and Stewart-Lockhart, Manual of Chinese Quotations, 284.

Si-nan, in Cantonese Si-lan, is Ceylon. See supra, p. 74, n. 2. Kién-pi is Kampar on the east coast of Sumatra, see supra, p. 71. Our author elsewhere says that pearls came from the Chola country (Coromandel), the Oman coast, the island of Kish, the Philippines, and Java. In Weï-shu, 102,18[b], pearls are mentioned among the products of Southern India, and are there called *mo-ni-chu* 35
(摩 尼 珠), *mani* being the Sanskrit word for «pearl». Edrisi, I, 375 et seq., says there were about 300 famous places in the Persian gulf where pearls were fished for. The fishermen lived on the island of Awal, the capital of which was called Bahrein. The fishing was principally carried on in August and September. See also Heyd, Hist. du Commerce, II, 648.

2) Ling-wai-tai-ta, loc. cit., remarks that the shark was so fierce and redoutable that 40
he was called «fish-tiger-dragon-fly» (魚 虎 蜓).

3) *Chu-mu*, literally 'pearl's-mother', is the pearl bearing oyster, the oyster in which a pearl has grown, a pearl producing shell. It stands for *chu-mu* (珠 牡) literally «pearl's pasture-ground», which appears to be the correct expression. Chöng-leï-pön-ts'au, 20,10, and Pién-tzï-leï-pién, 77,7. «Mother of pearl» is *yün-mu-k'o* (雲 母 殼), at least at the present day. 45

35.

CH'Ö-K'Ü (硨磲).

The *ch'ö-k'ü* comes from Kiau-chï. It has the appearance of a large cockle shell (蚌). The inhabitants of the coast grind the shell and, owing to
5 its (scolloped) surface, the cups they make are called «lotus-leaf cups» (荷葉杯). Its surface is smooth and clean, like that of a cowrie shell (珂玉). The lower part of the calyx of the largest specimens is worked into cups of up to three inches in thickness, and the remnants and chips are still useful for making rings, trinkets and other trifles.

10 According to the Buddhist books this substance was considered as a very valuable jewel; nowadays it (i. e., what is called *ch'ö-k'ü*) is only an ordinary sea delicacy (海錯). We do not know for certain whether it is identical with the ancient *ch'ö-k'ü*.

Note.

15 Ku-kin-chu (fourth century, A. D.) says (5[b]): «The Emperor Wu-ti of the Weï made bridles of *ma-nau* (cornelian) and wine bowls of *ch'ö-k'ü*.» At that time the term *ch'ö-k'ü* was applied to a cornelian or violet coloured gem, in which sense it is used by early Chinese Buddhist writers as the equivalent of Sanskrit *musāragalva*, which Childers, Pali Dictionary, 241, says was a sort of cat's-eye; but Monier Williams, Sansk. Engl. Dict., says it was a kind
20 of coral. See also Eitel, Handbook of Chinese Buddhism, 102.

The word *ch'ö-k'ü* is probably not Chinese. There is an Uiguric word *tscheku* meaning «a large spiral shell, prized as a jewel» Klaproth, Sprache und Schrift der Uiguren, 22. Radloff, Wörterbuch d. Türk-Dialecte, III, 2036, gives *čökö* «the button worn on Chinese officials' hats», and *čökölü* «Chinese officials». These words may have been borrowed from the Chinese. Hüan-tsang
25 (Si-yü-ki, 8,25[b]) writes the word 車渠 and uses it in the sense of *musāragalva*. The Weï-shu, 102,12[a], mentions *ch'ö-k'ü*, along with amber and cornelian, as a product of Po-ssï (Persia). It would seem that it was only in the eighth century, or even later, that this word came to have its present signification. Confirmation of this seems to be given by Liang-shu, 54,16[a], where we read of the kingdom of P'o-li (in the Malay Peninsula) presenting as tribute to the Emperor cups of
30 *lo* (螺杯 or «conch cups»), probably the same as the *lién-yen-peï* mentioned by Chóu K'ü-feï. The word *ch'ö-k'ü* does not, it is believed, occur in Liang-shu, *lo* is used instead. «Big shells and *ch'ö-k'ü*» are mentioned by T'ang-shu (221[B],13) as products of Fu-lin.

In the Sung period this name was applied to a very large sea shell. Ling-wai-tai-ta, 7,8[b] says that in the Southern Ocean there was a kind of cockle shell (蚌) called *ch'ö-k'ü*, which was like
35 a big *han* (蚶 a big bivalve shell with scolloped surface. It was from one to three feet and over across and increasing in value with the size. Cups and vases were made out of them. In another passage of the same work (6,3) it is said that the cups like a lotus-leaf and which were broad and shallow, were called *lién-yen-peï* (瀲灩盞杯 «billowing-waves cup»).

It seems likely that the *ch'ö-k'ü* of commerce was procured from many large shells
40 found in the waters of the Philippines, and the Indian Archipelago, some nacreous, others white. In Sumatra there is a very large one called *keemo*; it is perfectly white and is worked up like ivory by the natives. Marsden, Hist. of Sumatra, 9.

K'o-yü, here rendered «cowrie shell», was also at one time, according to some authorities, a smooth, pure white, cornelian-like stone.

36.

IVORY (象 牙).

Siang-ya, or ivory, comes from several countries of the Ta-shï and the two countries of Chön-la and Chan-ch'öng. The Ta-shï product is the better, and that of Chön-la and Chan-ch'öng is inferior. Among the Ta-shï countries it is   5 only at Ma-lo-mo that one finds any large supply.

The elephant lives in the depths of the hills and the remotest valleys, but every now and then he comes out of the wild into the plains and tramples down everything, so that man is afraid to come near him.

Elephant hunters make use of bows of extraordinary strength and pois- 10 oned arrows. When hit by an arrow the elephant runs away, but before he has gone a *li* or two, or a little more, the arrow poison acts and the animal falls down dead. The hunters follow him, remove the tusks from the carcass and bury them in the ground. When ten tusks or more have been collected, they are brought to the Ta-shï, who ship them to San-fo-ts'i and 15 Jï-lo-t'ing (日 囉 亭) for barter.

Large specimens weigh from fifty to an hundred catties. The tusks which are straight and of a clear white colour and which show a pattern of delicate streaks come from the Ta-shï; whereas the produce of Chön-la and Chan-ch'öng consists of small tusks of a reddish tint, weighing only from ten to 20 twenty or thirty catties, and of tips of tusks, which can only be made into scent holders (香 疊). Some people say that elephants are caught by decoys, and I presume that the tame elephant is used for this purpose.

Note.

Besides the countries here mentioned, our author states elsewhere that ivory was procured 25 from various countries in the Malay Peninsula, from Sumatra, Java, and Coromandel. The principal source of supply was the Berbera and Zanguebar coasts. Ma-lo-mo, or Merbat, was only the great entrepot of the ivory trade. Conf. Pön-ts'au-kang-mu, 51ᴬ,₁₀—₁₁.

Our author's apparent ignorance as to the method of capturing elephants is strange as he has told us in a preceeding chapter (supra, p. 117) the way followed by the Arabs. Ling-wai-tai-ta, 30 9,₁–₂, describes also the method followed in Tongking for capturing elephants, their management in captivity, their intelligence, etc.

Masudi, Prairies d'or, III, 8, says the negroes of East Africa (Zendjs) killed great numbers of elephants for the ivory which was sent to Oman and shipped thence to China and India, so that very little reached the Moslim countries. See also Marcel Devic, Le Pays des Zendjs, 35 179—187.

Gerini, Researches, 627, thinks that Jï-lo-t'ing was very likely Jelatang on a small stream, a little to the south-west of the present Jambi town in Sumatra. Conf. supra, pp. 62, 67.

37.

RHINOCEROS HORNS (犀 角).

The *si*, or rhinoceros, resembles the domestic cattle, but it has only one horn. Its skin is black and its hair scanty; its tongue is like the burr of a chestnut. Fierce and violent in its temper, this animal runs so quickly that you may imagine it is flying. Its food consists solely of bamboo and other woods. Since he rips up a man with his horn, none dare come near him, but hunters shoot him with a stiff (硬) arrow from a good distance, after which they remove the horn, which in this state is called a «fresh horn» (生 角), whereas, if the animal has died a natural death the horn obtained from it is called a «dropped-in-the-hills horn» (倒 山 角). The horn bears marks like bubbles; the horns which are more white than black are the best.

Note.

The rhinoceros is already mentioned in Shan-hai-king, 10,4, where it is called *si-niu* (犀 牛). Ling-piau-lü-i (written in the T'ang dynasty) gives (2,10) an interesting description of the different varieties of rhinoceros of Indo-China and of the peculiarities of the horns of each. When one of the horns is high up on the head, the animal is called *ssi-si* (兜犀), when one horn, and that a rather small one, is down on the snout, the animal is called *hu-mau-si* (胡 帽 犀). The largest kind of rhinoceros is the *to-lo-si* (墮 羅 犀), or *to-ho-lo* (墮 和 羅) rhinoceros, as the name is written in T'ang-shu, 222C,10ª, whose horns attain a weight of seven or eight catties. Gerini, Researches, 830—831, says To-ho-lo was a district on the Gulf of Martaban.

Another classification of rhinoceros is mentioned in the Kiau-chóu-ki (交 州 記 possibly of the fifth century A. D.) as quoted in Tung-si-yang-k'au, 1,10b. This work divides them into water-rhinoceros and mountain-rhinoceros, the former, it says, have three horns, the latter two. Conf. Pön-ts'au-kang-mu, 51A,13—15.

Our author in the first part of his work, besides mentioning rhinoceros in Tongking, Annam, and the Malay Peninsula, says the horn was also a product of Java, India, and the Zanguebar coast of Africa; he does not state they are found in Sumatra. The finest horns came, according to him, from the Berbera coast.

Masudi, op. cit., I, 385, says that in his time there was a great trade in rhinoceros horns with China from Rahma in India, which was probably about Dacca or Arracan. See also Reinaud, Relations, 28—30. The method followed in killing rhinoceros was described by the Arab envoy to China in A. D. 973. See supra, p. 118. Asiatics believe that rhinoceros horn detects the presence of poison, as does also tortoise-shell.

The belief in the formidable nature of the rhinoceros' tongue was old and widespread. Marco Polo (II, 265, 271—272) says of them: «They do not mischief, however, with the horn, but with the tongue only; for this is covered all over with long and strong prickles and when savage with any one they crush him under their knees and then rasp him with their tongue.»

38.

CASTOREUM, CIVET (膃 肭 臍).

(The drug called) *wu-na-ts'i* comes from the country of K'ié-li-ki (伽 力 吉 Kalhat?) of the Arabs. (The animal called *wu-na*) resembles in shape a *hua* (猾). Its legs are as long as those of a dog; its colour is either red or 5 black. It moves as if it were flying. Hunters stretch nets near the sea-shore to catch it. What is taken from its scrotum and mixed with oil (取 其 腎 而 漬 以 油) is called *wu-na-ts'i.*

P'o-ni (渤 泥 Borneo) is the only foreign country in which it is very abundant.   10

Note.

According to the Pön-ts'au-kang-mu, 51B,17–18, this animal was known in China as early as the first century of our era, when it was mentioned in the Shuo-wön (說 文) under the form *ku-na* (骨 貀). In the T'ang period the form 骨 豽 (or 訥) was also used. This word, the Pön-ts'au says, is a foreign term (番 言). «The *ku-na*», it goes on to say on the authority 15 of the eighth century writer Ch'ön Ts'ang-k'i (陳 藏 器), «was found in the countries of the Si-fan (西 番 Tibet) and of the T'u-kué (突 厥 Turks). The people of Western Asia (胡 人) called it *a-tz'ï-p'o-t'a-ni* (阿 慈 勃 他 你). It resembled in shape and size a fox, though a little bigger. It had a long tail. Its testicles (臍) were like musk, of a yellowish red colour and like decayed (or soft) bone.»   20

Li Shï-chön then goes on to say that «according to the T'ang-shu the animal called *ku-na* is found in Ying-chóu (營 州) of Liau-si (i. e., in southern Manchuria). It was also found in the Kié-ku (結 骨 Kirghiz) country. The I-t'ung-chï (一 統 志) says that *wu-na-ts'i* came from the Nü-chï (女 直 Northern Manchuria) and the San-fo-ts'i countries. The animal is like a fox, its legs are as long as those of a dog. It moves as if it were flying. What is taken 25 from its scrotum mixed with oil is called *wu-na-ts'i.*» Cf. T'ang-shu, 117B,12b.

From the above (the last two phrases of which are, however, a quotation from Chau Ju-kua) it seems clear that, at the time of which our author writes, there were two drugs known to the Chinese by the name of *ku-na-ts'i* or *wu-na-ts'i*, but of widely different origin. The one was derived from Northern Asia, from Manchuria to the Kirghiz steppes, the other was 30 brought to China by the Arabs of Oman, who called it *a-tz'ï-p'o-t'a-ni*, in which we have no difficulty in recognizing the Arabic word *al-zabād*, our «civet». Hearing that the drug procured from the *ku-na* and from the animal in the country of the Arabs was secreted in a somewhat similar way in both animals, the Chinese, quite naturally, gave both products the same name, though that brought them from Northern Asia was not civet, but castoreum, the oily and strong- 35 scented liquor secreted by the beaver. The word *ku-na* or *wu-na* is eastern Turki *kuna,* Russian *kunitsa,* the marten, or skunk. Radloff, Wörterbuch d. Türk-Dialecte, II, p. 910. As used by the Chinese, the name seems to have been applied to the whole family of Mustelidae, and also to the beaver, on account of the castoreum.

Chau's remark that the **wu-na** resembled the fabulous animal called *hua*, seems the 40 result of a copyist's error, as shown by the quotation of our text in the Pön-ts'au given above. All the authorities quoted in the Pön-ts'au agree that the animal resembled a fox.

The next two phrases of our text, as well as the last one of the chapter, refer to another animal from which was derived a substance used medicinally by the Chinese, and which, at an early date, was taking the place of the genuine *wu-na-ts'i*, which at all times was largely 45 falsified, according to the Pön-ts'au. This third *wu-na-ts'i* producing animal was a seal, a «sea-dog» (海 狗), or «black dragon» (水 烏 龍), and the authorities quoted in the Pön-ts'au (loc.

cit.), show that it was found in the Sea of Korea, the Eastern Sea, and down to the Malay Peninsula, where, according to Li Sün (李 珣) of the T'ang, «the K'un-lun people (崑 崙 家) shot it with arrows, removed its outer scrotum (外 腎) a nddried it in the shade for an hundred days. Its perfume was sweet and very strong.» In view of the above, there seems no
5 valid reason for supposing that the drug supplied by the sea-dog, and known by the name of *wu-na-ts'i*, may not have been principally procured from the coast of Borneo, as stated by our author, although it is remarkable that he makes no mention of the fact in the chapter devoted to that region.

At the time the Pön-ts'au-kang-mu was written, in the latter part of the sixteenth cen-
10 tury, genuine *wu-na-ts'i* must have nearly disappeared from the Chinese market — as had long before *an-si-hiang*, *su-ho-yu*, and other drugs originally brought from the West — in competition with similar but cheaper products from nearer countries, and *hai-kóu-shön* (海 狗 腎), or «sea-dog scrotum», had taken its place in the Chinese pharmacopœia, where it has since remained as the identical substance known in olden times as *wu-na-ts'i*. See Bretschnei-
15 der, Ancient Chinese and Arabs, 12, and Mediaeval Researches, I, 149—150, also Porter Smith, Chinese materia medica, 54.

Our author's reference to *wu-na-ts'i* being procured from K'ié-li-ki, which there seems good reason to identify with the important mediaeval port of Kalhat on the Oman coast, is interesting, for Abyssinia and Arabia had long been the principal centres of production of civet. In the
20 sixteenth century, and probably for centuries before, civet was one of the principal articles of export from Zeila on the Somali coast, Chau's Pi-p'a-lo. See Portuguese expedition to Abyssinia in 1541—1543, pp. 140, 232 (Hakluyt Soc. edit.).

39.

KINGFISHERS' FEATHERS (翠 毛).

25 *T'sui-mau*, or kingfishers' feathers, are got in great quantities in Chön-la, where (the birds) are brought forth in nests built by the side of lakes or ponds in the depths of the hills. Each pond is the home of just one male and one female bird; the intrusion of a third bird always ends in a duel to the death. The natives taking advantage of this peculiarity, rear decoy birds, and walk about with
30 one sitting on the left hand raised. The birds in their nests noticing the intruder, make for the (bird on the) hand to fight it, quite ignoring the presence of the man, who, with his right hand, covers them with a net, and thus makes them prisoners without fail.

The river Ku in Yung-chóu (邕 州 古 江) is also the habitat of a bird called
35 *jung-ts'ui* (茸 翠 downy kingfisher), covered with soft blue feathers all over the back, which are used by luxurious people as an ornament, the feathers being twisted and woven into each other so as to resemble long nap satin (毛 段).

Although, of late years, the use of this luxury has been strictly forbidden by the government, the well-to-do classes still continue to add it to their dress,
40 for which reason foreign traders, in defiance of the law, manage to smuggle it in by concealing it in the cotton lining of their clothes.

Note.

The two first paragraphs of this article are substantially a quotation from Ling-wai-tai-ta, 9,11[b]—12[a].

Sung-shǐ, 153,10,16, states that prior to the year 1107 «fine brocade of kingfishers' feathers» (翠 毛 細 錦) was included in the list of dress materials presented to officials of certain   5 grades by the Emperor. In 1107 the Emperor forbade it in an Edict in which he said: «The Ancient Rulers in their governmental measures extended the principle of humanity to plants, trees, birds and beasts. Now the depriving of living creatures of their life, in order to get their plumage for a perfectly frivolous purpose, is certainly unworthy of the kindness extended by the Ancient Rulers to all creatures. We therefore order the officials to stop the practice on pain of 10 punishment.»

Kingfishers' feather are still largely used in China to make ornaments for the head. They are still imported from Tongking.

A river called Ku-kiang, flows near Nan-ning-fu in Kuang-tung — which in the Sung period was called Yung-chóu-fu. T'u-shu-tsi-ch'öng, 6,1442. Ling-wai-tai-ta (loc. cit.) reads 15 Yu-kiang (右 江), and this is one of the names of the Nan-ning West River, which quite close to this city is formed by the two branches 'Left River' and 'Right River' (Yu-kiang). Hirth, China Review, III, 47—48.

40.

PARROTS (鸚 鵡).   20

Ying-wu are procured in Chan-ch'öng where they are found of all colours. This is the kind of bird which, in the time of the emperor T'ai-tsung of the T'ang dynasty (A. D. 627—650), was presented to our Court by Huan-wang. In the Annals they are said to have been able to complain of cold, for doing which the Emperor gave orders to return them to their home. The 25 country of Huan-wang is the same as Chan-ch'öng.

In K'in-chóu (欽 州) both white and red *ying-wu* are found of the size of small geese. Birds with plumage covered with dust like the wings of a butterfly are called «white *ying-wu*»; those showing deep scarlet colour with a tail resembling that of a black kite are called «red *ying-wu*».   30

Note.

The *ying-wu* is a large parrot; the smaller varieties are called *ying-ko* (鸚 哥鳥). Kuang-tung-sin-yü, 20,7, calls a specially clever variety of parrot *pa-ko* (嘞 哥) and *pa-pa* (嘞 嘞). This last name, which is in common use in Fu-kién for small parrots, may be derived from the Arabic name for parrot *babaga*, and the last character, *ko*, in the two preceding names 35 may perhaps also be traced to that word.

The whole of this article is taken from Ling-wai-tai-ta, 9,10[b]. P'ing-chóu-k'o-t'an, 2,5[b] notes that white parrots that could speak were for sale in Canton. Presumably such parrots were a rarity in China at that time.

The parrots sent to the Emperor T'ai-tsung of the T'ang were of two kinds, of variegated 40 plumage, and white. T'ang-shu, 222[C],1[b].

41.

AMBERGRIS (龍 涎).

«In the Western Sea of the Ta-shï there are dragons in great number.
Now, when a dragon (*lung*) is lying on a rock asleep, his spittle (*hién*) floats
5 on the water, collects and turns hard, and the fishermen gather it as a most
valuable substance. Fresh ambergris is white in colour, when slightly stale it
turns red, and black when it is quite old. It is neither fragrant nor bad-
smelling, it is like pumice-stone, but lighter. The statement that a special
perfume is derived from ambergris, and the other statement to the effect that
10 the odour of ambergris can bring out all other scents, are both erroneous.

«Ambergris does not affect the properties of perfumes in any way, either
by improving or by spoiling them; it merely has the power of keeping the
fumes together. When a quantity of genuine ambergris is mixed with incense,
and is being burned, a straight column of clear blue smoke rises high up into
15 the air, and the smoke will not dissipate, and those present (座 客) could
cut the column of smoke with a pair of scissors. This is occasioned by the
virtue left in the ambergris by which the dragon exhales cloud-borne buildings» (蜃 氣 樓 臺 之 餘 烈 也).

Note.

20   This article is a quotation from Ling-wai-tai-ta, 7,9. Conf. what our author said concerning
ambergris in the sea near the Somali coast (supra, p. 131). Yu-yang-tsa-tsu, 4,3[b], calls it *o-mo*,
which is Arabic *'anbar* (supra, p. 128). Edrisi (I, 64) says that the best ambergris comes from
the Sea of Oman. «It is a substance which flows from springs in the depth of the sea, just as
naphta flows from the springs of Hit. When the waves of the sea are raised by a storm, amber
25 is thrown on the coast. Some people have thought that it was the excretion of an animal, but it
is not so; it is as we have stated....» Conf. also Masudi, Prairies d'or, I, 333—334. See also
Marcel Devic, op. cit., 188—194. A thirteenth century Chinese writer calls this substance
sa-pa-ïr (撒 巴 爾). Bretschneider, Mediaeval Researches, I 152. *Sa-pa-ïr* is Persian
shahbūy (شهبوی) «royal perfume», erroneously read *shahbarī* (شهبری). Vullers, Lexicon,
30 s. v. *shahbūy*. See also Farhang-i Shu'ūrī, Constantinople, 1100, II, fol. 139, v. A fifteenth century
Chinese work mentions a Lung-hién-sü, or island, in the sea of Lambri, at a distance of a full
day from Sumatra, where the ambergris was sold. Groeneveldt, Notes, 100. Gerini, Researches, 691, takes Lung-hién-sü to be a transcription of Lam (p'u) yang, an old name of the island
of Pulo Bras.

35   The last phrase of this article refers to the mythological belief held in China from very
early times that certain mythical monsters, dragons, frogs, etc., blew out clouds of vapour in which
were temples and pagodas. Ambergris, or «dragon's spittle» lends itself to this belief. Vapour or
smoke which can carry a temple or pagoda must perforce be of very great density, hence the
connection between the dense smoke of this incense, in which ambergris is mixed, and the dragon
40 exhaled cloud-borne buildings. See Pei-wön-yün-fu, 64,5.

42.

TORTOISE-SHELL (瑇 瑁).

The *tai-meï* resembles the *kui-yüan* (龜 黿). Its back is covered with thirteen plates regularly marked with black and white spots and lines, their edges jagged like a saw. It is without feet, in lieu of which it is provided 5 with four fins, the front fins being longer than the hind ones, serving as paddles when moving about in the water. These fins, as well as the head, are marked like the plates. The plates of old animals are thick and show the black and white parts of the pattern quite clearly, whereas young specimens have thinner plates with an indistinct pattern. There is no foundation for the 10 story that these patterns are produced by the animals being lashed to fury so as to stir up the blood. They are caught on moon-light nights during the autumn. Their flesh is edible. They come from P'o-ni, San-sü, P'u-li-lu and Shö-p'o.

Note. 15

The *kui-yüan* is, according to Williams, Syll. Dictionary, the great sea-turtle. Ling-wai-tai-ta, 10,2, after describing the big turtle found in the sea near K'in-chóu, the westernmost port of Kuang-tung, and which it calls *pi-tai-meï* (鼊 瑇 瑁), says: «the shell of *tai-meï* has, like it, thirteen plates, but the story that the distinctness of the pattern on the plates is a result of the animal having had its blood lashed to fury is, of course, false.» 20

In preceding passages our author says that the best tortoise-shell, and also the largest quantity of this product, came from Pi-p'a-lo (Berbera coast). He says it was also procured from Socotra, the Celebes and the Moluccas. Crawfurd, Hist. Indian Archipelago, III, 444, says the tortoise is found in greatest abundance on the east coast of the Celebes, the coasts of the Spice Islands, and those of New Guinea. 25

Hóu-Han-shu, 118,12[a] mentions tortoise-shell as a product of India. The Ling-piau-lü-i, 1,4[a], quoting the (T'ang?) Pön-ts'au, says that *tai-meï* detects the presence of poison as well as bezoar stones. Conf. Pön-ts'au-kang-mu, 45,8[b]—9, and Marcel Devic, op. cit., 187—188.

_____

43.

BEES-WAX (黃 蠟). 30

Huang-la, or «yellow wax», comes from San-sü, Ma-i, Chön-la, San-fo-ts'i, and such like countries. The habitat of the bee producing it is in the depths of hills and the remotest valleys of the interior, where it builds nests in old trees, on the banana plant, or in caves in the rocks. The insect is somewhat larger than the Chinese bee and is darker in colour. The natives 35 in those foreign parts approach them by covering their bodies with a leather coat, drive out and disperse the swarm by making a smudge of foul-smelling grasses, when the nest is taken away and the honey squeezed out. What remains of the nest is the wax, which is melted into a form and reduced to 5 proper shape.

Some dealers adulterate the substance by mixing with it lime and rock-salt (鹽 石). The produce of San-fo-ts'i is the best; the next quality comes from Chön-la, and the poorest from San-sü, Ma-i and P'u-li-lu.

Note.

10   Besides the countries here mentioned, we learn from the first part of this work that bees-wax was also procured in Tongking, Tan-ma-ling in the Malay Peninsula, western Borneo, the Celebes and Moluccas, from northern Formosa, and from Ha·nan, the wax from the last named country being of very poor quality.

       Crawfurd, op. cit., III, 438 says that «bees' wax constituted a very valuable aud consi-
15 derable article of commerce in the Archipelago. The greatest supply is obtained in the islands furthest to the east, and, above all, in Timur and Flores. The trade is principally with China and Bengal.»

GENERAL INDEX.

ships go to Kalah, 18; efforts of government to develop foreign sea-trade, 19; results of this policy, 19; sea-going ships, methods of navigation, 27—28; traders to the Arabs' country change ships at Ku-lin, 91; trade with realm of Arabs conducted through San-fo-ts'i, 114; from Fu-kién living in Sin-lo, 169, line 39; from Ts'üan-chóu rarely go to Jï-pön, 171; trade with Li of Hainan, 177; settlers in Hai-nan, 181, 182, 183; method of making glass, 227.

Chintzes, coloured, made in Nan-p'i, 88.

Chola dominion, — see Chu-lién.

Chonen Fujiwara, — see Tiau-jan.

Chóu, Marquess of, 180; establishes markets in Hai-nan, 181.

Chóu K'ü-feï, author of Ling-wai-tai-ta, 22; quoted on the foreign countries trading with Canton, 22—24; quoted on the oceans and countries of the West, 25—27; his description of sea-going ships, 33—34; use made of his work by Chau Ju-kua, 36—38; his use of the name San-fo-ts'i, 63; quoted on the Arabs, 119—120, 121; quoted on Meï-lu-ku-tun, 141—142.

Chóu-pau-lung, an island or headland near the port of San-fo-ts'i, 100, n. 11.

Christians, of India, 105, 106; their chief, the patriarch of Baghdad, 105; of Syria, captives in Persia, 109—110; of Malabar, possibly visited China, 112—113.

Chrysanthemum, time of blooming in Hainan, 179.

Chu-ai, one of the ancient divisions of Hainan, 175, 176.

Chu-ko Wu, Marquess, temple in Pagān dedicated to, 58; his inventions for war operations, 111, 113.

Chu-lién, the Chola dominions, the Coromandel coast, a vassal of San-fo-ts'i (Palembang), 59; also called Southern India, 93; position of capital of, 93—94; no relations between, and China, 94; how it can be reached, 94; the great city of, 94; the thirty-two *pu-lo* of, 94-95; punishment of crimes in, 95; ceremonies at banquets in, 95; the dress and food of the prince of, 95; marriage customs in, 95; taxes in, heavy, 95; the army of, 96; methods of warfare, 96; products, 96; the relations of, with China, 96; envoys of, ranked with those of K'iu-tz'ï (Kúcha), 96; is the Ma'abar of the Arabs, 98; other Chinese names of, 98; rule of, over Ceylon, 98; the mission of 1015, 99, n. 3, 100, n. 11; sovereigns of, 99—100, n. 6.

Chu Ying, his mission to Indo-China, 6.

Chu Yü, author of P'ing-chóu-k'o-t'an (q. v.) when he lived, 16.

Chung-ka-lu, — see Jung-ya-lu.

Chung-li (Somali Coast), 130; the people of, dress, food, occupations, 130; the only country producing frankincense, 130; sorcerers of, 130—131; flocks of birds of passage in, 131; mortuary customs in, 131; whales, how used in, 131; dragon's-blood, tortoise-shell and ambergris come from, 131.

Cinnabar, imported by Persians to China, 16; a product of Kiau-chï, 46; imported to Shö-p'o, 78; its use in Su-ki-tan, 83; exported from Ki-shï, 134.

Cinnamon, imported to Aden from China, 4.

Civet, procured from K'ié-li-ki, 234; exported from Zeila on Somali coast, 235.

Cleanliness, in eating of Moslims in Canton, 17; habits of, of people of Chan-ch'öng, 47; customs connected with, in Chön-la, 53; about hair and nails among Arabs, 116.

Climate, of Chan-ch'öng, 47; of Chön-la, 52; of San-fo-ts'i, 60; of Nan-p'i, 88; in Arabs country, 115; of Ts'öng-pa, 126; of Ki-tz'ï-ni, 138; of P'o-ni, 156; of Hai-nan, 177, 178—179, 180.

Cloves, imported into Ceylon, 3; into Aden, 4; a product of San-fo-ts'i, 61; imported to Si-lan, 73; a product of Shö-p'o, 77; a product of pirate islands near Shö-p'o, 84; exported to Nan-p'i, 89; exported to Yung-man, 133; a product of Hai-nan, 176; varieties of, 209.

Coast, «Lower» and «Upper», countries, explanation of terms, 79, 204.

Cobalt blue, — see Wu-ming-i.

Cock, fighting, in Shö-p'o, 77.

Cocoanuts, imported at Aden from China, 4; principal food of Nicobar islanders, 12; juice of, drunk in Chan-ch'öng, 48; grown in Chan-ch'öng, 48; wine of, in San-fo-ts'i, 60; grown in Shö-p'o, 77; wine of, in Shö-p'o, 78; a product of Ku-lin, 89; a product of Chu-lién, 96; wine of, in P'o-ni, 155; a product of Hai-nan, 176, 183; description of, 214; wine made from juice of, in Nan-p'i, 214; origin of Chinese name for, 215.

Coir-palm, bark of, used to thatch houses in Sin-t'o, 70.

Comoro islands, — see Kan-meï.

Compass, when first used in navigation, 28—29; its use in navigation in twelfth century, 32; reference to use of, 176.

Conch shell, ground pieces of, used as money in P'öng-k'ié-lo, 97; pieces of, ground sharp used as knives in Yen-t'o-man islands, 147.

Constantinople, possible reference to, 141, 142.

Copper, exported from Calliana, 3; imported to Canton, 16; household utensils in Si-lan of, 73; used in alloy for Shö-p'o currency, 78; white, used in Shö-p'o, 78, 81; a product of T'ién-chu, 111; exported to Ts'öng-pa, 126; household utensils of, in Sin-lo, 167; temple bells, made in Sin-lo, 168.

Copperas, imported to Shö-p'o, 78.

Coral, imported by Persians to China, 16; imported to China in tenth century, 19; imported to San-fo-ts'i, 61, a product of Chu-lién, 96; a product of Ta-ts'in, 103; comes from Wu-ssï-li, 140; found off coast of Mo-k'ié-la, 154; two kinds of, on coast of P'u-li-lu (Philippine Islands), 162; description of, mode of fishing, 226

Cornelians, imported by Persians to China, 16; imported to China in tenth century, 19; used to ornament palaces of king of Si-lan, 72; a product of Ta-ts'in, 103; pillars of, in palace of king of the Arabs, 115.

Cosmas Indicopleustes, his knowledge of China, 2, 5; describes trade of Ceylon with China, 3; his reference to Kulam-Malé (Quilon), 12.

Cotton, fabrics, exported from India, 3; fabrics imported to Aden, 4; tree, and *ki-peï*, products of Kjau-chï, 46; *ki-peï*, a product of Chan-ch'öng, 48; figured stuffs of, in Chan-ch'öng, 48; fabrics,

and ceremonies attending trading in P'o-ni, 156—157; with islands near P'o-ni, 158; in Ma-i, 159—160; customs of, in San-sü (Philippine Islands), 161—162; of Liu-k'iu, 163; of Sin-lo, 168; lumber, of Japanese with China, 171; with Hai-nan, 177; between Li of Hai-nan and Chinese, 183.

Tree, of gold and jewels, in palace of king of Si-lan, 72.

Trengganu, — see Töng-ya-nöng.

Ts'au, the country of, indigo from, 217; asafoetida from, 225; its capital Ghazni, 225.

Tsi-ki (Tiz ?), a dependency of the Arabs, 117, 122.

Ts'öng-pa (Zanguebar), a dependency of the Arabs, 117, 122, 126; is south of Hu-ch'a-la, 126; people of, are of Arab stock, 126; food of people of, 126; products of, 126; trade of, 126.

Ts'öng-t'an, a country in the Southern Ocean, possibly same as Ts'öng-pa, description of, 127, n. 4.

Tsiau-shï island, the Hon Tseu island near Tourane, 8.

Ts'ién-mai, a dependency of San-fo-ts'i, 62; possibly in N. Sumatra, 66; like Tan-ma-ling, 67.

Ts'in-lun, a merchant of Ta-ts'in, comes to China, 5.

Ts'ing-lang-kan, a variety of coral found on coast of P'u-li-lu, 162, 226.

Tsu-ko-ni, Alexander the Great, builds tower of O-kön-to, 146; visits Ch'a-pi-sha, 153.

Tsu-la, the girafe, in Pi-p'a-lo, 128, 129, n. 6.

Tsushima, silver mines on, 171, 175, n. 22.

Ts'üan-chóu, foreign settlement in, 14; administration of foreign settlement in, 16; where situated, 16; Arab trade goes to, 17; called Zaytun by the Arabs, 18; foreigners abandon, during troubles in ninth century, 18; its foreign trade at end of tenth century, 19; official godowns for foreign imports at, 20; distance from, to Chanch'öng, 47; distance by sea from, to Chan-ch'öng, 47; distance to Chön-la, 52; distance by sea from, to San-fo-ts'i, 60; distance from, to Shö-p'o, 75; natives of Nan-p'i residing in, 88; distance from to Lan-wu-li and Ku-lin, 89; distance from, to Chu-lién, 94; priest from T'ién-chu comes to, and builds a shrine, 111; the Pau-lin-yüan in, 111; the Ta-shï live north-west of, 114; Arab living in, built Moslim burial ground, 119; P'o-ni (Borneo) south-east of, 155; distance from, to Liu-k'iu, 162; raids on district of, by savages of P'i-shö-yé, 165; Jï-pön lies N. E. of, 170; Japanese junks bring lumber to, 171; cotton its principal import from Hai-nan, 185; great consumption of lakawood at, 211; people of, use musk-wood to make furniture, 212.

Ts'ui-lan-shan, fifteenth century Chinese name for Nicobar islands, 12.

Tu-huai-sün, a dependency of Chön-la, not identified, 54, 56.

Tu Huan, his King-hing-ki quoted about Fulin, 104, 108, n. 14; his account of Fu-lin, 108—110.

Tu-kang, a ship captain, his temple in Lingshui, in Hai-nan, 181, 188, n. 28; literary examinations held at temple of, 182.

Tu-lau, headmen in Hai-nan called, 177; explanation of term, 186, n. 8.

Tu-man (Tuban in Java), 85.

Tu-nu-ho, a dependency of Nan-p'i, 88; possibly the Tāna of the Arabs, on Salsette island near Bombay, 90.

Tuan Ch'öng-shï, author of the Yu-yang-tsa-tsu, 28.

Tubers, grown in Nan-p'i, 88; used as ferment in Hai-nan, 176.

Tui-tau, in Japanese Tsushima, silver mines on island of, 171, 175, n. 22.

Tun-t'ién, north of Chu-lién 4000 li, 94; probably a copyist's error for Tun-sun on the southern extremity of the Malay Peninsula, 99.

T'un-li-fu, a dependency of Chön-la, not identified, 54, 56.

T'un-mön, Mount, passage out to sea from Canton, 10, 24.

Tung-ki, a dependency of Shö-p'o, 83.

Tung-nan-ki-wön, work of fourteenth century quoted, 16—17.

Turmeric, imported by Persians to China, 16; people of Ku-lin anoint their bodies with, 89; derivation of Chinese name of, 91—92; people of Nan-ni-hua-lo smear themselves with, 97.

Turtles, abundant in Shö-p'o, 77.

Tush, imported by Persians to China, 16; — see T'óu-shï.

Typhoons, in Hai-nan, 177, 186, n. 7.

Tzï-köng, a kind of lacquer found in Chön-la, 55.

Tzï-shui-tsiau, a canna (?) from Chu-lién, 96.

Umbrella, Chinese, kittysols, exported to Chön-la, 53; silk, carried over king of San-fo-ts'i, 60; black or white, carried over king of Su-ki-tan, 82; silk umbrellas and kittysols sold by foreign traders in Tan-ma-ling, 67; of peacock feathers in Nan-p'i, 87; carried over king of Ta-ts'in, 103; of the ruler of Ta-ts'in, possibly a reference to the *biruna* of the patriarch, 107; black, of ruler of Ki-shï, 134; black, of king of Pai-ta, 135; as present in P'o-ni, 156; white, used by chiefs of Ma-i, 159; silk umbrellas brought to San-sü, 161.

Urgendj, — see Au-kién.

Value, relative, of gold and silver, in Ling-ya-ssï-kia, 68; relative, of gold and silver in Ku-lin, 89; do. in T'ién-chu, 113, line 45.

Vinegar, imported into Chön-la, 53.

Wa-li, possibly Laos country, its trade centers in Chan-ch'öng and Chön-la, 25; a dependency of Chön-la, 54; was sixty days from P'u-kan, 59.

Wa-mu, colloquial name of sapan-wood, 217.

Walls, of bricks, round San-fo-ts'i, 60; palisade, round Tan-ma-ling, 67; of Lu-meï, 141; palisade, of P'o-mi, 155.

Wan-an, also called Wan-ning and Ling-shui, in Hai-nan, 181; Chinese settlers in, 181; the aborigines of, 181; the temple of Captain Tu-kang, 181—182; source of river of, 182.

Wang Kün, his voyage from Canton to Siam, 8.

Wang-shö-ch'öng, T'ién-chu of, Central India, 26; said to be in Pin-t'ung-lung, 51; said to be west of Ta-li, 97; means Magadha, 101.

War, customs as to, in Chan-ch'öng, 47; preparation for, in San-fo-ts'i, 60; customs as to, in San-fo-ts'i, 63; people of Nan-p'i fond of, 88; people of T'ién-chu cowards in 111; conntrivances for, used in T'ien-chu, 111, 113; Japanese unused to, 171.

INDEX

OF

UNUSUAL FOREIGN NAMES AND TERMS

OCCURING IN

CHINESE TEXTS.

sion of A. D. 1015 on voyage from Malay Peninsula to San-fo-ts'i, 100, n. 11.

昌化 *Ch'ang-hua*, in Hai-nan, 176.

長腰嶼 *Ch'ang-yau-sü*, Pulo Senang or Bam Island, 64.

朝霞 *ch'au-hia*, — see *kiau-shö-yé*.

質 *Chï*, the Singapore Straits, 11.

哲地 *Chö-ti*, the Chittis of Malabar, 89.

眞臘 *Chön-la*, Champa, Kamboja, 52, 54, n. 1; — see *Ki-mié* and *Kan-pu-chi*.

眞里富 *Chön-li-fu*, a dependency of Chön-la, the present Chanthabun on the lower Menam, 53, 56.

眞蒲 *Chön-p'u*, a dependency of Chön-la, possibly the same as Chön-li-fu (q. v.), 56.

舟寶龍 *Chóu-pau-lung*, an island or headland near entrance to port of San-fo-ts'i, 100, n. 11.

朱崖 *Chu-ai*, an ancient administrative division of Hai-nan, 175, 176.

珠利耶 *Chu-li-yé*, Choliya, identical with *Chu-lién* (q. v.), 98, n. 1.

注輦 *Chu-lién*, the Chola dominion, or the Coromandel Coast, 93; — see also *Ma-pa-ïr* and *So-li*.

厨 (or 除) 幭 *ch'u-* (or *shu-*)*mi*, Arabic *jum'ah* «assembly» (on friday, for prayer in the mosque), 138, 139, n. 2.

重迦盧 *Chung-kia-lu*, a variant of Jung-ya-lu (q. v.), a portion of western Java, 62, 66, n. 19.

中理 *Chung-li*, the Somali coast; the name may be derived from *Zang* or *Zenj*, 130.

方丈 *Fang-chang*, the «Cube House» the «House of Allah» (Bayt Ullah) or Kaaba, at Mecca, 125, note.

馮牙囉 *Föng-ya-lo*, in Amoy dialect *Bang-ga-lo*, probably Mangalore, 88, 90, n. 8.

佛羅安 *Fo-lo-an*, a dependency of San-fo-ts'i, 62; Beranang, W. coast Malay Peninsula, 65, n. 16, 69.

佛逝 *Fo-shï*, 11, 63, n. 1, — see *San-fo-ts'i*.

弗利剌河 *Fu-li-la-ho*, probably the Mináb river on which stood Hormuz, 14.

拂菻 *Fu-lin*, situated in the west of the Chan (苫) country (q. v.); it was also called Ta-ts'in according to Tu Huan, 104.

縛達城 *Fu-ta ch'öng*, the city of Fostat, the modern Cairo, or Baghdad, 14, n. 3.

海梅脂 *hai-meï-chï*, a product of Hai-nan; unidentified, 176.

海膽 *Hai-tan*, the Acta, the Negritos of the Philippine Islands, 161.

翰林 *han-lin*, title of an officer of the king of Nan-p'i who watched over his food, 88.

黑水 *Heï-shui*, probably the Irrawadi river, 26, called 黑水淤泥河 *Heï-shui-yü-ni-ho*, «Black-water-muddy river»; formed the frontier of P'u-kan, 59, n. 1.

禧寧 *Hi-ning*, a dependency of Java, (Shö-p'o), 83; possibly the Singhasari of the Javanese, 86, n. 7.

蝦猱丹 *hia-nau-tan*, a tree of Shö-p'o, inner part of which was used to make a liquor, 78; *hia-nau* probably Malay *anao*» the gomuti palm, 81, n. 13.

行勤 *Hing-k'in*, the Bonze, travels to the West, 117.

興瞿 *hing-k'ü*, also written *hing-yü*,

and *hün-k'ü* (q. v.), Sanskrit *hingu*, asafœtida, 225.

訶陵 *Ho-ling*, or Western Java, 11.

形虞 *hing-yü*, Sanskrit *hingu*, asafoetida, 225.

熏渠 *hün-k'ü*, Sanskrit *hingu*, asafoetida, 225.

何蠻 *Ho-man*, a sailor, probably Arab, of Ts'üan-chóu, at beginning of seventh century, who discovered Formosa, 163, n. 1.

霍悉那 *Ho-si-na*, Ghazni, the capital of Ts'au (漕), 225.

胡茶辣 *Hu-ch'a-la*, Guzerat, a dependency of Malabar (Nan-p'i), 88; 92.

鶻莽 *hu-mang*, Persian *khurmā*, the date, 210; see also *k'u-lu-ma* and *k'u-mang*.

歡斯 *Huan-ssï*, the family name of the kings of Liu-k'iu, 162.

黃麻駐 *Huang-ma-chu*, a dependency of Java (Shö-p'o), 83. Not identified.

火齊 *huo-ts'i*, a stone like talc, probably isinglass, 111, 113, n. 11.

血碣 *hüé-kié*, Cantonese *hüt-k'it*, possibly Arabic *kātir*, dragon's-blood, 198.

鑑 *i*, a weight of gold, equivalent to 20 taels, 73, 74.

一支 *I-chï (I-ki)*, in Japanese Iki(shima), 173, n. 7.

伊祿 *I-lu*, in Cantonese *I-luk*, Irāk, a dependency of the Arabs, 117.

伊麻羅里 *I-ma-lo-li*, a country or island between Chan-pin (q. v.) and Kulo (q. v.), on the west coast Malay Peninsula, 100, n. 11.

伊都 *I-tu*, also written 怡土, in Japanese Ido, in Chikuzen, 173, n. 7.

夷勿 *I-wu*, a dependency of Java (Shö-p'o), 83.

日麗 *Jï-li*, a dependency of Chan-ch'öng, 49.

日麗胡 *Jï-li-hu*, an island near P'o-ni, possibly Gilolo, 157.

日羅亭 *Jï-lo-t'ing*, a dependency of San-fo-ts'i, 62; not identified, 65, n. 6.

乳酪 *ju-lo*, usually «milk», but when used in connexion with Mongol and Turkish countries, «dried sour milk» or *kurut*, 102, n. 19, and 139, n. 1.

軟布兜 *juan-pu-tóu*, a litter or hammock carried by four men, in Chan-ch'öng, 47; other names of same, 50, n. 4; also written 軟兜 *juan-tóu*, 72;—see *pu-tai-kiau*.

戎牙路 *Jung-ya-lu*, in Western Java, but east of Sin-t'o; a dependency of Shö-p'o, 62, 66, 83, n. 19; also written *Chung-kia-lu* (q. v.). Probably the Janggolo of the Javanese, 86, n. 7.

甘羅 *kan-lo*, a fruit of Chu-lién, not identified, 96; is also called *kan-mau-sun* (甘茂孫), 100, n. 9.

甘眉 *Kan-mëi*, a dependency of the Arabs, 117; possibly the Comoro islands, 122, n. 13.

甘琶逸 *Kan-pa-i*, in Cantonese *Kŏm-p'ā-yat*, the city of Cambay, the Kambayat of the Arabs, 88, 90, n. 8.

澉浦 *Kan-pu* (or *fu*), near Hangchóu in Ch'ö-kiang, Marco Polo's Ganfu, 20, n. 3.

甘孛智 *Kan-po-chï*, the name given Kamboja during the Ming period, 54; it was also written 聚埔寨 *K'ién-pu-chai*.

吉蘭丹 *Ki-lan-tan*, a dependency of San-fo-tsʻi, 62; identified with Kalantan, 65, n. 4.

吉里門山 *Ki-li-mŏn-shan*, Pulo Krimun, north coast of Java, 85, n. 2.

吉羅達弄 *Ki-lo-ta-nung*, the products of Nan-pʻi were exported to China by way of this place, 88; it is not identified, but was probably on the extreme N. E. coast of Sumatra, 91, n. 10; — see *Ku-lo*.

雞籠島 *Ki-lung-tau*, Hen's nest (or Koh-rang-kai) island, 8.

吉蔑 *Ki-mié*, Kamboja, according to the *Tʻang-shu*. It is probably a transcription of *Khmēr*, 54, n. 1.

吉貝 *ki-peï*, or 古貝 *ku-peï*, Sanskrit *karpāsa*, Malay *kapas*; cotton, 218; — see also *ku-chung*.

記施 *Ki-shï*, a dependency of the Arabs, 117; the island of Kish (Keis) in the Persian Gulf; other forms of name, 134, n. 1.

吉陀 *Ki-tʻo*, a port probably of northwestern Sumatra, its ships traded with Ku-lin, 89, 91, n. 16.

吉瓷 (or 慈) 尼 *Ki-tzʻï-ni*, a dependency of the Arabs, 117; probably Ghazni; — see *Ho-si-na* and *Kʻié-shö-na*.

吉陽 *Ki-yang*, in Hai-nan, 176.

迦拘勒 *kia-kü-lö*, Arabic *kākulah*, the cardamom, but used by Chinese as name of nutmeg, 210.

加羅希 *Kia-lo-hi*, a southern dependency of San-fo-tsʻi, probably in Malay Peninsula, 52, 54, 62, 66, n. 10.

加麻延 *Kia-ma-yen*, Calamián, one of the Calamianes islands, N. E. of Pa-

lawán (Philippine Islds.). It was one of the San-sü (q. v.), 161.

加蒙 *kia-mŏng*, presumably the go-muti palm; sap used in Pʻo-ni to make liquor, 155.

加八山 *Kia-pa-shan*, an island or headland presumably on S. W. coast of Malay Peninsula, 100, n. 11.

加突 *kia-tʻu*, a sea-going ship, the *katur*, used on the south-west coast of India, 30, n. 2.

甲子門 *Kia-tzï-mŏn*, the point of present junk passage on Canton coast called Cupchi Point, 24.

交趾 *Kiau-chï*, Tongking, 45—46.

憍奢邪 *kiau-shö-yé*, Sanskrit *kausheya*, silken stuff, 218; use of term by Chinese, 219, lines 13 et seq.

交洋 *Kiau-yang*, Sea of Kiau-chï, the China Sea, 23.

羯布羅 *kié-pu-lo*, Sanskrit *karpūra*, camphor, 194 n. 1.

愷野 *Kié-yé*, Arabic *Kâhirah*, «the Victorious», the modern Cairo, 144.

伽古羅 *Kʻié-ku-lo*, possibly same as earlier Ko-ku-lo (q. v.) in Malay Peninsula, 222, line 7.

伽藍山 *Kʻié-lan-shan*, the Nicobar islands, 12; — see *Tsʻui-lan-shan*.

伽力吉 *Kʻié-li-ki*, a dependency of the Arabs, 117; presumably Kalhát, 122.

伽闍那 *Kʻié-shö-na*, probably Ghazni, 139, line 14; — see *Ki-tzʻï-ni*.

伽多羅 *kʻié-to-lo*, Sanskrit *khādira*, acacia catechu, 196, n. 1; *to-kʻié-lo* occurs, it may be Sanskrit *tagara*, cassia auriculata.

監篦 *Kién-pi*, a dependency of San-

麻 霞 勿 *Ma-hia-wu*, Mohammed, 116, 120, n. 7, 135.

麻 逸 *Ma-i*, in Cantonese *Ma-yat*, Mait, «the country of the Blacks», the Philippine islands, or a portion of them, 159, 160, n. 1.

馬 喏 *Ma-jö* or, *Ma-no*, an island near P‘o-ni, possibly Mahono, 158.

麻 嘉 *Ma-kia*, Mecca, a dependency of the Arabs, 117, 124.

麻 蘭 *Ma-lan*, a dependency of Chön-la, possibly identical with Ma-lo-wön (q. v.), 56.

麻 萵 *Ma-li*, Bali, a dependency of Java (Shö-p‘o), 83, 86, n. 7. see *Pa-li*.

麻 哩 抹 *Ma-li-mo*, i Amoy dialect *Ma-li-bwat* (Malabar?), 88, 90, n. 8.

麻 離 (or 囉) 扷 *Ma-li-* (or *lo-*) *pa*, Merbat on the Hadramaut coast of Arabia, 25, 115, 119, n. 2.

麻 囉 弗 *ma-lo-fu*, the style of the king of Ta-ts‘in, 102; transcribes presumably *Mar Aba*, a title of the patriarchs of the Nestorians, 105.

麻 囉 華 *Ma-lo-hua*, in Cantonese *Mā-lō-wā*, Malwa, a dependency of Malabar (Nan-p’i), 93.

麻 囉 奴 *Ma-lo-nu*, probably *Maláyu*, our *Malays;* lived by piracy, were cannibals, 150.

麻 羅 間 *Ma-lo-wön*, a dependency of Chön-la, the Malyan of Cham inscriptions, but not located, 53, 56, n. 10.

麻 尼 *Ma-ni*, an Arab envoy to China in A. D. 1003, 118, 123, n. 20.

馬 八 兒 *Ma-pa-ïr*, Ma‘bar of the Arabs, the Coromandel coast, or Chu-lién (q. v.), 98.

麻 東 *Ma-tung*, a dependency of Java (Shö-p‘o), 83; possibly the Medang-kamolan of the Javanese, 86, n. 7.

蠻 山 水 *Man-shan-shui*, a river, presumably in Kamboja, passed by Chu-lién mission of A. D. 1015 on voyage to China, 100, n. 11.

茂 門 王 *Mau-mön Wang*, in Arabic *Amīr-al-Mu’menīn* «Commander of the Faithful», 14; — see also 119, l. 20.

帽 山 *Mau-shan*, Pulo Rondo or Pulo Way, off Acheen, Sumatra, 74.

眉 路 骨 (惇) *Meï-lu-ku-(tun)*, the capital of Lu-meï, not identified; may be Arabic *mulhidūn* «Infidels», points to Constantinople or Rome, though details concerning it seem to apply to Damascus, 141.

眉 思 打 華 酒 *meï-ssï-ta-hua-tsiu*, a drink (or drinks?) of the Arabs made with honey and spices, 116, 120, n. 6, 127, n. 4.

彌 蘭 *Mi-lan*, the Indus river, called *Nahr Mihrān* by the Arabs, 13.

密 徐 籬 *Mi-sü-li*, the capital of the Arabs, 115; *Misr* of the Arabs, Egypt, 120, n. 3; — see *Wu-ssï-li*.

迷 思 耳 *Mi-ssï-ïr* (Misr of the Arabs, Egypt), 120, n. 3;—see *Wu-ssï-li*.

密 坦 羅 *Mi-tan-lo*, Sanskrit *Mitra;* a Western priest who came to China about A. D., 984, 114, n. 5.

篾 阿 抹 *Mié-a-mo*, in Cantonese *Mit-a-mat*, the style of the capital of Nan-p‘i; may possibly be Malabar, 87, 89, n. 2; — see *Ma-li-mo*.

門 毒 *Mön-tu*, probably near Quinhon, 10. Not identified.

默 伽 獵 *Mo-k‘ié,-la*, Cantonese

Mak-k'e-lap, Arabic *Maghreb (el-akṣà),* 154.

摩剌耶 *Mo-la-yé,* Sanskrit *Malaya;* Kulam-Malé, (Quilon), 12.

沒來 *Mo-lai,* Kulam-Malé (Quilon), 12;—see also *Ku-lin, Kü-lan, Mo-lo-kü-ts'a, Mo-la-yé.*

昧履支 *mo-li-chï,* Sanskrit *marīcha,* black pepper, 223.

莫良 *Mo-liang,* a dependency of Chön-la, possibly identical with Ma-lo-wön and Ma-lan (q. v.), 56, n. 10.

摩勒 *mo-lö,* in Cantonese *mo-lak,* used as a foreign name of frankincense, 196, n. 1.

秫羅矩吒 *Mo-lo-kü-ts'a,* Sanskrit *Malakûṭa;* Kulam-Malé, Quilon, 12.

末盧 *Mo-lu,* Japanese Matsura, 173, n. 7.

沒石 *mo-shï,* — see 麻茶 *ma-ch'a.*

摩娑石 *mo-so-shï,* bezoar stone, 90, 131, 141.

摩地那 *Mo-ti-na,* Medina, 125.

摩賊 *mo-tsö,* — see 麻茶 *ma-ch'a.*

木俱蘭 *Mu-kü-lan,* Mekran, a dependency of the Arabs, 117, 122, 224.

木瓜 *Mu-kua,* the Mukuva or fishermen caste of Malabar, 89, n. 1.

木蘭皮 *Mu-lan-p'i,* Arabic Murâbiṭ, the kingdom of the Al-Murâbitûn or Almoravides, 142.

木蘭皮 *mu-lan-p'i,* the bark of the *maratha-maram* of the Tamils (*Pentaptera tomentosa,* Rox.); a product of Ceylon, yields a black dye, its ashes are used as lime with betel-nut, 73, 75, n. 9.

目連 *Mu-lién,* the Arhat Maudgal-yâyana, 51.

那羅稽羅洲 *Na-lo-ki-lo-chóu,* Sanskrit *nārikera,* «cocoanut»; the Nicobar islands, 12.

那勿丹山 *Na-wu-tan-shan,* an island between Coromandel coast and the northern (?) coast of Ceylon, 100, n. 11.

南尼華囉 *Nan-ni-hua-lo,* a country of India, 96; situated probably in Sindh, 102. Nahrwāla in Guzerat, according to Gerini.

南毗 *Nan-p'i,* the country of the Nairs, the Malabar coast, 89.

牛論 *Niu-lun,* a dependency of Java (Shö-p'o), and adjacent to Su-ki-tan, 83; probably the same as Ku-lun (q. v.).

奴國 *Nu-kuo,* probably Naka, Chikuzen, in Kyûshû, Japan, 173, n. 7.

奴發 *Nu-fa,* Dhofar, a dependency of the Arabs, 116, 121, 195.

奴孤 *Nu-ku,* a dependency of Java (Shö-p'o), 83. Not identified.

遏根陀 *O-kön-t'o,* Iskanderiah, Alexandria in Egypt, 146.

巴吉弄 *Pa-ki-nung,* possibly Busuanga island, Philippine Islds. It was one of the San-sü (q. v.), 161.

巴姥酉 *Pa-lau-yu,* possibly the island of Palawan, Philippine Islds. It was one of the San-sü, 161.

琶離 *P'a-li,* Bali, a pirate state, 84; Chau uses the form *Ma-li,* (q. v.).

巴林馮 *Pa-lin-föng,* Palembang, also written 淳淋邦 *P'o-lin-pang,* 62, 63.

巴哪大山 *Pa-na-ta-shan,* — see *Pau-lau-an-shan.*

唎唎 *pa-pa*, Arabic *babagha*, parrot, 236.

八廝里 *Pa-ssï-li*, a dependency of Chön-la, possibly the same as Po-ssï-lan (q. v.), 56.

拔沓 *Pa-t'a*, a dependency of San-fo-ts'i, 62; possibly the Battas in N. Sumatra, 66, n. 8.

拔颶 *Pa-yü*, a country probably on the Guzerat coast, 13.

百花園 *Pai-hua-yüan*, a dependency of Java (Shö-p'o), 83; possibly the Pejajaran of the Javanese, 86.

白蓮 *Pai-lién*, Bahrein, in Persian Gulf, a dependency of the Arabs, 117.

白蒲延 *Pai-p'u-yen*, the Babuyan islands, Philippine Islds., 160.

白達 *Pai-ta*, in Cantonese *Pāk-tāt*, Baghdâd, a depenency of the Arabs, 117; other forms of name, 135, n. 1.

保老岸山 *Pau-lau-an-shan*, a high mountain on coast of Su-ki-tan (Central Java), 82; identified with Tanjong Pautuman, 85, n. 2; it was also called *Pa-na-ta-shan* (q. v.).

貝多 *peï-to*, Sanskrit *patra*, leaf, but more particularly the leaf of the *Borassus flabelliformis*, 111, 114, n. 4.

盆泥末換 *Pön-ni-mo-huan*, Beni Merwân, the last Omayyad Caliph, 117.

奔陀浪 *Pön-t'o-lang*, on the coast of Cochinchina, Panrang, 11; — see *Pin-t'ung-lung*, *Pin-t'o-ling*, and *Pin-t'óu-lang*.

蓬豐 *P'öng-föng*, Pahang, a dependency of San-fo-ts'i, 62, 65.

彭湖 *P'öng-hu*, the Pescadores, they were in the district of Ts'üan-chóu-fu, 165.

鵬茄囉 *P'öng-k'ié-lo*, a country of India, its capital was Ch'a-na-ki, (q. v.), 97; possibly «the kingdom of Balhara» of the Arabs, 102, n. 14.

弼離沙 *Pi-li-sha*, Bharoch?, a dependency of Malabar (Nan-p'i), 88, 90.

毗陵茄 *pi-ling-k'ié*, said to be a foreign word meaning «cubeb» (*piper cubeba*), 224.

琵琶洲 *Pi-p'a-chóu*, island off entrance to port of Canton, 101.

弼琶囉 *Pi-p'a-lo*, Berbera coast, a dependency of the Arabs, 117, 128.

畢撥棃 *pi-po-li*, Sanskrit *pippali*, the long pepper, 223.

弼斯羅 *Pi-ssï-lo*, Basra, a dependency of the Arabs, 117, 137.

毗齊 *Pi-ts'i*, a dependency of Chan-ch'öng, 49. Not identified.

毗喏耶 *P'i-no-yé*, a dependency of the Arabs, 117; the Ifrîkiya of the Arabs; the coast of Tunis and Tripoli, 122, 226.

毗舍耶 *P'i-shö-yé*, a district or people of southern Formosa, 163, 165; the name may possibly represent *Visaya* or *Bisaya*, 166.

賓窣 *Pin-su*, Pasuri, the Fansur in al-Ramny, Sumatra, of the Arabs, 193.

賓陁陵 *Pin-t'o-ling*, Panrang coast,—see *Pin-t'ung-lung* and *Pön-t'o-lang*.

賓頭狼山 *Pin-t'óu-lang-shan*, cape Panrang or Padaran, 101.

賓頭盧 *Pin-t'óu-lu*, the Arhat Piṇḍola Bhāradvaja; gave his name to Pin-t'ung-lung (Panrang), 51.

po-lü, and *sha-mo-lü*, (q. v.), Persian *shāhballūt* — «royal oak», 215, note.

蒲 盧 歇 *Pᵘu-lu-sié*, the Arab who opened relations between Borneo (Pᶜo-ni) and China, 159, n. 13; also called P'u-a-li (q. v.).

菩 薩 蠻 *Pᵘō-sat-man*, in Cantonese *Pᶜō-sāt-mān*, Arabic *Mussulman*, 16.

蒲 端 *Pᵘu-tuan*, possibly identical with Pᶜu-kan (Pagān), 59.

撒 巴 爾 *sa-pa-ïr*, Persian *shahbarī*, (correct form *shahbūy*), ambergris, literally «royal perfume», 237.

三 佛 齊 *San-fo-ts'i*, Çri-Bhöja, the Serboza of the Arabs, the north-eastern coast of Sumatra, Palembang, 60, 63, n. 1.

三 合 溜 *San-ho-liu*, «three-joint currents», rapids in channel between Leï-chóu peninsula and Hai-nan, 176.

三 濼 *San-lo*, a dependency of Chön-la, possibly an early transcription of the name Syâm, later on transcribed *Sién-lo*, our Siam, 53, 56, n. 10.

三 泊 *San-po*, a dependency of Chön-la, 56, n. 10; — see *San-lo*.

散 絲 *san-ssï*, a flower of Chu-lién; not determined, 96.

三 嶼 *San-sü*, or «Three Islands», belonged to Ma-i, Philippine Islds., 161; see *Kia-ma-yen*, *Pa-lau-yu* and *Pa-ki-nöng*.

沙 糊 *sha-hu*, Malay *sagu*, sago, 61.

沙 華 公 *Sha-hua-kung*, pirates on islands near Shö-pᶜo, the «Orang laut» or «Men of the sea» of the Malays, 150.

沙 沒 律 *sha-mo-lü*, Persian *shāhballūt*, «royal oak», 215.

上 下 竺 *Shang-hia-chu*, the island

of Pulo Aor, 23; also called T'ién-chu (q. v.).

十 二 子 石 *Shï-ïr-tzï-shï*, rocks N. of Carimata island, S. W. coast Borneo, 24.

施 曷 *Shï-ho*, in Cantonese *Shï-hot*, Shehr, a dependency of the Arabs, 116, 121, n. 12, 195.

室 利 佛 誓 (or 逝) *Shï-li-fo-shï*, 63, n. 1; — see *San-fo-ts'i*.

施 那 幃 *Shï-na-weï*, an Arab of Ts'üan-chóu who built a charnel-house for Moslims, 119.

十 宿 *Shï-su*, in Cantonese *Shap-suk*, Arabic *Yûsuf*, Joseph, descendant in the third generation of Pᶜu-lo-hung (Abraham), 144, 145, n. 3.

師 子 國 *Shï-tzï-kuo*, Singhala, Ceylon, 12; — see *Si-lan*.

師 子 石 *Shï-tzï-shï*, Pulo Sapatu, or Pulo Cecir de Mer?, 8, n. 2.

設 馬 *Shö-ma*, Japanese Satsuma, 173, n. 7.

闍 婆 *Shö-pᶜo*, Java, 75, 78, n. 1.

蚍 臍 桑 *shö-ts'i-sang*, a flower of Chu-lién, not determined, 96.

勝 鄧 *Shöng-töng*, a district of Sumatra near present Deli, 11.

水 澳 *Shui-au*, a village in Ts'üan-chóu-fu, 165.

細 蘭 *Si-lan*, Ceylon, a dependency of San-fo-ts'i, 62, 66, 72; also written 急 蘭 *Ki-lan*, and 錫 蘭 *Si-lan*, 74, n. 2; older forms used by Chinese, 74, n. 2.

細 輪 疉 山 *Si-lun-tié-shan*, the Serendib of the Arabs, Adam's Peak in Ceylon, 73, 74, n. 8.

西 龍 *Si-lung*, possibly the island of Céram, 157.

西棚 *Si-p'öng,* a dependency of Chön-la, not identified, 54.

相公 *siang-kung,* the ruler of Tan-ma-ling in the Malay Peninsula, was addressed by this title, 67.

象石 *Siang-shi,* Tinhosa island?, 10.

暹 *Sién,* in Cantonese *Ts'īm,* Siam, 56, n. 10.

新州 *Sin-chóu,* the capital of Chan-ch'öng, 47, 49, n. 3.

新拖 *Sin-t'o,* Sunda, a dependency of San-fo-ts'i, also written *Sun-t'a,* (q.v.) 62, 66.

新頭河 *Sin-t'óu-ho,* the Sindhu or Indus river, 13;—see also *Mi-lan.*

鎖 (also written 所 and 娑) 里 *So-li,* the Cholas of Coromandel or Chu-lién, 98.

斯加里野 *Ssï-kia-li-yé,* Sicily, 153.

思蓮 *Ssï-lién,* a dependency of the Arabs, 117.

思魯瓦 *Ssï-lu-wa,* Surabaya, in Java, 85.

司馬傑 *ssï-ma-kié,* title of a minister of state in Shö-p'o, 76.

司痳烟 *Ssï-ma-yen,* Ishmael, son of Abraham, 113, n. 2.

思酥酒 *ssï-su-tsiu,* a drink of the Arabs made with sugar and spices; probably the *sharāb* or *sherbet* of the Arabs and Persians, 115.

蘇吉浪 *Su-ki-lang,* a small island outside of Ki-yang in Hai-nan, 176.

蘇吉丹 *Su-ki-tan,* Central Java, between the Sundas and Tuban, 82, 85; sometimes used to designate Shö-p'o (Java), 78.

素丹 *su-tan,* Arabic *Sultan,* title of a ruler among the Arabs, a tributary of Ta-ts'in, 103.

孫他 *Sun-t'a,* the Sundas, in Western Java, 84; — see *Sin-t'o.*

打綱 *Ta-kang,* a dependency of Java (Shö-p'o), 83.

大泥河 *Ta-ni-ho,* the Patani river, E. coast Malay Peninsula, 65.

打板 *Ta-pan,* Tuban, Java east of Su-ki-tan; it was also called Jung-ya-lu, (q.v.), 82, 84.

大食 *Ta-shï,* Cantonese *Tai-shik,* Persian *Tazi,* or *Tadžik,* the Arabs, 114, 119, n. 2.

大秦 *Ta-ts'in,* the Roman Orient, but Baghdad as used by Chóu and Chau, 102, 104, n. 2

大坐敢兄 *ta-tso-kan-hiung,* title of a minister of state in Shö-p'o, 80.

毾㲪 *t'a-töng,* a product of T'ién-chu, 111; a woollen texture.

儋耳 *Tan-ïr,* an ancient administrative division of Hai-nan, 175, 176.

丹戎武囉 *Tan-jung-wu-lo,* a dependency of Java (Shö-p'o), 83; in fifteenth century the Javanese called S. Borneo Tanjong-pura, 86, n. 7.

單馬令 *Tan-ma-ling,* a dependency of San-fo-ts'i, 62; probably about mouth of Kwantan river, E. coast Malay Peninsula, 67.

薔薇 *tan-po,* or 薔葡 *tan-p'u,* an abbreviated form of *chan-po-kia* (q.v.).

淡水江 *Tan-shui-kiang* or «Brackish river», in the Nan-p'i country, or Ceylon; cat's-eyes found in it, 88, 229.

膽逾 *Tan-yü* (?), an island near P'o-ni, 158.

談馬顏 *T'an-ma-yen*, probably the island of Botel Tobago off the S. E. coast of Formosa, 163.

毢 *töng*, an animal, not identified; its skin used as a seat by king of T'ién-chu, 110.

墱 *töng*, in Sanskrit *tola*, a small weight. It seems in this work to be used as a dry measure, 68, 131.

登流眉 *Töng-liu-meï*, Ligor?, a dependency of Chön-la, 53, 57.

登牙儂 *Töng-ya-nöng*, Trengganu, a dependency of San-fo-ts'i, 62, 65.

藤蘿 *t'öng-lo*, a fruit of Chu-lién, not identified, 96.

遞角場 *Ti-kio-ch'ang*, port on Leï-chóu peninsula coast facing K'iungchóu in Hai-nan, 176.

第辣撻 *Ti-la-ta*, a dependency of Chön-la, not identified, 56, n. 10.

提羅盧和 *Ti-lo-lu-ho*, probably on Mekran coast near entrance Persian Gulf, 13. It was also called *Lo-ho-i* (q. v.).

底勿 *Ti-wu*, island of Timor, a dependency of Java (Shö-p'o), 83; also called 底門 *Ti-mön*, 156.

柢鴉 *ti-ya*, the name used in Chanch'öng to designate a litter with one pole and borne by four men, 50, n. 4; — see *juan-pu-tóu*.

提風 *Ti-yü*, possibly the port of Taïz on the Indus, 13.

奝然 *Tiau-jan*, in Japanese *Chōnen;* a Bonze who visited the Court of China in A. D. 984, 171, 175, n. 23.

天竺 *T'ién-chu*, India, 13; — used in a restricted sense, 110, 112, n. 1.

天竺山 *T'ién-chu-shan*, Pulo Aor 23, 100; see also *Shang-hia-chu*.

多骨 *to-ku*, said to be a foreign name for the cardamom, 222, line 8.

陁盤地 *T'o-pan-ti*, Damiath of the Arabs, Damietta on the eastern branch of the Nile near its mouth, 142.

陁婆華 *T'o-p'o-li*, an Arab shipmaster who visited the Court of China, beginning eleventh century, 118, 124, n 23.

塊羅綿 *tóu-lo-mién*, or «*tūla* cotton», from Sanskrit *tūla*, cotton, 217, 219.

鍮石 *t'óu-shï*, «tush», copper, or an alloy of copper, produced in Persia, 81, n. 14.

層拔 *Ts'öng-pa*, Zanguebar, a dependency of the Arabs, 117.

層檀 *Ts'öng-t'an*, Zanguebar?, a country in the «Southern Ocean», possibly same as Ts'öng-pa, p. 127, n. 4.

積吉 *Tsi-ki*, a dependency of the Arabs, 117; possibly Tiz on the Mekrān coast, 122.

焦石山 *Tsiau-shï-shan*, Hon Tseu island near Tourane, 8.

千里長沙 *Tsién-li-chang-sha*, «Thousand-li-banks», east of Hai-nan, 176.

潛邁 *Ts'ién-mai*, a dependency of San-fo-ts'i, 62; possibly in N. Sumatra, 66 (7).

青琅玕 *ts'ing-lang-kan*, a variety of coral, 162, 226, Note.

青木香 *ts'ing-mu-hiang*, putchuck, 221.

徂葛尼 *Ts'u-ko-ni*, in Cantonese *Ts'ō-kot-nī*, Arabic *Dhu-l-karnein*, Alexander the Great, 146.

徂蠟 *ts'u-la*, Arabic, *zarāfa*, the girafe, 128, 129, n. 6.

翠藍山 *Ts'ui-lan-shan*, the Nicobar islands, 12.

杜懷潯 *Tu-huai-sün*, a dependency of Chön-la, not identified, 54.

都老 *tu-lau*, a head-man in Hai-nan, 177.

杜嚕 *tu-lu*, probably an abbreviated form for *turushka* or *tu-lu-sö-kién* (q. v.).

咄魯瑟劍 *tu-lu-sö-kién*, Sanskrit *turushka*, Indian olibanum, the resin of the *Boswellia Serrati*, 196, n. 1, 201, line 18.

猪蠻 *Tu-man*, Tuban, in Java, 85; — see *Ta-pan*.

都奴何 *Tu-nu-ho*, a dependency of Nan-p'i, possibly the Tana of the Arabs, on Salsette island near Bombay, 88, 90, n. 8.

對島 *Tui-tau*, in Japanese Tsushima, the island of, on which silver was mined, 174, n. 11, 175, n. 22.

吞里富 *T'un-li-fu*, a dependency of Chön-la, not identified, 54.

屯門 *T'un-mön*, passage leading out to sea from Canton, 10, 24.

東岐 *Tung-ki*, a dependency of Java (Shö-p'o), 83. Not identified.

崴裏 *Wa-li*, possibly Laos, 25.

崴木 *wa-mu*, colloquial name for *su-mu*, sapan-wood, 217.

萬里石床 *Wan-li-shï-ch'uang*, «Myriad-li-rocks», (south-)east of Hai-nan, 176; the Macclesfield Banks, 185, n. 4.

王舍城天竺 *Wang-shö-ch'öng T'ién-chu*, Central India, Magadha, 26; a Wa g-shö-ch'öng said to be in Pin-t'ung-

lung, 51; less than forty stages west of Ta-li (Yün-nan), 97.

文單 *Wön-tan*, a section of Chön-la during the T'ang period, 57, n. 12.

甕蠻 *Wöng-man*, in Cantonese *Ung-mān*, Oman, a dependency of the Arabs, 133; the second character is sometimes erroneously written 篱 *li*, 117.

微芮 *Weï-jui*, a dependency of Chan-ch'öng, 49. Not identified.

尾巴 *weï-pa*, in Cantonese *mi-pa*, the nipa palm, 84.

五指山 *Wu-chï-shan*, a peak in the Li-mu-shan of Hai-nan, 184, 189, n. 39.

烏刺 *Wu-la*, Sohar in Oman?, 14; — see *Wu-pa*.

烏里 *Wu-li*, a small island outside Ki-yang (Hai-nan), 176.

烏麗 *Wu-li*, a dependency of Chan-ch'öng, 49.

勿里馬 *Wu-li-ma* (?), an island near P'o-ni, 158.

無離拔 *Wu-li-pa*, in Cantonese *Mō-lī-pat*, Malabar, 223.

烏馬拔 *Wu-ma-pa*, a dependency of Chan-ch'öng, 49. Not identified.

無弄山 *Wu-nung-shan*, a hill in Töng-liu-meï, on which Sakyamuni Buddha manifested himself, 57, 58.

勿拔 *Wu-pa*, Sohar?, a dependency of the Arabs, 117.

無石 *wu-shï*, — see 麻茶 *ma-ch'a*.

無西忽盧華 *Wu-si-hu-lu-hua*, a centenarian Arab living in Canton, 118.

勿斯离 (or 里) *Wu-ssï-li*, a dependency of the Arabs, 117; *Misr* of the Arabs, Egypt; — see also *Mi-sü-li*.

勿 斯 離 *Wu-ssi-li*, Al-Mawṣil, Mosul, 25, 140.

沃 沮 *Wu-tsü*, an island in the Great Ocean inhabited by women, 152, n. 2.

饒 洞 *Yau-tung*, Yortan, south of Surabaya, Java, 85.

啞 巴 閑 *Ya-pa-hién*, Ispahan, 202; — see *Ya-ssï-pau-hién*.

啞 四 包 閑 *Ya-ssï-pau-hién*, Ispahan, a dependency of the Arabs, 116, 121, n. 12.

羊 山 *Yang-shan*; Pulo Gambir, 101.

瑤 蓮 蟬 *yau-lién-ch'an*, a flower of Chu-lién, not identified, 96.

邪 馬 臺 *Yé-ma-t'ai*, in Japanese Yamato, 173, n. 7.

餘 甘 *yü-kan*, a fruit of Chu-lién, not identified, 96.

鬱 金 *yü-kin*, Cantonese *wat-kam*, old sound *hat-kam*, Persian *karkam*, Arabic *kurkum*, curcuma, 89, 91, n. 17.

于 達 布 *yü-ta pu*, «cloth of *yü-ta*», presumably ramie fiber fabric, a product of Ma-i, 160.

越 裏 *Yüé-li*, a dependency of Chan-ch'öng, 49. Not identified.

Errata and Addenda.

P. 12, line 46, read Pʻo-lo-mön.

P. 13, note 2, add: Dr. Bretschneider's opinion is fully corroborated by Tsʻau Chau (曹昭) who, in his Ko-ku-yau-lun (格古要論), written in 1388, says (4,12): «*Pin-tʻié* comes from the Western Foreigners (西蕃). On its surface are spiral designs; some has a design like sesamum seed, and (some like) snow flakes. When sword blades are being burnished and polished, gold wire is used to gild them (用金絲礬礬之), and these designs (in gold wire) are plainly visible. The price (of such blades) is greater than (their weight in) silver .... Imitation *pin-tʻié* has designs in black; it must be carefully examined».

P. 37, line 13, read O-kön-tʻo, An-tʻo-man, Chʻa-pi-sha, Mo-kʻié-la.

P. 37, line 17, read Pin-tʻung-lung.

P. 37, line 18, read Pi-pʻa-lo and Ki-tzʻï-ni.

P. 37, line 20, read Kʻun-lung-tsʻöng-kʻi.

P. 38, line 8, read Pan Chʻau.

P. 38, line 22, read Kʻau-ku-pién.

P. 48, line 13, read *po-tié*.

P. 51, line 31, read *kʻién-lung*.

P. 53, line 26, read 熟 香.

P. 55, line 33, read Ling-k'ié-po-p'o.

P. 61, line 30, read 熟.

P. 62, line 14, read P'öng-föng.

P. 70, line 36, read 東 瓜.

P. 75, line 28, read irreconcilable.

P. 76, line 11, read 柴 歷 亭.

P. 85, line 34, eleventh character, read 卽.

P. 89, line 28, read Chö-ti.

P. 90, line 43, read 狼 奴.

P. 94, line 25, read Ku-t'an ...

P. 94, line 27, read P'o-lun ...

P. 95, line 2, read P'a-li-p'a-li-yu.

P. 95, line 5, read Po-lo-yé.

P. 95, line 14, read T'ién-chu-li.

P. 102, note 15, add: The J. R. A. S. for April 1911, pp. 437—445, contains an article by Col. G. F. Gerini on the subject of the Nan-ni-hua-lo of Chau Ju-kua. The author identifies it, with great plausibility, with the «well-known mediaeval kingdom of Nahrwāra, Anhilwāla or Aṇhilvada in Gujarāt, which flourished between c. 746 and 1298. A. D.»

P. 102, line 33, read 軨 軒.

P. 196, line 25, after the word to-k'ié-lo, add: Hung Chu in his Hiang-p'u (1,15ᵇ) gives, however, this latter form on the authority of the Shï-shï-hui-yau (釋 氏 會 要), and says it means «root perfume» (根 香). It may be Sanskrit tagara, which is Cassia auriculatis.

P. 215, line 41, read ballût and shah-ballût.

P. 219, line 31, add: The Ko-ku-yau-lun (4,23ᵃ) refers to tóu-lo-kin, or tūla brocade, as a velvety tissue, from five to six feet broad, made from the contents of the seeds of the so-lo (莎 欏 Sanskrit sāla) tree, and procured from the Southern and Western Foreigners, and also from Yün-nan. It also mentions si-yang-pu (西 洋 布 «Western Ocean cloth») as a snowy-white tissue, seven or eight feet broad.

P. 235, line 22, add: John Saris (1605—1609) noted that «the best (civet) is that which is of a deepe yellow colour some-what inclining to the colour of Gold, not whitish, for that is usually sophisticated with grease ....» Purchas, His Pilgrimes, III, 504. (Mac Lehose edit.).

Although the *wu-na-ts'i* from Borneo here mentioned was unquestionably a secretion of the sea-dog, the true civet-cat may also have been found there. Three centuries later Juan Gonzalez de Mendoza mentions it as very abundant in the neighbouring islands of the Philippines. Purchas, op. cit., XII, 147.